ACLE

'Austin M[...] *[...] of Fire*, cricket balls and petrol bombs, Sloane Rangers and *Boys from the Blackstuff* . . . Andy Beckett's lively and even-handed account of two years in the life of modern

'A lucid account . . . Andy Beckett writes with vivid, even-handed clarity in this excellent book' Sean O'Brien *Times Literary Supplement*

'Takes us back to the first three years of that decade, showing how the new individualist zeitgeist extended deep even into those parts of society most opposed to Thatcherism' Lorien Kite,

'A breezy and very intelligent anatomy of the years 1980–82 . . . Beckett is as interested in [...] television production companies and [...] lands as he is in monetarism, the Falklands [...] on the trade unions'
Jonathan Derbyshire, *Prospect*

ABOUT THE AUTHOR

Andy Beckett writes for the *Guardian*. He has also written for the *Economist*, *The New York Times* magazine, the *London Review of Books* and the *Independent on Sunday*. His previous books are *When the Lights Went Out* and *Pinochet in Piccadilly*.

ANDY BECKETT

Promised You a Miracle

Why 1980–82 Made Modern Britain

PENGUIN BOOKS

PENGUIN BOOKS

UK | USA | Canada | Ireland | Australia
India | New Zealand | South Africa

Penguin Books is part of the Penguin Random House group of companies
whose addresses can be found at global.penguinrandomhouse.com.

Penguin Random House UK

First published by Allen Lane 2015
Published in Penguin Books 2016
001

Set in 9.35/12.48 pt Sabon LT Std
Typeset by Jouve (UK), Milton Keynes
Printed in Great Britain by Clays Ltd, St Ives plc

A CIP catalogue record for this book is available from the British Library

ISBN: 978–0–241–95688–5

www.greenpenguin.co.uk

MIX
Paper from responsible sources
FSC® C018179
FSC www.fsc.org

Penguin Random House is committed to a sustainable future for our business, our readers and our planet. This book is made from Forest Stewardship Council® certified paper.

For Sara, Lorna and Gillen

Contents

PART FIVE
A New World

Prologue: Ron's Chair

One lunchtime in early 1981, Ron Arad left the office for his break and didn't come back. He was working for an architect in Hampstead, a small practice in a dead-end street. There were half a dozen staff and not many commissions: London, like Britain, was in recession, the worst for half a century. The practice, which was based in the architect's undemonstrative, bunker-like modern house, survived by doing home renovations in Hampstead and the handful of other north London suburbs that were still wealthy enough to afford them. As a recent recruit and the most junior employee, Arad was assigned the most repetitive drawings.

From the studio's small windows, the only visible life was people walking past to collect parcels from a Post Office depository at the end of the street, which was otherwise completely residential; and the trees of Hampstead's lovely, slightly isolated hilltop, fretting in the wind. Arad had just turned thirty. He had a beard and a hippyish, sleepy manner, with a voice that seldom rose above a mutter. But his quick eyes betrayed a restlessness. He especially hated his job in the afternoons.

It was eight years since Arad had arrived in London, as an Israeli art-school graduate with successful, doting artist parents and a hunger for English bohemia. Between 1974 and 1979 he had studied at the Architectural Association, an internationally famous central London institution where brilliant students and professors came up with multi-coloured visions of the British future, almost none of which were ever built. He approached the AA more like a second, leisurely stint at art school than a professional training: alternately skiving and showing off, intermittently producing confident, faintly science-fiction drawings that were more provocations than actual designs. For one of his final projects, he conceived a school for a site near Southend in Essex. The town was one of the swelling commuter settlements east of London where a new, politically pivotal working-class Toryism was gestating. From the air, Arad's notional complex of buildings looked like a hammer and sickle.

In 1980 he drifted into the Hampstead job, his first as an architect. People from his year at the AA were already there and persuaded him to join them. But within months he realized that the work – and working for someone else – did not suit him. The day he walked out, he gave no warning. At the end of the morning, he simply left work and, instead of turning left as usual out of the dead-end street towards the centre of Hampstead, with its cosy lunchtime cafes full of other dreamers and its decaying bookish mansions full of liberals and left-wingers – including the hapless Labour leader Michael Foot – he turned right: towards central London.

It was a fine day and the busy road ran downhill. Arad ate up the wide pavement with his rolling, slightly bear-like stride. As he descended, so did the housing stock: from the vast Edwardian semis of south Hampstead to the subdivided, peeling terraces of Belsize Park, to the gloomy mansion blocks and looming towerblocks of Chalk Farm. After about a twenty-minute walk, the road ended. Ahead was a giant drum of Victorian brick: the Roundhouse, a legendary counterculture performance space in the 1960s and 1970s, now about to go bust. And to the right of it, half-hidden from the street, wedged against a railway line, was a narrow scrapyard.

By 1981, previously packed inner London districts such as Chalk Farm had been depopulating and deindustrializing for decades. The population of the capital had shrunk by two million – over a fifth – from its peak in 1939, and the once great city was gap-toothed with empty spaces, often filled by scrapyards and other entropic enterprises. The Roundhouse yard dealt mainly in dead cars. There were piles of them, their carcasses almost worthless but their interiors, yet to be crushed, often intact. Arad spoke to the owner of the yard, who was Greek, an immigrant like him, and walked in.

At the AA, Arad had developed an interest in 'readymades': everyday objects, often industrially produced, which celebrated twentieth-century artists from Marcel Duchamp to Andy Warhol had transformed into strange and suggestive artefacts by placing them in unintended combinations or wildly out of context, Duchamp's up-ended urinal-in-a-gallery being the most cited example. In the late 1970s Arad had begun poking around in London fleamarkets and scrapyards, including the one in Chalk Farm, without knowing exactly what he was looking for or what he would do with it. But this lunchtime, he suddenly found it: a pair of red leather car seats, still in perfect condition, inside a defunct Rover 2000.

The Rover 2000 was a great boat of a saloon car, admired and state-of-the-art when introduced in the early 1960s. But its later models had grown steadily out of date, as Rover was absorbed into the nationalized conglomerate British Leyland, and became tangled up in bureaucracy and bad industrial relations. By the time it ceased production in 1977, the car was cumbersome and anachronistic-looking – one metaphor, of the many available, for the country's post-war industrial slide. By the early 1980s, fleets of Rover 2000s were beached in British scrapyards.

Yet Arad saw potential, not melancholy, in the car seats. They were well crafted and curvy and wide, like gentleman's club armchairs that had been adapted for automotive use. They had a ribbed central section that you sank into, which felt cool on your back, surrounded by a thick, enclosing band of firmer cushioning. A simple black lever to one side made them recline. After a little haggling, he bought them for £29 apiece. He extracted them from the car himself – he was good with tools – and took them back to an artist's studio he had recently begun renting for as yet undefined future projects.

The studio was a couple of miles south, in Covent Garden. For much of the 1970s, the area had been dominated by a dying, then derelict fruit and vegetable market, but by 1981 it was being redeveloped as a theatrical new retail district largely aimed at tourists. On the fringes of the area, though, there were still shabby, half-abandoned side streets with spaces that artists and edgier businesses could afford. Nosing about, Arad had discovered a small, high-ceilinged warehouse, owned by the Greater London Council and used occasionally for storage by a nearby maker of stage props. The GLC had an immense, lightly overseen property portfolio, the rent was low, and the props maker agreed to split it with him. Arad brought in his car seats and got to work.

He decided to turn them into armchairs. Taking a dozen short tubes of metal scaffolding and a dozen cast-iron brackets, called Kee Klamps – a British brand first introduced in the 1930s for building milking stalls for cows – Arad assembled two rectangular cradles. Then he paid a London engineering firm a small sum to bend four further lengths of tubing into C-shapes. He attached the C-shapes to the longest sides of the cradles, tube ends facing down. The cradles now stood evenly on the floor of the warehouse, faintly sinister-looking, like four-legged spiders.

Next Arad fixed a car seat to each cradle. With the soft leather jarringly framed by industrial metal, the assemblage was an odd hybrid; but he felt immediately that it worked. As furniture, it was solid-feeling and low to the floor, the smooth tubing perfectly supporting your elbows. And as art, it suggested scavenging, ingenuity, the eking out of old luxuries – it felt right for the threadbare country Britain seemed to have become.

Arad called his creation Rover Chair. He resolved to make more and sell them from his studio, for £99 each. After his time at the AA, he knew people with adventurous tastes. And arty Covent Garden streets like his were beginning to attract other suitable foot traffic that he intended to draw in – people going to the area's scattering of galleries and nightclubs, shooting the occasional pop video, visiting an isolated boutique. So he made the studio double as a showroom, enticingly untidy and creative-looking, with metalworking equipment and Rover Chairs in various states of assembly, their seats sourced from other scrapyards, scattered about. He named the whole enterprise One Off.

At first, the chairs barely sold. People would come in and peer at them, but that was all. Even in fashionable London, the market for such ostentatiously designed modern objects was tiny and fickle. And in early 1981, in the fifth consecutive quarter of recession, £99 was a lot for a chair: not much less than the average weekly wage. Arad survived by doing more prosaic work with Kee Klamps, custom-building metal bed frames and storage units for people, taking advantage of the tail end of the late 1970s vogue for industrial-looking, 'high-tech' home furnishings. His studio was often freezing; when the weather warmed up, it crawled with wasps.

During the many days with no visitors, he would lock the doors and smoke dope, or just hang around and draw. He was good at not thinking too much about the future. Then, on Boxing Day that year, he was in the warehouse alone when there was a rap on the doors. He told whoever it was that the showroom was closed. The knocker persisted: he said he wanted to buy Rover Chairs, not one but several. Arad opened up. A short, twinkly young Frenchman stepped into the studio. He was a friend of a friend but not somebody Arad recognized.

It was the fashion designer Jean Paul Gaultier. He was in the early stages of his 1980s ascent, and he liked to come to Covent Garden to see what its more daring inhabitants were wearing and making. He told Arad he wanted six chairs for his home and paid for them upfront.

Thirty-two years later, Arad finished telling the Rover Chair story in careful fragments – none of the versions I had read of it was ever exactly the same – and allowed himself a brief, sly smile. We were sitting at a table in another ex-industrial London building, a couple of hundred yards from the old site of the Chalk Farm scrapyard. Arad still talked in a mutter. In baggy striped trousers, sharply tapered at the ankle, a long rainbow scarf looped over a black T-shirt, and floppy leather shoes with red laces, he still looked like a cross between a hippy and a hopeful 1980s creative. His eyes still darted about.

But in most other ways he moved in a different world now. On the table in front of us, heavy catalogues gleamed, from recent Arad exhibitions in galleries around the world. Either side of us there extended a labyrinth of workshops and studios and showrooms, with almost every detail of every room – shelves, walls, doors, floors – in Rover Chair-style curves and raw edges. Self-consciously casual young men sat at deluxe computers, or stood clustered in impromptu meetings. Their accents were international and so were the projects under discussion: an asymmetrical tower block in Tel Aviv, a wobbling multi-storey public sculpture in Toronto. At Ron Arad Associates in the hot autumn of 2013, as all over the London economy, business was booming in ways scarcely imaginable in 1981.

Arad stopped making Rover Chairs in 1989. They now sell for up to £5,000. The prototype of another, later, slicker chair design of his, he mentioned in passing, 'changed hands in New York last year for about a million and a half'. Besides furniture and architecture, his company had diversified into sunglasses, glassware, coffee makers; even its logo had won an award, he added with a faux-casual chuckle.

I asked whether he had any politics, and whether they had changed at all since he first set up his business. 'I'm still progressive, liberal, left wing,' he said with sudden earnestness. 'Still sort of a hippy. I subscribe to the *Guardian*, not the *Daily Telegraph*.' He gave one of his gnomic pauses. 'In the 80s, business for me was a necessary evil.'

Introduction: 'A Small Number of Determined People'

On 6 July 1979, two months after taking power thanks to the biggest electoral swing between the main parties since the Second World War, Margaret Thatcher made a speech at Trinity College, Cambridge. The audience was friendly: a Conservative Party summer school. Thatcher was enjoying the fleetingly good opinion polls and feelings of omnipotence usually granted to new British prime ministers, and the title of her speech was appropriately ambitious: 'The Renewal of Britain'.

She began in the stirring, slightly windy tone that had characterized her big speeches since becoming Tory leader four years before:

> Britain is a great nation ... Britain has been in dire straits before, and she has recovered. She will recover again ... Our decline compared with other countries may show up most clearly in economic statistics. But that does not mean that the remedy lies only in economics ... The mission of this government is much more ... It is a recovery of our self-confidence and our self-respect ...

Then she became more intriguingly specific:

> Nations depend for their health ... upon the achievements of a comparatively small number of talented and determined people ... The ideas which will make for better lives for everyone in ten years' time are now in the minds of [those] individuals ... locked up there for the moment. If we can create the right national mood, those ideas will flourish.

Ron Arad's scrapyard epiphany was two years in the future. But in 1979 Thatcher's own character and career already offered a model of sorts for her proposed elite of national saviours. She was fifty-three years old, young for a prime minister by post-war standards. Despite her buttoned-up dress sense and careful, coached enunciations, her basic manner was frank, impatient, aggressive – in private as well as in public. She walked and ate fast, and slept little. According to her long-standing adviser and confidant Robin Harris, she was 'immensely strong in the arms. There was not a stuck window or jammed door that she could not shift.' As prime minister, she often worked in a particular high-backed chair in her official study; gradually, Harris noticed, her restless feet ground out a hole in the carpet.

During her twenty years as an MP prior to Downing Street, Thatcher had coped with the crushing maleness of Westminster, where the proportion of female MPs remained under 5 per cent. She had toppled Edward Heath as Tory leader in 1975: when the result was announced, the Conservative historian John Ranelagh records that an unnamed vice chairman of the party blurted out, 'My god! The bitch has won!' She had gradually cornered the dogged and canny 1976–9 Labour government led by Jim Callaghan. And she had gradually convinced the British radical right that a political and economic revolution they had dreamed of for decades was at last about to happen, with her as its frontwoman. 'She absolutely had this "Let's go for the mountaintops" attitude,' recalled John Hoskyns, a brilliant but tactless ex-army officer, computer tycoon, and deviser of national rescue plans whom she made head of the influential Downing Street Policy Unit in 1979. 'That's really what got me in there with her.'

Yet in a nation as old and self-doubting as late twentieth-century Britain, revivalist talk from prime ministers was not new. In 1964, Callaghan's Labour predecessor Harold Wilson had been elected on a promise to re-energize the country through the 'white heat' of new technology. In 1970 Heath had been elected promising 'to change the course of history of this nation'. Neither attempt ended well. Wilson lost power after six years, widely despised, leaving a still old-fashioned industrial economy and a forcibly devalued currency. Heath lost power after four, humiliated, with the trade unions he had vowed to curb more dominant than before.

Many analysts of Britain's seemingly unstoppable downward modern trajectory expected Thatcher to do no better. After her first two years in office, these pessimists saw no reason to change their minds.

'Britain has now been in decline for a hundred years,' wrote the historian Andrew Gamble, in a brief but persuasive 1981 book called *Britain in Decline*, 'the most observed and analysed decline in modern history. Few explanations have not been proffered, few causes not dissected, few remedies not canvassed at least twice . . . There have been periods of recovery . . . [but] at every crisis . . . the prospects for lasting recovery have looked bleaker, the straitjacket of decline tighter . . . The caravan is still on the road, but few believe it has much further to go.'

In the summer of 1981, the coldest and darkest for a decade, the sharp-eyed, socially conscious travel writer and novelist Jonathan Raban decided to buy a small boat and sail around the ragged British coastline, coming ashore whenever he fancied to explore the ancient ports and navy towns which for centuries, but no longer, had made Britain an imperial and economic superpower. 'Economic recession meant that half the boats in England were up for sale,' wrote Raban in *Coasting*. 'The margins of England [were] lined with these men and their rotting boats. Redundant in many more senses than one.' Britain, he generalized, had become a country with 'a thin, hurt and sullen look . . . troubled, inward'.

Raban put to sea in February 1982. His stop-start voyage lasted a year. But within a few weeks of setting out, his sense of Britain began to change. Visiting Lymington, a previously 'spinsterly' Hampshire town on the south coast, he was astonished to come across 'a solid mile' of marinas, with large yachts 'wedged into their slots . . . shark-nosed and white'. Nearby, 'The windows of Lymington's quayside restaurants were bright, slap-happy collages of credit cards.' Something was stirring in the supposedly moribund British economy, Raban began to realize: 'The marinas represented just a small tithe of the profits to be made in Mrs Thatcher's England . . . the rich pickings of the property business, the money markets, the motor trade, North Sea oil.'

Haltingly but emphatically, the locations in *Coasting* shift from melancholy, backward-looking places to ones that are looking brashly ahead. The book ends with Raban holed up writing in Essex, the quintessential 1980s boom-time county. 'The place was a hive of tiny, tax-free private enterprises,' he observes. 'Everyone was in work.' It is now 1985. He thinks back to the Britain of 1981: 'It was hard to believe that I was now living in the same country.'

A profound change came over Britain in the early 1980s. It was a change as wide-ranging and abrupt as any since the Second World War. And we are still living with the consequences – happily or otherwise.

One dimension of the change was party-political. In 1981 the Conservatives had lost four of the previous six general elections, and looked highly likely to lose another: that December, a Gallup poll gave Thatcher an approval rating of 25 per cent, the lowest for a prime minister since records began. Yet after 1981 the Conservatives won three general elections in succession, the first two by huge margins, and held power for another decade and a half – the longest continuous period spent in office during the twentieth century by any British political party.

In 1981 the first significant new British party for almost a century was founded. The Social Democratic Party (SDP) split the left, and altered the country's electoral geometry in the right's favour, for more than a generation. Also in 1981, the previously dusty business of London government was transformed. A loose-tongued young Labour radical with a fondness for the *Godfather* films, Ken Livingstone, snatched the leadership of the Greater London Council. The cacophonous experiment in racial, sexual and gender politics that followed has been largely forgotten or caricatured – 'the loony left' – but its ideas still pervade Britain: from the multiculturalism of modern school life to the equal opportunities policies of big companies.

London's modern dominance of Britain also started in the early 1980s. With the establishment of the London Docklands Development Corporation in 1981, the capital's long-fading eastern riverfront began to be remade, from an emptied-out flatness of silent quaysides and rubble to a dream, or a nightmare, of humming glass towers. On the foggy backwater of the Isle of Dogs, the corporation helped create an international financial centre – Canary Wharf – which would come to rival the City of London and tilt the whole capital eastwards. Meanwhile the old City acquired a new transatlantic rawness and swagger. In 1982 the London International Financial Futures Exchange opened. Its model was the yelling, jostling trading pits of Chicago at their most macho.

In 1981 the famously sharp-elbowed and profitable estate agent Foxtons was founded by a dapper twenty-eight-year-old ex-soldier, Jon Hunt. Its first office, which unlike other estate agents stayed open deep into the evening, was in a former Italian restaurant in Notting Hill in west London. During the 1960s and 1970s the slopes of Notting Hill, with their towering, subdivided terraces, had been a haven for bohemians and squatters from all over Europe. But in 1981 one attitude to property was usurping another.

The wider British geography of wealth and power was also shifting. While London was rising, much of the rest of the country, and the north of England in particular, was losing political and economic leverage – leverage it had enjoyed since the Industrial Revolution a century and a half earlier. The first Thatcher government had a sometimes Darwinian view of the British regions: an abrupt break with the local subsidies and decentralization schemes of mid-twentieth-century Whitehall. This new attitude was most coldly expressed towards the struggling, increasingly turbulent port city of Liverpool. In July 1981 the chancellor Geoffrey Howe wrote a private letter to Thatcher, arguing that with Liverpool 'the option of managed decline is one which we should not forget altogether. We must not expend all our limited resources in trying to make water flow uphill.'

The early 1980s were a time of hard-headed realism – or political and personal self-interest masquerading as such – as well as start-ups and idealism. In pop music, which still offered clues then to what millions of Britons were thinking, with record sales still enormous and music weeklies almost as popular as national newspapers, the otherworldly or raw styles of the 1970s gave way to a new glossiness and careerism. Rising bands such as the Human League and Scritti Politti fundamentally rethought their sounds and looks, and their reasons for being. In the late 1970s, Scritti Politti's singer Green Gartside had lived in a squat and written lyrics inspired by the Italian Marxist theorist Antonio Gramsci. In 1981 he announced, 'What has meaning is what sells.'

Television, the other sensitive social motion detector of late twentieth-century British culture, became more fascinated by commerce as well.

In 1982, Channel 4, the first new British TV channel for a quarter of a century, began broadcasting, fed by a whole new economy of independent production companies. At first, most of them were little more than a few frustrated ex-BBC staff with cameras bought on credit and a roomful of desks; but their sometimes innovative programmes and cheapskate working practices shaped Channel 4, and British broadcasting as a whole.

One of the most successful of the early 'indies' operated from a former banana warehouse in the London Docklands enterprise zone, an area intended by the Thatcher government to become a showpiece for a more liberated capitalism. The company came up with the vicious political puppet satire *Spitting Image* – with a hawk-nosed latex Thatcher as its presiding monster. Her government had hoped the new production companies would become model Thatcherite entrepreneurs, but many of them became something less biddable but more politically useful: people who fought against her government's ideas in public while they absorbed them and adjusted to them in private. You could call them hypocrites; or you could call them modern Britons.

In the early 1980s, after decades of post-war decline and drift and crisis – real and imagined – Britain was more receptive than usual to such a remaking. Many people wanted to hear a new national story. I was one of them. I turned eleven in 1980. That year, my family moved back to England after my father finished an army posting in Germany. I was becoming interested in politics. I was not a Tory, or a supporter of any other party yet, but I was patriotic, in the way of eleven-year-old boys who read Britain's nationalistic newspapers and watch too many Second World War films, which then still marched in formation through the television schedules. I was susceptible to the idea of a national revival – not least because it sounded more exciting than the narrative of retreat and the need to accept it, which I had overheard for years whenever grown-ups talked about the state of the country.

During the 1960s and 1970s one closely watched symptom of Britain's supposed decline had been the sagging value of the pound against the American dollar. There was a recurring fear in Whitehall and the British media that the exchange rate would drop to parity or even go into an unspecified but catastrophic 'free fall'. In late 1980 the pound unexpectedly shot upwards instead towards $2.50, and I can remember the excitement and pride I felt. As a patriot herself, and desperate for any sign of what Hoskyns called 'turnaround', Thatcher was also thrilled suddenly to have a strong currency. In fact, the effects of the surge were in many ways disastrous. Hoskyns told me, 'I remember talking to companies who said, "We had been clinging on to the edge of the cliff, and now we've gone – because of the high pound. Our export business has been absolutely wiped out."'

Much of the first Thatcher government was a revolution in its early, hit-and-miss, most revealing stages – not the remorseless and in some ways predictable programme of consolidation that Thatcherism became after her first general election landslide in June 1983. In the early 1980s she and the era's many other iconoclasts were often tunnelling away in the dark, largely or completely unaware of other, parallel or divergent underminings of the status quo. In March 1981 the SDP was officially launched in an ornate hired hall in Great Queen Street near Covent Garden. Almost directly across the street, at the Blitz nightclub, a clique of London clubbers and future pop stars had spent the previous two years staging their own much-photographed breakaway: spurning the often dour mass youth fashions of the 1970s for a new peacock individualism – dressing as pirates or matinee idols – which would dominate the coming world of sheeny pop videos and street-fashion journals. But you will not find even the tiniest mention of the Blitz in SDP memoirs.

However, the rebels had a lot more in common than standard accounts of the period usually allow. In the early 1980s the radicals and dreamers of the 1970s, from Arad to Livingstone to Thatcher, finally got to do and run things rather than just issue manifestos. In modern Britain's often placid peacetime history, many would-be revolutionaries have not been so lucky – or unlucky, as it may have seemed to Livingstone and Thatcher for much of 1981 and 1982.

By Britain's usual, incremental standards, things often happened fast in the early 1980s: the Falklands War went from humiliation to triumph in seventy-four days. Yet some of these feverish episodes would change the national psyche for decades. The Falklands campaign gave British governments, both Conservative and Labour, the

House of Commons, most of the British media and many voters a taste for military aggression in pursuit of liberal-sounding causes – the right to self-determination, removing dictators – that did not even begin to fade until the coalition's abortive attempt to 'intervene' in Syria thirty-one years later.

Over three decades on from the first Thatcher government, we still live in the more outward-looking, market-driven, materialistic, mercurial, energetic and colourful, lonely and cruel, charismatic and polarized country that it messily brought into being. Elsewhere in the rich world and beyond, from Poland to New Zealand, much of the social and economic landscape has been formed, directly and otherwise, by the policies that Thatcher's administration pioneered.

Why exactly did Britain change so much and so influentially in the early 1980s? What did the transformation feel like – for both the transformers and the transformed? What was created, and what was destroyed? Was all the change caused by the Thatcher government? Or was some of it driven by forces that pre-dated, or even opposed Thatcherism? Who benefited, and who was left behind? Was the transformation permanent? Or was it a dead end?

In Britain and elsewhere, it remains unusual to ask most of these questions. Despite the 2008 financial crisis, and the subsequent and deepening doubts about the City of London banking practices that began in the 1980s; despite the dwindling of the Thatcherite dream of mass home ownership; the spreading unease about modern inequality and alienation and social fragmentation; the increasingly patchy performance of deregulated, Thatcher-influenced economies across the West; the growing inability of these economies to deliver better living standards for the majority; and partly as a consequence of all this, the shock election of Jeremy Corbyn in 2015 as Labour's first left-wing leader since the early 1980s, with Ken Livingstone's fierce deputy in those years, John McDonnell, becoming Corbyn's shadow chancellor, and the wily Livingstone himself returning to prominence as a Corbyn advisor – despite all these prompts, the first, most pivotal years of her rule remain under-examined. Even when she died in 2013, and the dam opened to release reservoirs of memory and commentary that had been building for a third of a century, the heroism or malignancy of 'Maggie' – a whole society's metamorphosis reduced to your view of a single person – was the only aspect of the early 1980s up for public discussion.

This book is an attempt to redress that. It is not intended to be a conventional, comprehensive history – twentieth-century Britain has plenty of those – nor a simple thumbs up or thumbs down for Thatcherism. Many Britons, including me, had and have more complicated feelings about what happened to their country in the tumultuous early 1980s – an ambivalence that has been largely written out of history. As well as overthrowings and zealotry, revolutions involve complicity, last-minute conversions, the acceptance – sometimes knowing, sometimes not – of new realities, and countless other forms of psychological rewiring. This book is partly about that revolution in the head: the shift in mass consciousness, haphazard but enduring, which helped turn Thatcherism from just another doomed Downing Street scheme for national revival into a rare modern example of a British government with social traction.

The book is also about how Britain was remade physically in the early 1980s: the hasty, shiny construction and the sweeping demolition. It is about the period's extraordinary concentration of important political, military and economic battles. It is about often forgotten or derided radical alternatives to Thatcherism, and how they, too, changed Britain – sometimes working directly against her government, sometimes unwittingly in step with it. Above all, this book is a portrait of a brief time when, to many Britons, on the left as well as the right, outside politics as well as within it, miracles seemed possible. In an old country such moments do not come along often.

PART ONE

Yearnings

I

A British Car to Beat the World

A beach somewhere in southern England at dawn. The sand is deserted. The sea is slack. Reddish-grey clouds hang ominously above. Four ships, military landing craft of the sort used in the Second World War, glide side by side towards the shore. They begin to open their bow doors like jaws.

A growling voiceover starts: 'Some of you may have noticed that for the past few years Britain has been invaded . . .' There is a tiny, hammy pause, then close-ups of the ships, revealing foreign flags and cargoes of neat little foreign cars: '. . . by the Italians, the Germans, the Japanese, and the French.' To stabs and rumbles of horror-film music, the landing craft beach themselves. Platoons of Volkswagens and Datsuns, Renaults and Fiats drive down onto the sand.

'Now,' says the voiceover, 'we have the means to fight back.' The soundtrack abruptly turns piping and upbeat, and there is footage of a spotless factory production line, devoid of humans, but with bold red robot arms dipping and pivoting around the silvery bodies of half-built cars: 'The new Austin Metro.' A small formation of hatchbacks, with big-eyed headlamps and cute bonnets, sweeps along a deserted motorway. A line of onlookers wave Union Jacks from a bridge above. The voiceover digresses for a moment about the Metro's unprecedentedly low fuel consumption and 'split-action rear seat'. Then the convoy leaves the motorway and enters a village.

The old houses are deep red, or pastel and half-timbered. Union Jack bunting is strung between them, with more flags attached to walls and windows. Ancient trees in full leaf catch a sudden shaft of buttery sunlight. As the Metros parade through the village, a stout old man in a 1940s flat cap and waistcoat, with three medals pinned to his chest, squints at the cars and then salutes them. 'Rule Britannia' plays on the soundtrack.

The Metros race out of the village and towards the coast. On the beach, the foreign cars scuttle back onto the landing craft. The British cars nimbly negotiate a narrow seaside track, throwing up dust, deep English greenery to either side of them. 'Rule Britannia' reaches its climax: 'Britons never, never, nev-er, will be slaves!' The Metros pour onto a grassy headland and stop dead, feet from the edge, forming a kind of mechanized phalanx, bonnets facing outwards. Far below them, the landing craft are slinking ignominiously away. Finally, the camera pulls back, to show the Metros in their defiant formation, atop blinding white cliffs, an unusually blue English Channel stretching away on three sides. 'The new Austin Metro,' concludes the voiceover. 'A British Car. To beat. The world.'

The advertisement was broadcast for two weeks in October 1980. I was startled and thrilled by its cheek and confidence. Britain had been in the Common Market for seven years; we had been sniggered at as 'the sick man of Europe' for much longer. Surely we couldn't say such crudely patriotic things any more? Or was the ad, I vaguely wondered, a sign that such feelings were going to be voiced a lot more from now on? Either way, it felt as if a taboo had been broken.

Lots of other Britons were struck by the ad too. According to the London agency that made it, Leo Burnett, '[Public] recall of the campaign, as measured by the British Leyland Continuous Advertising Tracking Study was at an unparallelled high', for a campaign selling cars, throughout October and into November. By April 1981, five months after the ad stopped showing, almost half of those surveyed could still recall it in detail.

In the early 1980s British cars still provoked strong feelings. Arad's Rover Chair played on the melancholy ones, the widespread sense that the automotive industry's days of craftsmanship and stylish design were long gone. The Metro and its bullish advertising played on a feeling that was less prevalent, more submerged: a hope that the good times could come again.

Tony Ball was one of the optimists. He had joined Austin in 1951, straight from school. His father had run a small Austin dealership in the market town of Bridgwater in Somerset since the 1930s. 'I had been *born* to the dealership,' Ball told me with reverence. 'I elected to go as an apprentice to the Austin Motor Company – it had an amazingly effective apprenticeship – with the intention of eventually going back home to Bridgwater to take over the dealership.'

But Ball was too successful and adventurous. Chosen as apprentice of the year, he was quickly initiated into all aspects of Austin's business, which since 1905 had been based around a labyrinthine plant at Longbridge, outside Birmingham. 'I worked in the legal department, in the drawing offices, on the factory floor, as a technical service correspondent – writing the letters of response to complaints [about defective cars] that came in . . . which is an art in itself, I can tell you!' In 1959, at the age of twenty-three, he was given responsibility for the press launch of the Mini. Dressed as a magician, he produced one of the revolutionary little cars out of a giant top hat; and then out of the car he produced three male and two female passengers, including his wife, his baby son, two white poodles, half a dozen suitcases and a set of golf clubs.

Ball was seventy-six when I interviewed him, and still working, though he had long since diversified away from the car industry into masterminding the official openings of stadiums and international sporting tournaments. He wore expensive buckled shoes, and his stories tended to have the polish and prolixity of the professional after-dinner speaker. We met at the agency that handled his bookings, in a luxuriously low-key set of central London offices where water glasses and glass tables and glass walls whispered high-status cleanliness. Yet Ball himself was warm, his face ruddy and open, his handshake attentive, and he still talked with intensity and fondness about the car industry and the models he had worked on. He had brought with him a well-preserved 1982 hardback about the Metro, and tapped the cover as he sat down: 'This marvellous little car! We got 8 per cent of the UK market through it. It was one of the most exciting times of my entire life!'

According to Ball and most industry historians, the two decades before the Metro had been disastrous for Austin. In the late 1960s, like the country's other major vehicle manufacturers, it was shoehorned into British Leyland, an improvised conglomerate that made too many similar models, and too few of them well. The Maxi, the Marina, the Allegro: these were grandfatherly cars, with stiff, upright designs that looked at least a decade out of date, and which were often fussy and under-powered. When they were on the road at all, that is: unreliability and shoddy assembly became BL hallmarks. In the early 1970s, the sheer size of the company briefly made it the fourth-largest car maker in the world; but then the 1973 oil crisis swept through the British economy, making manufacturing and motoring much more expensive and toppling ungainly giants such as BL into near-bankruptcy. The company was hastily nationalized in 1975 and put on a drip of government subsidies. A cost-cutting programme closed many Austin dealerships. Ball was horrified: 'I felt sick.' He flushed. 'The dealers had been *figures of some importance in their communities*, in every town and city in the country. Now we were giving our representation, on a plate, to the opposition, at a time when our industrial relations and production quality were at their lowest level.' Many of the sacked dealers immediately acquired franchises to sell foreign cars.

Throughout the 1970s, the Renault 5, Volkswagen Polo and many other innovative, imported small cars arrived in Britain – in vessels less dramatic-looking but much more capacious than landing craft – while BL soldiered on with the increasingly out-of-date Mini. One BL scheme to replace the car collapsed in the late 1960s, another in the mid-1970s. All the while, the company's share of the overall British car market dwindled alarmingly fast, particularly in the late 1970s. It fell by almost a third between 1977 and 1980. And Longbridge, the oldest working car factory in Britain, became a byword for industrial dysfunction: bodged-together buildings that were never replaced, tunnels left over from wartime production where fires broke out, touchy workers perpetually seeking excuses for disputes and stoppages, led by the plant's cunning, smartly dressed union convenor Derek Robinson, better known as 'Red Robbo'. British Leyland's seemingly ever-deteriorating performance, its seemingly ever-escalating neediness, particularly exasperated Margaret Thatcher's more austere advisers. In 1980 one of the sternest, John Hoskyns, wrote in his diary that the company should be 'liquidated'.

But the uselessness of BL had always been a bit of a caricature.

Here and there in the organization, talent and good ideas remained. In late 1977 work began on yet another successor to the Mini. Time was short: the next general election was due in less than two years, the Conservatives were favourites to win it, and BL needed an exciting new car if it was to look like a company worth subsidizing rather than closing. Development funds were also limited: instead of a purpose-built engine, the new car had to make do with one that 'went back to 1949,' wrote the automotive historian Eric Dymock. 'It was created [originally] . . . for the Austin A30, then went into the Morris Minor II in 1952. It was turned through 90 degrees and fitted in the Mini for 1959 . . . and reappeared [in the new car] in 1980.'

The body of the as-yet-unnamed vehicle was designed in three intense months. To save time, modelling clay was applied to a mock-up of one of the earlier, rejected Mini replacements. Yet despite all this scrimping and recycling, the new car was intended to be more modern and upmarket, more aerodynamic and fuel-efficient – the 1973 oil crisis and another oil price surge in 1979–80 made that a priority – than any previous small BL model. Meanwhile the company chairman, Michael Edwardes, made an additional demand of the designers: he wanted a 'cheeky' car, a car 'with an aura'.

Edwardes was one of the first of a new type of boss in the nationalized industries, foreign and demanding. He came from a swaggering South African corporate background: 'I never eat breakfast,' he wrote in his account of his times at BL, *Back From The Brink*. He was appointed to run the company by the British government in 1977, just as the car project was getting under way. Labour were still in power, but under the never very left-wing prime minister Jim Callaghan they were increasingly focused on cutting Whitehall spending and making state-owned companies more competitive. In a *Times* interview in 1980, Edwardes laid out his vision for BL: 'entirely new standards of quality and reliability . . . every automated advantage . . . the removal of restrictive practices . . . demanning by 30,000 jobs . . . new levels of productivity to put us on a par with the best Europeans'. Many BL trade unionists saw the 'Edwardes Recovery Plan', as it was officially known, as a malign and economically misguided management conspiracy. 'Edwardes will not be satisfied,' warned a 1979 pamphlet published by the rising left-wing group Militant, who had a substantial shop-floor presence in BL, 'until he has reduced Leyland factories to the level of slave camps.'

At Longbridge, where the new car was developed and manufactured, 'It was an exciting time, but it was also too harrowing for some,' writes Graham Robson in the car's official history. 'The hours worked were horrendous . . . [Austin chairman] Harold Musgrove says, "Some people couldn't take the strain . . . We had to move them out . . ." The management team came up with a working rule. If possible no one ever slept on a problem, if it could be solved that night.'

In 1979 Leyland experienced 234 strikes or shorter stoppages; in the first half of 1980, 126. At Longbridge the workers, when provoked, would pour out of the plant and assemble across the road in Cofton Park, a natural amphitheatre of municipal grassland. Derek Robinson would address them, big-shouldered and rousing, and industrial action would be agreed by a show of hands. But under Edwardes the management gradually became more wily. Ball provided some of the nous. He had spent much of the 1970s away from Leyland, working for another car company in South Africa, where he had got to know Edwardes. But in 1978 Ball had been persuaded to return to BL as head of sales and marketing, and also with a more free-ranging, liaising, smoothing-over role. He helped work out a way to outflank Robinson: 'In several major wage disputes, we contacted every employee personally, with a letter sent to their home address.' Ball knew that strikes were harder to support alone at home, or in front of your family, than in the crowd at Cofton Park. By November 1979 the management felt strong enough to sack Robinson, for the relatively trivial offence of signing a pamphlet opposing the Edwardes plan. In February 1980 a Cofton Park rally refused to back a strike for his reinstatement.

The company's ultimately successful battle with Robinson was watched with interest by the new Thatcher government. Ball, ever the networker, was a former schoolmate and 'personal friend' of John Biffen, her chief secretary to the Treasury from 1979 to 1981 and trade secretary from 1981 to 1982. Biffen regularly came to Longbridge. Ball remembered: 'He would say to me, "We want to know how you're getting on. We're behind you. Don't give up on what you're trying to do with Red Robbo."'

The government also sent emissaries to Longbridge to check on the car project. One part of the plant interested them in particular: the New West Works. An immense, smooth-skinned, flat-roofed square box, covering seventeen and a half acres, it loomed over the oily muddle of the rest of Longbridge like a landed alien spacecraft. Opened by Prince Charles in October 1980, the building was designated solely for production of the new car, and it cost £285 million – according to BL the single biggest-ever British investment in car production. Unlike the usual cramped, multi-level Longbridge halls where vehicles were awkwardly jigsawed together by men with welding guns – a method, writes Robson, 'first used at the end of the Second World War' – inside the new facility there was a clean, open-plan space populated largely by robots. The production line was intended to be even more efficient than the much-admired automated systems used by the great motor companies of Japan and continental Europe. The car it would create, promised Edwardes, in an uncharacteristically airy moment of utopianism, would be 'a child of information technology'. On 4 October 1980, four days before the vehicle's launch, the influential car magazine *Motor* summarized the situation more baldly: 'No other car in the long history of the British motor industry has been as important.'

Motor's rival weekly, *Autocar*, explained the pressures: 'One can't talk about [the car] without talking politics ... Even before it was conceived, every kind of meddler, from the informed to the ignorant, from spurned industrialists to revolutionary union leaders and publicity-seeking Members of Parliament, had their say about the car, the cost of the project, and how and where it should be made. [The car] had every possibility therefore of being a "committee car" of the worst kind.'

The vehicle that finally emerged from the New West Works, after years of rumours and media guesses, some of them deliberately orchestrated by BL to build interest, was indeed full of compromises. But they were shrewd ones. The car was angular in places and cosily rounded in others; affordable but not too plain; fresh and contemporary-looking but reassuring. Inside, it was ingeniously roomy – more spacious than its rivals despite a shorter body – and had a novel touch: rear seats that divided unequally for folding down. In an era that increasingly valued consumerism and choice, being able to fill your car with more different configurations of shopping and passengers had a strong appeal. Even the elderly engine performed well: a review of the car in *Motor* found that it was faster and more economical than its competitors.

A final success was the car's name. Usually at BL, names were chosen by an outside branding firm, and then painstakingly discussed by the many layers of Leyland management. But this time, in a clever piece of shopfloor co-option, the entire Longbridge workforce was balloted on a shortlist of three names: Match, Maestro, or Metro. Just over half of the workforce responded – a better turnout than in many union elections – and Metro won by 267 votes, a margin of just over 1 per cent over the second choice, Maestro. The name chosen sounded urban, modern, clean and efficient, and surprisingly European – the Paris Metro – given all the nationalistic feelings bound up in the car. Now all Leyland had to do was persuade people to buy it.

Riskily but astutely, Ball decided to make the company's long decline part of the sales pitch. The Metro would be promoted as a 'rebirth' for BL, he told Robson in 1980, 'to prove to the world that although we had been down on our knees, we were now capable of bringing BL back'. Beyond that, the car was intended to be 'the first step towards . . . the re-establishing of the credibility of a *British* motor industry'; and beyond that, even more ambitiously, a first step towards a broader national revival: 'to bring out an in-born feeling of pride everybody in the country [has], that, when our backs are against the wall, we can really fight our way out of trouble'.

Thirty-two years later, half an hour into our interview, Ball raised a meaty hand above the glass table between us, and began to speak more slowly than before, weighing his words: 'I'm a great patriot myself. And I believe there is a very genuine and very deeply felt patriotic element in everyone. There is a need to feel proud of Britain. There is a fear that Britain is not what it was. In 1980, with the Metro, I felt' – he smacked the table – 'Britain needs something like this!' He looked grave: 'It showed a country coming back from the brink – at a time when everything had been so bleak.'

Then a more knowing expression crept across his face, and his voice speeded up again. 'There is so much going for this wonderful country. If you can . . . tap into the feeling that people have along those lines – it may be for a commercial purpose, admittedly – but . . . people do want to see a product that the country can be proud of, that is seen to be part of our ingenuity as creators and manufacturers.' He grinned. 'In 1980, I thought, "Why not rattle the patriotic drum?" It is going to be for the benefit of everybody in this country if we succeed.'

A key part of the task was given to a foreigner. Gerry Miller was a raspy young New Yorker who had grown up thinking about cars: 'Everyone on my block could tell you what year and model as they drove past.' His other formative interest was Britain. In 1966 he had come over to study at Sussex University, then entering its mind-expanding heyday, and he enjoyed his degree and the 'sex and drugs' so much that he stayed in the country. In 1970 he drifted into writing ad copy, liking the money and the fact that he was good at it, just as 'London was becoming really exciting – taking over from New York as the centre of the advertising world.' In 1973 he joined Leo Burnett.

The agency, which had the Mini account, worked regularly for British Leyland. Miller was not impressed by BL: 'They were geniuses at making really bad cars. Oh God, they were so ugly! We used to go up there [to Longbridge] all the time. I wouldn't say the people there were the sharpest tools in the box. It was very heavily bureaucratic. The smarter British Leyland people didn't have the confidence or stature to be heard. And you couldn't drive up there in anything but a British Leyland car.'

He took a sip of his espresso and looked disdainful. We were in a stark, hipsters' café with whitewashed walls and teetering stools, in Soho in central London. Miller had chosen the venue. He lived back in America now, but he was in London for a reunion with old colleagues, and he still dressed like a typical ad man: carefully and neatly but slightly younger than his age, a black Kangol flat cap subverting a crisp striped shirt. The brim emphasized the assertive jut of his nose. Unlike Ball, he spoke in quick, fat-free sentences. Setting the scene for his involvement with the Metro, he said, 'It was sort of failure time for Britain: the end of the 1970s. They said to me, "You're gonna work on this new car."'

In the first half of 1980, a few months before the Metro's launch, Leo Burnett set up secret focus groups of people who had recently bought other, often foreign hatchback models. When shown the Metro, they were impressed. Then a second set of focus groups were convened, involving a greater proportion of BL customers, to find 'the emotional hook', as *The Leo Burnett Book of Advertising* (1984) put it – something which would give the Metro an appeal beyond the empirical. 'The research,' the agency concluded:

> identified an emotional desire to buy British and, in particular, a strong undercurrent of positive feeling for British Leyland: people very much wanted to see BL get it right again ... But whereas in the past people would automatically buy British on the assumption that they were getting a superior product, in 1980 this was no longer the case. Much as they wanted to, they simply did not believe they would get a superior product, especially from British Leyland. So, while the product [the Metro] was right ... Disbelief had to be overcome. Of the various [advertising] concepts shown, a 'British car to beat the world' ... struck exactly the right note of pride in heritage and of British success for a change. It had the capacity to overcome the underlying disbelief.

Miller remembered the focus groups. 'You'd say, "This car will go 12,000 miles between services"' – unusually far for a hatchback then – 'and people would say, "That's good." But you're not making an emotional connection. Yet when you said, "This is a great *British* car", that was much more potent. They could be proud again. As soon as you got that, the campaign fell into place. It gave you music, an attitude, how the brand should talk, what sort of words it should use.' Leo Burnett's analysis matched Ball's notion of the Metro as a vehicle for patriots, in all senses. The agency's copywriters, Miller among them, got to work.

For several weeks they immersed themselves in English history, looking for heroes and resonant phrases to use in the campaign. Their choices were predictable and jingoistic – references to and quotations from Nelson, Wellington, Churchill – but shrewd. 'In advertising,' said Miller, more expansive now as his espresso got to work, 'the consumer really is in charge. You're just coming up with something they're looking for. And we gave them what they were looking for ... They needed to feel good.' Rocking forward on his stool, looking into the whitewashed middle distance of the café, which was half filled with cool young Britons pitching business ideas to each other, he spoke for a moment as if to the gloomier collective unconscious of 1980: 'When was the last time you felt really good about yourself? That was in the war!' Then he turned back to me: 'People were less sensitive then about the Second World War. You could let yourself go, and say "Fuck those foreign cars, they're German!"'

Didn't he feel a bit odd pushing these British buttons, as a foreigner? 'I found it easy. It was a sort of submerged patriotism on my part, because I couldn't express my American patriotism.' And how did he feel about the political tone of the Metro campaign, the way it so perfectly dovetailed with all Margaret Thatcher's talk of national revival? Miller shrugged. 'I'm an old union person from New York. I understand that unions are there to help the weak and vulnerable. I thought of British Leyland like I thought of General Motors back home: decaying. Create more jobs – I thought that was the real achievement of the Metro ad.'

Filming began in August 1980. The village the cars were shown driving through was a composite of two, Lavenham and Kersey in Suffolk, exquisite tourist favourites that in many ways were already theatre sets for the portrayal of an idealized Englishness. Deftly, Leo Burnett and British Leyland treated the shoot as both a big secret – Metros transported to Suffolk disguised under special black covers, security guards discouraging photographers – and a sneak preview: the cars were briefly parked in a line along Lavenham High Street, and passers-by were able to peer in through their side windows. A 'spokesman for BL at the scene', reported the *Ipswich Evening Star*, told local journalists that the shoot would move on to Dorset next. Another spokesman gave out some of the Metro's technical specifications.

In the last weeks before the car's public launch, the whole project was wrapped tighter and tighter in the flag – literally in the case of the first teaser ads in the press, which featured a Union Jack-swathed Metro and the sub-Churchillian slogan, the first of many in the campaign, 'This could be your finest hour.' During August and September, groups of motoring journalists were introduced to the Metro at – of course – the Churchill Hotel in central London. Even more pent-up Leyland dealers had the car unveiled to them on a specially chartered cruise ship. It sailed from Liverpool to the Isle of Man and back across a wild autumnal Irish Sea, while one of Ball's trademark pieces of 'industrial theatre' unfolded to its captive audience. 'The car was hidden behind the bulkhead of the ship's theatre,' he told me. 'Onstage, there was a giant British Leyland logo. The stage revolved, the logo disappeared, and the car came out, to the tune of "Land of Hope and Glory". And I swear to you' – Ball let his voice crack a little – 'there wasn't a dry eye in the house. Hard-bitten dealers – in tears of joy!'

At Leo Burnett, the *Book of Advertising* records, there were 'internal worries that we might be going over the top', but these reservations were quickly put aside. In the national press, there was a rumour that at least one Metro had fallen off the white cliffs during the making of the TV ad. Ball quickly denied it, and then characteristically turned the story into an opportunity for more publicity. He claimed that a parody of the ad planned by Dave Allen, then a hugely popular BBC1 comedian, had envisaged a Metro slipping off the edge; but that BL had not allowed it to be filmed.

More seriously, during October and November some workers on the Metro production line turned restive. First, in the launch week, 'A group of fitters refused to allow less-skilled men to work with them, and downed tools,' The *Sun* reported on 9 October. For a whole day, 'Work halted on finishing touches to the Metro' – finishing touches such as the vacuuming of the cars for any stray parts, a practice that was supposed to signify a big jump in quality over previous BL models.

Then, during the crucial first weeks of full Metro production, 500 workers were temporarily laid off after a dispute over the supply of seats for the car by outside companies. On 22 November, according to the *Daily Mail*, 'Scores of [these] workers . . . chanted "We want work", broke windows and doors . . . Pallets of components were overturned and unfinished Metros slightly damaged.' Afterwards, writes Graham Robson, 'A few members of the workforce were disciplined, fined, or even sacked . . . In the end things returned, somewhat uneasily, to normal.' Longbridge's industrial relations problems had not been erased simply by sacking Red Robbo.

Yet that autumn, the media frenzy around the Metro smothered such doubts. Even the communist *Morning Star* giddily compared the New West Works' automated production line to something from *Star Trek*. The *Guardian*, usually deeply sceptical about the economy's prospects under Thatcher, hailed the Metro as 'the first step of a ladder which can lead to industrial health and, possibly, prosperity'. The *Daily Mail* called the car a 'British miracle', performed 'in record time, and within a rigid budget' by a manufacturer 'moving 40 years forward in one step'. There was even praise from the great car-making countries of continental Europe, despite their taunting by the TV ad. The Parisian daily *Le Matin* described the Metro as 'the ideal small car, which many European constructors would have liked to have created'.

A week after the launch, the annual British Motor Show opened in Birmingham. The lavish, crowded Metro stand received one particularly significant visitor. Margaret Thatcher posed a little stiffly beside a car in one of her primmest suits. Ball took advantage and pinned a Union Jack badge – 'I found out subsequently that it had been made in Taiwan' – to her lapel. Then, relaxing, Thatcher gave interviews from behind the wheel, her piled-up hair inadvertently showing off the Metro interior's generous ceiling. 'It's a lovely little car,' she told the *Sun*. The Metro was, she added, part of 'British industry's fightback'. The following week, she drove one along Downing Street.

Another early adopter of the new car attracted even more attention. When Prince Charles had opened the Metro plant at Longbridge in October 1980, he had been offered a test drive. The thirty-one-year-old Prince of Wales loved cars, and for twenty minutes he tried out a tomato-red model with a sunroof and cream go-faster stripes. It had the least powerful engine of any Metro, a frugal, slightly feeble one-litre, but he enjoyed himself regardless. Afterwards, Ball and his marketing subordinates delicately suggested to the Prince's staff that, given the Metro's importance to the nation, the car might usefully find a royal home. 'It was done purely on the basis that we did with so many celebrities – that personalities should be seen in our cars,' Ball told me. 'It was all done very diplomatically and certainly not in a . . . bribing manner at all.'

The following month, press photographers started to spot the car in prosperous parts of west London, pluckily nosing through the traffic jams, or nipping past the puce mansion blocks of Kensington and Earls Court. Yet Charles was not in it. Its driver was a young woman with a heavy, slanting haircut and a tendency to stall: Diana.

2

The Year of Flags

In Britain as the 1980s began, great hopes and yearnings were invested in a few vulnerable projects. The Metro was one; the relationship between the heir to the throne and Lady Diana Spencer was another.

When it started in July 1980, he was thirty-one and she was nineteen. Diana had never been abroad, apart from a homesick term at a finishing school in Switzerland. She had grown up in rural Norfolk and Northamptonshire, then at eighteen moved to the capital, into an old-fashioned west London world where young upper-class women still marked time before marriage as if they were Jane Austen characters. She tried nannying, kindergarten and ballet teaching, and cookery – 'My fingers were always in the saucepans,' she told her biographer-cum-confessor Andrew Morton later – while living in various smart shared flats owned by her mother. The Spencers were an ancient family with royal connections: Diana was an eleventh cousin to Charles. She had a worldly side, knowing how to alternate usefully between shyness and cheekiness, and how to look her best – head dipped, liquid gaze upwards – in front of a camera. But in other ways she was still '19 going on 15', as a royal servant later described her. Before Charles, she had never had a serious boyfriend.

Before Diana, he had had many girlfriends, perhaps too many. They included, two years earlier, Diana's older sister, Sarah; Amanda Knatchbull, the great-granddaughter of his great-uncle and mentor Lord Mountbatten, who had advised him in 1974 to 'sow his wild oats and have as many affairs as possible before settling down . . . [with] a suitable and sweet-hearted girl'; and Camilla Parker Bowles. She and Charles had met in 1970, and in 1980 they were still sporadically but intensely involved.

But by then she was married, and he urgently wanted to be as well. 'The media will simply not take me seriously until I do get married,' he wrote in a letter to an unnamed close friend in April 1979. 'At the moment I'm convinced that they see me [only] as "marriage" or "bird" fodder.' That anxiety was increasingly shared by the royal family and its advisers during the 1970s, as the prince's twenties passed in what the tabloids presented as a glossy blur of womanizing and polo matches and skiing holidays, with frequent photos of a tanned and shirtless royal heir giving off a whiff of decadence amid the decade's hardships. In 1978 Mountbatten warned Charles against 'beginning on the downward slope which wrecked your Uncle David's life and led to his disgraceful abdication and his futile life ever after'. 'Uncle David' was the previous Prince of Wales, later Edward VIII. The following year, Mountbatten was blown up by the IRA. 'I have lost someone infinitely special in my life,' Charles wrote in his journal.

He first met Diana while he was going out with Sarah, and was intrigued by her youth and her unselfconsciousness in his presence. Diana told Morton that Charles invited her to his 30th birthday party at Buckingham Palace in 1978; and saw her 'off and on with Sarah' during the late 1970s. Then, in July 1980, she was invited by a friend to a house party at a country estate in Sussex:

> I was asked . . . 'Would you like to come and stay for a couple of nights . . . because we've got the Prince of Wales staying. You're a young blood, you might amuse him.' The first night, [Charles and I] sat down on a bale at the barbecue . . . I said: 'You looked so sad when you walked up the aisle at Lord Mountbatten's funeral.' The next minute he leapt on me practically . . . I wasn't quite sure how to cope . . . Anyway we talked about lots of things and . . . that was it . . . He said: 'You must come to London with me tomorrow.'

Within a few weeks the relationship was in the papers. 'He's In Love Again! Lady Di Is The New Girl For Charles,' announced the *Sun* on 8 September: a reporter had spotted Diana half-hidden behind a tree near the remote Scottish royal residence at Balmoral while Charles fished nearby. Back in London, whenever she went out in her Metro, Diana was tailed so incessantly and by so many reporters that she taught herself to go through every traffic light just as it was turning red – or sometimes borrowed another car. In private, in her besieged flat, 'I cried like a baby to the four walls. I just couldn't cope ... because I got no support from Charles and from the Palace press office.' By early 1981 she had also 'realized there was somebody else around' in his romantic life, meaning Camilla. And yet, when he proposed to her regardless that February, Diana, flattered, still nineteen, as excited by the idea of the relationship as by the relationship itself, said yes. 'I said: "I love you so much, I love you so much." He said: "Whatever love means ..." And he ran upstairs and rang his mother.'

On 24 February the engagement was announced. The United Kingdom was into its second year of recession. There were 2,463,300 people officially unemployed, the highest total since 1933, one of the worst years of the Great Depression, and the figure was rising frighteningly quickly. Even more than usual, the press treated happy royal news as a much-needed diversion. 'For a nation more than ever starved of symbols of hope and goodness in public life,' commented the *Daily Telegraph* on 25 February, 'the Royal example ... becomes more important.' *The Times* wrote contentedly but also a little riskily, given Charles's complicated personal history, 'It is fitting that the Prince of Wales should enter married life when one considers the extent to which the monarchy is now regarded as an exemplar of family life.'

A few days later Diana moved out of her flat and into Buckingham Palace. The wedding had been set for 29 July: five months away. For much of this interlude, she felt brittle. Cut off from her west London friends and flatmates – 'For God's sake, ring me up,' she wrote in a final note that she left for them – she found the grey, inscrutable Palace lonely and imprisoning. Despite her country-house upbringing, the courtiers baffled and alienated her, with their professional reserve and perpetual concern for hierarchy and protocol. And she baffled them, unsure exactly what role to give to a sometimes giggly teenager who liked soap operas, especially the cheap motel saga *Crossroads*, but who was about to become the first Princess of Wales since before the First World War. Meanwhile Charles disappeared for several weeks on an interminable official visit to Australia, New Zealand, Venezuela and the United States. Day by day, the enormity of what she had committed herself to sank in.

She lost weight. 'The first time I was measured for my wedding dress I was 29 inches around the waist,' she told Morton. 'The day I got married [five months later] I was 23 and a half inches.' She began to suffer from the eating disorder bulimia: 'The week after we got engaged, my husband [to be] put his hand on my waistline and said, "Oh, a bit chubby here, aren't we?" and that triggered off something . . . and [so did] the Camilla thing . . . The first time I made myself sick, I was so thrilled because I thought this was the release of tension.'

There were murmured suggestions from the press that she was finding the engagement period an ordeal: assessing her wedding-day performance, *The Times* wrote of 'composure entirely regained after the strain of recent days'. At the wedding rehearsal, a BBC outside-broadcast team saw and filmed Diana in tears, according to the BBC's official historian Jean Seaton, but deliberately did not pass on the news or the footage to any BBC colleagues.

Occasionally, the media were more candid. The day after the rehearsal, the *Sun* carried a front-page picture of her with Charles, coming down the steps of St Paul's Cathedral, where the ceremony was to take place. Gripping his hand tightly, she wore a slender summer dress that hung off her like a sail from a mast, and revealed bony wrists and shins – almost a different person from the fleshy, drooled-over teenager of her first press appearances. 'Darling Di, you're lovely,' read the *Sun*'s headline, 'but promise us you won't lose one more pound.' Charles, lean himself, seemed suddenly heavyset and middle-aged beside her, as he strode purposefully forward in a pinstriped suit, its cut baggy and old-fashioned, his broad, froggy mouth set and preoccupied. The headline writer chose not to mention that the couple were looking resolutely away from each other. According to Morton, two days before the wedding Diana 'seriously considered' calling it off, and said so to her sisters over lunch. With country-house bluntness they replied, 'Your face is on the tea towels, so you're too late to chicken out!'

The Prince's official biographer, Jonathan Dimbleby, records that there were 971 different commemorative wedding items. Among them were Charles and Diana's 'heraldic devices' cast in limited-edition gold and silver ingots – not the most sensitive souvenirs, given the economic circumstances – and a scale model of a Metro, advertised as 'A British Car For A Royal Occasion'. There was a faintly desperate air to the cashing-in. Four days before the wedding, Dennis Barker of the *Guardian* wrote:

> Makers and sellers of flags and bunting reported that buying had been conservative. Mr James Smith, managing director of Black and Edgington, who have installed the flags [along the wedding procession route] in the Mall, said: '... The impression was there at an early stage that people were not going to spend much money on decorations. Business houses are under pressure.' Mr Smith estimated the demand had been only a tenth of that for the 1977 Silver Jubilee.

'Immediately off the actual [procession] route,' Barker continued, 'there was practically no decoration at all.' In Manchester city centre, 'only modest decoration was visible'; in Edinburgh, there were 'few flags'. Two days before the wedding, *The Times* revealed that the government's decision to make the day – a Wednesday – a public holiday had not been universally welcomed: 'Many firms were reluctant to pay their workers, arguing that they could not afford it at a time of recession.'

The rest of the press, more unreservedly royalist, with extensive resources committed to the wedding, tried to will a great occasion into being. In the week before the ceremony, along the swept-clean, tree-sided tunnel of the Mall, the same few fanatical wedding-watchers – mainly women, mainly white, with flasks of tea and stoical smiles – were repeatedly interviewed by different newspapers about their pavement camping strategies and hopes for the royal couple. Away from London, the government tried haphazardly to create a sense of national celebration. Beacons were lit on the eve of the wedding, *The Times* reported, 'on the same sites used to warn the nation of the approach of the Spanish Armada'. The navy's traditional rum ration, 'abolished as an economy measure in 1970', was restored for the day itself. There was a sense of a nation rummaging around in its past for suitably patriotic symbols, and coming up with strikingly military-tinged odds and ends.

But a haphazard celebration could still stir up something. The evening before the wedding, a fireworks display in Hyde Park in central London was attended by so many people – the police said more than half a million – that a crush developed afterwards at the park exits and more than 1,200 people were slightly injured. Along the Mall that night, and on the usually orderly lawns of Green Park and St James's Park to the immediate north and south, a semi-anarchy of moonlit picnicking and drinking and football-style chanting – 'Lady Di, Lady Di, Lady Di' – was permitted by the authorities. The weather had turned suddenly warmer, always a great London loosener, and the perceptive journalist Ian Jack, covering the wedding for the *Sunday Times*, sensed 'a new kind of British behaviour, ribald and self-mocking', in London's staid royal quarter.

The bride-to-be had been moved to the Queen Mother's official residence, Clarence House. 'They put me in a bedroom overlooking the Mall,' recalled Diana, 'which meant I didn't get any sleep.' That night she also 'had a very bad fit of bulimia'. At eight o'clock on her wedding morning, the police estimated the crowd at 900,000. By the time she was escorted up the Mall towards St Paul's, in prickling sunshine, in a goldfish-bowl coach that was too small for her whale-tail of a dress, to a ceremony described by the presiding Archbishop of Canterbury Robert Runcie as 'the stuff of which fairy tales are made', the global television audience, attracted by the rarity of a genuinely significant royal wedding, was estimated at 750 million.

'The crowds buoyed you up,' Diana told Morton later. On the day, *The Times* felt the same, seeing 'crowds drawn from the many nations over which the British Throne holds titular sway as well as lost colonies'. In truth, as with all royal processions in London, many of those behind the police barriers were actually tourists. They did not necessarily have any imperial or commonwealth connections, or any wider loyalty to Britain at all. But for a day it was possible for patriots to believe again that London, even Britain, was the centre of the world. The crowds bawled 'Rule Britannia' for the banks of foreign TV cameras.

Two days earlier, the royal yacht of the same name had sailed from Portsmouth, the tattered old naval city sixty miles away on the south coast, heading for a honeymoon rendezvous with the royal couple at another resonant British citadel, Gibraltar. Hundreds of cheering people lined Portsmouth's fortified sea wall to watch *Britannia*, built when Britain still had an empire, steam past. The day after the wedding, *The Times* concluded, 'The national response to the royal marriage is itself a source of hope.' The *Guardian* saw such sentiments as wishful thinking: 'Radiance and romance may bring a smile, even momentary cheer. But they change nothing. There is . . . no new national spirit to be tapped . . . Two people who seem to be in love' – the 'seem to be' was well judged – 'got married . . . [but] the pageantry was simply pageantry.'

Within a few days the wedding was gone from the serious papers. But even as the *Guardian* was dismissing the possibility of a 'new national spirit', another, less predictable patriotic surge was under way. Its trigger was something almost as charged with national symbolism as a royal marriage, at least for the English: cricket.

In early July 1981, England were on an almost unprecedented losing streak in their great imperial sport. In Test matches, the often attritional, sometimes mesmerizing, occasionally electrifying five-day contests that then still dominated the sport, they had won only two games since Margaret Thatcher had been elected over two years previously. In Australia, in the southern hemisphere summer of 1979–80, England were swatted aside by their oldest rivals 3-0 in a three-match series; in the English summer of 1980 they were lucky to lose a five-match series only 1-0 to the West Indies, the alliance of former Caribbean colonies, most of them British, which was beginning to dominate world cricket. Only rearguard actions and the loss of play to rain kept the margin respectable. The crowds were thin. In the winter of 1980–81, England played the West Indies again, this time in the Caribbean. Again they lost, but this time the sense of a former overlord being humbled was more explicitly political. In Guyana the government revoked the visa of one of the England players, Robin Jackman, on the basis that he regularly played and coached in apartheid South Africa, and the match was cancelled.

Back in England for the 1981 summer season, the team was presented with the most charged and high-profile set of fixtures of all: a home series against Australia. There were six Test matches, an unusually large number, stretching from mid-June into September; and an English sporting press primed by all the recent defeats to administer even stronger doses than usual of mockery and moralizing fury.

By 1981 the England team was a motley assortment. It reflected a dip in talent that, as with many of the country's other underlying problems, had become apparent in the mid-1970s. There were green youngsters such as Graham Dilley, a gangly bowler who delivered the ball like an unreliable catapult; veterans such as the cussedly slow batsman Geoff Boycott, and the careeringly fast bowler Bob Willis, who had bad knees but a terrifyingly distant stare when his game clicked; and finally a captain, Ian Botham, who had been arguably the best player in the world until given the captaincy in 1980 – and bafflingly mediocre ever since.

Even by the standards of professional cricketers, 'Both' was a complicated figure, full of the neuroses and eccentricities that such a drawn-out, capricious sport instils. A northerner, he played for the most showbiz of southern county teams, Somerset, alongside several West Indian superstars. A Conservative supporter in an era when Toryism (and cricket) often had an openly racist edge, he was known for his outspoken friendships with black cricketers. Literally colour-blind, a claustrophobic, a bearer of grudges, sometimes overweight, before becoming captain at the precocious age of twenty-four he played regardless like someone with no insecurities whatsoever. A slingy, muscular bowler who could make the ball bend wickedly in the damp English air, he performed sometimes with cunning and sometimes with adrenalized bravado. He took wickets with both brilliant and terrible deliveries, and with record-breaking regularity. When he batted, he was even more of a comic-book hero. In the flimsy England batting order, he usually came in seventh, the last of the team's proper batsmen before the pokers and the flailers. When he went out to bat, England were often in trouble; Botham's job was to launch counter-attacks and improbable recoveries, or at least go down fighting. Like Thatcher, he relished confrontations. With a quick eye, an extra-heavy bat and long, loose arms, he would swing hard: sometimes in smooth, straight textbook arcs, and sometimes with cruder, clubbing strokes, like a village cricketer on steroids. 'Beefy', as he was also known, was a hairy six foot two, and looked like a more handsome version of Obelix, Asterix's mountainous sidekick. Like Obelix, Botham appeared not always to know his own power.

Then he became England captain and the fairy tale stopped. Instead, there were increasingly distracted, anonymous performances, and a leadership style that lacked spark. Yet by 1981 Australia were also vulnerable. Their captain, Kim Hughes, was young and green too. Most of his players had little experience of England's idiosyncratic playing conditions. His team was factional, full of rivalries carried over from Australian domestic cricket, and some of the best players were absent, having defected to a breakaway international tournament organized by the Australian media magnate Kerry Packer.

The first Test match of the England-Australia series was played at Nottingham, in dim, finger-chilling weather. Batting was difficult. England held the initiative, tentatively and briefly, then lost it and never quite got it back. After four days of progressively smaller, eked-out batting scores, Australia won narrowly. Botham had another forgettable match, scoring 1 and 33 and taking only three wickets. He was retained as captain for the next game; but solely, it seemed, for the lack of an alternative.

The second Test was at Lord's, the often stiff, always status-conscious headquarters of English cricket. England played fractionally better – they drew – but again the weather was dismal and the cricket mediocre. On the second day, after play had been called off early because the light was too feeble, cushions were thrown onto the pitch by the crowd, including by some of the usually prim Lord's members. Frustration at the England team was becoming unusually strong and universal. When Botham batted, he scored 0 in both innings. Walking off the pitch after getting out a second time, he wrote, 'I approached the members sitting in their seats in front of the pavilion . . . Most of them sat unmoving, staring straight ahead.' After the game, he resigned the captaincy; soon afterwards the selectors announced they would have sacked him anyway.

To replace him, they chose the most different kind of cricketer imaginable. Mike Brearley was a part-time psychotherapist who lived in Highgate, then one of north London's more intellectual suburbs. A public schoolboy with two degrees from Cambridge, he had been a successful England captain in the late 1970s, renowned for his perceptive man-management and clever placement of fielders; but after the 3-0 thrashing by Australia in 1979–80, aged thirty-seven and beginning to approach his sporting retirement, Brearley had given up the captaincy to concentrate on his therapy. Now, in 1981, a year and a half older, prematurely grey-haired, he was being recalled. The sense of a short-term fix, of options being exhausted, of a failed iconoclast being replaced by an establishment figure: if there was a wider metaphor here, perhaps for the prospects of Prime Minister Thatcher, it was not reassuring.

Nor was the venue for the next match. Headingley in Leeds can be the bleakest of English Test cricket grounds: unlovely stands exposed to the Yorkshire weather, cold players enduring cutting Yorkshire banter, the pitch often an enemy to batsmen yet an unreliable friend to bowlers. In 1981 the ground had a particularly notorious recent history. Six years before, a Test against Australia had been abandoned at its climax after protesters, seeking the release of George Davis, an East End villain wrongly convicted for an armed robbery, poured oil on the pitch and made it unplayable. Subsequent Tests in 1978, 1979 and 1980 were all ruined by rain.

On 16 July 1981, under another heavy Headingley sky, Brearley led England out onto the field. He had lost the toss, and Australia had chosen to bat first. The pitch was dry, too dry – in cricket, pitch preparation is never an exact science – and would get worse for batsmen as the match went on, as cracks opened, the ball hit them, and either jumped or shot along the ground. Yet for the first two days of the game Australia batted quite comfortably. England bowled without much luck or accuracy: fielders spilled catches, good deliveries just missed the stumps, bad deliveries were patiently picked off. From the crowd, there was silence and sporadic catcalls.

I watched it all from my parents' television room. We were living in the Hampshire commuter belt, two hundred miles south of Headingley and in another England altogether, in a palatial but institutional army house with wooded grounds and chilly staff, my father's questionable reward for a recent promotion. I was home for the holidays from boarding school, where I had started following Test cricket properly two years earlier, in the middle of the Botham craze, as an anxious nine-year-old looking for carefree heroes. I had memorized his match-winning triumphs down to the last detail. But those days seemed gone. As I sat alone on our sticky army sofa in a trance of exasperation and boredom – the default mode of the frustrated cricket supporter – the Australians inched to 401, an almost impregnable score in the circumstances.

The one small consolation was a spell of bowling late in the innings from Botham. Running in with some of his old bounce, he took six wickets, his best performance since his pre-captaincy glories. But it felt defiant, not match-altering; and all the more so when England's turn to bat finally came: they made 174, Botham top scorer with a token-feeling 50. Australia, having outscored England by 200 or more, had the right to make their opponents 'follow on' – bat again immediately – an ordeal and a humiliation in Test cricket that usually meant rapid defeat. Only once, when England beat Australia in Sydney in 1894, had a Test team followed on and gone on to win.

On the third evening at Headingley, England plodded out to bat again, and almost immediately lost a wicket. Then the gloom closed in and play was called off for the day. Minutes later, reported the *Sun*, 'Four men barged their way into the pavilion' – spectators looking for the match umpires who had halted play. The umpires had gone, but 'The men were met by Alan Martin, marketing director of [the series' sponsors] Cornhill Insurance. Martin said, "They were not yobs and were not drunk. But they were extremely angry."' After the cushion-throwing at Lord's, the atmosphere around the England team was souring further. the *Sun* gave its own verdict on the day's play: 'PATHETIC!'

A strange lull followed. The next day, a Sunday, was a rest day: in 1981 Test matches still featured them, a residue of less fraught sporting eras. Botham had a house not that far from Headingley, in the north Lincolnshire countryside. After play ended on the third day, he put on a barbecue for the players of both sides. Boozy off-field fraternizing between opponents was usual during Test matches, and everyone who came to the barbecue would have the rest day to sleep it off.

The Australians arrived in a cocky mood, the England players less so. 'It was a rather subdued event at first,' Botham later wrote. Most of the England team expected to lose the match soon after play resumed on Monday, and some expected their Test careers to end at the same time. But after enough beer, escapism trumped introspection: there was an England–Australia rugby scrum on the lawn, more drinking until dawn, then some messing around on quad bikes.

This mood of silliness and resignation spilled over into the match. Before play restarted on the Monday, Botham, Willis and several other England players checked out of the team hotel in Leeds: professional cricketers travel constantly, and they wanted to save time when defeat came. By mid-afternoon, that outcome seemed even more certain: all England's good batsmen were out except Botham, and England needed to score an unlikely 92 more runs just to make Australia bat again. Botham was joined at the crease by Dilley, an impulsive batting novice of crude strength but little judgement, who had been one of the quad bikers the day before.

The ground was half-full, finally warming in a faint sun after days of grey, and with the end of the match seemingly in sight, a demob-happy feeling took hold. 'Picca [Dilley] and I tried to see who could play the most idiotic stroke,' Botham recalled. Botham himself had borrowed the weightiest bat he could find, while the hulking Dilley had a bat that looked too small. They slashed and swiped, carved and hoicked, swung at the ball more like bad golfers or baseball players than international cricketers. And even their mis-hits started to race away. 'We felt like men in a play,' remembered Botham. 'Everything had a dreamy feeling . . . like a mad interlude in a serious drama.' The Australians, their dressing-room bath already full of champagne bottles ready to be covered with ice, were at first amused, then irritated, then alarmed. In his biography of the Australian captain Kim Hughes, Christian Ryan wonders: 'How [Botham's] windmill wind-ups . . . evaded hands and stumps so repeatedly defies rational explanation . . . England's turnaround was so fast, so implausible to the fieldsmen . . . that it became almost an hallucinatory experience, as if they were onlookers not participants.' Ryan quotes Hughes's teammate Graham Wood: 'I still have nightmares about that Test . . . It kept rolling on and on and on.'

In the crowd, with each ball that was battered to the boundary, an intrigued murmur began to stir; then defiant cheers; then a football-ground roar. Union Jacks were produced – in the royal-wedding summer, there were a lot of them about. Botham grinned as he batted, his longish, late 1970s rock-star haircut sweaty and matted. When

Dilley was out, after the wildest hour and a quarter of his batting career, the other England bowlers produced unusually defiant innings of their own as Botham, playing slightly more responsibly as the match's possibilities opened out, stretched his score almost inconceivably to 149 not out.

I missed the whole thing. After the first three days of the game, I had been sent on a long-arranged visit to family friends in the Scottish countryside, where cricket was less of a priority. Driving back to their house with them after a cold day trip to Edinburgh, the first I heard of events at Headingley was a thrilling blurt from the car radio: 'Botham scores a century, and England live to fight another day.' The next day's *Sun* seized on it hungrily as a national allegory: 'The Bulldog Breed bared its teeth again . . . as Ian Botham and Graham Dilley gave the Australians a "V" sign Winston Churchill would have been proud of.'

And yet, most cricket reporters and England supporters did not expect the fightback to make much difference: Australia only needed 130 runs to win. For most of the morning of the fifth day, the game slid back towards anticlimax. A scattered crowd watched: barely 2,000 in a ground with a capacity of 16,000. Australia got the first 56 runs batting as they had in their first innings, steadily and almost bloodlessly, losing only one wicket. England again bowled impotently. Australia now needed 74 with nine wickets left. Only schoolboy cricket teams missed such targets.

Then Bob Willis, who had failed to take a single wicket in the match and was feeling his age – thirty-two, autumnal for a fast bowler – asked Brearley if he could bowl with the Headingley wind shoving behind him. Brearley, dismissed by the Headingley crowd and the tabloids since his return as captain as ineffectual and over-intellectual, now used a little of his therapist's shrewdness: he told the insecure Willis he could bowl downwind only if he forgot about accuracy and did so as fast as possible.

At 12.40 p.m., Willis began to pound in on his bad knees, spindly legs pumping, one arm flapping, white man's Afro wilting, possessed eyes staring – 'I was in a trance of some kind,' he recalled – and immediately his deliveries began to hit the cracks in the pitch and spit wickedly upwards. A cricket ball can be dangerous, especially when moving at over 80 miles an hour, and the Australian batsmen were caught between protecting their hands and faces and protecting their wickets. They began to play jumpily and get out. Wickets fell in panicky clusters: four by 1 p.m., eight by 2 p.m.

As England went from doomed to in with a chance to the verge of triumph, Headingley filled and got louder – 'Both-am! Both-am! Will-is! Will-is!' – even louder than during Botham's innings the day before. Away from the ground, on high streets from Kent to Glasgow, small crowds of people were seen outside television rental shops – Britain's still-cautious response to the age of consumer electronics – watching and then shouting as Willis charged in and the Australian batsmen flinched and the England fielders clung to the sort of catches they had fumbled three days earlier. In London, 'Stock Exchange trading [came] almost to a standstill,' reported the *Daily Telegraph*, 'as people watched the match on television.'

The Times pointed out that traders needed a lift: 'The general economic outlook offered little in the way of comfort. The latest unemployment figures showed a further increase ... and confirmed fears of three million unemployed before long ... [Trading] conditions were again described as thin ... Sentiment remained drab ... Small amounts of nervous selling persisted.' Yet starting at 2 p.m., when the eighth Australian wicket fell and an England victory became probable, there was a modest rally in the FTSE share index, which until then had been falling.

At 2.20 p.m. Willis flattened the last Australian batsmen's middle stump and England had won. The margin was a narrow but not sensational 18 runs, yet the crowd swamped the pitch like football hooligans. They taunted the Australian team coach as it left, and bellowed out 'Jerusalem' in front of the pavilion. The England players appeared briefly on the balcony, Willis's expression still completely glazed; then they quickly headed for the M1 and the treadmill of their next matches. 'It wasn't until you were driving down the motorway,' Dilley remembered later, 'and people were beeping their horns at you and waving and giving you the thumbs up that you realized what had been achieved ... Given the state of the country in 1981 it was something that people could latch onto.' Peter Willey, an England batsman who had played only a minor part in the victory, found the response 'unbelievable': 'It was like winning a world war.'

The following day the front page of the *Daily Telegraph* read: 'Australians Meet Their Agincourt'. Inside the paper commented: 'England won against odds that were at one stage quoted at 500 to one. Perhaps, reflecting on this apparent impossibility, Mrs Thatcher may sleep a little easier.'

A fortnight later, in the next Test at Birmingham, Australia spent three days painstakingly setting up another dominant position. Then Botham took five wickets in a manic half hour, and England won. It was 'the noisiest [Test] ever played in England, reckoned the home players,' recorded Ryan, 'as if the [royal] wedding guests had decamped from St Paul's Cathedral and flocked to Edgbaston for the reception.' Even the determinedly patriotic *Daily Mail* was astonished: 'We had considered writing about the mounting threat of a national rail strike . . . or the stratospheric losses of British Airways. The last thing we had in mind was another stirring leading article about cricket.' A fortnight after that, in mid-August, at the penultimate Test in Manchester, with England on their way to defeat yet again, Botham conjured 118 runs in a display of *Boy's Own* hitting that outdid Headingley and almost every other innings in Test history. England won the game, and with it the series.

Throughout July and August, Brearley received 'at least fifty letters a week' about the matches. 'There were occasional hints,' he wrote, 'that the dramatic and precarious successes by the national team had some intangible effect on national morale . . . One card read, simply, "A wonderful tonic for England in these hard times." "People keep writing us off," went another. "But they need not, while cricket continues."'

The series ended on 1 September. Two months later, England went to India for their next series – and lost: beginning a sequence of mixed-to-terrible results that would last for over twenty years. Like the royal wedding, 'The Incredible Tests' of the summer of 1981, the title of an instant, blow-by-blow, but somehow tepid book that I bought that autumn, fleetingly revealed and altered aspects of the national mood. But they offered no suggestions as to how the country might more deeply and lastingly remake itself. Britons could not all be Bothams – gifted and charismatic enough, and lucky enough in what they did, to be able to reverse years of decline in an hour or two. Nor, increasingly after 1981, could Botham himself; despite playing Test cricket for eleven more years, he never quite recaptured the wider public imagination or his 1981 Ashes form.

Yet there was one more patriotic craze in 1981, also superficially to do with sport, which lasted much longer than a few weeks and spread a slightly more realistic message about national revival.

Chariots of Fire was a film about competition: its dilemmas, its costs, but also its potential for self-fulfilment. 'I was very interested in the competitive nature of athletics – beating one's best, beating one's previous time,' the director Hugh Hudson told me later. The film was also interested in competition against others, and the possibilities that success opened up: 'I don't think it would've been made if they hadn't won.'

'They' were Harold Abrahams and Eric Liddell, British runners and rivals who took gold at the 1924 Paris Olympics. Abrahams won the 100m, Liddell the 400m. Abrahams was Jewish at a time of widespread British anti-Semitism; Liddell was a devout Christian who refused to run on a Sunday, and so had to switch from his favoured 100m to the 400m. Famous in the 1920s, Liddell died in 1945 and Abrahams in 1978, by which time they and their Paris deeds had been largely forgotten.

'There was a single paragraph on Liddell in a book I found on the history of the Olympics,' remembered David Puttnam, the producer of *Chariots of Fire*, when we met four decades later. In 1981, Puttnam was forty, but already an experienced hustler in the ramshackle village that was the British film industry. Like Hudson and an increasing number of the industry's youngish talents, he had started out in advertising, with its better commercial and international prospects. In the early 1960s, Puttnam had been a groovily connected young ad executive, close to the Beatles and David Bailey. But by 1970 that London scene was over, and Puttnam left advertising for the theoretically more fulfilling business of making movies. He had a natural dealmaker's voice, soft but insistent, steadily more Hollywood-style bouffant hair, and sporadic successes: he produced *Bugsy Malone* in 1976 and *Midnight Express* in 1978. Yet the British film industry seemed a place of steadily narrowing horizons. In 1979, sixty-one British films were made; in 1980, thirty-one; in 1981, twenty-four.

In response, Puttnam tried periodically to establish himself in America. It did not go well. By Hollywood standards, his drive, charm and track record were unremarkable, and the effort of trying to prove otherwise exhausted him and gave him asthma-like symptoms. In early 1977, feeling too ill to go to the office, he was in a rented house in Los Angeles, watching the incessant California winter rain and looking for reasons to avoid reading film scripts, when he glanced along the shelves of books and was intrigued by one on the Olympics. Dipping into it, he came across the Liddell paragraph.

As a boy, Puttnam had loved sport, the Olympics in particular. 'My dad was in charge of still photography at the '48 [London] Olympics. For the '56 Olympics, in Melbourne, I created my own Olympics, done with Subbuteo men, including keeping record books of the winners.' But in the 1960s such straightforward worship of sporting stars had gone out of fashion in some British quarters. Raw, disillusioned films such as *The Loneliness of the Long Distance Runner* (1962) and *This Sporting Life* (1963) instead portrayed sport as brutal, often pointless, and a way for the powerful to distract the powerless. Left-leaning politically, Puttnam in some ways admired the acclaimed director of *This Sporting Life*, Lindsay Anderson, and his equally revered producer, Karel Reisz. Yet by the late 1970s Puttnam had wearied of what he saw as their 'dyspeptic' view of Britain. 'I was consciously looking for a film [to make] that would allow people to imagine a better place, out of this crappy world.' In the story of Liddell and the 1924 Olympics, Puttnam felt he had found his subject: 'He was a little-fancied Brit, an underdog, and in running he found transcendence.' Puttnam also sensed that these themes might now go down well with the public. 'If you'd made *Chariots* in the 1960s, it would've been booed off the screen. But by 1981 it was the low point of Thatcherism. The country *badly* needed a lift.'

By the time we spoke he was Lord Puttnam, a busy and high-profile Labour peer, and practised at making such pronouncements. We met at an immaculate Westminster restaurant. He wore a dark grey suit, but his hair was still longish and when he crossed his legs he revealed pink socks. 'There is still a lot of the 60s left in me,' he said. He was keen to emphasize that *Chariots of Fire*'s version of the Liddell and Abrahams story, although slightly more heroic than the reality, with some minor feats invented and time frames compressed, was never intended as nationalistic propaganda: 'As far as I was concerned, the most important thing was that they were both outsiders, and they didn't do what was required of them.' Yet he conceded the film was meant to be emotional and populist: 'I knew from advertising that the way to capture attention was through broad strokes.'

Hudson had never directed a feature film when Puttnam hired him for *Chariots of Fire*. But in advertising and documentary-making Hudson had a reputation as a clear and muscular visual stylist. *Fangio: A Life at 300 km/h*, a film he made about the 1950s Argentinian racing driver Juan Manuel Fangio, had won a cinema release in 1979. 'He [Fangio] was a *hero*,' Hudson told me. 'He became a good friend. I spent a year with him.' Even more than Puttnam, Hudson was fascinated by sporting achievement. 'I went to the '48 Olympics. Fanny Blankers-Koen [the legendary Dutch athlete] won four golds. Fantastic!'

Whereas Puttnam was a middle-class north Londoner from the aspiring outer suburbs, Hudson had learned about sport on the playing fields of Eton, following his father and grandfather. Five years older than Puttnam, Hudson was a more complicated character. He had loathed aspects of Eton: 'I couldn't keep up with those people – the super-elite. And I saw the way they treated Jews and scholarship boys.' Straight after school, he joined the army, for its 'egalitarianism' and opportunities for adventure. In 1956, aged twenty, 'I was in a tank regiment, embarked to go to Suez. I wanted to fight.' But the notoriously misconceived British military expedition was called off before he could.

A faint air of unfulfilment still hung over Hudson. He was friendly at first on the phone, a deep, rich voice full of enthusiasm for *Chariots of Fire* – 'I hope it still has a message for today' – but then his agreement to meet gradually receded into a maze of further, gloomier calls – '*Chariots* was used, and misunderstood' – and increasingly gruff last-minute cancellations. We finally met in London on a dark spring lunchtime. His house was in Chelsea, a lovely thin Georgian terrace facing a huge square. The house was surrounded by the former residences of Tory politicians – the address where Margaret Thatcher plotted her path to power in the 1970s was three streets away – and by the current prize assets of the foreign property investors and City professionals that she had done so much to liberate. Hudson came to the door in a baggy shirt and pale jeans, a lean, long-faced seventy-five-year-old, hair tousled, almost spiky: he looked like a Chelsea bohemian from the old days, before the bankers arrived. The house had been in his family for generations, and its deep, open-plan living room and study had black floorboards, antiques and a desk at the far end. Hudson sat down at it, in front of a laptop, one foot bobbing, and answered my questions in terse sentences between glances at the screen.

In 1978 he first read an early version of the *Chariots of Fire* script, written by the politically orientated English actor and screenwriter Colin Welland. 'I thought it would be a small English film about two runners,' Hudson said. But the project soon broadened. 'I was ambitious – there's nothing wrong with ambition. And I like beautiful imagery.' From its early scene of the runners training, dressed in angelic white, caught between ecstasy and agony on a grey-gold sweep of British beach, Hudson gave the film an unashamedly romantic look: somewhere between sunlit period drama, the slow-motion climaxes of the more arty kind of action movie, and the most lavish British TV advertising – the beach scene was a calmer echo of the Metro ad.

'Running is eternal,' said Hudson, reverently, looking up from his laptop. 'And the film also has a sort of elegiac quality. You can't avoid that. It is set in an England that is regretfully gone.' He paused with typical ambivalence. 'Maybe.' Yet neither he, nor the screenwriter Welland, nor Puttnam wanted the film to seem a museum piece. 'It was necessary to have something contemporary in it, to bring it into the ken of the public, give it a charge.' So for the soundtrack Hudson hired the Greek electronic composer Vangelis, with whom he had worked on ads and documentaries since the 1960s. Vangelis wrote a stately, pulsing, sad-euphoric theme for the film that sounded like a lusher and more sentimental version of records by the German electronic band Kraftwerk, who were hugely successful in the late 1970s and early 1980s. In March 1981, unusually and ambitiously for a film score, the piece was released as a single, with an accompanying video including clips from the film.

Other novel elements of the film grew out of the politics of its makers. Hudson, Puttnam and Welland were all on the left, but by the early 1980s Puttnam and Hudson had reservations. Puttnam thought Labour was too extreme and that trade unions had too much power. Hudson, meanwhile, developed contradictory feelings about Thatcher. 'I hated her. I think she destroyed so much, frankly. She made this country a service country. But' – he bobbed a foot – 'she stood by what she believed. That's an admirable quality.'

Like Puttnam, Hudson was open to the idea of a national revival. 'It was the 80s now. We were coming out of the [era of] the three-day week. We capitalized on that with *Chariots*. It showed things that were good about Britain. It was flag-waving in places – it got highly criticized for that. But what's wrong with liking a country? Everyone likes their own country.'

The film presented Britain in the 1920s as a place in flux, both traumatized and full of new opportunities. 'There was turmoil then – unemployment, war damage, the General Strike – just as there was turmoil in 81,' said Hudson. 'But the runners are standing up for their own beliefs. Abrahams is fighting for his place in our society.' In one of the key scenes, the intense, impatient runner is summoned to dinner with the authorities at his Cambridge college, to be reprimanded for his use of a professional coach at a time when the amateur ethic still reigned. The angry young man and his smoothly patronizing seniors sit down in a quintessentially stuffy Oxbridge room, all ritual tableware and heavy panelling. The master of the college, played, significantly, by the great social pessimist Lindsay Anderson, says to Abrahams reproachfully: 'Your aim is to win at all costs.'

'Perhaps you would rather I played the gentleman, and lost?' Abrahams responds.

'To playing the tradesman, yes,' says the master.

A few seconds later, Abrahams wipes his handsome mouth with his napkin, and abruptly stands up to leave. 'Gentlemen,' he says. 'You yearn for victory just as I do, but achieved with the apparent effortlessness of gods. Yours are the archaic values of the prep school playground. You deceive no one but yourselves. I believe in the pursuit of excellence. And I'll carry the future with me!'

The scene could almost have been scripted by one of Margaret

Thatcher's speechwriters. Elsewhere, the film was more ambivalent about self-improvement. It portrayed Abrahams as never quite settled or satisfied, even after winning his gold medal. By showing him struggling against subtle and unsubtle anti-Semitism – 'tradesman' – the film also helped make his story palatable for liberal audiences. But *Chariots of Fire* was tub-thumping enough – starting with its title, a quote from 'Jerusalem', a poem long claimed by British Conservatives – to alienate or baffle some of Puttnam's circle. 'I knew people at the *Sunday Times* magazine, a group that was quite sort of 60s. Two months before we released the film, hoping to get a good spread in the magazine, I arranged a screening. About twelve of them turned up. And they hated it! Not one scrap of enthusiasm. I was absolutely devastated.' The radical gay film-maker Derek Jarman, who since the 1970s had been directing bleaker, more adventurous state-of-the-nation movies, later dismissed *Chariots of Fire* bitchily but lethally: 'muscular Christianism and jingo[ism], crypto-faggy Cambridge stuff . . . lots of running nowhere in slow-motion . . . rewriting history [from] far away in Hollywood.'

The film almost failed to get a cinema release. One of its financiers was Dodi Fayed, Diana's future boyfriend – Britain can be a small and tangled place – and he became anxious about his investment, so the film was offered to the American television network ABC Sports instead. The network said no. *Chariots of Fire* was a film about a foreign country of middling importance, set in the distant past, with a first-time director and no stars.

Finally, in mid-April 1981, the film was released in cinemas over the Easter weekend, a perfect date for its religious and resurrectionary themes. Alexander Walker, the much-followed film critic of the London *Evening Standard*, was captivated: 'It puts you in direct touch with sentiments so long unexpressed . . . love of country, fear of God . . . modesty in victory.' But other critics were not. In America, the even more influential Pauline Kael disapproved of the film's 'mildewed high moral tone' and 'manufactured, go-to-the-mountain poetry' – a poetry, she noted with typical astuteness, of the kind that usually 'sells products'. And yet, she conceded, 'The picture works.'

It took a while for the public to notice. 'Opening business was not great,' remembered Puttnam. He and Hudson spent the Easter weekend in the Isles of Scilly, on the escapist, pseudo-tropical island of Tresco, half-hiding from any news about their film and half-desperate for it. 'The first cinema *Chariots* played in was a 600-seater, the Odeon Haymarket in London. We heard on the phone that it was only two-thirds full on the Easter Monday. I thought the film was over.'

Yet its lyricism and emotional intensity left a mark on those who saw it: enough word-of-mouth was generated to keep it in the cinemas. The film's patriotic themes and a dearth of other British releases made it a rallying point for the industry's supporters, and it was chosen for a Royal Command Performance. Meanwhile the Vangelis single and video acted as an increasingly potent advertisement for the film, and vice versa. The single got to number twelve in the UK charts and number one in the United States. 'I remember going shopping on the King's Road [in Chelsea],' remembered Puttnam, 'and after I'd walked in and out of about five shops, including the butchers, and it was playing in every single shop, I started laughing.'

In May the usually seen-it-all Hollywood trade magazine *Variety* published a piece on *Chariots of Fire* headlined 'Hope Of A Dispirited Britain'. Fortuitously, an actual revival in British running gave the film a further claim on the zeitgeist. At the 1980 Olympics, after a track medal famine for much of the 1970s, two skinny, pale British rivals in the Liddell-Abrahams mould, Steve Ovett and Sebastian Coe, had won gold in the 800m and 1,500m respectively. Ovett, gaunt and staring and explosive on the track (Coe was more of a glider), even had something of Abrahams about him. In August 1981, with *Chariots of Fire* still playing in cinemas, and Ian Botham in the process of almost single-handedly overwhelming the Australians, Coe and Ovett broke the world record for the mile three times between them, in a single, breathlessly reported nine-day period. British sport had seldom seemed so heroic.

Chariots of Fire began to be screened at Conservative Party fund-raisers. In 1982 the film's British audience reached three and a half million – an influential one in fifteen of the whole population – and higher Tory powers took notice. Puttnam, always a good networker, had known Margaret Thatcher's less forbidding journalist daughter Carol since the 1970s: 'I met her at a do in Australia. We got on very well, and sort of stayed in touch.' In December 1982 he was summoned to meet her mother at Chequers. 'There was a very strange mix of people, including the chairman of Sainsbury's and Andrew Lloyd Webber. I was introduced to the prime minister as a triumphant film-maker.' Puttnam smiled half-modestly in his plush restaurant chair. 'She was always very nice to me after that, right through to her last days in power. Whenever I bumped into her, she said' – he slipped into a passable impersonation of her heavy diction – '"*He-llo*, David, how are you?"'

In April 1982 the film magazine *Screen International* reported that Ronald Reagan, another embattled right-wing head of state with an appetite for heroes, was also a *Chariots of Fire* fan. In America the film had made $31 million, five times its smallish budget, then a record for a foreign production. On 29 March, at the Oscars, against strong competition it won Best Picture, Best Screenplay, Best Original Score and Best Costume Design. Accepting the screenplay award, Welland, a thickset man from Lancashire crammed into his tuxedo, with a walrus moustache and a cloud of curly hair – a less Hollywood figure it was hard to imagine – made a delighted, manic four-line speech. 'You may have started something,' he concluded. 'The British are coming!'

PART TWO

Morbid Symptoms

3
The Liverpool Model

In the early 1980s, optimists about Britain set great store by its successful exports: of hit films, pop music, even oil, as the North Sea deposits discovered a decade or more earlier finally began to flow in even more plentiful quantities than the thirsty country required. For much of the post-war period, Britain had imported more goods than it exported; the resulting trade deficits had become widely seen as a sign of approaching economic doom, that a once-great trading and manufacturing nation could no longer make its way in the world. In 1980 this pattern went into reverse: that year, and in 1981 and 1982, there was a rare British trade surplus in goods.

Yet the economic commodity most valued by the first Thatcher government was an import. It was not an industrial product but something much more modern, an intellectual product, a theory: monetarism.

Roughly defined – and only brave people define it precisely – monetarism says that governments can only control inflation, and therefore ensure a healthy economy, if they control the amount of money circulating in their country. Since inflation means money becoming less valuable, the way to make money more valuable, and therefore reduce inflation, is by restricting the amount of it available.

Most economic historians say the theory first germinated in the 1930s, at the University of Chicago, probably the leading twentieth-century laboratory of modern right-wing ideas. For years, monetarism then spread its tendrils steadily but largely unnoticed through American economics departments, before finally flowering during the 1960s in the more conspicuous hothouses of Anglo-American academia, political think tanks and the thoughtful parts of business journalism.

By then rising inflation was beginning to threaten the West's long post-war boom. Monetarism appeared to offer a solution. In 1980 the BBC broadcast 'Free to Choose', a surprisingly watchable imported television series showcasing the thinking of the American radical right, presented and co-written by Milton Friedman, a University of Chicago professor with deceptively merry eyes and a folksy drawl. 'Inflation is like alcoholism,' the gnome-like Friedman explained. 'When you start drinking, or when you [the government] start printing too much money, the good effects come first. The bad effects only come later. When it comes to the cure, it's the other way round. When you stop drinking, or you stop printing money, the bad effects come first, and the good effects only come later. That's why it's so hard to persist with the cure. [But] every country that has been able to persist with the policy of slow monetary growth has been able to cure inflation.' The latter, monetarist approach was 'scientific', Friedman assured viewers, with a certainty that made him sound, improbably and momentarily, like the most doctrinaire sort of Marxist.

Monetarism was a dull word but it had dramatic implications. For Friedman and other right-wingers, it meant drastic cuts in government spending. Such spending had risen across the world during the mid-twentieth century as countries established or expanded welfare states. Yet Friedman was not at all squeamish about saying that these protections should be slashed, nor about which governments he advised to do so. In 1975, to widespread outrage, he had publicly visited Chile, where the vicious military dictator Augusto Pinochet, who had overthrown the elected left-wing government of Salvador Allende two years earlier, was already being guided by right-wing Chilean graduates of the University of Chicago known as 'the Chicago Boys'. Friedman met Pinochet, and advised him to move the country even further away from Allende's free-spending policies in order to control inflation. Pinochet's pioneering austerity experiment provoked massive and recurring social unrest. When the dictator used water cannon, torture and state murder to keep it in check, Friedman neither publicly supported nor condemned the repression that Chile's 'Chicago School' policies appeared to necessitate.

Friedman saw Britain as another case, equally important but different, for what he called the monetarist 'shock treatment'. 'The Thatcher government is a kind of experiment,' he said in October 1979, 'in whether it will be possible, in a democratic society that has gone as far [leftwards] as Britain has gone . . . to set [that society] on a new road.'

From the 1940s to the mid-1970s, Labour and Conservative governments alike had followed economic policies that ignored the strict rules of monetarism, when Whitehall was aware of monetarism at all, in favour of a more forgiving theory: Keynesianism. The left-leaning Cambridge economist John Maynard Keynes had argued that governments should alleviate the slumps that periodically came with capitalism by increasing, not decreasing, the amount of money in the economy. Keynesianism, or at least the sometimes approximate version applied by Whitehall, worked reasonably well for three decades, ensuring that the grinding, socially devastating Depression of the 1930s which had helped form and popularize Keynes's ideas did not recur, and that most Britons got steadily richer. But by the mid-1970s, Whitehall Keynesianism was yielding diminishing returns, with inflation and unemployment rising and economic growth stuttering. On the British right, and even on the left, a growing number of thinkers and doers abandoned Keynesianism for monetarism.

In 1976 Denis Healey, a shrewd, sometimes shameless Labour chancellor, set a target for annual growth in the money supply, and cut government spending. The Conservative Party's monetarists, such as Thatcher's future chancellor, Geoffrey Howe, were privately impressed – and also alarmed, especially when the economy and Labour's poll ratings started to recover during 1977 and 1978. But then the approach of the general election caused Healey, ever pragmatic, to relax his stern new monetarist habits for a pre-election splurge. Thanks to the strike chaos of the 1978–9 Winter of Discontent, Labour lost anyway. The way was clear for the Tories to administer the monetarist medicine in full.

The new prime minister was neither a pure ideologue nor an instinctive political adventurer. Her bolder lieutenants nicknamed her 'cautious Margaret'. She was often, justifiably, slow to accept the electoral viability of the new right-wing economics. Healey's dalliance with monetarism had lost as well as gained Labour support, alienating voters angered by the accompanying cuts. It was also likely that the economic recovery of 1977–8 owed as much to an upswing in the business cycle and North Sea oil as to any magic formula from Milton Friedman. And yet, Thatcher's hairshirt temperament, and her upbringing as a grocer's daughter in Grantham in Lincolnshire, with all its skilfully publicized small-town grafting and careful budgeting, had given her a taste for puritanical, seemingly commonsensical economic arguments, of which monetarism was one. At a Press Association press conference in late 1980, she was challenged on whether monetarism was a bit too novel and dogmatic. She snapped back: 'It isn't a new-fangled theory. It is as essential as the law of gravity.'

Monetarist targets could be met, at least in theory, in three ways. As well as cutting public spending, countries could raise interest rates or taxes, each of which would have the effect of reducing the amount of money in circulation. Between 1979 and 1981 the Thatcher government tried all three methods, often simultaneously, while devising and publicizing a set of monetary targets, which it named the Medium-Term Financial Strategy, a phrase that tried hard to suggest rigour and neutrality. As a globe-trotting intellectual superstar – he had won the Nobel Prize for economics in 1976 – Friedman was too busy to be closely involved. Instead, much of the technical and intellectual support for this risky economic venture came from the tiny community of British monetarist academics. One of them was Alan Walters, a quietly spoken man with an icy blue gaze who had been a frequent and sympathetic visitor to Pinochet's Chile, and who became Thatcher's chief economic adviser on 1 January 1981. Another was a former PhD student of Walters with a voice like sandpaper and a machine-gun laugh, Patrick Minford.

Walters died in 2009. But two years later Minford was still working, at Cardiff University. It was a boiling June afternoon, and his glassy corner office was smallish and low-ceilinged, crammed full of books with faded spines, including both volumes of Margaret Thatcher's memoirs, prominent near his desk. Immediately outside his open window, trains rattled past distractingly in the first proper sunshine of the summer; occasionally during our interview the monetarist debates of the early 1980s seemed rather a dry topic.

Yet Minford was compelling company. Sixty-eight, dressed in tweed and stripes like a Thatcherite intellectual from central casting, he had big hand gestures and a loud voice with an almost metallic edge. Thatcher's heirs in the coalition government were finding the economy a struggle, but Minford's faith in right-wing economics remained undiminished: 'No one says, "We don't want modern medicine, because a few patients died."' Out came the machine-gun laugh.

At the start of the 1980s, Minford was teaching at Liverpool University. He had moved there in 1976, after a dozen years steadily purging himself of the left-wing politics and Keynesian economics he had learned at Oxford. As well as academia, he had worked in Whitehall, in Washington DC, and in the former British colony of Malawi, and had acquired a near-certainty about how 'real-life economics' functioned, as well as 'a certain nationalism'. During the final, disastrous months of the Heath government in 1974, he explained, 'I was in Washington – at the time of the three-day week. I looked back at Britain in disbelief. Part of me thought, "We must get this country back on its feet."'

Like Walters, with whom he'd remained in touch, and an assortment of other previously isolated radical right-wing thinkers, Minford was drawn into the Conservative ferment created by the failure of Heath. 'I came into contact with Mrs Thatcher and Keith Joseph . . . in about '78. I got roped in by Keith Joseph. I think he must've read something I'd written . . . She was very friendly to me, and I was very impressed by her personality. She had grit. I felt, "This [Thatcherism] is great. This is going to work."'

The intense, questing Joseph was a key Thatcher ally and one of the first senior Conservatives to be persuaded by monetarism. He invited Minford to an ideas meeting for the 1979 election manifesto, also attended by Thatcher and Howe, and soon the Conservatives were regularly asking Minford to do work for them. Once Walters started at Downing Street in 1981, Minford said, 'I was constantly in touch with him. I was providing him with consultancy on macroeconomics. I'd meet him in Number 10. We would discuss unemployment, whether interest rates were too high, the overall economic situation.'

What Minford offered was particularly enticing, even in an increasingly competitive market for new Conservative ideas: an analysis which seemed to prove that monetarism would work in Britain. He called it the Liverpool Model.

'Economics problems are just like engineering problems,' he explained briskly. In the late 1970s and early 1980s, he went on, Liverpool University had a single mainframe computer. 'In the social sciences, no one much used it. I kind of schmoozed the computer director. Computer directors always like to expand their empire, so he gave us [Minford and a few research assistants] loads of time on the mainframe.' They used it to build a model of how he believed the British economy functioned. 'We would set the model up, and then we would simulate it, with shocks of various sorts' – such as changes in overall government spending, or in the level of welfare benefits, or tax rates, or wages. 'And then the data would speak.'

When the data 'spoke', it appeared to provide reassuring conclusions for monetarists and the British radical right in general. In a strikingly short 1981 pamphlet titled 'The Problem of Unemployment', Minford wrote: 'Estimates based on the Liverpool Model suggest that a combination of a 15 per cent cut in real social security benefits . . . and a reduction in the union [wage] mark-up to its level in the mid-1960s . . . would reduce unemployment in the UK by around 1.5m by the mid-80s.' In a May 1982 lecture in the City of London, titled 'The New Classical View of the Economy', he made another large claim: 'To cure inflation permanently you require that cuts in public borrowing [and therefore public spending] and money supply be permanent . . . The cure can be effected with minimal disruptive effects . . . if a government with credibility in the pursuit of such cuts is expected.'

The final word was a giveaway. Minford's model drew heavily on another assertive mid-twentieth-century American economic theory: rational expectations. Like monetarism, the theory came from the Midwest, but it was easier to explain. Its originator, John Muth, was a young assistant professor of mathematical economics at Carnegie Mellon University in Pittsburgh when, in 1961, he published a paper on the business practices of hog farmers. What he discovered was that, far from being helpless economic simpletons who merely reacted to the constant rise and fall in hog prices, as the economists who had previously deigned to study them had assumed, the farmers were in fact quite sophisticated in their gathering of information about the hog market, and about where prices were likely to go next. It was this information-gathering, and the 'rational expectations' it generated, that kept them in business.

Muth half-hid his finding in a thicket of calculations and cautious verbiage. But his conclusion had a populist appeal – the little guy knows best – and especially for right-wingers who believed that free markets produced good decisions. Walters became an enthusiast of Muth's work around 1970, and Minford not long afterwards. By the mid-1970s, with the wider world of economic and political ideas now moving firmly rightwards, Muth had become influential, and his 1961 arguments were applied more and more broadly: to the behaviour of the whole economy, and to politics.

If people had 'rational expectations' about changes in the economy, and adapted their behaviour accordingly, Minford argued, then they would also be influenced by the economic approaches of governments – not so much by their individual policies as by what he called their 'policy reflexes', their deeper strategic or psychological instincts. The more clear-sighted and determined the government – the more obvious its 'reflexes' – the more it would influence economic behaviour. One way for a government to attain this influence, or 'credibility' as Minford and other right-wingers called it, was to have a stark and unshakeable overall plan, such as monetarism. Another was to have a prime minister with consistency and unflappability, with what he called 'grit'. Margaret Thatcher, he believed, was such a leader. 'Policy reflexes are not easy to describe,' he said in his 1982 City lecture, 'but everyone knows what they are trying to describe when they say "Mrs Thatcher would not do this."'

Between 1979 and 1982 her government made a great show of being unyielding. 'You turn if you want to,' she told the 1980 Conservative Party conference, delivering the line a little clumpingly, but with its reference to the infamous U-turns of her predecessor and enemy Heath still cutting and defiant. 'The lady's not for turning.' In March 1981, despite the recession, her chancellor Geoffrey Howe sharply raised taxes in the budget by freezing income-tax allowances at a time when inflation was running at a feverish 13 per cent. Three hundred and sixty-four economists, a substantial proportion of the entire British profession, from grand old Keynesians to thrusting youngsters, signed a letter to *The Times* in protest. There was 'no basis in economic theory' for the government's economic strategy, the letter thundered. 'Present policies will deepen the depression, erode the industrial base of our economy and threaten its social and political stability . . . The time has come to reject monetarist policies.'

A tiny chorus of right-wing economists and commentators spoke up for the government. Minford did so loudest. Thirty-three years old, only five years into his first university job, he swiftly produced an article for *The Times* dismissing the letter from the 364 economists – many of them more senior, and from better-known institutions than Liverpool's relatively obscure economics department – as 'nonsense'. To their warning that the government's economic policies would devastate British industry, he replied confidently: 'There is no evidence that those [companies] with sound long-term prospects are going to the wall. Instead, we have seen rationalization, a reduction in over-manning.' Margaret Thatcher was relieved and delighted by Minford's intervention. 'I . . . wrote to congratulate him,' she recalled in her memoirs, 'on his brilliant defence of the Government's approach.'

Minford's zeal was reinforced by how he saw the city he taught in. Liverpool University is just north of Toxteth – or Liverpool 8 as residents prefer to call it, after its postcode. During the nineteenth century, when the city was one of the richest ports in the British Empire, Toxteth's criss-crossed rigging of streets had housed merchants and sea captains, in terraced Georgian mansions of fine brick and cream stucco, set along boulevards with self-congratulatory names such as Upper Parliament Street. But by the 1980s this prosperous, prestigious world, like the sea captains, was long gone: bombed in the Second World War alongside Liverpool's docks, half a mile downhill by the River Mersey; partially redeveloped after the war as low, boxy council houses and blocks; and partially left to rot.

Most of the surviving mansions had been subdivided and rented out or simply boarded up. Flaking, damp, buddleia sprouting like unkempt hair from their basements and back walls, they faced stretches of waste ground, where uncleared rubble from the war mixed with fly-tippings and dogshit. Drains backed up and grass grew to knee height. Inhabited streets ended abruptly, or degenerated into roofless shells, broken into and stripped for their lead and copper. Confident Victorian churches and public buildings, some functioning, some abandoned, stood like islands under a sky that seemed too open, too unobstructed for a city landscape. After dark, prostitutes used the shadows.

Between 1971 and 1981 alone, the population of Toxteth fell by over a third. In extreme form, the area exemplified the wider decline of Liverpool. By 1981 it had been sliding economically for almost a century. Since the Edwardian era, the city's commercial zenith, its long chain of working docks, with their colonnaded quays and warehouses like palaces, had been thinning and corroding. Britain's maritime trade had moved steadily to other ports, on the east coast not the west, closer to Europe. Since the 1970s, the factory jobs that were meant to replace the dock work had been disappearing too, with Liverpool plants increasingly regarded as disposable branch facilities by manufacturing conglomerates based elsewhere. Since the 1950s, Liverpool's population had been dropping faster than in any other city in the country: from a peak of almost 900,000 to under 500,000 in 1981.

Much of Liverpool was still handsome, with its bright estuarine light and its steep city-centre hills, stacked with centuries of grand buildings from past booms. It still had cultural leverage and charisma, with its ongoing tradition of clever pop music from the Beatles to mouthy new bands such as Echo & The Bunnymen; and a quick-passing football team, Liverpool FC, that was in the middle of a period of unprecedented dominance of both the English and European game.

Yet all this swagger was, at best, inadequate compensation for, and at worst, a distraction from the depopulation and the decaying economy. Early 1980s Liverpool, even more than the country's many other tatty, depopulating cities, could be seen as a warning: the fall of Britain writ large. 'It was just like having a case study on your doorstep,' said Minford, from the safe distance of his Cardiff office. 'The British disease in its terminal phase. Productivity – hopeless. Union militancy – very strong. Living on benefits – the norm. I saw whole streets doing that at first hand.' On weekday lunchtimes, he and

Liverpool University colleagues used to go to a pub on the northern edge of Toxteth. 'You had to be a bit careful. But in many ways it was very instructive.'

Once he became known nationally as one of the government's few academic cheerleaders, Minford had to be rather more careful. By the early 1980s Liverpool, previously politically fickle, was moving strongly leftwards, with the aggressive Labour splinter group Militant surging in municipal elections, and the number of local Conservative MPs rapidly collapsing. The last Tory lost his seat in 1983, the same year Militant took effective control of the city council. In his Toxteth pub from 1981 onwards, Minford said, more quietly than usual, 'There was a bit of aggro.' Then his impregnable grin returned: 'Mostly quite friendly aggro. Liverpool's a funny place . . . There was this kind of feeling, "He may be in the enemy team, but at least he's in Liverpool!"'

Minford actually lived in Birkenhead then, across the Mersey, but only a few minutes' drive away from the city. During 1981 he began to get anonymous phone calls. '"We know where you are" sort of thing,' he said, quiet again, fiddling with the cap of a mineral-water bottle. 'We got kind of threats and things, so we went ex-directory. The police were alerted. We didn't want to encourage people to turn up on the doorstep.'

Other political enemies were slightly more subtle. 'I was regarded with a mixture of contempt and hatred by colleagues in the profession,' said Minford. He waved a meaty hand: 'I just wrote them off. I just thought, "It's lucky I don't want to get a [university] chair anywhere else. I've got my chair in Liverpool. No one can stop me!"' In his department there were other monetarists, yet in the wider university the theory became controversial. 'One of our colleagues in the sociology department organized a trade union march on the economics department, with placards and stuff, saying "Hang Minford".' How did that make him feel? 'I thought it was a good joke, actually.' Rat-tat-tat went his laugh.

But in 1981 there was at least one problem with the defiant arguments deployed by Minford, by the government's other ideologues, and by Margaret Thatcher herself. It was not clear that her policies were working, in Liverpool or anywhere else. On 23 January, Geoffrey Howe sent her a brief official minute, the tone and contents of which would become wearyingly familiar as the year went on. It began:

> This minute is to amplify my warning of the picture which the public expenditure totals will present . . . The last round of public expenditure discussions in Cabinet ended with the programmes so much higher than we hoped. There have been further increases since . . . Main reasons for the further increase this year are the larger take up of special employment measures . . . Next year, the main increases come also from the special employment measures . . . There is no doubt that these figures . . . will disappoint our supporters . . . We can point to the recession as one cause . . . I am sure, however, that these totals are not acceptable . . .

Howe wrote as he spoke, in a mumbling, understated, sometimes euphemistic style: 'special employment measures' meant unemployment benefit. But the bad news and even panic in his orderly paragraphs was unmistakable. Despite his mild, consensual manner, which Thatcher found increasingly exasperating, in the end fatally so, Howe had been a believer in shaking up the economy and British society with it for much longer than she had, since the late 1950s. But now he seemed to be losing confidence. Across the top of his first page, Thatcher wrote in thick pen, her impatient, upward-slanting sentences and slashing consonants almost obliterating his typescript: 'I cannot just do nothing about this. We appear to have no control over expenditure.'

For much of 1981, the intricate national transformation programme based on monetarism, rational expectations theory and the Liverpool Model appeared to be malfunctioning disastrously. In many ways, the crisis originated with monetarism itself. Attractively simple in crude outline, in practice monetarism raised far more questions than it answered. How exactly should a government measure the amount of money in the economy? Did the amount of money in the economy really set the level of economic activity, or was it vice versa? Was the use to which that money was being put, what economists called its 'velocity', also important? If a government applied the recommended monetarist remedies, would there be side effects? And how long would the medicine take to work?

At the latest, the Thatcher government would have to seek re-election in three years' time, in May 1984. And such a full five-year term was unlikely. The previous three governments, buffeted by the ongoing worldwide economic turbulence that had begun in the 1970s, and weakened by the growing impatience of modern voters, had lasted an average of only three years. In the early 1980s even monetarism's true believers saw difficulties ahead. Friedman had warned about the theory in his TV series 'Free to Choose': 'The bad effects come first, and the good effects only come later.' Thatcher's strategist John Hoskyns put it more colourfully when we met in 2011: 'My favourite quote is from George Schultz: "The economist's lag is the politician's nightmare." And it is – an absolute nightmare. You've done the right thing, and it's going to be 18 months before people realize.'

Schultz was the American secretary of state under President Reagan in the 1980s. Confrontational, boldly right-wing and deeply unpopular in 1981, the Reagan administration had much in common with Thatcher's – unlike the centrist or left-wing governments in power in the world's other prominent democracies. The two premiers became famously close allies. Yet American support for Thatcher was not wholly reliable. In 1981, despite following a monetarist strategy of its own, the Reagan administration openly derided how the British one was going.

On 27 February, Radio 4's *Today* programme offered its large audience of British opinion-formers a recent recording of Reagan's Treasury Secretary, Don Regan, telling a Congressional Committee: 'We think that our programme is much more sensible, much more comprehensive, and with a greater degree of chance of success than the British experience.' Regan then summed up for the uninitiated: 'Our money is going to stay under control.'

But which money? Anyone attempting to define the money supply immediately entered a labyrinth, haunted by elusive letter-number hybrids: there was M0, also known as the monetary base, which was meant to represent the cash in the economy; M1, which included some bank accounts as well; and M3, which included all bank accounts but not money in building societies. All of these measures were, to a degree, contrived and incomplete. To make matters worse, Alan Walters recorded, 'Because of industrial action by civil servants, the preparation of statistics on the money supply ... was much delayed and distorted.'

For much of 1980 and 1981, the monetarists in the Thatcher government – to say nothing of the many people in her government who did not believe in monetarism at all – were split and sometimes paralysed by fierce, factional debates, involving ministers, advisers, foreign economists and the prime minister herself, about which measure of the money supply should be at the centre of economic policy. Thirty years later, Howe remembered the rows well. 'The argument about whether it was M1, M0 or M3 showed how difficult the technicalities of monetarism were,' he half-whispered, when we met in a murky meeting room in the House of Lords. Did he think monetarism had originally been sold as too simple a scheme? 'It's true. It doesn't destroy the basic premise. But to make monetarism work, there's a great deal of' – Howe searched for the right euphemism – 'judgement.'

And even when a money-supply measure was settled on, it rarely behaved as the government hoped and predicted. In the section of Howe's painstaking memoirs covering the second half of 1980, he writes, 'I had warned in my Budget speech ... [about] some overshoot in the sterling M3 figures. When it happened the size of this phenomenon astonished us all. In July *and* August, sterling M3 grew by almost 5 per cent in each month – more than ... our target for the entire year.'

For a government that had loudly promised to run the economy in a more realistic, modern way, replacing what it caricatured as the naive and obsolete policies of the Wilson, Callaghan and Heath administrations, the errors and blind spots of British monetarism were embarrassing and highly damaging. The rigid money-supply targets seemed at odds with the increasing volatility, complexity and interconnectedness of a late twentieth-century economy. Indeed, some of the latter traits were simultaneously being reinforced by other Conservative economic policies, such as allowing banks to lend more, and allowing the differences between banks and building societies to blur. As it would demonstrate in areas of British life beyond the economic, the Thatcher government, often self-defeatingly, wanted both to liberate and to control.

Minford sighed in his hot office. 'She wasn't very good at economics. Sometimes, she'd get the economics completely wrong. It was a big problem trying to get her back on track.' At Oxford University in the 1940s, Thatcher had studied chemistry, a more reliable science. From 1979 to 1981 Minford took part in seminars to help her fill the gaps. 'She was quite concerned about all the details of economic policy that seemed to be going wrong. Why wasn't the money supply tighter? Why wasn't any of it working?'

To many people, the most obvious sign that Thatcher's economic strategy was misfiring was the rate of unemployment. When she took office, 1,299,300 people were officially jobless in the United Kingdom. That total was already alarming by post-war standards: between 1945 and 1970 the annual average had never exceeded 650,000. During the 1970s the figure had worsened because of broader economic shocks such as the 1973 oil crisis, which quadrupled the price per barrel and hurt all Western countries. Yet growing unemployment was also the product of a longer-term and more profoundly disruptive economic trend that particularly affected Britain. The manufacturing industry that supported much of the north and many cities was suddenly disappearing.

Early on in the 1973 film *O Lucky Man!* a typically gleeful portrait of a declining Britain directed by Lindsay Anderson, the main character, a travelling coffee salesman played by Malcolm McDowell, visits Cochranes Amalgamated Steel & Iron Works, a fictional plant somewhere in the northeast of England. The complex looks well kept, with a spotless canteen and trimmed lawns, but its actual machinery of rusty pipes and tanks looks decades old. The whole place is deserted except for a cleaner in the canteen. 'They're closing us down,' he explains to the coffee salesman. McDowell's character gives a look of bug-eyed, naive amazement: 'Closing you down? Why? Five thousand men?' All around the two men stand gleaming, empty tables, as if the employees have just been vaporized. 'That's right,' says the cleaner, deadpan. He patiently draws out the word: 'Re-dundant.'

Throughout the 1970s and with unprecedented speed, manufacturing conglomerates of all nationalities closed their British factories in favour of foreign ones that were more modern, more efficient, or offered cheaper labour – and sometimes all three. In the 1982 edition of his best-selling series of books *Anatomy of Britain*, the veteran social observer Anthony Sampson described a shift in corporate culture that he said had begun well before Thatcher's election: 'Chairmen and chief executives . . . no longer feel responsible for the continuing security of their workers.' In 1978 a less patrician but equally perceptive social commentator, the rising Liverpool playwright Alan Bleasdale, began writing a television drama series about the consequences. The unemployed protagonists of *Boys from the Blackstuff*, set in Liverpool, were shown lost in lonely mazes of drink, shame, domestic violence, or madness. Most of the series was scripted while Labour were still in power.

Also in 1978, the Conservatives cleverly used the jobs crisis to undermine the Callaghan government with a cutting poster campaign based on the slogan 'Labour Isn't Working'. Tellingly, Margaret Thatcher may have had some misgivings about the tactic. According to her aide Robin Harris, 'She feared – although she did not openly admit it at the time – that attacking Labour's unemployment figure . . . was disingenuous.' If she became prime minister, 'She knew that it was more likely to rise than fall, as monetary discipline began to bite.'

Which was exactly what happened. By the end of 1980, the official jobless total was 2,244,000 – a startling increase of almost a million people in the year and a half since Thatcher's election. By the end of 1981, the total had shot up to 2,941,000. During 1982 it burst through the three-million mark. It did not lastingly fall back below that figure until the middle of 1987.

Unemployment on this scale – three million jobless was almost one in seven of the working population – had not afflicted Britain since the 1930s. Even half a century later, for most British politicians and much of the population, the mass unemployment of the Great Depression remained the definitive modern peacetime trauma. Heath's economic contortions as prime minister were due largely to his desperation not to preside over a repeat of the hard times he had seen and read about in the 1930s, as the son of a sometimes struggling carpenter and as a socially conscious young Tory. In 1971, when the unemployment total had suddenly leapt towards a million, he had almost completely abandoned his initial, relatively tough economic approach as premier, which had included an ambition to withdraw state support from 'lame duck' industries, in favour of greater subsidies for exactly those same industries.

Yet some in the Thatcher government saw the ballooning unemployment figures very differently. For them, upheaval in the jobs market was unavoidable. In fact, it was desirable. In 1985 Alan Walters wrote of the early 1980s: 'The overmanning notorious in British manufacturing was substantially reduced . . . Britain [was] closing her industrial museums.' That last sentence had the cruel sureness of the true revolutionary.

I asked Howe how he felt about what happened to manufacturing during his tenure. 'It didn't have an easy time,' he said, softly, in the panelled gloom of the House of Lords meeting room. 'But' – his voice hardened – 'it was a consequence of their performance over the previous decade . . . and by the inescapable discipline we were imposing. Things had needed treatment for a long time.' Had he been worried at the time about the political consequences of mass joblessness? He wrinkled his tortoise-like brow: 'Unemployment, it was a worry, yes. One's expectation was that it would start to move in the right direction. But one didn't know when that great day would come.'

'That great day' – the phrase had a chilling jauntiness. I asked Howe whether, at the time, he had felt for those who were made redundant. He explained that he had grown up in a declining steel town, Port Talbot in Wales, in the 1930s. 'One had been directly exposed to the areas of hardship. All one could do [in the early 1980s] was explain that it was a consequence of mismanagement, on both sides, in the past.' So he had felt no guilt as chancellor for the social consequences of his actions? He rubbed a shirt cuff with a finger. 'One didn't have any reason to doubt what we were doing. Because it was intellectually correct . . . The key illnesses were being tackled. We were getting reports back from our ambassadors abroad. The sick man of Europe was being seen as undergoing some sort of cure.'

In Cardiff, Minford was characteristically blunter. 'Unemployment had been concealed in the 70s by massive subsidies to' – the word came out as a hiss – '*useless* industries. When this was being put right in the early 80s . . . the unemployment came out of the cupboard.'

Yet he conceded that the sheer scale of the shake-out had surprised him. The initial versions of the Liverpool Model had assumed, as did many Thatcherites, that Britain's 'natural' rate of unemployment was low, and that therefore purging the economy of inefficiencies with monetarism would mean, at worst, hundreds of thousands of redundancies – rather than millions. 'In the Liverpool Model we were too optimistic about the speed with which the economy would . . . come right,' Minford admitted. 'Although we were closer than many of the pessimists.' He paused, untypically. 'The bit we were way out on was unemployment.'

Thatcher herself did not share Heath's fear of unemployment. A decade younger, she had only been a child in the 1930s, and had grown up in more comfortable circumstances: no crowds of the hungry jobless besieged her father's two upmarket grocery shops in busy Grantham. Yet in the early 1980s, in private, she was perplexed and alarmed by the explosion of unemployment. Her strategist John Hoskyns told me, 'She was at her wits' end: "Why is unemployment so high? Why are we losing all these jobs?"'

In 1981 Nigel Lawson was a smoothly self-assured, eagerly monetarist treasury minister, who would replace Howe as chancellor two years later. In his otherwise unrepentant memoirs Lawson acknowledges the social turmoil caused by the mass redundancies: 'Well-established workers who had been earning good wages found themselves unemployed for the first time in their lives.' These middle-aged people, mostly men, unprepared for the indignities of the dole office, the scrutiny by officials behind grilles, the inching, shaming queues, were joined by another, much younger generation of the jobless: school leavers. The mid-1960s had been peak years for the British birth rate. By the early 1980s almost 100,000 extra teenagers a year were looking for work.

Unemployment became a political and cultural preoccupation, far larger than it had been even during the most listless, fearful years of the 1970s. On the BBC1 nine o'clock news, lists of major redundancies were sombrely read out every night during the early 1980s, as if they were wartime casualty figures. On the long, steeply sloping roof of the Greater London Council's offices at County Hall in central London, directly facing the Houses of Parliament, and the camera lenses of countless journalists and passing voters, the GLC's provocative and PR-savvy new leader Ken Livingstone arranged for giant digits to be propped up and regularly updated, announcing the capital's ever more catastrophic jobless total.

In the autumn of 1982, *Boys from the Blackstuff* was finally broadcast on BBC2. Filmed on innovative lightweight cameras that roamed the overgrown quaysides and litter-strewn voids of inner Liverpool, the five episodes often felt less like a drama than a documentary. Some of the besieged characters were based on real people. The series was such a hit that it was shown again only two months later, this time on BBC1, which had previously rejected the script as too downbeat. In Liverpool the effects of monetarism, and of the economic policies that flowed from it, were being graphically demonstrated – but not as Minford and his computer model intended.

4
Wait Until Dusk

In Toxteth unemployment had been high for decades. But during 1980 and 1981 it surged. According to the 1981 census, in the Granby electoral ward, which included Toxteth, 39.6 per cent of men were jobless. A 1989 report on race relations in Liverpool by Lord Gifford, a radical QC, and Wally Brown, a well-informed Toxteth black activist, concluded that for much of the 1980s 'the real Black youth unemployment figure in the Liverpool 8 area [was] between 70–80%'. The figure for young black men – the least favourite recruits of employers in the city – was almost certainly even worse.

By the early 1980s, the narrow triangle of Toxteth, only a few minutes' walk from one side to the other, had effectively become Liverpool's ghetto. The process had started in the early twentieth century, when the district's cheapening property and proximity to the docks had drawn merchant seamen, many from East and West Africa, to settle there. They stayed and intermarried. Jimi Jagne's family was typical: 'My mother was Chinese, born in Liverpool. My dad was a joiner from the Gambia.' By the time Jagne was born, in 1964, Toxteth had a large minority of mixed-race and black inhabitants, over a quarter of all its residents, by far the largest concentration in the city.

In many ways they brought life to the surviving streets. In discreet, unused rooms in the huge houses, from the 1940s onwards they had set up illegal drinking clubs and nightclubs. By 1981 most of them had licences, but many retained an edge: 'Straightaway you were going downstairs into a basement,' Jagne remembered when we met in 2011, 'and you've got these ... *inhabitants* like you might find in a film, or in a small, shady place in Havana. Nocturnal creatures that you don't find in mainstream Britain. You can have a smoke [of marijuana], you can buy a smoke down there.' In 1982 John Cornelius, one of a trickle of white bohemians who for decades had been moving into Toxteth just as much of the local white working class was moving out, published *Liverpool 8*, a fond but double-edged non-fiction portrait of the area's rackety nightlife and streetlife, and its underlying tensions. 'Warm nights in this part of town,' he wrote, 'can mean trouble.'

Crime in Toxteth was actually no worse than in other poor areas of Liverpool. 'Setting cars on fire and the smashing of stolen cars are . . . activities long since adopted by white and black young people in many parts of the inner city, as well as in peripheral estates,' found a 1982 report on Liverpool by the Evangelical Coalition for Urban Mission. But Toxteth, with its unusual racial mix, its perceived otherness, was the area of the city that became notorious for lawlessness and other transgressions. In the 1950s Liverpool newspapers sometimes called it 'the Jungle'. In November 1978 the Chief Constable of Merseyside, Kenneth Oxford, wrote in the BBC's *Listener* magazine about

> . . . the problem of half-castes in Liverpool. Many are the product of liaisons between Black seamen and white prostitutes in Liverpool 8, the red light district. Naturally they grow up without any kind of recognisable home life. Worse still . . . the Negroes will not accept them as Blacks, and whites just assume they are coloureds. As a result, the half-caste community of Liverpool is well outside recognized society.

Even by the standards of the 1970s and 1980s, Oxford was an authoritarian, socially conservative senior policeman, with a taste for making sensationalist state-of-the-nation pronouncements. But in the Liverpool of the time his views on race and Toxteth were not unique. In 1989 Gifford and Brown concluded that 'racial discrimination in Liverpool is uniquely horrific', and that it required 'tremendous courage . . . to establish oneself as a Black family outside of the confines of Liverpool 8'.

Growing up in Toxteth in the 1970s and early 1980s, said Jagne, 'I was told by the other black kids, "Don't go here. Don't go past here. Because the skinheads will get you."' He was a scrawny, slightly nervous child, and almost the only time he crossed this invisible cordon in his free time was on Saturday afternoons, to go shopping in the city centre. On the other afternoons he would stay in Toxteth and watch a regular border ritual: 'Older black kids called themselves the Afros or the BIA – Black Is Ace. After school hours, they'd gather in an area on the edge of our community where there'd been some houses knocked down . . . where there were lots of stones and bricks lying around. We used to call these areas olahs – I don't even know how it's spelled, but I know it meant a battleground. Kids would come up [there] from the white areas . . . and they'd just launch half-bricks at one another. Guys would be carried off with huge gashes.'

In 1981 Merseyside Police had four black officers out of a total force of 5,000. Sometimes the police descended on Toxteth like an occupying army. They used the 'sus' laws, an increasingly contentious set of stop-and-search powers derived from the Vagrancy Act of 1824, which gave policemen the right to act against anyone they suspected of 'intent to commit an arrestable offence' in 'any street' or 'place of public resort'. Officers would sweep young black men off Toxteth's street corners and pavements – even from outside their own homes – and into patrol cars. Sometimes policemen referred to these operations among themselves as 'going farming'. Once harvested, 'suspects' could be searched for drugs, or knives, or stolen goods; they could be charged with vague offences such as resisting arrest, or threatening behaviour; or simply harassed and intimidated.

By his early teens, Jagne still lacked confidence. He passed the 11-plus, but was too overawed by grammar school to take up a place. Instead he became a studious but beleaguered pupil at a heavily white secondary modern north of Toxteth, more interested in Charles Dickens than fights with his taunting classmates. One darkening winter afternoon in 1978, shortly after the publication of Kenneth Oxford's 'half-caste' article, he began his walk home from school as usual. Wearing his uniform and carrying a schoolbag, he was passing Liverpool's huge, blood-red brick Anglican cathedral, which guards a hilltop just beyond the northwestern boundary of Toxteth, when:

> . . . An Austin Allegro started crawling alongside me. There were two police officers in it, and it was a marked [police] vehicle. One of them wound down the window, and asked me where I was going. I explained

> that I'd just come from school . . . The car stopped. One of the officers got out . . . He put his hand on my shoulder, and touched my bag . . . He said, 'I'm going to look inside it.' I was too small, and too young, and too naive to argue. I just let him take it. He opened it, and there were some exercise books, my PE kit, and a towel. And he said, 'Have you robbed any of this?' I said, 'No.' Some of the books had my name on the front. 'I've got to ask you some questions,' he said. 'You've got to get in the car.' I said: 'Why? Where are we going?' He said, 'I've got to take you to the police station. If you don't come, you'll get into trouble.' I said, 'I don't want to. I want to see my mum. I live round the corner.' He said, 'I'm not interested in all that. Get into the car, *you black swine*!' . . . So I got into the car. I knew that on [nearby] Admiral Street there was a police station . . . We drove past it, and carried on. And carried on. Then we were along Aigburth Road [south of Toxteth] and I didn't know the area at all. We drove through Aigburth and then through Garston, and into Speke, which was the very south of the city. It was just a wasteland then, mainly mud. They drove off the road . . . By that point of time it was dark. In the car, one of the policemen had been turning round to me, making threatening faces and saying things – I can't remember what now, because my mind had gone blank. I was scared absolutely shitless. On the wasteland, he pulled me out of the car, and . . . emptied my bag into a huge puddle. Then they pushed me into the puddle, and started laughing, and said, 'That's what you get, *you daft little black cunt!*' And just got into the car and drove off.

Jagne walked home in his cold and filthy clothes, with his ruined homework, hours late, too scared and ashamed to tell his furious mother what had happened. Soon afterwards, for the first time, he began to become 'a little bit politicized'. He read up on the slave trade, in which Liverpool, and some of Toxteth's original mansion-owners, had played a central role. He discovered the writings of the American black radical Malcolm X, and 'hung around' with older Toxteth boys who had become militant Rastafarians. In July 1980 he left school and went on the dole.

Without work, without much money, without many daytime amenities, and without access to the rest of the city; unpredictably harassed by the police; largely ignored by Liverpool and national politicians – young male Toxteth stood around under the flaking Georgian porches and on the overgrown street corners, and waited for diversions. Jagne was one of those waiting. 'Everybody would rush to a [police] incident if they got word of it.'

At about 9.30 on the mild, showery Friday evening of 3 July 1981 a young black man on a motorbike, chased by an unmarked police car, reached the corner of Granby Street and Selborne Street in the middle of Toxteth. The man was local, but has never been officially identified. The policemen suspected his motorbike was stolen. At the street corner, a favoured spot for people to gather and pass the time, the motorcyclist lost his balance and fell off. The officers tried to arrest him. But a small crowd surrounded them, suspecting an instance of police harassment, and was quickly swelled by other angry residents. At least eight more patrol cars arrived. According to Jagne, who was in the crowd, now about forty strong, 'Police started threatening, shoving. And then a [police] baton struck someone. So some guys started picking up stones. Bricks started flying over.' In the mêlée, the motorcyclist broke free and ran off; and one of the crowd, Leroy Cooper, another young black local, from a family with a well-known history of friction with the police, was arrested for assaulting officers.

For the next few hours three or four groups of youths, a dozen people in each, roamed Toxteth throwing stones at any police vehicle that passed within range. At least half a dozen had their windscreens smashed. The next day, from dawn, Toxteth was flooded with police. Many residents took it as a sign that the policing of their neighbourhood would from now on be even harsher. Meanwhile news and rumours spread about the Cooper incident. And some residents began to think about a stronger response than stone-throwing.

Three months earlier, in Brixton in south London, one of several other rundown British inner-city districts made combustible by rising unemployment, racial tensions and over-policing, a botched police operation similar to the Toxteth motorbike confrontation had led to three days of rioting, the fiercest in Britain for half a century, which was reported around the world. Two hundred and ninety-nine policemen were injured. Jagne and his friends were transfixed by the Brixton coverage: 'We talked about it for weeks and weeks and weeks. All the circumstances that led to Brixton were exactly the same, mirrored ours . . . The impression we got from Brixton was that although there were youths arrested, there were also police officers injured – and it focused a lot of attention on that black community. And those two things appealed to us enormously.'

On 4 July, the day after the Cooper incident, what Jagne and others called 'the uprising' began in Toxteth. Jagne was involved from early on. Thirty years later, wearing a big Afro and a tight corduroy worker's jacket, he still looked like a 1970s or 1980s black radical, rather than the respectable community activist and entrepreneur he had since become. We started our interview in a café at the Albert Dock in Liverpool, a cleaned-up and restored Victorian complex where maritime trade has been replaced by tourists; but Jagne quickly suggested we walk the mile to Toxteth and continue talking there. When we reached Upper Parliament Street, which was still gappy and gaunt and poor, like much of Toxteth, he stopped. Then he recalled the events of July 1981 with gusto.

The action usually started just after dark. 'Each evening, some of us would walk out into Parliament Street in balaclavas. Or we'd drive [stolen] cars out into Parliament Street from side streets and set them on fire. I felt for the people who were on the buses that went along Parliament Street – they would look out of the windows, absolutely terrified . . . But all we wanted was to get the street clear. You don't do that by politely asking buses and passing cars, "Can you divert?" You've got to take the street now.'

An arena had been created. Now the police could be drawn into it and confronted. The rioters put out the street lights by repeatedly kicking the metal plates that covered their fuses. Then they looked for weapons. Some of the best came from a regeneration scheme that had begun in Toxteth earlier that summer. On one stretch of Upper Parliament Street, fist-sized rocks were piled up, ready for use as landscaping material. Excavators and a bulldozer were parked, and not securely locked. Along nearby Grove Street, once one of Toxteth's finest, a long screen of scaffolding covered the front of several Georgian terraces.

The piles of rocks became stocks of missiles. The Grove Street scaffolding was unscrewed, and the poles made into improvised lances.

The bulldozer was hotwired, and used to build barricades out of stolen cars; and also to plough through more of the scaffolding, scattering and freeing more poles. An excavator was hotwired, and turned into a sort of armoured car. Other vehicles were commandeered: milk floats stolen from the local dairy, throttles jammed open with concrete blocks so they could become driverless battering rams; rental cars seized from a local hire business; even a fire engine. A school was broken into, and javelins were taken out of the sports cupboard. Spiked metal railings were broken off from the front gardens of Toxteth mansions. A local tyre depot was looted for barricade materials. Derelict properties supplied bricks and planks of wood. From inhabited houses came sledgehammers, chisels, baseball bats, bicycle handlebars – and milk bottles for making into petrol bombs.

Jagne quickly learned how to assemble and use them. 'The bottle had to have a wide enough neck. You filled the bottle about two-thirds of the way up. Then you needed plenty of length on your rag. Somewhere with some light, from car headlights or a streetlight that was still working, you lit the rag and put it in the bottle at the last minute. And then you threw the bottle like a javelin' – standing on the pavement of Upper Parliament Street, with lunchtime cars going past, he mimed the action – 'so the petrol jumped up the rag, and didn't spill onto you.' When the bottle hit something or someone, it sprayed a 20-foot area with broken glass and burning fuel. 'It was a really evil device,' said Jagne, dropping his voice. 'Did I think I was gonna kill someone with one? I'm not a violent person, but it did cross my mind.'

During the riots up to 1,000 policemen at a time were deployed in Toxteth, brought in from as far away as Cumbria. Across the broad, exposed width of Upper Parliament Street, in the near-darkness, with the only light coming from flaming cars and buildings, with burglar alarms shrieking from looted shops, and broken glass underfoot, and the smell of spilled petrol and spilled, looted alcohol, and oily smoke from barricades of burning tyres, the policemen formed into long, thin lines – sometimes advancing, sometimes static, sometimes retreating, rarely ready for what they were encountering.

Jeff Ashcroft was a constable with ten years' policing experience, working in Wallasey, a dormitory town across the Mersey on the Wirral. On 5 July 1981, he told the BBC later,

> I was on an afternoon shift, a normal sort of day, looking forward to a nice cold pint. Then [that evening] a sergeant hurried around in a van, quickly picking up as many officers as possible. We were told that youths in Liverpool at a place called Toxteth had started to riot. I laughed, thinking this was some sort of joke . . . When the van arrived in a side street at the bottom of Upper Parliament Street, we could hear this . . . animal-like howling mixed with the sound of breaking glass. We lined up and were quickly given a riot shield, something I'd only seen before on the news from Belfast. Following a very nervous sergeant, we walked around the corner . . . There before us stood row upon row of ambulances, police vehicles and officers . . . lit by a strange flickering light . . . We were forced to stand there as stationary targets, because senior officers hadn't a clue how to handle the situation . . . We'd been issued with a stupid little plastic face guard that fixed to the front of our helmets. Those old helmets offered no protection at all from flying bricks, stones and bits of iron railings . . . You never saw them coming. I grew to like the petrol bombs – at least you could see them . . .

The standard police uniforms worn initially at Toxteth were not fire-resistant. Many officers had only a small type of riot shield, a narrow octagon that protected the torso but little else. After the first three days of street battles, Merseyside Police received 400 military-style helmets from the Ministry of Defence, but even these proved inadequate: a gap between the helmet and its visor let in splashes of burning petrol. 'It was something of a shock,' commented Margaret Thatcher in her memoirs, 'to contemplate the kind of equipment the British police now required.'

Their Toxteth opponents were much better adapted to the frightening new world that seemed to have come into being. While the lines of policemen edged up and down Upper Parliament Street, crouching, ducking, weighed down by their equipment, between 100 and 400 rioters darted back and forth in front of them, picking up and throwing missiles at them, building barricades, sometimes sprinting to within a few yards of the police shields, sometimes raising their arms in triumph. They were almost all male. Jagne saw 'a few tomboys', and shocked journalists spotted a few children; but men in their teens and twenties dominated. Many of them, but not all, were black or mixed-race. They wore trainers and drainpipe jeans, tracksuit tops or short casual jackets: the fashions of young Liverpool in 1981, football and sportswear-driven, aspirational, influenced by what Liverpool fans had seen in slick continental boutiques while travelling to European matches; but also good clothes, flexible and anonymous, for running from policemen. Some rioters also wore partial face masks made out of bandanas or towels or bedding. But most made no attempt to disguise themselves. There was no CCTV, and either side of Upper Parliament Street there was the overgrown, bashed-about geography of Toxteth, baffling to outsiders. Jagne recalled: 'If you were being chased by a policeman, you had the advantage. You'd know, for example, that if you'd run so far along a back entry, it's this part of the wall that you jump over, because you know that this empty house has got a door that isn't locked, and you can run through, and you can be on the next street. The policeman's standing around, figuring out which way you went, and you're gone.'

On several occasions, for hours at a time, the police simply cordoned off parts of Toxteth and left them to the rioters. Looters saw their opportunity. Some were local, but many were not, and their social make-up and what they took made it clear that Toxteth was not the only economically desperate area of Liverpool. David Thompson, a Toxteth rector, told the *Liverpool Echo*: 'I saw grown women carrying baskets out of chemists. Old-age pensioners and whole families were looting.' In mid-July, during a lull in the rioting, he organized an amnesty for the return of looted goods. No items were handed back.

The absence of police also meant that buildings could be torched. One hundred and fifty were burnt down in the first four days of rioting. Some were carefully chosen. On a prominent corner of Upper Parliament Street was a grandiose former cinema and ballroom, the Rialto, built in the 1920s. Doris Day and the Beatles had once played there. Now it housed a less uplifting antiques shop, Swainbank's. In 1975 the white owner had complained in print: 'All I see around me are layabouts . . . especially those half-caste kids. They break into my place nearly every day and steal something.' On the night of 5 July his business was petrol-bombed.

The fire that ate its innards was so hot that the building's twin copper roof cupolas glowed before collapsing.

A hundred yards along the street, another resented landmark was the Liverpool Racquet Club. It had opened in 1877, to offer the wealthy of Toxteth and the wider city a members' club and facilities for gentlemanly sports such as racquets and Eton Fives. As Toxteth had declined around it, the club and its clientele had endured – provocatively so, some felt. Jagne remembered 'Jags, the occasional Rolls parked outside. No one from here had ever been inside. There were a lot of rumours about what went on in there, about freemasonry, judges, the police . . . We felt very strongly that this riot was the black man lashing back: not only at the police, not only at the establishment, but at everything we thought was bad about Britain.' The club was set alight and destroyed.

Sometimes the violence had an overtly party-political element. On 16 July the Conservative MP for Liverpool Wavertree, Anthony Steen, pointed out in the Commons that the controversial owner of Swainbank's was 'a former Tory councillor', and that during the riots 'the Sefton Park Conservative club, over a mile away [from Toxteth], had a petrol bomb thrown at it. Thatcher's Tea and Coffee House, run by my local Conservative association, had all its windows smashed.'

As the disorder continued, deep into July, the rioters grew more organized. To Jagne, 'It wasn't just people piling in and going mad. People were quite smart. It wasn't something that was discussed, but eventually everybody seemed to realize . . . that if there were others coming up to [attack] the [police] cordons, you'd back off, take a bit of a rest. And then when you could see that the number [of attackers] was starting to lessen, because people were getting tired, you'd step up to the plate, make sure that the number was consistent.' The police had to be kept penned back: 'If they got on top of the situation, they could end it. We couldn't afford for that to happen.'

In July 1981 Jagne was only seventeen. Just before the riots, he had got his first good job, as an apprentice electrician. And yet, 'I became increasingly involved, night after night. At first, there was a bit of scepticism towards me [from the other rioters], not only because I was so young, but because I looked like a kid. I didn't shoot up until I was 18. But I was out there, and I was starting to make suggestions to them, and some people would go along with them. I would say, "We need people to go over there." Or: "The bombs that have just been made – take them to the other side of the road."'

Rioters charged the police lines with lengths of scaffolding like medieval horsemen. They drove an excavator at officers. They attacked fire engines. They hacked at police vans with axes. They picked up and used abandoned police helmets and riot shields. They seized a fire hose, and turned it on officers as a water cannon. Some other Toxteth residents watched approvingly from the pavement or their front door-steps or balconies. On 28 July the *Echo* reported, 'One pensioner in his slippers . . . standing next to an overturned truck, shouted fiercely, "Don't burn the cars, burn the coppers!"'

Between 468 and 781 policemen were injured – official estimates see-sawed amid the chaos. Two hundred and fourteen police vehicles were destroyed or damaged, a toll closer to a medium-sized tank battle than a civil disturbance. Chief Constable Oxford quickly decided that more assertive tactics were required. At about 3 a.m. on 6 July, one of the wildest nights of rioting, police fired tear-gas canisters for the first time on the British mainland. The Home Secretary, Willie Whitelaw, said afterwards that the projectiles were intended 'for use against armed besieged criminals', and had been designed 'to detonate against walls and other hard surfaces'. Their manufacturer had warned that they should not be fired directly at crowds, but at Toxteth this advice was ignored. Half a dozen people were hit, not all of them rioters. One of the innocent victims was a professional footballer with Southport FC, Philip Robins, who was left with wounds to his back and chest, one egg-sized and an inch deep, and one much larger. 'He said he had been lucky,' *The Times* reported. 'If the wound just below his throat had been any higher he could have choked to death.'

Chief Constable Oxford also supplemented the vulnerable, thin-skinned police vans with tougher, more nimble Land Rovers, similar to those used by the army in Northern Ireland. He ordered his officers to drive directly at rioters, break up the swarm and isolate and seize individuals. 'I have tried low key policing,' he told the *Echo* on 28 July, 'and to put it crudely these people have spat in my face.' That night David Moore, a twenty-two-year-old disabled man, not a local, who walked with a dragging limp and had been visiting his sister in Toxteth – amid the riots, life had to go on – was crushed against a wall by a police van. He died that night in hospital. Two officers from the vehicle were later acquitted of manslaughter.

By late July, nearly four weeks since it started, 'the uprising' seemed almost to have become self-sustaining. There were flare-ups and lulls, there were periods of recuperation and escalation, there was violence and counter-violence. For Jagne, 'The rest of the world had stopped. My life was all about this [riot]. I wasn't going into work. I didn't phone into work. I couldn't say, "I'm not coming in because, basically, I'm rioting."'

In their report on the riots, the Evangelical Coalition for Urban Mission described 'a mood of anger and violence mixed with an excitement running through the community'. According to the *Echo* on 6 July, even Kenneth Oxford recognized that the rioters were in a 'state of euphoria'. In her memoirs Thatcher wrote of Toxteth and Brixton: 'High animal spirits, usually kept in check by a whole range of social constraints, had been unleashed.' She went on: 'What perhaps aggravated the 1981 riots into a virtual saturnalia was the impression given by television that . . . rioters could enjoy a fiesta of crime, looting and rioting in the guise of social protest . . . These are precisely the circumstances in which young men riot, and riot again.'

Jagne saw the riots in completely different terms. 'For us, they were the first major breakthrough. We stepped forward and said, "We're here, and this is how we feel."' But his sense of their momentum was similar to the prime minister's: 'You never thought of a time frame for the riots. They were never planned to end.'

From the Liverpool University campus, a few minutes' walk to the north, you could clearly see the flames. A police cordon, effective for once, protected the university and the rest of the city centre – but not all the university staff. 'One of my colleagues in the economics department,' remembered the campus's most famous Thatcherite, Patrick Minford, 'was living in one of the riot streets. Either me or Kent [Matthews, a colleague and fellow monetarist] was in touch with him during the trouble. As the rioters were coming down the street . . . where they burnt the Racquet Club . . . we went round to his house.

We decanted him to another street that was out of the path of the rioters. He went to stay with another colleague.'

I asked Minford whether the riots had given him any second thoughts, at the time, about monetarism and the Thatcher government. Only weeks before the disorder, in his pamphlet 'The Problem of Unemployment', he had written, 'Unemployment is . . . unlikely to cause major social unrest.' Yet while racism and unjust policing had clearly been the riots' long-term causes, it was hard to argue that the new and staggering level of joblessness in Toxteth under Thatcher played no part; after all, there had been no riots there under her immediate predecessors.

For once, Minford lost his fluency. 'Well . . . I think that, you know . . . the riot was pretty alarming.' Then his bulldozing certainty returned: 'The thing is, I think the behaviour in Liverpool really pointed up the sanity of Margaret Thatcher's policies. All she had to say was, "Look, the policies are working, and there's nowhere more in need of them than Liverpool."'

The prime minister arrived in the city on 13 July. Ten days after the beginning of the Toxteth riots, and over two years into her premiership, it was her first trip to Liverpool. It was not a sure-footed performance.

Before Toxteth erupted, there had been over a year of warnings about the potential for 'civil disturbances' in the city and in the many other British places with high unemployment and tense race relations: from the Home Office, from the cabinet's official think tank, the Central Policy Review Staff, from the Anglican bishop of Liverpool, David Sheppard, and the Roman Catholic archbishop of Liverpool, Derek Worlock, from the Liverpool MP David Alton, from Liverpool teachers and community organizations and trade unions. Yet as late as 30 June 1981, four days before the first brick was thrown, Thatcher had brushed off a request from Liverpool politicians to see their city's problems for herself: 'I am sorry I cannot take up your challenge in the immediate future. I will, however, bear it in mind when I next consider which of the very many demands for regional visits I receive to accept.'

Even once the riots started, she seemed unsure how to treat Liverpool. A plan to visit on 8 July, and possibly try to calm the situation with an on-the-spot party political broadcast, was abandoned at the last minute – officially because of a diary clash, but in reality because of worries about her security. Instead, she recorded the broadcast many miles away, in the cocoon of a BBC studio in central London. Bolting a few sketchy sentences about 'events in Liverpool' onto a longer homily about the 'pressing concern' of unemployment, while refusing to acknowledge that the two might be connected, she sounded alternately patronizing, panicky and uncaring. 'Not for the first time,' commented the usually Tory-supporting *Times*, 'she was unable to strike the right note when a broad sense of social understanding was required.' The *Sun* was blunter. A cartoon showed Thatcher, as always neatly dressed and coiffed, looking with a fixed, uncomprehending smile at a riot-ravaged landscape. A line of smoking ruins spelled out the words 'Act Now'. A caption added with broader menace: 'The Writing On The Wall'.

On 13 July, with little advance publicity, she left Downing Street by car at 6 a.m. Her husband Denis accompanied her, as he often did for particularly stressful expeditions. She wore all black and looked tired. 'The last ten days,' she told journalists later that day, 'have been the most worrying of my administration.'

After a high-speed drive north, she met Kenneth Oxford in Liverpool at 8.30 a.m. and was escorted to Toxteth. Over the previous few days the violence had temporarily receded. The TV crews whose trembling footage had startled British and foreign viewers had mostly departed; and the smell of charring and spilled petrol and alcohol was becoming fainter. Yet the prime minister barely got out of her official car. Instead, for forty minutes she was driven around the main streets, peering through armoured glass at a new landscape that in places was like something from the London Blitz: blackened bones of buildings, glassless windows, unidentifiable melted deposits on pavements, sudden new empty spaces.

She spoke briefly to customers at a hairdresser's. Rather than the riot damage, physical or psychological, what struck her most about the area, she said in her memoirs, was the quality of the housing – 'by no means the worst' – and 'the litter' and 'untended' grass, 'some of it almost waist high'. In the large official and private homes she had inhabited in recent years, in richer parts of England, a well-kept garden had always been one of her priorities. After looking at Toxteth she wrote, 'I asked myself how people could live in such circumstances without trying to clear up the mess and improve their surroundings. The young people [who had] got into trouble,' she concluded like a naive schoolmistress, 'had plenty of constructive things to do if they wanted.'

Next she went to Liverpool Town Hall. Several hundred protesters had gathered outside. Tomatoes and toilet rolls were thrown at her. The police had to link arms to hold back the crowd as she passed. Once inside the Town Hall, she spent three hours with Liverpool councillors, church leaders and Toxteth community figures. She was 'amazed', an official minute recorded, at the latter's 'hatred for the police'. She unconvincingly insisted to the Toxteth representatives that 'She had not heard a word from Mr Oxford against [their] local community.' As for their community and city's wider problems, 'Resources had been poured into areas like Liverpool.' The *Echo* reported that the prime minister also asked the councillors 'why no decision had been taken about the Liverpool Ring Road. It had, said Labour leaders, informing an apparently surprised PM that they'd scrapped it.' Minutes later, after a total of five hours in Liverpool, she set off in her official car back to London. On 27 July, a fortnight after her visit, the Toxteth uprising restarted.

Meanwhile a less ferocious but less predictable disorder raced across England. During July there were riots and smaller, copycat actions against police and property all over Merseyside – in Kirkby, Netherly, West Derby, Speke, Halewood and Cantril Farm; in the multiracial inner city districts of Chapeltown in Leeds, Moss Side in Manchester, and Handsworth in Birmingham; and in similar areas right across London – from Southall, Hounslow, Notting Hill and Acton in the west, to Hackney and Leytonstone in the east, Wood Green, Stoke Newington and Dalston in the north, and Battersea, Balham, Clapham, Streatham, Lewisham, Woolwich and Brixton in the south. There were flare-ups all over the Midlands – in Wolverhampton, Leicester, Nottingham, Coventry and Derby; the north – Birkenhead, Blackburn, Bradford, Ellesmere Port, Fleetwood, Preston, Sheffield, Huddersfield, Halifax, Hull, and Keswick in the Lake District; the West Country – Bristol, Cirencester and Gloucester; the south – Bedford,

Reading, Luton, Harlow, High Wycombe, Aldershot, Maidstone, Tunbridge Wells and Slough; and on the south coast – Portsmouth and Southampton. From tough garrison towns to soft commuter towns, from supposed tourist idylls – Keswick! – to stoical ex-milltowns, from decaying places to rising ones, from tense places to supposedly contented ones, much of built-up England seemed suddenly to have become ungovernable.

On 13 July, the day Thatcher went to Toxteth, *The Times* replaced its usually aloof leading article with something more emotional, headlined 'Where Are We Going?':

> The riots of the past week are a severe blow ... One of the qualities upon which we have been accustomed to pride ourselves as British people has been the orderliness of our way of life. We may no longer have an empire. We may no longer be the workshop of the world. We may even have difficulty paying our way. But this is still ... [a] society renowned for tolerance and gentleness. Now that too seems to have been exposed as a false dream. It is at times like this that the sap of a nation can dry up so as to paralyse all its endeavours ... The impression has been created that all that lies ahead is the prospect of slogging through, which is not exactly a vision to uplift the spirits of a dejected people. The Government has only itself to blame ...

The following day, despite Thatcher's Liverpool trip, the pound sank fast on the foreign exchanges: 'Dealers said that fears about a breakdown in law and order in Britain were being widely expressed in foreign centres,' *The Times* reported.

Between late 1980 and early 1982, damning verdicts on Thatcher's premiership were everywhere: in left-wing and right-wing papers, in broadsheets and tabloids, in books and television series, in Britain and abroad. Many read like obituaries. 'What at the time of her election seemed like an innocent enthusiasm now seems like a risible delusion,' wrote the usually measured political columnist Peter Jenkins in the *Guardian* in November 1980. 'Thatcherism doesn't work.' In the 1982 book and BBC series *On Britain*, the revered Anglo-German sociologist Ralf Dahrendorf bracketed together the Thatcher and Heath governments – a humiliating comparison for Thatcherites – as attempts 'to transform a solidarity society into one of individual competition . . . Both failed.'

In March 1981 a leader in the right-leaning *Sunday Times* described Britain as 'Mrs Thatcher's Wasteland . . . a new and dispiriting environment . . . where our oil bonanza is dissipated on preserving a fruitless stagnation.' The piece continued, 'Opposition to the government's entire economic strategy is being loudly articulated by every lobby and interest group in the land, from the brewers to the banks, from road interests to oil, from the CBI to the TUC.' The paper wrote off the prime minister as out of her depth: 'The failure of Mrs Thatcher's economics is a failure of vision. Hers is a view that might suit a branch bank manager, who believes all he need do is set an overdraft limit and then lecture his customers into meeting it.'

In February the influential American magazine *Time* put Thatcher's troubles on the cover. 'Is she leading the country out of the wilderness or into it?', the article inside asked. It quoted Thatcher: 'Things will get worse before they get better.' It also asked Milton Friedman himself about her monetarist experiment. 'Unfortunately,' he said, drily but woundingly, 'actual practice has not conformed to policy.'

In January 1982 even the Institute of Economic Affairs (IEA), a British think tank that had been arguing for a radical right-wing government since the 1950s and had been close to Thatcher since the 1960s, turned on her version of monetarism. 'The rhetoric has often been admirably monetarist, [but] the execution . . . has been clumsy to the point of incompetence,' wrote David Laidler, a monetarist academic, in the IEA journal. 'To treat the economic policies of the Thatcher government as monetarism is a little like treating the economic policies of Brezhnev as an experiment in applied Marxism.'

Leonid Brezhnev was the leader of the Soviet Union, seventy-five years old, seventeen years in power, increasingly immobile in public, increasingly a byword for failing government. He would be dead within ten months. During 1981 and early 1982 many in Whitehall did not give the Thatcher government much longer.

Some of the strongest doubters were in the government itself. John Hoskyns was one. The head of the Downing Street Policy Unit titled the chapter of his memoirs dealing with early 1981, 'It's Not Working'. Thirty years later he still had mixed feelings about Thatcher's abilities. 'She was a very limited lady,' he told me. 'No great brain. And terribly insecure. Much more insecure than people realize . . . She hated being in the wrong. She couldn't bring herself to say, "I should've started thinking about this earlier."'

I met Hoskyns at his house in rural Suffolk, which was more modern and hard-edged than Thatcher's cottagey tastes would ever have accepted. 'We built this in '75, '76,' Hoskyns said casually; in a polo neck and canvas shoes, sitting languidly in a glass-ceilinged room, he seemed at first more like a retired art historian than a retired radical.

In the early 1980s he was sometimes a dashing presence in Downing Street, with well-tailored suits and the sort of officer-class manners and good looks that Thatcher often found appealing in male subordinates. Yet, like Minford, he was a maverick and a zealot. Public service ran deep in the Hoskyns family. Half a dozen ancestors had been MPs, Tory and Liberal. His father was killed by the Germans in 1940, leading a battalion in a sacrificial rearguard action to protect the retreat from Dunkirk. Hoskyns joined the army as soon as he was old enough, in 1945, months before the end of the war. He did no fighting.

For a dozen years afterwards the patriotism, organizational precision and gentlemanly pleasures of life in a 'toffish', polo-playing armoured regiment were enough for him. 'The armed forces were in those days just about the only aspect of the United Kingdom of which people did not feel slightly ashamed,' Hoskyns wrote in his memoirs. But peacetime soldiering, apart from 'a more interesting interlude in Kenya during the Mau Mau emergency' – the undeclared but brutal end-of-empire war – gradually bored him. In 1957 he left the army.

His inquisitive mind and experiences with military technology had given Hoskyns an interest in 'stuff to do with the future', so he joined the American computer company IBM, which was then just setting up in Britain. As he travelled to America and around Europe on IBM business, his conviction that Britain was backward and failing was reinforced. One symptom of this backwardness, he thought, was the difficulty British companies had managing computer projects. In 1964 he left IBM to set up a software engineering consultancy. By the early 1970s, Hoskyns Group had become one of the top half dozen such British companies, but his view of the state of the country, and particularly of the economy and how government functioned, had only darkened. In 1974 he began selling off his company. The same year, influenced by the then-fashionable business and academic concept of systems analysis, which sometimes sought to express the workings of complex phenomena in flow charts, he drew an inky one-page diagram of 'the UK Economic Problem'. Like monetarism, like the Liverpool Model, it attempted to corral the semi-anarchy of a modern capitalist economy into a neat pattern of cause and effect. Some of the British weaknesses that the diagram's interlocking arrows pointed to were predictable – 'inflation', 'union attitudes'; but others were more intriguing – 'changes in individual attitudes', 'UK spared European wartime upheaval'.

'In Britain in the 1970s,' Hoskyns told me, 'we were all settling for string quartets on Sunday afternoons. What we needed was a bit more vulgarity, a bit more get-up-and-go. In the 1980s, you'd say to people' – he raised his voice almost to a parade-ground shout – '"We're going to fight 'til we die to save this bloody country!"'

During the 1970s other former military officers with similarly strong ideas about the state of Britain, such as the founder of the SAS, Colonel David Stirling, and General Sir Walter Walker, considered drastic, undemocratic solutions – possibly even a military coup. Hoskyns grimaced. 'I met one or two of them. Absolute fools. I thought, "I wouldn't mind being with them in the jungle, but that's it."' Instead, he approached politicians.

Hoskyns was 'a floating voter', and rarely a Tory one. The first politician he contacted, in 1974, was Dick Taverne, a former Labour minister and MP. Taverne had recently resigned from the party and set up the Campaign for Social Democracy: a new, centrist party intended to take voters from Labour, which was then beginning to move strongly and lastingly leftwards. Hoskyns joined the campaign's committee. When the campaign fizzled out in 1975, he attached himself instead to a group of Labour-supporting businessmen who were looking for ideas, as he put it, on 'how the economy could be saved and rejuvenated'. Again, the association was brief, from 1975 to 1976, and came to nothing. The Labour government of the day was swamped with problems; Hoskyns and the other businessmen were, he wrote later, with revealingly haughty frustration, 'unable to get the Prime Minister or his colleagues to focus their minds on our recommendations.'

In the autumn of 1975 Hoskyns began talking to the Conservatives. He showed them his diagram. Its essentially right-wing assumptions, sense of utter conviction, and implied call for drastic solutions all appealed to Thatcher's fiercer advisers. After some bumpy initial meetings with Thatcher herself, who preferred not to be lectured but to do the lecturing, Hoskyns and his ideas also won over the Tory leader. 'John,' she wrote, 'had strong powers of analysis and helped formulate our economic strategy in Opposition . . . In government he repeatedly compelled ministers to relate each problem to our overall strategy of reversing decline. He kept our eye on the ball.'

At first the Downing Street Policy Unit had three staff and a poky office. But under Hoskyns it constantly fired out memos and policy papers, which were blunter and more provocative than the usual Whitehall advice. Responding to the Toxteth riots, a Policy Unit paper in September 1981 wrote off Liverpool as 'a dying sub-economy'. This abrasiveness was quite deliberate: 'We did none of the usual "Ministers will be aware . . ." and "Colleagues will understand that . . ."; instead, just "We got this bit right" and "We got this bit wrong", and "Unless we do the following, we might as well pack up and go home."' From the prime minister downwards, the Thatcher government was often self-dramatizing, sometimes to good effect. Hoskyns was not an MP, and did not ultimately need her favour: he had lots of contacts outside politics, and plenty of money. Even more than the other Thatcherite insiders, he was free to play the drama queen.

He helped write Thatcher's speeches, organized seminars for her and for ministers, and 'produced odd ideas for Geoffrey [Howe]'. Hoskyns worked up to nineteen hours a day, going back to a flat in Clapham in south London to sleep – or to read more policy papers in bed. At the end of the week, he would drive to East Anglia, through the depopulating, exhaust-grey suburbs of early 1980s east London, through the expanding, increasingly Tory-voting Essex commuter towns, and out to his Suffolk house, which had a small lake and secluded grounds, but where a phone call often awaited from the chancellor, or a summons to see Thatcher at her weekend country residence, Chequers, three hours' drive away in Buckinghamshire.

Hoskyns found the business of government both incredibly exciting and incredibly difficult. Dealing with civil servants was 'like pushing on a piece of string. There was no machinery for doing *anything* – except what was already going on.' Nor did he get on well with ministers: 'Most of the people in her first cabinet – absolutely useless. Completely defeatist about everything.' Above all, he was ground down by the almost perpetual air of crisis that enveloped the Thatcher administration: 'We were so quickly into hard times. By the end of '79, there must have been a lot of people [among the public] saying, "What the hell's going on? We thought life was going to get better, but it's beginning to get worse." And then 1980 and 1981: worse still.' In his memoirs, Hoskyns described the process of creating a functional government in the early 1980s as like 'trying to pitch a tent in the middle of a landslide'. He resigned from the Policy Unit in April 1982.

As often with struggling governments, events abroad seemed to gang up on Thatcher too. Between 1979 and 1981, just like the unlucky Heath half a dozen years earlier, she was cursed with an oil crisis. The 1978–9 revolution in Iran had overthrown the pro-western Shah, whose regime had supplied 5 per cent of the West's oil. Iranian production was disrupted, and panic-buying began on the world oil market. In 1980 a still-febrile Iran was opportunistically invaded by its neighbour and rival, Iraq, another major oil producer. The ensuing, protracted war caused oil output to collapse in both countries; further panic-buying followed; the global oil price almost quadrupled, and during 1980 six of the world's biggest seven economies went into recession.

As in the 1970s, a higher oil price also meant higher British inflation. When Thatcher had taken office, after three years of belatedly successful Labour anti-inflation measures, the rate had finally fallen to 10 per cent: still high but considered economically and politically acceptable. By mid-1980, the figure had shot back up to 22 per cent – almost as bad as under Labour in the mid-1970s, a period which Conservative propaganda had spent years portraying as utterly disastrous. Inflation did not drop below the figure Thatcher had inherited for almost another two years.

For a government whose monetarist approach was meant to deal with inflation above all else, this was humiliating and deeply unsettling. Hoskyns recalled a frightened meeting of senior ministers and advisers at Chequers in January 1981: 'Terry Burns, Geoffrey [Howe]'s chief economic adviser, said, "All the big numbers are running away from us."'

These numbers included the opinion polls. In March 1981 the usually loyal *Daily Telegraph* reported that that month's harsh Budget was the most unpopular for thirty years – quite a nadir, given the amount of bad news delivered by British chancellors since the 1950s. The government's broader ratings were just as dire. In December 1981, Gallup put the Conservatives at 23 per cent. None of Britain's 1970s governments, frequently despised as they were, had ever fallen that low in the polls.

In public, in her armour-like suits and heavy make-up, Thatcher remained fluent and defiant – 'the lady's not for turning' – but in private she sometimes seemed overwhelmed by her predicament. 'She was completely bombed out in the summer of '81,' Hoskyns recalled. That August, although she disliked holidays – she often spent parts of them working, or returning early – she abandoned Downing Street and Chequers and went to Cornwall for a few days. There she stayed with David Wolfson, a businessman, friend and confidant who was the unpaid chief of staff of her political office.

Wolfson wrote to Hoskyns afterwards. 'The picture I got,' Hoskyns told me, 'was of Margaret almost as a zombie. Not talking. Going and sitting on a seat at the end of the garden. In a dark night of the soul . . . thinking, "It's all gone wrong. I don't think it is going to come right. I'm the most unpopular prime minister ever. I will go down as a total disaster."'

5
Doom City

Many Britons had a feeling of dread in the early 1980s. Even more than the most unsettling years of the 1970s, the previous post-war peak for social turbulence and talk of national crisis, the early 1980s carried a sense of things coming to a head: in politics, in the economy, in the inner cities, in race relations, in international relations. Some commentators even feared for the survival of British life itself. 'We are entering the most dangerous decade in human history,' wrote the historian E. P. Thompson in a hurriedly published pamphlet in 1980. 'The extinction of civilized life upon this island is probable.'

Thompson was a long-established left-wing public intellectual, wild-haired and gauntly good-looking, with a thrillingly theatrical prose style. Yet his warning was hard to dismiss as just polemic. 'Protest and Survive', as his pamphlet was titled, was a response to a recent official booklet and series of public-information films, *Protect and Survive*, which in their euphemistic Whitehall way were even more frightening.

On 10 March 1980 the BBC current affairs programme *Panorama* broadcast the films to an audience of 7.7 million. Using animation, bright colours, simple diagrams and montages, cheery synthesizer music and a slow, carefully enunciated, repetitive voiceover, they might have been aimed at primary-school pupils, except that their subject was what civilians should do in the event of a nuclear war.

'If an attack is expected,' the first film began, the public would hear 'a rising and falling note' in the distance, like an air-raid siren. 'When you hear the attack warning, you and your family must take cover at once . . . If you cannot reach home in 10 minutes, take cover in the nearest building . . . If you are caught in the open, lie down.' The voiceover continued: 'After an attack, you may have to stay in your home for about 14 days.' The film showed a model of a small detached house, a little charred on one side but otherwise as cosy as a child's drawing, with a steep red roof and a chimney poking out. 'Do not go outside,' the voiceover went on, 'until you are told it is safe . . . Advice will be given to you over the radio.' Three words flashed up in capitals: 'STAY AT HOME'.

The film explained why: 'Nuclear fall-out can settle anywhere, so no place in the United Kingdom is safer than any other.' There was a graphic of radioactive dust twinkling down over a pretty farm gate and field like deadly confetti. Instead, housebound citizens should build 'a fall-out room' inside their home, away from outside walls or roofs. 'Making a refuge is not difficult. The main things you need are' – the voiceover slipped into a kind of infantilizing note form – 'shovel, boxes . . . earth, bricks, sand'. As if for a very elaborate children's den, walls should be made out of piled-up mattresses; ceilings out of doors taken off their hinges; further insulating layers out of suitcases and binbags filled with soil. Then the shelter should be stocked: 'Food, mostly in tins . . . [or that] you can eat cold' – there was a shot of a packet of Rich Tea biscuits and a tin of ham – '. . . water: seven gallons per person . . . books and magazines to pass the time . . . clock and calendar . . . box of dry sand [and] cloths for wiping plates and utensils . . . buckets, preferably with lids: line them with plastic bags, and try to rig up some kind of seat across the bucket . . . dustbin: keep just outside fall-out room . . . brush or shake off any fall-out dust you may have picked up.'

Spending weeks in a low-roofed shelter a few dozen feet square, the film conceded, would be 'cramped' and 'uncomfortable . . . Most of the time you will be resting . . . It will not be easy for you to keep clean – but cleanliness is essential to prevent sickness. Pour some disinfectant into the toilet. It will cut down the smells and keep off flies.' As for nutrition, 'You may not be able to replace your stocks of food for a long time . . . Eat the smallest amount you can.'

In its concluding moments, the film finally admitted that far worse things than these would happen to civilians. 'Arrangements will be made to treat any people who are ill or injured. Listen to your radio. Details will be given.' The vagueness and passive voice of the first and last sentences were not reassuring. But nor was the precision of what followed: 'If anybody dies while in your fall-out room, move the body to another part of the house. Label the body with name and address, and cover it as tightly as possible.'

The *Protect and Survive* public information campaign, which also included radio ads and newspaper pull-outs, had been first conceived and drafted by the Central Office of Information between 1974 and 1976. It was the middle of the Détente era, when East–West relations softened and anxieties about nuclear war unknotted a little after three decades of post-war tension. The *Protect and Survive* material was secretly produced and stored away. One of the booklets was eventually placed in the House of Commons library, but MPs were forbidden to make copies or show it to the media. If a nuclear conflict became likely, the official thinking went, the films and literature would be quickly distributed on a massive scale: the printing of between ten million and twenty million pamphlets was envisaged. The *Protect and Survive* ideas were even incorporated into a Queen's Speech, drafted in secret in March 1983, to be delivered in the event of an imminent nuclear conflict:

> Now this madness of war is once more spreading through the world and our brave country must again prepare itself to survive against great odds . . . We all know that the dangers facing us today are greater by far than at any time in our long history . . . But whatever terrors lie in wait for us all . . . if families remain united and resolute, giving shelter to those living alone and unprotected, our country's will to survive cannot be broken.

The *Protect and Survive* film and documents were released in 1980, after protracted media pressure; the draft Queen's Speech not made public until 2013. Yet all this secretive official planning managed to leave a cloud of questions unanswered. In what circumstances, exactly, were the population to start building and stocking their private fallout shelters? Why couldn't the government provide bomb shelters, as it had in the Second World War? How many fall-out rooms were likely to survive nuclear blasts anyway? And how were millions of people in a congested, panicking country meant to get home 'in ten minutes' once the sirens sounded? Was 'about 14 days' a credible estimate of how long it would take for the fallout to drop below lethal levels? What sort of government would be left to advise – or compel – the public on such matters? What else would survivors find when they emerged from their windowless bolt-holes?

Some of these questions were probably impossible for any government to answer honestly and convincingly. But the flimsiness of the advice in *Protect and Survive* showed with terrifying clarity how far Whitehall's plans for protecting Britons from nuclear attack had fallen behind the strategies being developed, in Britain and abroad, for how those weapons might be used.

For over a quarter of a century, since the early years of the Cold War, there had been a consensus in Whitehall that building government shelters for the civilian population was simply too expensive for a country with fifty million citizens and a declining share of the world's wealth. A few smaller, richer countries such as Switzerland did complete mass shelter-building programmes, but Whitehall did not change its mind. In 1980 a Home Office working party estimated the cost of protecting every Briton at £70 billion; the government's entire annual spending was around £100 billion.

Yet by 1980 the context for such calculations seemed to be shifting dramatically. In December 1979 the Soviet Union had invaded Afghanistan. The following summer, the United States and sixty-four other countries, overwhelmingly Western or West-aligned, boycotted the Moscow Olympics in retaliation. That autumn the sometimes crudely anti-Soviet Ronald Reagan was elected US President, defeating the more conciliatory Jimmy Carter. In 1983 Reagan told the American National Association of Evangelicals that the Soviet Union was 'the focus of evil in the modern world'. The Détente era was emphatically over.

John Nott was Margaret Thatcher's defence secretary from January 1981 to January 1983. 'When I was at the Ministry of Defence,' he told me, 'we were completely transfixed by the Cold War. The Russians . . . were really running ahead. They were increasingly catching up with technology, and they had an overwhelming superiority in numbers, in tanks, planes, everything . . . They had a huge, overwhelming force that we would never have been able to resist without nuclear weapons.'

This picture of surging Soviet strength was actually open to question – as their slow-motion defeat in impoverished Afghanistan would demonstrate – but it became a potent orthodoxy in the United States and Britain, not just among politicians, defence bureaucrats and the military, but also in the wider world. In 1981, as an eleven-year-old with an army father and a small boy's unthinking fascination with military hardware, I bought a lavish, just-published hardback in W. H. Smith. *The Balance of Military Power* had a foreword by the Secretary General of NATO, Dr J. M. A. H. Luns, and page after page of photos, often snatched and grainy, and all the more frightening and exciting for it, of the latest Soviet tanks, bombers and nuclear missiles, bulging and gigantic or rakish and futuristic, as they were paraded through Moscow or took part in military exercises that looked like mock invasions. 'The USSR continues to field new and more capable [nuclear weapons] systems,' ran a typical passage in the main text, written by a small committee of Western defence journalists and military officers, 'to the point where a first-strike might, at some time in the future, seem to be feasible.'

The bland technical phrase 'first strike' increasingly haunted discussions about nuclear weapons in the early 1980s. Previously in the Cold War, it had been widely assumed by strategists, politicians and the public on both sides that the nuclear arsenals of NATO and the Soviet bloc were so powerful that using even a minute fraction of them in an East–West conflict would provoke instant and crushing retaliation, and only achieve, as a less euphemistic nuclear war term put it, 'mutually assured destruction' – usefully abbreviated to MAD. Yet by 1980 there were signs that this uneasy but enduring equilibrium might be weakening. Both sides were increasingly exploring the possibility of launching their nuclear weapons so swiftly and accurately at the other's nuclear arsenal that a devastating response could not follow, and that military victory would therefore be won.

Some of this was just contingency planning, and had been quietly going on deep inside the war bureaucracies since at least the early 1960s. But in the early 1980s both sides also appeared to be taking steps to turn first strike into a practical option, deploying new, more mobile, more accurate and stealthy 'tactical' nuclear weapons, such as the Soviet SS-20 and the American Tomahawk Cruise Missile, which seemed specifically designed for this sort of warfare. More alarmingly still for Britons and other Europeans, these deployments were not in the traditional nuclear citadels of the United States and eastern Russia, but in western Russia and western Europe. Since the new weapons had a shorter range than traditional, larger nuclear missiles, their targets were likely to be confined to one continent. In October 1981, Reagan was asked by a gathering of newspaper editors whether he could foresee a 'limited' nuclear war, waged only in Europe. 'I don't honestly know,' the American president answered with typically unsettling casualness. 'I could see where you could have the exchange of tactical weapons against troops in the field [in Europe] without it bringing either one of the major powers to pushing the button [to attack the other].'

In the early 1980s it was commonly assumed that an East–West war would begin with a massive Soviet tank attack across the West German border. When we lived in West Germany between 1978 and 1980, a few hours from that border across flat fields that were perfect for tank manoeuvres, my father would disappear for days at a time on army exercises that, as far as he was willing to talk about them, appeared to be for precisely such a scenario. On 26 January 1981 the *Daily Mail* carried a recruiting advertisement for the British army: a full-page photo of a Soviet tank grinding through Kabul in Afghanistan, dwarfing a parked car. 'Next?' asked the none-too-cryptic caption. 'Will Russian tanks roar across the plains of Germany?' Later, my father told me that his exercises used to take place directly across the border from an enormous Russian military training area. Twice a year the Soviet Union rotated the soldiers stationed there, sending hundreds of thousands back to Russia and bringing in replacements. Officially, these troop movements were so that the soldiers could help with the Russian wheat harvest; but to my father and his outnumbered NATO comrades these manoeuvres always looked indistinguishable from a mobilization for war.

Much of the West's response to a Russian invasion would have been launched from Britain. An important member of NATO and an intimate American ally, from 1979 Britain also had a premier who was sometimes as aggressively anti-Soviet as Reagan. 'The Russians are bent on world dominance,' Thatcher had claimed in 1976 in one of her first resonant speeches as Tory leader. Britain also housed Western Europe's biggest concentration of nuclear weapons: British submarines with Polaris missiles, American jets carrying atom bombs and, from 1983, Europe's first cruise missiles, based at Greenham Common in Berkshire. Dozens of other American-controlled airbases and electronic eavesdropping facilities were scattered all over Britain.

In short, the country was an obvious target for a Soviet first strike. From the late 1970s, British popular culture began to wake up to the possibility. In 1978, *The Third World War: August 1985* was published, a novel whose authorship was credited to 'General Sir John Hackett and Other Top-Ranking NATO Generals and Advisors'. Hackett had actually retired from military service ten years earlier, but had commanded the substantial British army based in West Germany. His novel was an uneven mixture of melodramatic battle scenes – 'nothing could stop the incoming waves' of Soviet tanks – technical military talk, crude right-wing propaganda, and surprisingly deft fictional game-playing, including photos of actual Soviet forces on manoeuvres and fake footnotes referring to other World War Three 'histories'. It sold more than three million copies worldwide. In Germany, well-thumbed copies lay around in the homes and cars of my father's friends and fellow officers. In 1982 the jacket of an updated edition announced that the novel had been 'chosen by President Reagan as one of the three most important books he read last year'.

One of the novel's more compelling chapters described 'the destruction of Birmingham' by a surprise Soviet nuclear attack. A million people are killed or injured, the city administration evaporates, and armed soldiers have to take over the blasted streets to stop looting and the complete collapse of law and order. At its conclusion, the book draws back from the abyss, with a peace settlement between East and West. In Britain a system of emergency government just about copes with the war crisis. But a pessimism about Whitehall's preparations for nuclear attack runs through the novel regardless: in none of its editions, even the updated 1982 one – all of them packed with references to actual defence policy – is there any mention of *Protect and Survive* and its supposedly vital recommendations.

Hackett's book was followed by an explosion of nuclear-war fiction, factual guides, exposés, investigations, polemics, pop songs, even comedy. There were Hollywood movies about nuclear weapons: *WarGames*, a 1983 box-office hit in Britain and America, won three Oscar nominations. Its well-researched story, including input from American military computer scientists, was about a teenage hacker who accidentally gets into a Pentagon supercomputer and triggers a nuclear-war simulation that almost becomes a real conflict. Like Hackett's book, *WarGames* ends happily; but disturbingly long stretches of its narrative suggested that an East–West nuclear mobilization, once initiated, would be very hard to stop. In 1983, when the regular rising and falling wail of a siren being tested on one of my father's army bases was enough to spook me a little every time, *WarGames* stayed with me for months after I saw it. Thirty years later, British government papers revealed that a 1983 NATO exercise, Operation Able Archer, involving troop movements in Germany and the use of airbases in Britain to simulate a Soviet invasion, was so realistic that the Russians came close to treating it as the prelude to an actual conflict. Soviet SS-20 missile launchers were put on alert and Soviet aircraft loaded with nuclear weapons. 'We cannot discount the possibility that at least some Soviet officials/officers may have misinterpreted Able Archer 83 . . . as posing a real threat,' concluded the British Joint Intelligence Committee after the crisis had subsided. An aghast Margaret Thatcher ordered civil servants to 'urgently consider . . . what could be done to remove the danger that, by miscalculating western intentions, the Soviet Union would over-react'.

In 1982 London Weekend Television broadcast *Whoops Apocalypse*, a six-part farce featuring a clumsy right-wing American president not unlike Reagan, a succession of ailing but fierce Soviet leaders not unlike Brezhnev, and a spiral of nuclear accidents and misunderstandings. The series climaxed darkly with Soviet missiles in the air and the American president about to launch an all-consuming retaliation. A spin-off book included a map of Britain after a nuclear attack: 'All persons in reinforced concrete shelters which they bought . . . at the time of the Afghanistan crisis would enjoy an additional life expectancy of approximately 37 seconds.'

Seemingly every British pop musician with a social conscience suddenly felt compelled to write an anti-nuclear song. Occasionally, black humour leavened them. 'Two Tribes', a knowingly bombastic and provocative 1984 number one by the Liverpool band Frankie Goes to Hollywood, had a video starring crude lookalikes of the American and Russian leaders, ineptly brawling. But more often the songs were grave and bleak: from 'The Earth Dies Screaming', a muted hit by the usually perky Birmingham reggae band UB40 in 1980; to 'Breathing', a beautiful stop-start single about inhaling radioactive dust, released by the usually otherworldly Kate Bush in the same year; to 'Hi Baku Shyo (Suffer Bomb Disease)', a hollow and sickly-sounding 1981 instrumental by the London avant-gardists This Heat.

The terrible things atomic weapons did to the human body, a subject often avoided by British artists and governments earlier in the Cold War, became an inescapable element – perhaps the central element – of the nuclear-war debate and culture of the early 1980s. 'Tissues are charred to black carbon', began a typical line in *A Guide To Armageddon*, an authoritative 1982 BBC1 documentary film about the effects on London of a notional nuclear bomb, of relatively modest one-megaton power, detonating above St Paul's Cathedral. 'Six hundred and fifty thousand' people would suffer 'major burns' in the 'first few seconds'. Winds from the blast would reach 'up to 2000 mph', bursting eardrums and turning buildings into storms of debris. The film cut between a photo of an old woman in a headscarf and footage of airborne glass flaying a pumpkin. 'When a [nuclear] fireball touches the ground,' the voiceover continued, 'tons of earth and debris are sucked up and made radioactive. For weeks, lethal dust drops out of the cloud . . . As it's blown by the wind, areas hundreds of miles away can be affected.' The film cut to an actor made up to look like someone with radiation sickness, with bleeding gums and hair falling out.

The same year, the celebrated British children's writer Raymond Briggs, author of gentle, happy-sad graphic novels such as *The Snowman* and *Fungus the Bogeyman*, published *When the Wind Blows*, about an elderly couple in an archetypal English cottage trying to survive a nuclear war. Deferential to authority, part-mesmerized by rosy memories of the home front during the Second World War, Jim and Hilda improvise a shelter according to the *Protect and Survive* principles, and squeeze in just before the Soviet missiles explode. They survive the blast, unlike their incinerated neighbours. But then they run out of drinking water and misunderstand the official advice about when it is 'safe' to leave their shelter. A brief expedition into the scorched outside world exposes them to fall-out. Back in the shelter, Jim and Hilda die slowly, vomiting, pale and dishevelled, increasingly terrified and totally alone.

Harrowing and angry though Briggs's best-selling book was – at the time I couldn't bear to read the last dozen pages – it missed one disturbing seam of potential material. During the 1950s, just as Whitehall was dismissing the idea of providing nuclear shelters for the public, it was also, secretly, in the middle of a major programme of tunnelling and excavation to create atom bomb-proof underground facilities for selected members of the civil service, government and military. Most of this work was completed by 1960, and the bunkers remained largely unnoticed, their small and anonymous above-ground structures – small winding sheds for lifts, unexplained railway-tunnel entrances – just more official property in a post-war Britain thick with government and military buildings. Then in 1982 Duncan Campbell, an investigative journalist with an interest in state and nuclear secrets and an appetite for underground trespassing, published *War Plan UK: The Secret Truth about Britain's 'Civil Defence'*. To the near-astonishment of reviewers, the polemical and well-documented book revealed that 'Across Britain . . . some distance below the ground . . . there are twenty thousand or more "desks" in war headquarters; half are in relatively well-protected central or regional government or military HQs and half in less well-protected district or county council HQs.'

From these bunkers, what Campbell called 'district dictatorships' would operate in the aftermath of a nuclear attack: twenty almost self-contained regional governments with extensive emergency powers, many of them handed to unelected 'County Controllers'. He quoted a 1973 Home Office circular, 'Machinery of Government in War': 'Post-[nuclear] attack decisions should not be compared with . . . peacetime decision-making processes of government. Inevitably post-attack plans would be crude and simple. The urgent decisions of County Controllers would be arbitrary, and, to some people, would appear harsh and inequitable.'

During the 1970s and early 1980s this authoritarian system was tested with increasing frequency in national civil-defence exercises, played out solely on paper, in part to avoid alarming or angering an increasingly anxious public. Campbell obtained many of the 'scenarios and diaries' generated by the participants, effectively official predictions of what life and government would be like in Britain during and after a nuclear war. During one exercise, 1978's Scrum Half – even at its most apocalyptic, Whitehall liked sporting metaphors – the County Controller for Essex sent a telex to superiors: 'Attempting to keep zombies separate from clear local residents.'

Campbell explained: 'The "zombies" in question were . . . the half million refugees from bombs on London' who the exercise predicted would be 'tramping northeast' into Essex. It was assumed that all would be fatally or seriously suffering from radiation sickness. Campbell went on, 'Later [during Scrum Half] the same Controller described plummeting police morale as the problems of controlling the public slipped beyond reach. Forty fire stations were besieged by mobs trying to get at their food supplies. Hundreds of prisoners were being held, with difficulty, by police, for crimes of murder and organized looting.' But at least one post-holocaust law-and-order problem was considered soluble. 'The "zombies" were put away out of sight to await their deaths – the County Controller minuted that he had "requested [the] military to hold irradiated cases at refugee camps".'

If the bomb dropped, was there any credible way that British civilians could escape all these horrors? In 1981, in a village in the West Country, some people thought they had found one.

Gastard in Wiltshire, a few miles east of Bath and south of the M4, is a blustery straggle of semis and bungalows and older stone houses. It has been a settlement since the early Middle Ages, and possibly since Roman times, but the current population is only just above 400; there is not much visible life except a pub and passing cars trying to get through the village as fast as possible along a knotty B road. For much of Gastard's recent history, the most interesting thing about the place has been out of sight, underground.

Starting in the mid-nineteenth century, beneath a low wooded hill a few hundred yards west of the village, a mine was sunk and excavated for the quarrying of Bath stone, which had the lovely shortbread richness favoured by local builders. The quarry was variously known as Pictor Monks, Eastern Monks and Eastlays. But by the 1930s demand had dwindled, as Bath's nineteenth-century heyday receded, the spa city stopped adding lavish buildings, and the Great Depression slowed the wider construction business. In 1934 the mine closed.

Yet the 1930s, like the early 1980s, were a time of military as well as economic anxieties. With Hitler in power in Germany and another world war becoming a possibility, in 1936 the British government bought Eastlays and two other nearby mines for £47,000. It began converting Eastlays into a fortified underground warehouse complex for explosives and ammunition.

Set in innocent-looking farmland, and between 60 and 100 feet below ground, Eastlays was shielded from air attack by thick layers of rock. Its passages and cavities extended in a kidney shape for 24 acres, the size of a small village. Over the next quarter of a century its pitted floors were levelled and rough walls smoothed and painted. Its ceilings, typically a generous 10 to 12 feet high, were strengthened with steel and concrete beams, resting on cathedral-like pillars. Heavy metal anti-blast doors were installed, along with miles of flame-proof and damp-proof electricity cabling: some parts of the quarry leaked heavily. An air-conditioning system and enormous fans were inserted to keep the temperature constant, at a chilly but tolerable 58 to 59 degrees Fahrenheit. Railway tracks were laid for munitions to be transported by wagon around the complex. And three gently sloping shafts were constructed connecting the facility to the surface, narrow and elegantly arched as station corridors on the London Underground, with steps and more tracks so that people and materials could move easily in and out, but angled so that the force of any bomb explosion on the ground above would not find its way, disastrously, down to the ammunition rooms.

During the Second World War, two thousand people worked in this supposedly secret complex. Intrigued locals quickly saw through an attempt to disguise it as an emergency food store, but it was not discovered or bombed by the Germans. By the 1940s Eastlays was one of half a dozen subterranean military facilities in the area; together they formed what Campbell called 'the greatest underground complex in Britain'. One clandestine burrow five miles west of the former quarry, the existence of which was kept secret until well into the 1960s, was equipped with thin bunks and giant kitchens as 'the main seat of government . . . in any future war'.

This part of western England is barely a hundred miles from London, along mostly fast roads. The prevailing wind blows from west to east, towards the capital and its concentration of Soviet targets: if these were attacked with nuclear weapons, there was a chance that this wind would keep Wiltshire relatively free of radioactive fallout. Contingency plans were made to rush the Whitehall elite and their staff there in the event of an impending nuclear attack, by car and special train, or a fleet of coaches, army trucks, or helicopters.

Yet at Eastlays in 1981 a radically different, entrepreneurial, somewhat less exclusive approach to surviving the apocalypse would be promoted. The opportunity for the venture was inadvertently created by Whitehall itself. From the 1950s onwards, it assumed that nuclear weapons diminished the need for huge stockpiles of munitions, and in 1962 Eastlays was emptied and mothballed. In 1972 the Heath government, increasingly short of money, and tentatively exploring the possibilities of what Thatcherites would later call privatization, finally decided that an unused ex-quarry, which needed to be continuously pumped dry and guarded, was an asset that would be better sold. An advertisement for Eastlays and a similar government property nearby was placed in the national press:

VAST UNDERGROUND PREMISES: WILTSHIRE
TWO PROPERTIES OFFERING UNDERGROUND CLEAN, DRY, LEVEL SPACE

Bold entrepreneurs were rare in 1970s Britain, and bidders were given two and a half years to submit their offers. In 1975 a consortium led by a farmer from nearby Somerset bought both properties. According to an article by Campbell in the *New Scientist* magazine, the buyers 'probably paid in excess of £100,000 – [the] original MOD price tag was nearer £1m'. For this relative bargain – the average price of ten houses then – the new owners acquired 70 acres of land and buildings above ground as well as the quarries' subterranean vastness, connected by a short, narrow track to the Gastard road. They began talking to a haulage firm in Doncaster about converting some of Eastlays into a high-security warehouse; and to a mushroom grower in Darlington about turning the rest into the largest underground mushroom farm in the world. 'Mushroom Plan for the Caves of Death,' reported the *Wiltshire Gazette & Herald*.

The local Highways Authority was sceptical that Eastlays was sufficiently accessible for the fleets of vehicles needed for such large-scale businesses. For five years the consortium tried to convince them. Meanwhile the locked quarry dripped and remained off-limits to villagers. Its faintly forbidding surface buildings, with their slits and massive military concrete, became gradually overgrown. In 1977 the eerieness and emptiness of the complex attracted the makers of *Blake's 7*, a BBC1 science-fiction series that would achieve massive popularity between 1978 and 1981 with its cheap but addictive evocation of an authoritarian, post-apocalyptic future. The BBC rented Eastlays to shoot the first episode: 'It was the most amazing place,' remembered the head of visual effects, Ian Scoones. 'You could drive tanks through there. It was almost an underground city, with bunkers all over the place. We drove the trucks and prop wagons right in, down a little grassy lane, and there behind the trees, were these enormous doors covered in ivy. The doors opened, and there were these gigantic underground tunnels.'

In the episode titled 'The Way Back', the quarry is infinite-looking and pale: branching, whitewashed corridors and receding doorways, fluorescent-tube ceilings and tiny breezeblock rooms, pools of light and larger shadows, thrums and silences. Deep inside, a meeting takes place between members of an anti-government resistance movement. The gathering is discovered by state security men wearing face masks and boiler suits. The rebels surrender but are massacred on the spot. Except the hero Blake: he hides in a dark corner and escapes.

In late 1980 the idea of Eastlays as a refuge began to form for real. That autumn the consortium abandoned their warehouse and mushroom-growing schemes. In November a pair of companies registered in the Channel Islands, Douvaine Investments Ltd and Rusepalm Developments, announced they wanted to buy Eastlays. Shortly afterwards, the *Wiltshire Gazette & Herald* reported, they bought the quarry for £450,000. Even allowing for the sharp inflation of the 1970s and early 1980s, the figure was puzzlingly large: four and half times what the consortium had paid only five years earlier for Eastlays plus another quarry. But the new owners of Eastlays had bigger plans. In January 1981 they announced to the local and national media that they planned to turn the quarry into the country's first nuclear-proof town.

During 1980, while much of British manufacturing was imploding, a small but ambitious new industry had sprung up, operating according to a firm Thatcherite logic. Since the government could not afford to protect the population properly from nuclear attack, ran this reasoning, people should do it for themselves. Some of the industry's ideas and key participants had their roots in the loose anti-government, pro-self-reliance movement that had suddenly spread across Britain in the troubled mid-1970s, with low-tax pressure groups claiming massive memberships, middle-class activists fetishizing private property, and ex-military men such as General Sir Walter Walker sketching plans to lead private armies against supposedly over-mighty Labour politicians and trade unions. Thatcher's election as Tory leader, and her promises to follow much of this agenda as prime minister, had robbed the movement of its impetus. But in the early 1980s, with her premiership in crisis, this brand of right-wing politics began to re-emerge, with the private citizen's need to defend himself or herself against Soviet nuclear attack as its new cause.

In January 1981 a new magazine appeared aimed at these British survivalists, titled *Protect & Survive Monthly*. The May issue's editorial gave a flavour of its underlying politics:

> Opposition to Civil Defence ... comes from ... the Labour Party ... Always we find the Labour Party and its fellow-travellers in the vanguard of the Surrender Lobby ... But let us suppose for a moment that the 'anti-C.D.' enthusiasts succeed in their aims, and as a result Britain is defeated and occupied by Soviet troops ... The Soviets invariably dispose of their dupes once they have fulfilled their purpose. The Gulag Archipelago will be filled to overflowing [with] defeatists, 'moles', trendy clerics, and the whole stew-pot of cranks, fools, and traitors ...

Yet the new civil-defence lobby and its associated industry also owed something to less overtly political British trends. The 1970s vogues for camping, caravanning and DIY – early signs of a more self-reliant, property-oriented society – had left millions of Britons potentially interested in nuclear-survival products. The pages of *Protect & Survive Monthly* were crammed with advertisements and advertorials: 'complete lightweight survival suit . . . £130 ex VAT'; 'Monthly Buyer's Guide to manufactured shelters'; 'pocket dosimeters . . . on the spot detection . . . of gamma radiation'; 'brand new Nuclear . . . gas mask with vomit clearance facility'; 'Firearms training by arrangement . . . seven day telephone service'. Many of the products were quite expensive: in 1981, £130 could have bought a bespoke suit instead of a survival suit. The accompanying articles also assumed a certain prosperity, with illustrations showing owners of large detached houses installing private nuclear shelters under croquet-sized back gardens. In January 1981 the *Daily Mail*, always a newspaper closely attuned to middle-class fears and aspirations, sent a reporter, Yvonne Roberts, to the first 'Ideal Nuclear Shelter Exhibition', held in north Yorkshire. Roberts was unimpressed. One shelter on show was little more than 'a dirt trench carpeted in wall-to-wall polythene patterned with puddles, and two mini-prefabs dressed in black plastic'.

Some of the refuges advertised in *Protect & Survive Monthly* looked more credible: they were imports from Switzerland, where the home-shelter industry was much more established. In 1980, while I was living in Germany, we visited family friends in Zurich. I was led downstairs, fascinated, to look at a tiny, spotless chamber off their basement. It had a door like a bank vault and the both reassuring and frightening air of a panic room.

The Eastlays project promised Swiss nuclear security on a mass scale. In early 1981 the quarry's new owners began distributing a glossy three-page prospectus of their plans for their subterranean acres. 'Rusepalm Shelters offers you and your family safety from nuclear fall-out,' declared the cover, the words superimposed on a photo of a mushroom cloud, tinted blood red. 'Apartments constructed within secure main shelter complex.' This refuge, the brochure continued inside, would be:

> one of the safest and best offered to the public in the world today . . . The apartments will be habitable as long as required after a nuclear attack . . . The main shelter will house up to 2500 family units, and

> there will be facilities for recreation and exercise even during a nuclear attack. Among the apartment owners will be doctors, nurses, social workers, craftsmen, sportsmen, teachers and experts in many fields but, most of all, responsible people, with families, and the will to survive a nuclear war.

These people would 'join together to form a friendly community'. But the apartments would to a degree be 'self-contained'. 'Designed for four persons', they would not be large – '13 feet by 14 feet': the size of a decent living room – but much bigger than the cramped survival cells envisaged in *Protect & Survive*. 'Multiple units' would also be offered. Each apartment would have 'lighting, power, heating, washbasin, bunks, radio connected to the main shelter control and communication centre, closed circuit television, storage compartments and fresh water supply'. An accompanying floorplan showed a squarish, open-plan room with thick outside walls, no windows, and a table and four chairs as its sole daytime furniture. However, the brochure went on:

> The main shelter will provide the following facilities for communal use: dining facilities for all main meals, fully lit corridors, showers, laundry, a library which will contain a mini-computer programmed with survival technology, updated from time to time, recreation rooms, medical centre, radio transmitter and receiver, security control room, air filtration/purification, monitoring and alarm system . . . main food and provision store, water storage tanks (additional to mains supply), electronic security system and fire fighting equipment . . . mains electricity with emergency power system installed . . . The complex has 41 acres of surface land upon which will be provided extensive parking space . . . in addition, there will be provision for helicopter landing . . .

Users of the Rusepalm Shelter Complex were expected to come from across the south of England, south Wales and the Midlands: the prospectus listed the distance to Bath ('5 miles'), Bristol ('23 miles'), Cardiff ('33 miles'), Birmingham ('110 miles') and London ('130 miles'), and details of which exit to take from the M4. Customers were expected to be comfortably off: '99 year leases are offered for a capital consideration of £8,000 for a standard unit' – about a third of the price of the average home in 1981. In addition, there would be a 'ground rent of £50 per annum for each standard unit' and an unspecified 'annual service charge', in order for 'the management company ... to maintain all vital services'. Rusepalm would also offer 'mortgage facilities – 25% down, balance over 5 years'. No interest rate was mentioned. In effect, reserving a family bolt-hole in case of apocalypse would require a minimum initial payment of £2,000, followed by ninety-eight years of annual fees, whether the end times arrived or not. What would happen once that period was up, assuming human life still existed in 2080, was not stated; nor whether those of a perpetually nervous disposition about the international situation – or simply intrigued by bunker life – would be permitted to reside at Eastlays full-time.

Alongside the neatly laid-out text, with subheadings also in blood red, were three recent photographs of the quarry interior. 'Taken prior to development', they included an entrance shaft and a corridor, both looking clean, well preserved and well lit. In two of the pictures was a lone figure: a woman of about forty, with a helmet of blonde hair and head-turning cheekbones, dressed authoritatively but a little incongruously for the setting in a grey suit, high heels, and a white blouse with a pussy bow of the sort that Margaret Thatcher increasingly wore. 'Introducing our Chairman,' read one of the captions, 'Maureen Whittart.'

'She was a really powerful character – larger than life, brassy, big, loud,' remembered Eran Bauer, a civil-defence writer and entrepreneur whom Rusepalm hired as a consultant. At the time, Bauer had a business selling anti-nuclear and other protective equipment, Civil Defence Supply Ltd., more solid than most of its competitors and based in Lincolnshire. When we spoke in 2011 it was still thriving.

In the early 1980s he was also a co-editor of *Protect & Survive Monthly*. Rusepalm contacted him through the magazine in late 1980, just before it commenced publication, and soon afterwards he met Whittart and another director of the company, Nicholas Fior. While Whittart was from the genteel army town of Camberley in Surrey, Fior was a London solicitor, slight and small and, at least in Bauer's view, dominated by her. 'He was very nice, mild-mannered and very intelligent. His legal practice was in Harley Street or nearby, and his offices were splendid. But I found it very entertaining to see how she bossed him around.'

In January 1981 Whittart arrived in Wiltshire, checked into a succession of good hotels, and began giving newspaper and television interviews about the Rusepalm Shelter Complex. That winter, as all over Britain, local interest in nuclear issues was already feverish. Labour councillors were campaigning to make Bath a nuclear-free zone, a common, often largely symbolic move in left-leaning British municipalities to ban the movement or siting of nuclear material, military or civilian. The *Bath and West Evening Chronicle* was carrying startling stories about the possibility of rationing at supermarkets and internment camps for 'subversives' in the event of a nuclear war. The pros and cons of nuclear disarmament dominated its usually parochial letters pages.

The response to the surprise announcement of the Eastlays scheme was usefully dramatic for Rusepalm's purposes. The *Wiltshire Gazette & Herald* called the planned refuge a 'Noah's Ark', then 'Doomsday City'. The Campaign for Nuclear Disarmament, which was highly active in the area, called the shelter a 'horrendous' idea, saying it would encourage the notion that nuclear wars were endurable. But CND seemed to accept that the refuge would work: it warned anyone planning to sit out a nuclear conflict there, 'You will be surviving in a frightful world.'

Rusepalm and its sister company Douvaine – their precise relationship was unclear – continued to feed irresistible titbits to the press. On 29 January the *Gazette & Herald* reported that 'Douvaine expect at least 48 hours' warning before the bombs drop and say they can get all 10,500 people to the site before the doors are finally shut ... A private security force will make sure anyone without a ticket is kept outside.' The paper quoted a previously unknown Douvaine director, Anthony Barron: 'We will issue a code system to the people who have paid to make sure they get in.' On 5 March the paper added that Douvaine expected 'intense traffic movements ... during a period of international tension ... It is estimated that 2,000 cars would move towards the site from all parts of the UK ... Coach pick-up points are planned from major towns to reduce the number of cars.'

For customers not taking part in this doomsday park-and-ride scheme, Eastlays would offer carefully positioned on-site car parking. 'I had all the plans drawn up,' remembered Bauer, 'with on-surface parking to the north of the site, should anything catch fire and fumes be drawn into the ventilation system, which was to the south of the site.' As local anti-nuclear activists had pointed out soon after the shelter scheme was announced, Wiltshire, despite the hopes invested in it as a haven from nuclear fall-out, was actually thick with probable sites for Soviet missile strikes. Apart from all the underground military facilities, there were army headquarters, Royal Air Force bases and ammunition dumps, all highly visible and vulnerable.

During early 1981, while Whittart orchestrated the publicity for Eastlays, periodically striding into Gastard and then disappearing back to the Home Counties or London, leaving reporters hungry for more, many of the more practical issues about the shelter scheme were left to Bauer. For weeks at a time, he left his home and girlfriend and business in Lincolnshire and moved into a pub a few miles from Gastard. He photographed and measured the quarry, and drew up a master plan of how the shelter units, which he called 'pods', would fit into its underground passages and chambers. 'I designed with a lot of communal spaces to enable free movement and to avoid claustrophobia.'

He also designed a demonstration pod to show the press and potential customers. The sprawling quarry had been divided into almost self-contained 'districts' by the War Office in the 1930s, and he wanted to develop them one by one, using deposits from customers to fund the work. As would become standard practice in the many British property booms and bubbles to come, the pods would be sold 'off plan' – before they had been constructed. Bauer calculated that the project needed to attract 1,200 deposits, leaving the shelter just under half-occupied, to be 'viable'. However, even with his roomy layout, the quarry was so vast – 'there were huge areas unconverted by the War Office' – that its eventual population could have been much larger, 'up to 25,000'.

As well as a consultant's fee, Bauer was promised shares and a directorship in Whittart and Fior's companies 'if', in his words, 'the scheme went well'. After a few weeks he realized that his job was too big to be done from a pub, and hired a static caravan. He had it deposited among the quarry's surface buildings, near one of the entrance shafts. The caravan was long and scruffy, off-white, anonymous, with no sign or logo to help explain what he and Rusepalm were up to. Bauer lived and worked in it 'for many months'. The caravan was so cold during early 1981 that the quarry's old caretaker, 'Ron, a local man who had the bunch of keys and knew the place backwards, often took pity on me, and invited me back to his house for meals.' An engineer from Liverpool called Ricky, who was involved in the project too, 'came down a few times' to see Bauer in his caravan. A few security men with walkie-talkies patrolled the overgrown quarry compound to deter unwelcome visitors. Otherwise, remembered Bauer, 'The site was locked tight. No one ever entered unless an appointment had been confirmed.'

Most of the time he was alone in the caravan, looking at his maps and plans. In some ways, he gradually discovered, 'The site was ideal. The geography and landmass shape between Eastlays and the surrounding MOD properties would have masked . . . direct flash and blast' from a nuclear explosion. But in other ways the task came to seem larger and larger: 'Two underground springs fell into the quarry and would have to be rerouted as no [radioactive] contamination would be allowed to enter. This alone would cost thousands of pounds; as would the re-engineering of the existing air conditioning, as blast valves weren't in place . . . never mind active filtration [of fall-out] . . . All in all, the cost would be millions.'

This work potentially meant jobs. Unemployment in the area, while below the national average, was climbing fast in early 1981, and the closure of many of the local subterranean military spaces since the 1960s had left Wiltshire with a lot of jobless quarry experts. There were also plenty of wealthier potential customers – West Country retirees, Bath and London commuters – only a short drive or even a short walk from the proposed shelter.

Or so you might have thought. In fact, 'There was complete uproar in the village when the proposal was announced,' remembered Norman Duckworth, a Gastard resident. At the time, and when we met three decades later, he lived in one of the nearest houses to the planned shelter. The quarry extended so far underground, under a field in front of his cottage, that one of its metal ventilation pipes stuck up like a periscope from the waves of ploughed soil, only 20 feet from his front garden.

'It's not a tight-knit community here,' continued Duckworth, an amateur historian with an airburst of white hair and a percussive laugh. 'But everyone sensed a scam. And once this woman appeared on TV . . . She was out to grab the moment! The whole scheme was so bizarre. It was feeding off a hysteria – the early 80s were strange times, if you think of it. The shelter could not have worked. These narrow roads' – he nodded out of the window of his fuggy living room, where we were having tea and chocolate biscuits, at the cars winding through the village – 'would've been blocked by weight of traffic, if people had fled to the shelter. And what would've happened if they'd got that lot down into the quarry, and then shut the doors to everyone else?'

In *Secret Underground Cities*, a well-informed history of subterranean British military sites, N. J. McCamley records that, 'In public houses around north Wiltshire there were many militant mutterings, much talk of the odds against the wealthy few ever taking up their places in "Doom City" in the face of a panicked population armed with pitchforks, rook-guns and a grim determination to survive.' On 12 February 1981 a letter to the *Gazette & Herald* predicted 'riots and probably deaths' in confrontations between the shelter's private security force and desperate locals if a nuclear emergency occurred. The next day the *Bath and West Evening Chronicle* reported, 'Four out of five people in Gastard are against [the project], claims a survey carried out by Corsham Young Conservatives.' Corsham was a few miles away. 'Only 4% of people said they would pay to use the shelter.' And on 6 March: 'a recent meeting of villagers heard that residents felt alarmed at the possible arrival of large numbers of outsiders . . . not only in the event of a nuclear attack, but also at times of great international tension . . . [putting] an unacceptable strain on the resources of the local community'.

At first, Bauer insisted to me that 'the real locals' in Gastard were more interested in the job possibilities. 'I was in touch with them . . . not the vociferous few who kicked up a lot of NIMBY noise.' But later he conceded that everyone except reporters and potential customers was kept away from the site 'because some locals were very hostile. I went about the area shopping and using pubs totally anonymously.'

According to Duckworth, the landlord of the Gastard pub that the developers sometimes used was 'a supporter' of the scheme. 'And they did collect a number of deposits. I know of a couple in the village who put down a deposit for them and their two children.' Duckworth grimaced: 'I knew the family – it was the kind of thing they were likely to do.' Hadn't he been tempted? He laughed. 'I grew up in Essex in the Blitz. During the Cold War, I was a volunteer in the Royal Observer Corps: sitting in holes in the ground, and told to monitor the drift of nuclear blasts if they happened, their width and speed. Then I was in the window-blind business; for a while, there was great demand for lead-lined curtains, which were supposed to keep out radiation.' By 1981, 'I was just totally fatalistic. If there was going to be a giant rotisserie, I'd rather be here at home with my wife, not down a hole!'

At the foot of the final page of the shelter brochure, an isolated line of text read, 'These apartments are offered subject to planning permission being granted.' On 29 January 1981 the *Gazette & Herald* reported that the chief planning officer of North Wiltshire District Council, Richard Hill, could 'see no major obstacles' to permission being given. On 5 March the paper reported that an 'outline' planning application had been submitted, for the development of 797,000 square feet underground and 41.5 acres above ground. 'Designs for the apartments are not shown . . . Detailed plans . . . will be submitted later.' The application included parking spaces for 'about 3,000' cars – 50 per cent more traffic than Douvaine had told the *Gazette & Herald* the shelter would generate, which implied that the underground population might grow in the future, or that Douvaine were a bit cavalier with figures, or both. But the application also promised that the belts of trees and fields around the quarry would be retained 'to hide [the] obvious surface installations' the shelter would need. Whether this sensitivity to landscape was to appease villagers or fool the Russians was not stated.

On 13 April, Corsham Parish Council considered the application. The council had also received a letter of objection to the development, said the *Gazette & Herald*, signed by a less than overwhelming 'five local residents'. But the council rejected the application unanimously. The chairman, David Henderson, told the paper that Douvaine had not planned enough parking spaces; had made no provision in the relative placement of those spaces and the shelter's ventilation system for a change in wind direction; and had given 'no details . . . about [road] access to the site, or concerning the treatment of sewage'.

None of these problems seemed insoluble. The application moved up the planning chain to the District Council. There the enormity of the questions the shelter scheme raised began to sink in. Hill wrote: 'During peacetime one would expect little activity on the site. The activities and difficulties would occur in . . . a context the exact nature of which cannot be accurately foreseen.' On 11 May the local MP, the Conservative Richard Needham, raised the matter in Parliament. Holding up a copy of the shelter brochure and reading out long extracts, he seemed equally bewildered. 'I am not sure whether "Rusepalm Shelters" is a hidden pun,' he said, 'on the confidence trick that the company may be attempting to play . . . or on the fact that the Russians may attack us.'

Needham condemned the Eastlays project, and the new nuclear-protection business in general as 'an illegitimate trade' that was 'trying to make money on . . . legitimate fears'. But he accepted that the Wiltshire planning authorities 'may find considerable difficulty in turning the application down'. Instead, he argued, it should be 'called in' – referred to the secretary of state for the environment. Whether the application was ultimately rejected or not, he pointed out, there were dozens of other old quarries, once military-owned and now derelict and privatized, that would appeal to nuclear refuge-building 'speculators'. It was unlikely that all such schemes could be stopped, so 'The Government must coordinate a policy towards such shelters . . . set standards and specifications . . . issue instructions on placement and access.'

The environment minister Giles Shaw replied for the government. 'Given the possibility of nuclear attack, I understand my hon. Friend's emphasis . . . [But] there is of course nothing new about communal shelters. A great many were constructed for use in the Second World War.' He skated over the fact that these were built by the government, not mysterious businesses registered in the Channel Islands. 'In relation to . . . calling in the application,' he continued, 'I am not persuaded that . . . it requires the Secretary of State to act.'

To Needham and others during the spring of 1981, 'Doom City' seemed unstoppable. But to Bauer it was beginning to feel very different. 'I was on-site for weeks at a time . . . on the promise of regular fees, and funding for real work, including building the demonstration pod. After three months, we were owed thousands, as were many other contractors and advisers. But all sorts of lame excuses began to be made.' Gradually, it became 'obvious we weren't going to get paid a penny'. Whittart appeared in Wiltshire less and less often. According to Bauer, she did not ever 'release any sign-up or deposit information' about how the sale of leases was going. No funds were even released for the construction of the demonstration pod.

By April, Bauer had had enough. On 10 April he told the *Evening Chronicle* that the Eastlays shelter would not be built. The paper tried and failed to contact Whittart. 'Douvaine's telephone number,' it discovered, 'is out of service.' The paper also found that Fior was being investigated by the Law Society, 'after an alleged breach of accounts rules' for solicitors. He was forbidden to practise while the investigation was going on; when it concluded, he was struck off. On 19 June he was declared bankrupt.

Whittart disappeared, possibly abroad, possibly to Spain. However many deposits Douvaine and Rusepalm actually collected, there are no reports of any being returned. 'I do believe that their intentions were initially genuine,' Bauer told me, 'but there must have been some sort of underlying problems or debts . . . that took over [the shelter project] and greed then became their driving force.' Or perhaps, as Needham suggested, the odd, ungainly names of the companies hint at what the project was really about. One anagram of Douvaine is 'naive duo'; anagrams of Rusepalm include 'maps lure' and 'sale rump'.

It took me almost three hours to drive from London to the quarry, even without the traffic challenges of an imminent apocalypse. At Gastard, I turned off the twisting main road onto the quarry track, which was pitted and for most of its length totally exposed, with open fields to each side. 'Private road', said a sign. Another mentioned CCTV and infra-red motion detectors. A third said: 'Report to security'.

Some of the quarry's above-ground buildings were little changed from 1981. There were military-looking bunkers and earthworks, and enigmatic industrial doorways. But the complex was less overgrown, and more modern metal sheds with conventional windows had been added. A large lorry was parked in a loading bay, and there were wooden pallets lying around. There were also more people than in 1981, walking purposefully back and forth and talking on phones, some in overalls, some in suits.

'Welcome to Corsham Cellars,' said the website for the quarry, 'home to many of the world's finest wines . . . Like any other high-value investment, fine wine needs to be stored under tight security. Our unique facility . . . is a "Fort Knox" for wine.' Corsham Cellars held approaching a million cases and had been profiled in the *Financial Times*. Britain had many more rich people in 2011 than in 1981, and asset accumulation rather than nuclear protection was on their minds.

But below ground some of the old Eastlays eerieness endured. The air was immediately damp and cold as I walked down the entrance shaft, which looked exactly the same as in photographs from the 1970s and 1980s. The steps were smooth, only wide enough for one person, and awkwardly shallow; I imagined thousands of terrified nuclear refugees trying to get down them in a hurry.

Near the foot of the shaft, a small office had been built for the cellars' supervisor, John Turner. On the wall was a map of the quarry dated 1981, with the name of Bauer's company on it. Despite a carpet, heater and tight-fitting door, a stony clamminess lingered. Keeping Bauer's living pods permanently warm and dry would have been a challenge. 'When we turned our huge dehumidifiers off once, all the walls went black and manky,' said Turner, a middle-aged, heavyset man who had worked in the quarry since 1991. 'When I started here, the place was a death-trap electrically. Wiring from the 30s. You got shocks when you changed a lightbulb.'

We left the office and turned onto one of the quarry's main passages. It had damp-speckled white walls, a smooth black floor, wide as three cars, and a flat ceiling along which pipes and cables snaked into the far distance, as if in some epic hospital corridor. For a few minutes we walked past stretches of shelving, with pallets of wine cases stacked on them, and occasional forklift trucks whirring back and forth. Then we entered a dustier, emptier realm. Doorways either side of the passage gave onto dark rooms with floors of rubble. A moth shot past a lightbulb. Monstrous fans and generators, ancient and military green, sat silent or still throbbing in the shadows. In the better-lit spaces, there were caricatures and graffiti drawn in delicate pencil on the walls: the 1940s Labour politician Nye Bevan and film star Errol Flynn. I thought about the nuclear refugees again, living down here for weeks or months or years, trying to sit out a third world war, surrounded by traces of how people survived the one before. Perhaps it would have been reassuring.

'I'm a caravanner,' interrupted Turner, 'and if there'd been a nuclear shelter down here, I imagine you wouldn't have hung around in the corridors. You'd have gone back to the warmth of your pod.' Back in his office, I asked him what he thought of the shelter scheme in general. He laughed. 'I'm ex-Royal Navy. I've dealt a bit with nuclear stuff. When you're in a ship, and you go into a fall-out zone, after a nuclear bomb test, you close the whole ship down, and spray water up over it to keep any dust off. So in 1981 you were looking at making this place airtight. Then where would the carbon dioxide from the pods have gone? And if you had got a big bomb hit upstairs' – he meant at ground level – 'it would've snapped the beds of stone above us.' He picked up a stack of beer mats from his desk, and made them splay outwards. 'The reinforced ceilings here were meant to protect you against 1000-pound bombs, not nukes. The whole roof would've come down.' On 29 January 1981, in a little-noticed remark about the proposed shelter to the *Gazette & Herald*, the Douvaine director Anthony Barron admitted: 'It is sited so it's unlikely to get a direct hit from a [nuclear] bomb – which it could not survive.'

Without a direct hit, Turner continued, 'You might've survived a few days down here' during a nuclear war. 'But Bath stone is permeable. We got leaks everywhere down here, cracks, fissures. Water would've got in.' That water would have been radioactive. He laughed again and swivelled in his scruffy office chair. 'They all would've died anyway!' In Britain in 1981 it would take more than a few entrepreneurs – if that's what they really were – to ease the terrors of the Cold War.

PART THREE

Stirrings

6
Winter Thaw

In 1965 a cocky, young, would-be Labour MP bought a home in Limehouse in east London. A public schoolboy and Cambridge graduate, he had a good job as a hospital doctor, and had previously lived among the millionaires of Belgravia. But he loved the Thames. When he heard that the wealthy banker Jacob Rothschild had acquired a row of dilapidated riverside terraces in Limehouse, to save them from demolition by a developer and then sell them to suitable buyers, he offered £3,000 for one.

The house was a rare early Georgian, four slender storeys, next to a pub on Narrow Street. A few yards from the house's back windows, working Thames barges sat at anchor, snub-nosed and muscular, sometimes six deep. Beyond the boats, a great glittery, muddy bend of the river opened out to the east and west: towards the giant docks of the Isle of Dogs, a century old and still seemingly thriving, and the distant Houses of Parliament. Limehouse was a tough area, poor, war-damaged and dense with tower blocks, but middle-class incomers had occasionally moved there. Half a century before, the future Labour prime minister Clement Attlee had lived in a flat in Narrow Street. The road, in short, was a good place for an apprentice politician – to ponder England's past, and to dream about shaping its future.

In 1966 David Owen was elected to Parliament. Labour were already in government, under the then popular and energetic Harold Wilson, and in the general election of that year they increased their majority from a feeble four to a powerful ninety-six. Anticipation about what could now be achieved ran especially high among the dozens of new Labour MPs: 'There was a huge amount of idealism in that entry,' Owen told me in 2012. 'We thought we were going to stop "stop-go"' – improve on the short-term, boom-and-bust economic policies that Britain had followed since the early 1950s. Yet even among these optimists Owen stood out. He was good-looking for a politician, with a film-star jaw and a bow-wave of dark hair, and a precocious public speaker, sometimes smooth, sometimes fiery. Hard-working and intellectually curious, he had a strong appetite for Whitehall policy papers and Anglo-German conferences. His own ideas, while sometimes right-wing by Labour standards, were forward-looking and eclectic: devolving power to Scotland and Wales, charging for some social services, discriminating in favour of ethnic minorities. Owen appealed to all sorts of voters: the seat he had taken from the Tories, Plymouth Sutton, had been Conservative for forty-two years of its forty-eight-year existence. And he was only twenty-seven. He appeared to have many of the attributes of a future Labour prime minister.

Over the next decade and a half, Owen and his socially adept American wife Deborah, a successful literary agent who represented Delia Smith among others, transformed their Limehouse home into one of London's most envied middle-class residences. It was much photographed by newspapers, with its exposed beams and cosmopolitan bookshelves and south-facing, sun-bleached riverside terraces, where the Owens messed around with their three children and made up nicknames for other British politicians: Neil Kinnock, then a young Labour left-winger, talkative and pointy-nosed, became Kinnochio. In 1972 the house acquired a touch of radical chic when the Owens allowed striking miners, who were picketing a nearby power station and damaging the Heath government, to stay in their spare bedroom for several weeks. 'They were incredibly neat and . . . considerate,' David Owen wrote afterwards, 'apart from the smell of fry-ups drifting up from the kitchen into our bedroom in the middle of the night when the night shift came back from picket duty.'

Outside the oasis of 78 Narrow Street, life for most of Limehouse did not get better during these years. The recessions of the 1970s and early 1980s left waterfront dereliction. All the nearby docks closed, with unexpected and catastrophic suddenness. The large local working-class population tried to cope, cut off by bad public transport from more fertile parts of London. Meanwhile in the country at large, Labour leaders and predominantly Labour governments struggled with national versions of these economic and social problems.

In 1967, after only a year as an MP, Owen co-wrote an article for the outspoken Labour journal *Socialist Commentary*, titled 'Change Gear!' It was, as he put it later, 'a comprehensive rebuttal of most of government policy'. The essay argued that Labour lacked 'drive' and 'strategic vision' in office; that the party was letting the state get too big and centralized, which was stifling Britons; and that among Labour's most loyal voters 'disillusionment' was setting in.

Despite, or perhaps because of his mutinous thoughts, and because the party lacked other young, telegenic stars, Owen was promoted fast. He was minister for the navy at thirty, a health minister at thirty-five, and foreign secretary at thirty-eight, in 1977. He did these jobs with zest and a hunger for attention. In between, when Labour were out of office, he resigned twice from party positions on matters of principle: in 1972, over Wilson's fickle attitude to British membership of the European Economic Community, which Owen strongly favoured; and in November 1980, over Michael Foot's left-wing Labour leadership in general.

By the early 1980s, all this activity had given Owen an unusually high profile and ambiguous reputation for a middle-ranking politician. He was charismatic and promising, or an arrogant ageing prodigy; too self-assured, or too tortured; a political loner, or politically lonely; fiercely loyal to his party, or impossible to work with; the latest in a long line of Labour right-wingers, or the bringer of a new kind of centre-left politics. Probably he was an unstable combination of all these things. What was certain, as 1981 began, was that Owen was forty-two and once again a backbencher, a role with which he was unlikely to be satisfied for long.

On the morning of 25 January, a milky midwinter Sunday, reporters and photographers gathered in the street outside his Limehouse home. They had been warned to expect a significant announcement. Inside the house were Owen, his wife, four political advisers, and three other well-known and increasingly unpredictable political players: Roy Jenkins, Shirley Williams and Bill Rodgers.

Like their host, Williams and Rodgers had been cabinet ministers in the Labour government that had lost power a year and a half before. Williams, fifty, famously charming, tousled and unpunctual, had been education secretary, a sometimes messy administrator but a highly effective public communicator. Rodgers, fifty-two, leaner and more reined-in, had been transport secretary, skilful at backroom manoeuvring and defending his budget, but disillusioned and burnt out by the government's end, when he was unable to stop striking trade unionists from paralysing parts of the transport network for weeks on end during the Winter of Discontent.

Again like Owen, both Williams and Rodgers had long been considered Labour right-wingers. Roy Jenkins was a more detached figure. A different generation from them, he was sixty, and in some ways seemed older still. He liked claret and spoke in courtly sentences, and nothing about his appearance – heavy-rimmed glasses, slicked-back receding hair, portly suits – suggested that it was not 1950. Back in the Wilson era, Jenkins had been one of Labour's stars: an innovative, lastingly influential home secretary who abolished the death penalty and helped legalize abortion and homosexuality; a more buttoned-up but canny chancellor; and a perennial plotter for the party leadership. But in 1976 he came third in a leadership election, and the same year he left Westminster to become President of the European Commission in Brussels. By the 1979 general election, despite growing signs in the polls of a close result, he had become so distant from Labour that he did not vote.

Yet now, in January 1981, Jenkins was about to enter British party politics again. But not as it had previously been played: he and the three other Labour misfits had in their minds the outline of a new party.

Traditionally, Labour did not react well to general election defeats. From its foundation, more than most British parties, Labour had been fractious with competing visions: gradual change or radical change; standing for the working class or a wider social coalition; preserving principles or achieving power. These tensions were often bad enough when Labour was in office, as Owen's grumblings during the first Wilson government had demonstrated, but when Labour lost power they were worse. Party unity could no longer be presented as for the good of the government or the country. On the contrary, party disunity could be presented as a necessity, however painful, for the generation of the new ideas that Labour needed to return to power, and to govern better next time.

Wilson's ejection from Downing Street in 1970 had prompted years of left–right recriminations and philosophical and factional jostling. When an exhausted Wilson finally stepped down as party leader in 1976, the first round of voting to find his successor produced a tellingly fragmented result. No candidate won even a third of the vote. There were two contenders from the left – the mercurial Michael Foot, who received the support of 29 per cent of Labour MPs; and the more relentless Tony Benn, who got 12 per cent. And there were no fewer than four contenders from the right – the calculating Jim Callaghan (27 per cent), the expansive Roy Jenkins (18 per cent), the domineering Denis Healey (10 per cent), and the cerebral Tony Crosland (5 per cent). It took two further rounds of voting to find a winner, Callaghan, who ended up with a less-than-sweeping mandate of 56 per cent. Barely three years later, after a Callaghan premiership that was often a skilful exercise in managing the party's competing personalities and ideologies, but not much more, Labour lost the 1979 election anyway, and the near-civil war of the early 1970s resumed with greater force.

By now the left was stronger. Partly this was because of a widespread sense that the Labour right had failed. Its ideas – using the state to help build a more just and robust capitalism; using the tax proceeds to entrench the welfare system; keeping Britain well armed and close to America – had dominated the Labour governments of the 1960s and 1970s. And those governments had not done that well. British capitalism had become only a little less callous and erratic. Welfare spending had often been insufficient or inefficient. Socialism, however you defined it, had not actually been delivered. Meanwhile the once-dazzling range of talent available to the Labour right had aged and dwindled. Jenkins drifted away from the party. Crosland died prematurely of a brain haemorrhage in 1977. Healey's rudeness isolated him from colleagues. Callaghan soldiered on as party leader for a year and a half after losing the 1979 election, finally resigning in November 1980.

The party membership dwindled too. In 1951, at Labour's peak as a social institution, it had about 800,000 members; by 1980, at least two-thirds were gone. Many Labour constituency parties were being run by a few dozen people, often elderly, sometimes disillusioned and going through the motions, sometimes simply disorientated by the less close-knit country Britain was becoming. One of the problems faced by Labour in its inner-city strongholds was that it was harder for these ageing activists to canvass people in tower blocks, with their sometimes broken or forbiddingly rundown lifts, than in the terraced housing the blocks had replaced.

A more left-wing Labour politics elbowed its way into the vacuum. Many of its practitioners were well versed in how to influence or take over an organization, such as a constituency party, through time spent as student activists or in determined, perpetually manoeuvring left-wing groups such as the Socialist Workers Party and Militant Tendency; these had grown from tiny sects to significant organizations during the 1970s. In 1973 Labour's National Executive Committee, itself already shifting leftwards, had lifted a long-standing ban on Labour members belonging to such bodies. One consequence was an increase in 'entryism', or people joining the party in order to increase the leverage of other groups. The *Guardian* commentator Peter Jenkins, no relation of Roy's but close to the Labour right, explained one common entryist technique: 'Keep the meetings going until all good moderate people had gone home to bed.'

In the autumn of 1980, the columnist attended the Labour conference in Blackpool:

> The foyer of the once-exclusive Imperial Hotel was like a Soviet permanently in session; the environs of the conference hall were ankle-deep in leaflets and revolutionary newspapers . . . Speakers who attempted to stand against the tide were subjected to venomous hissing. Healey, particularly, was denounced as the man 'who led the advance against working people', under the Callaghan government. On the fringe the Left drew huge crowds. Tony Benn moved from meeting to meeting . . . to be greeted with revolutionary adulation. In a keynote speech to the conference, tumultuously received, he promised that the next Labour government would . . . nationalize industries, control capital and

> introduce industrial democracy [worker involvement in management] 'within days' ... restore all powers from Brussels to Westminster 'within weeks', and – to loudest cheers of all – would abolish the House of Lords.

In a column immediately afterwards Jenkins wrote, 'Political liberty is now at threat in Britain, for I cannot feel confident that it would long survive the coming to power of the people who have taken hold of the Labour Party.' Such dire warnings about the emergent Labour left had been circulating more and more widely since the 1970s: first within the party; then among Conservative propagandists and their press and business allies; then out in the mainstream of reasonably politically aware, self-consciously 'moderate' Britons.

In many ways this portrayal of the left was exaggerated and unfair. As Owen himself conceded, a little belatedly, in an article for the Labour-focused magazine the *New Statesman* in January 2011, 'It was not unreasonable for those on the left to try to shift the balance of power in the party closer to their views in the aftermath of electoral defeat.' The Labour right did exactly the same, and just as ruthlessly, during other periods, such as the long, left-crushing leadership of Tony Blair. It was just that the right's preferred bullying techniques were less public: the vicious spin doctor's phone call rather than the party conference catcall.

However, in the charged, ideologically polarized political atmosphere of the early 1980s, with the worsening Cold War giving a paranoid edge even to mainstream party politics, few were prepared to give the Labour left the benefit of the doubt. Tony Benn grew into a particular demon. Once upon a time – and he would ultimately become this again – he had been the sort of Labour politician with whom people who don't like Labour feel comfortable. Born Anthony Neil Wedgwood Benn, he had been privately educated and came from a grand old political family: his father William Wedgwood Benn, originally a Liberal MP, had defected to Labour, been made secretary of state for India, and then a peer as Viscount Stansgate. Benn junior started out as a right-wing Labour MP in the 1950s. He became an eager and efficient minister of technology in the 1960s, always crisp on television, and only moved left towards the decade's end.

But when Benn changed political direction he precisely caught Labour's militant wave, and rode it expertly through the 1970s and into the early 1980s. This move was not pure calculation. Even in his relatively right-wing days, he had been hostile to nuclear weapons and the upper-class world from which he came, renouncing the peerage he inherited from his father. During the early 1970s, however, Benn's radicalism became much more thorough. In 1972 he changed his preferred public name to the more proletarian Tony Benn. From 1974 to 1979 he ostentatiously played the dissident cabinet minister. His ambitious, sometimes astute policy ideas – an Alternative Economic Strategy to insulate Britain from the worst of international capitalism, a sovereign wealth fund to make the most of Britain's North Sea oil revenues – were ignored by Wilson and Callaghan, but noisily promoted by Benn regardless. His opposition to their often cautious approach to government was explicit; but his party following was too strong, and their premierships too fragile, for him to be sacked.

Then circumstances moved further in his favour. Labour's defeat in 1979, Thatcher's struggles as prime minister, Callaghan's resignation as Labour leader in 1980 – all these suggested to some that the time was imminent for Benn to take over the party and then the country. The right-wing press began to panic. 'Why Labour Leaders Tremble at the Relentless Advance of Benn's Army', began a *Daily Express* piece on 22 May 1981. The same day the *Sun* asked: 'Mr Benn – Is He Mad Or A Killer?' The paper also called him 'Ayatollah Benn', as if he was the equivalent of Iran's ferocious new revolutionary leader. Benn's 'local Mullahs', said the *Sun*, 'babble slogans inciting mob thinking.' It became commonplace for right-wing journalists, and sometimes centre-left ones, to claim that Benn, who had been standing for election for almost thirty years, wanted to turn Britain into a police state. Peter Jenkins called him 'sinister' and 'demagogic'.

Like Thatcher, Benn had a public speaking style – soft voice, hard eyes, mesmeric rhythms, utter conviction – which was distinctive and compelling, and, depending on your politics, either inspirational or terrifying, whether in extended set-pieces at party conferences or in brief extracts on news programmes. He became the de facto leader of the new Labour left. He shared their conviction that the party's key decisions, such as its choice of leader and deputy leader, what its election manifesto said, and how accountable MPs were to their constituency parties, should be opened up to a much wider range of interest groups, such as local activists and the unions – groups that in the early 1980s just happened to be increasingly left-influenced.

On 24 January 1981, at a one-off 'special conference' held in the cacophonous hangar of Wembley Arena in London, the party agreed that in future its leader and deputy leader would be chosen by an 'electoral college', in which the unions and constituency parties had 70 per cent of the votes and MPs only 30 per cent. It seemed a system tailor-made for left-wing candidates in general and Benn in particular. Shirley Williams, David Owen and Bill Rodgers were all at the Wembley conference. Owen was photographed sitting on some stairs in the hall, away from the other delegates, with an expression on his face of ostentatious fury. The next day, the three disillusioned Labour politicians convened with Roy Jenkins in Limehouse.

At Owen's house, while the press waited, they and their four advisers talked and wrote and rewrote in one of the upstairs rooms, all morning and deep into the afternoon, trying to come up with a short document that would sum up and announce a new political project, without prematurely fixing its precise details or giving too much away. At lunchtime they stopped for wine and cheese and salad, and so that Williams could be interviewed on Radio 4's 'The World At One'. Williams, naturally enthusiastic and frank, was more open about her intention to leave the Labour Party than they had intended. 'We all roared with laughter,' remembered Owen. 'Those were good days. We could disagree, and still have good fun.'

By teatime, after eighteen drafts, with the deadlines for the evening news and the next day's papers fast approaching, a page and a half of text had finally been agreed. Deborah Owen typed it up, and copies were hurriedly made. According to David Owen, copies were produced for distribution to the media using some of his wife's carbon paper; according to other accounts, the politicians were forced to use the photocopier at the gilded Savoy Hotel, four congested miles upriver to the west. In 1981 photocopiers were becoming common – but not in the East End.

Eventually, reported Alan Rusbridger for the *Guardian*, 'An emissary popped out of Dr David Owen's house . . . and dished out three copies of the glad tidings.' Inside the house, the politicians, frazzled, euphoric, rushed to prepare themselves for the photographers. Williams had to borrow a smart blouse from Deborah, which had a yellow geometric print and was slightly too big. Rodgers stuck to a blue crewneck jumper with his shirt collars poking out, like an off-duty polytechnic lecturer. Jenkins wore one of his habitual baggy dark suits. Owen wore a suit too, but paler and more informal, with a check and wide lapels. They looked like people from the 1950s, 1960s and early 1970s – not from the 1980s.

They decided that the house was too small for an indoor photocall; nor was Owen keen for his home to act as an outdoor backdrop. A fine eighteenth-century terrace was not the best place, perhaps, for left-of-centre politicians to make a mould-breaking announcement. So, despite the fading light, they agreed to walk to another location. 'On the stroke of 4pm,' wrote Rusbridger, 'they emerged blinking at the barrage of flashguns' – there were also television cameras – 'and made off down the street.' They walked fast: Rodgers on the left, staring ahead, Williams on the right, arms folded, perhaps against the cold – she had not thought to put a coat on – and Jenkins in the centre, occasionally turning around, with a chuckling, man-of-the-world expression, to say something to the small crowd of reporters and photographers who were slightly comically trying to keep up. Owen strode along a few yards behind his three new colleagues, hands in his pockets.

For a minute or so, they all headed west down the straight, treeless canyon of Narrow Street, past old brick warehouses and taller blocks of council flats. 'A car screeched to a halt and the driver yelled out, "Up the Tories",' Rusbridger reported; otherwise, there was so little traffic in this depleted, grey-brown landscape that much of the crowd just walked in the road. The collective mood was a mix of self-consciousness and jollity. The politicians had announced that they would not answer questions; but the journalists, enjoying the novelty of the situation, not least of a day away from their usual Westminster territory, tried anyway.

The text issued to them had declared portentously, 'We propose to set up a Council for Social Democracy.' One of the reporters asked what exactly it was. Rusbridger recorded what followed: '"I think the statement makes it perfectly clear," said Dr Owen. "Well, what was a council?" "It's a very useful body," replied Mr Jenkins. Were they still members of the Labour Party? "I'm sorry . . . It's all in that beautiful statement," said Mr Rodgers.'

When the politicians reached a small bridge over a disused dock entrance, they stopped. Immediately to the south, over a cracked, shoulder-high old wall, there was a glimpse of the Thames, the remaining light reflecting off it – enough light and scenery for the photographers, hoped Owen, who had chosen the spot. On a thin, uneven pavement, the politicians lined up, again with Jenkins in the middle and Owen at a slight remove, standing on the far right of the group and sometimes looking off to one side while the others grinned for the cameras. The wind off the river made Williams' and Rodgers' hair flap around. In their four clashing outfits, without a coat between them, the politicians looked like four charismatic individuals, excited, interesting, enjoying each other's company – but not yet a team, and possibly a little impractical and eccentric. 'Photographers fired away,' wrote Rusbridger, 'uncertain whether they were illustrating a footnote or a chapter in history.'

The press release tried strenuously to sound momentous. Titled 'The Limehouse Declaration', it announced early on: 'Our intention is . . . to reverse Britain's economic decline . . . [and] to create an open, classless and more equal society.'

This transformation, it promised, would satisfy both iconoclasts and traditionalists: 'We want more, not less, radical change in our society but with a greater stability of direction.' And both free-marketeers and socialists: 'Our economy needs a healthy public sector and a healthy private sector . . . We want to eliminate poverty . . . without stifling enterprise.'

The Council for Social Democracy would be less centralizing and bureaucratic than Labour: 'Our public services . . . must be made more responsive to people's needs.' It would also be less cruel than the Conservatives: 'We do not accept that mass unemployment is inevitable.'

In order to succeed, the Council would need 'the support of men and women in all parts of our society . . . [from] politicians who recognize that the drift towards extremism in the Labour Party is not compatible with the democratic traditions of the party they joined and [from] those . . . outside politics who believe that the country cannot be saved without changing the sterile and rigid framework into which the British political system has increasingly fallen in the last two decades'.

As a manifesto, the document left a lot to be desired. Although brief, it was not a quick read. Its sentences and rhythms were lumpy, clogged up with remnants of old drafts. For a supposedly universal rallying cry, it spent too much time on Labour Party matters. For a state-of-the-nation assessment, it touched too briefly on the convulsive social consequences of monetarism and Thatcherism. It barely hinted at how its authors' enormous, hard-to-reconcile objectives – 'eliminate poverty . . . without stifling enterprise' – could be achieved. Finally, it did not spell out whether the clunkily named Council for Social Democracy was going to be a new political party, or just a pressure group within an old one. And if it was a party, who was going to lead it?

At first, none of the project's shortcomings seemed to matter. On 5 February, a full eleven days after the Limehouse event, the Council for Social Democracy took its next, halting step, placing an ad in the *Guardian*. It was not a whole page but an unappealing half-page strip, inky and dense: little more than a list of public figures who were declaring their support, a reprint of the Limehouse Declaration, and a coupon for readers to return to a London PO box if they, too, wished to show support or make a donation. Yet the ad's list of names was quite impressive. There was Michael Young, the famous sociologist and co-founder of the Open University; the leftish supermarket magnate David Sainsbury; the steadily more right-wing trade-union leader Frank Chapple; the noted *Guardian* columnist and social reporter Polly Toynbee; the analyst of Britain, Anthony Sampson; the pioneering female rabbi, Julia Neuberger; the former deputy Labour leader George Brown; the former Labour trade secretary Edmund Dell; the veteran economist and former government adviser Alec Cairncross; the radical barrister and former government adviser Anthony Lester. Many of these signatories, generally drawn from the more left-leaning, thoughtful parts of the Establishment, had intimate knowledge of Britain's post-war struggles, as participants or observers or both. They might be part of the problem; or, if the Council for Social Democracy took off, they might be part of the solution.

Through February and March the new body metamorphosized into a parliamentary party. Fourteen MPs defected to it, thirteen from Labour and one from the Tories, and started sitting together in the Commons. Over the rest of 1981 another thirteen Labour MPs joined them; and in 1982, two more. In all, twenty-eight MPs came over from Labour, over a tenth of the Labour total. In addition, thirty-one former Labour MPs joined the new party, including eight former cabinet ministers; and eighteen Labour peers. It was the largest parliamentary desertion since 1886, when seventy-eight MPs had left a Liberal government in opposition to its support for Irish Home Rule. That split subsequently helped keep the Liberals out of power for almost twenty years.

The Council for Social Democracy, self-evidently, could not be the new party's name. The founders discussed alternatives: Centre Party, Radical Party, Progressive Party, Progressive Labour, Democratic Labour – even New Labour. The first three were rejected as too vague; the last three as too Labour. By mid-March, with an impatient media jumping the gun and referring to the Labour defectors as 'social democrats', the name Social Democratic Party, or more informally the Social Democrats or SDP, was chosen without a formal decision ever being made.

The name was lengthy by British standards, and foreign-sounding: Germany already had a left-of-centre party with almost the same name, the SPD. Just as confusingly, the phrase Social Democratic Party also contained echoes of previous, short-lived British political projects: the ex-Labour MP Dick Taverne's abortive mid-1970s centre party, the Campaign for Social Democracy; and the Social Democratic Alliance (SDA), a minor Labour pressure group set up in 1975, which was obsessed with the threat to the party and the country from the radical left – a stance the SDP would inherit, together with the SDA founders and Taverne himself.

In other ways, too, the SDP was an idea riskily long in the hatching. What the Limehouse Declaration called a 'realignment' of British politics had been a recurring dream for some activists and politicians since shortly after the 1900 foundation of the Labour Party, which had lastingly divided non-Tory voters between itself and the Liberals in ways that often let in the Conservatives. Later, during the 1960s, after decades as an insignificant third party that alternated confusingly between right-wing and left-wing stances, the Liberals settled on a more coherent centrist politics and started to win a double-digit share of the vote again in general elections. Hopes began to rise of a Liberal–Labour alliance. During the 1970s, Liberals campaigned alongside Labour Europhiles, such as Jenkins, in favour of Britain's EEC membership. During 1977 and 1978 the Lib-Lab Pact, a formal Commons arrangement, helped keep Callaghan's teetering government in office. Finally, during 1979 and 1980, Jenkins, Rodgers, Williams and Owen – 'the Gang of Four', as the media began calling them – all said and wrote things, and held meetings at each other's attractive residences, privately and then less privately, which hinted more and more strongly that they planned to work together outside the Labour Party. By the time they made their move in 1981, some were heartily sick of the Gang of Four and their manoeuvres. 'What a ghastly quartet this is,' wrote Ian Gow, Thatcher's private secretary, in January 1982, after a fellow Tory MP had forwarded him the SDP's first Christmas card.

The photo showed the party's founders posed in flattering half-shadow, arms purposefully folded, gazes intent and level, hair tidied and styled. They looked like senior management consultants rather than the mismatched quartet of academics and bank managers that had revealed itself to the media at Limehouse. A prominent caption said, 'Photograph by [Lord] Snowdon', the famous aristocratic portrait-taker. Beside the picture was the SDP logo: three underlined letters in rounded, unstuffy, rather 1970s capitals, coloured an alternating blue and red on a white backdrop – a patriotic combination in keeping with the Limehouse Declaration's promise to 'save' the country, and a cheeky pinching of both Labour's and the Conservatives' traditional colours.

The SDP's official launch was held at the Connaught Rooms in central London on 26 March 1981. The venue was away from Westminster, between the rebranded Covent Garden and bustling, clerical Holborn; but in almost every other way the event was studiedly conventional. Most of the Grand Hall, with its corporate-event decor, all chandeliers and cream and gold pillars, was filled by craning ranks of reporters – far more than had been at Limehouse. Onstage, in front of four large SDP logos, sat the four party founders, the three men grave and immaculate, Williams a little more ruffled. The press conference began at 9 a.m., and the Gang of Four's carefully enunciated answers were heard in reverent near-silence. Also facing the journalists, but to the side of the stage, and mute, like prisoners being paraded, were two rows of defecting MPs. 'Everything went with a zing,' Owen wrote afterwards.

After the launch, a party bureaucracy was rushed into being. Excitement and novelty explained some of the released energy – the flood of volunteers to the party's first headquarters in Westminster, the recruitment of 80,000 members in the first year – but so did a widespread sense that 1981 was a very good year to launch a new party; and that such a moment might not come again for a long while.

In April, Tony Benn announced a challenge for the Labour deputy leadership. The post was held by Healey, whose disdain for colleagues and position on the right of the party made him vulnerable. And beating him seemed a likely prelude to greater things. Michael Foot, spindly, scholarly, and in his late sixties, had won the Labour leadership unconvincingly six months earlier. He had defeated Healey – considered by many outside observers to be much more appealing to the public, precisely because of his suffer-no-fools personality and lack of left-wing ideology – by only ten votes in a secret ballot of Labour MPs. Several of those who voted for Foot, it has been credibly claimed since, planned to defect to the SDP and wanted to sabotage their old party. Either way, Foot quickly became regarded as a weak, stop-gap leader – easy meat for an ambitious deputy.

The Benn–Healey contest lasted almost six months, from April to September 1981. It dominated the life of the party and how Labour was perceived by the outside world. To the delight of the SDP and the Conservatives, Benn was remorselessly portrayed as a loopy extremist by his Labour foes: the left-winger Neil Kinnock, who was beginning to shift rightwards, dismissed Benn's radical policies as 'a fantasy that insults adult intelligence'.

A few weeks into the campaign, Benn began to feel tingling in his hands, and a spreading stiffness and pain in his arms and legs. In June 1981 he was hospitalized, and rumours began that he had been poisoned. He was eventually diagnosed with Guillain-Barre Syndrome, a rare nervous disease with uncertain causes, though thought at the time to be triggered sometimes by toxic metals. Benn discussed the possibility with doctors that he had been exposed to arsenic. He also had dark thoughts about how that could have happened. 'I wondered if the security services wanted to stop me winning,' he told me, without any prompting, when I met him by chance in London in 1994. I had gone to his home office to see a girlfriend who was one of his researchers. Benn chuckled, a little mirthlessly; then he gestured around the large basement room, which was dotted with bookshelves and half-finished mugs of tea, of which he famously drank over a dozen a day. 'In the end,' he continued, laughing more genuinely, 'I found out the cause was coffee whitener! I'd been using it instead of milk in my tea, to save time during the campaign. The manufacturers had never considered that anyone would consume so much of it.'

Benn was in hospital for almost half of June 1981, too weak to campaign. Three months later, on the first day of the Labour conference, it was announced that he had won 49.574 per cent of the vote for the deputy leadership. Healey had won 50.426 per cent. Abstentions by Kinnock and a few other 'soft left' anti-Benn MPs; hostility or a lack of enthusiasm towards Benn from some union leaders, often in defiance of their members; a diffuse sense that Benn had harmed the party by standing – together, all this had been just enough to stop him. The Labour right treated the result as both a triumph and a narrow escape. But the party looked utterly split, and the left, while defeated, had also demonstrated its growth from a marginalized faction to a near-majority. In the short term at least, the election result was a gift to the other parties, and especially the SDP.

'Jenkins was an old man in a hurry,' said Owen, with typical bluntness, as we sat in his exquisite Limehouse living room. 'This was his one chance. He had geared himself to think, if he could become SDP leader, he could almost become PM in one.' At party meetings, Jenkins started talking about 'the breakthrough', or 'the bweakthwoo' as Owen called it behind his back, imitating Jenkins' speech impediment. 'If you believed in the bweakthwoo,' said Owen, pursing his lips, then switching instantly from languid mockery to a lingering soreness, 'you would make any sacrifices, even of SDP independence.'

Despite Owen's misgivings, during 1981 Jenkins quickly manoeuvred the party into an electoral partnership with the Liberals. The SDP-Liberal Alliance was even more of a mouthful and an organizational challenge than the Social Democratic Party. But Jenkins felt the pact gave the SDP a chance of seizing power at the next general election.

For much of 1981 such hopes did not seem far-fetched. In the first opinion poll after the Limehouse Declaration, the Liberal and Social Democrat vote shares, if you added them together, made a promising 26.5 per cent, less than 10 per cent behind both the Conservatives and Labour. By mid-March, even before the SDP's official launch, this combined share was up to 32 per cent, ahead of the Conservatives, and only just behind Labour. In October the SDP-Liberal Alliance, formalized over the summer, took the lead: its 40 per cent rating was enough, in theory, to win a majority in Parliament. Then in December 1981, in a survey by the respected pollsters Gallup for the Tory house journal the *Daily Telegraph*, the Alliance hit 50.5 per cent: enough for an electoral landslide, on a scale not seen since at least the 1940s – and an astonishing 27 per cent ahead of both Labour and the Conservatives. At the Liberals' annual conference three months earlier, their usually measured leader David Steel had told delegates, 'I have the good fortune to be the first Liberal leader for over half a century who is able to say to you . . . go back to your constituencies and prepare for government.'

Much of this sensational momentum was created and sustained through by-elections. The Alliance took advantage of these volatile showcase contests with the glee of all astute British political insurgents. In June 1981, Jenkins ran for the supposedly safe Labour seat of Warrington. A working-class town in the north of England did not seem a wise choice for a plummy cosmopolitan who had walked away from the Commons for Brussels, and who retained a part-time job and private office at the smart bank Morgan Grenfell in the City of London. But Jenkins knew how to charm voters with whom he had little in common: he had previously held a Labour seat in an industrial part of Birmingham for twenty-seven years. In Warrington, to general astonishment, he almost won. In March 1982 he tried again, this time in even more gritty Glasgow. The seat was Hillhead, Conservative-held, with a mixture of wealthy and very poor residents, and Labour and the Scottish National Party also locally strong. Jenkins beat them all.

In November 1981, Williams took Crosby, an even more improbable target: a comfortable coastal town outside Liverpool complete with yachts and private schools and a huge Tory majority of 19,000. The SDP campaign there, as in the other by-elections, formidably combined eager volunteers, a famous candidate and a crusading aura. Williams criss-crossed the constituency in a convoy of vehicles blasting out the theme from *Chariots of Fire*. Her winning vote share was 49 per cent – unusually high for a three-party contest, and almost exactly the same as the Alliance's dizzy score in the national polls.

Just as disconcertingly for the other parties, Crosby, Hillhead and Warrington showed the Alliance appealing to all kinds of voters, in very different areas of the country. Part of this appeal was modernity. While the Liberals had a lot of historical baggage, and the Gang of Four all had their political back stories, the SDP sought to present itself as something fresh and in tune with a changing country – 'a genuine party of the 80s', in the words of the political academics Ivor Crewe and Anthony King, who were both involved with the SDP early on. Another sympathetic historian, Hugh Stephenson, elaborated: 'The guiding principles were ... the party must not be in the thrall of any paymaster such as the trades unions, or industry and commerce; it should be open and consultative ... it should use the latest in computerized administrative techniques.' A database of members was to be created, with the task contracted out to the Midland Bank. Donations by credit card were to be facilitated – another innovation, in the filing-cabinet world of early 1980s British politics – in order to obtain most of the party's funding from ordinary citizens.

To raise more money, and the party's profile generally, the SDP set up a marketing department. It made plans to sell goods and services to its members far beyond the usual tribal knick-knacks, including insurance and 'general household and personal goods'. As a start, the SDP members' newsletter offered mail-order merchandise including shopping bags and, for £12, an 'italic script reproduction on parchment paper of the Limehouse Declaration, individually hand-signed by the Gang of Four'. Even the first appearance of these national saviours was thus commodified. It was a sign of the times.

7
'London's Ours!'

The SDP was not the only new political force in Britain in 1981. Another also announced itself in London. It would ultimately change the capital and, in some ways, the whole country. But it would get a much less friendly media reception.

From April 1977 to December 1980, BBC1 broadcast a hit sitcom about the most absurd political figure it could imagine. Set in the tidy inner suburb of Tooting in south London, among municipal statues and florists and elderly ladies in headscarves, *Citizen Smith* was about a local chancer, Wolfie Smith, not quite young any more, who had delusions that he was Britain's revolutionary left-wing saviour. Wolfie presided over a tiny, hopeless sect called the Tooting Popular Front. Sometimes they pursued stupid schemes, such as invading the House of Commons in a stolen tank, without realizing that Parliament was in recess. Much of the time, Wolfie just talked. 'Can you imagine,' he said, wide-eyed and breathless, to one of his bemused comrades in the pilot episode, 'all the oppressed masses taking to the streets in one festival of the people? Snotty-nosed kids dancing a ragamuffin dance of freedom; plumbers with machine guns; black blokes with 'and grenades, rabbis with flak jackets.'

One of the many good but unsubtle jokes was that Wolfie's radicalism was pretty skin-deep. Beneath the rhetoric, his interests and attitudes were just the same as any of the era's mob of laddish sitcom characters. He liked beer, birds and money. He disliked wine, vegetarians and foreign food. He made saloon-bar quips about gayness and ethnic accents. The implication was that left-wing politics had nothing to say about such non-class issues; or that it was just a threadbare set of poses, a passing phase.

Another, related joke was that Wolfie's radicalism was out of date. He wore a shaggy, hippyish Afghan coat and flared jeans, and carried an acoustic guitar, like some refugee from the 1970 Isle of Wight festival. He had a haircut, beret, badge and T-shirt that gauchely paid homage to Che Guevara, even though Che had been dead since 1967. Yet for all the nudge-nudge humour, some of which even I got as a ten-year-old in 1980, *Citizen Smith* was lifted by a certain poignancy. Its writer, John Sullivan, was himself from south London, and based Wolfie on someone he had known. The show caught well the feeling of a political movement that had over-extended itself and passed its peak, but was being kept alive by dreamers and latecomers who had yet to realize.

The one problem with the programme was that the state of the London left was the exact opposite. During the 1970s and the start of the 1980s, while Sullivan was conceiving and perfecting his socialist Walter Mitty, elsewhere in the south London suburbs – indeed sometimes in Tooting itself – a vigorous new left-wing network was quietly forming. At its centre was a slight and deadpan man from nearby Streatham. Like Wolfie, he was youngish, and had been partly formed by the liberations and cultural explosions of the 1960s. Like Wolfie, he had the gift of the gab and a conviction that his political work was part of a global struggle. Like Wolfie, he sometimes wore an Afghan coat.

Ken Livingstone was born in 1945, just before the end of the Second World War, to working-class Tory parents. Both these facts would be quietly important to his noisy political career. His father was a merchant seaman, and during the war his ship was torpedoed; he spent several days on a life raft in the Arctic sea. 'The war left me with a real worry,' Livingstone told me. 'Could I and my generation ever be as effective as theirs had been? This was Britain making the right choice under Churchill, to fight on . . . You felt inadequate by comparison.' This preoccupation with the Second World War and Churchill's role in it was shared during the 1970s and 1980s by many Tory radicals, including John Hoskyns and Margaret Thatcher herself; like them, Livingstone would acquire a huge appetite for changing Britain.

His Conservative parents, to whom he remained close, also made him different from Labour tribalists. He did not join the party until the age of twenty-three. Through his mother and father, too, he learned that London was increasingly a place of complicated and fluid political opinions. On the one hand, his parents were so implacably right-wing that they refused to buy a television until the arrival of ITV broke the BBC's state-backed monopoly. On the other, Livingstone records admiringly in his autobiography, 'Dad travelled the world, working side by side with men of all races and religions . . . He had none of the racism so common in those times.'

Livingstone's father died suddenly in 1971, at the age of fifty-six. Livingstone was stricken – 'it was twenty years before the pain began to fade' – and also felt his own intimations of mortality: 'Dad's early death taught me not to play safe.' Livingstone had been a Labour Party member for only three years, leftism belatedly awakened by the war in Vietnam, and by the poverty and anti-colonial movements he encountered while travelling in Africa. But already he considered himself different from other would-be politicians.

'Before politics, my interest was in science,' he explained when we met in 2013. 'I spent eight years working [as a lab technician] at the Royal Marsden [hospital] with brilliant scientists . . . We were looking for a cure for childhood leukaemia, and there were two rival camps . . . But no one in science says, "Well, you can't say that."' Livingstone wanted to bring this exploratory, results-based approach into the often rigid and over-theoretical world of left-wing politics. 'I broadly wanted a socialist society, but I didn't have a fixed view of how it was going to work.'

The young Livingstone did have strong political dislikes, however. One was the social conservatism that often ran through the post-war Labour Party: to him, the anti-immigration Callaghan was 'a terrible old racist'. Another was the restrictive, stuffy city he felt London had become: 'God, it was so boring. In the 60s, I used to go with a friend to the bookshops in Charing Cross Road, play records, and then go for an Italian dinner. Then we'd wander from pub to pub. It'd be nine o'clock and you'd be walking through Leicester Square, and it'd be empty. And my mum, who'd been on the stage in the 30s, always said that, then, things went on all night, buses ran all night, restaurants were open.'

In 1971 he became a councillor, in Lambeth, a politically unstable borough to the immediate east of Tooting. After taking the council from the Tories in that year's local elections, 'the Labour group launched into a vicious struggle between left and right in which I was an enthusiastic participant.' Livingstone, on the party left, quickly realized that he had the stomach and patience for factional politics. 'I love meetings and plotting,' he wrote later. He described the first two *Godfather* films as 'an honest account of how politicians operate'.

In early 1970s Lambeth the Labour left failed to seize the council; but its young, politically inexperienced comrades were elected to enough important posts to test out some iconoclastic policies. As vice-chairman of housing, Livingstone 'wanted tenants to get involved in managing their estates'. When he started to give them a say, 'Some of them asked to see the terms and conditions of the [unionized] residential caretakers so they could check that they were doing their job . . . But the deputy director [of housing] warned that the unions would strike if I agreed to it.' Livingstone had to back down. But he drew a conclusion that showed him already moving away from Labour orthodoxies: 'The bureaucrats had colluded with the unions to block the first step in transferring power to tenants.'

His desire to decentralize power, to loosen Labour up, to make the party readier to enter alliances with other political and social groups, was partly instinctive and partly hard-headed. 'I'd always hated that traditional Labour movement approach that if you're not in the Labour Party we'll ignore you,' Livingstone said to me. 'You could understand how that worked when Labour was getting half the vote nationally, and there were massive trade union structures. But by the time I came into politics, the two main parties were getting less than 80 per cent of the vote, and a whole range of issue groups had sprung up.' Across London, the traditional sources of Labour support were dwindling. Over 395,000 manufacturing jobs were lost between 1971 and 1984. But other potentially sympathetic social groups – immigrants, squatters, left-leaning gentrifiers – were moving in. This was particularly true of the tatty, modestly off, terrace and tower-block inner districts where Livingstone and his fellow Labour left-wingers cut their teeth.

His approach to coalition-building was both promiscuous and guarded. Whether dealing with apolitical community groups, single-issue campaigners such as environmentalists, hard-left sects such as the Workers' Revolutionary Party, or Labour factions of all kinds – with the Labour right, he could be conciliatory as well as vicious – 'You never had a formal alliance,' Livingstone said. 'People worked with you on issues. I took the broad view that Winston Churchill took, that you had an alliance with Stalin to defeat Hitler. That's just the way politics is: constantly shifting. What I found interesting when I was doing the autobiography was that there's no permanent friendship in there. People who you were totally close to, and working with . . . end up hating you. There are no permanent alliances in electoral politics.'

From 1971 until 1981, from the age of twenty-six to thirty-six, childless, charming, always working, usually dressed in skinny denim or corduroy rather than the traditional Labour councillor's jacket and tie, Livingstone moved deftly and swiftly upwards through the then little-reported world of London municipal politics. In 1973 he was elected to the Greater London Council, the capital's ungainly but ubiquitous local authority, for the south London constituency of Norwood. Even for a politician, he was an unusually attentive reader of opinion polls and local electorates, and shortly before the 1977 GLC elections he realized that the Conservatives, resurgent across London, were about to take his seat. He slipped off to the safer one of Hackney North and Stoke Newington. In 1980 he co-founded a monthly journal to rally the Labour left on the GLC and in the wider capital, with the slyly neutral title *London Labour Briefing*.

In 1977 the Conservatives duly took control of the GLC, as Livingstone had predicted they would. But he also knew that parties rarely held the electorally fickle council for more than one four-year term. In addition, he knew that GLC elections, like all local elections, tended to produce revolts against the party in national office. So he watched with interest as the Thatcher government took power in 1979, and then become more and more unpopular. During 1980 and 1981 many Labour left-wingers believed, he wrote later, 'that Thatcher [was] so bad that Labour would have a walkover' in the next general election. 'But I feared that a leader with firm beliefs and money from North Sea oil would be hard to dislodge.'

Yet the next GLC election, Livingstone judged, would be a

different matter. 'I expected Labour would win the GLC in 1981.' In preparation, he became 'an oppositional figure with a loose group of followers,' remembered Michael Ward, a brainy young left-wing Labour councillor in Wandsworth in south London during the late 1970s. 'From shortly after the 1977 election, Ken was not so quietly recruiting a cadre of people to come on the GLC. It was horses for courses. Different people were entered for different races. I went for Wood Green' – the opposite side of London from Wandsworth – 'because I knew the party members there. [The Conservative] David Mellor gave this wonderful denunciation of us as "peripatetic extremists", which is a badge I've worn with pride ever since.'

Ward lived on the edge of Tooting. Another young left-winger who became an important member of Livingstone's circle, Valerie Wise, lived for a time in Tooting itself. She was the daughter of a well-known former Labour MP, Audrey Wise, but otherwise not an obvious GLC candidate: recently arrived in London, she was in her early twenties but seemed younger, with huge spectacles and an unguarded manner. Yet Livingstone spotted potential. 'He saw me as a good organizer,' Wise told me. 'Ken and Michael Ward helped me get selected. Ken said, "It's good to go for a marginal seat, because you only want to be there [on the GLC] if we win power."'

During 1980, Livingstone, Ward and Wise used to have lunch together at an Indian restaurant in Tooting, Ward remembered, 'and start to plot things and work things out'. They were safely out of earshot of their political enemies and political journalists, who were miles away in central London. 'Ken wanted to be leader of the GLC,' said Wise, 'and he needed the left to come together.'

The same year she moved to a flat owned by her mother in the Barbican in the City of London. After a decade and a half as a glacial, much-mocked building site, the gigantic residential and arts complex was finally almost complete, and a good place to impress political visitors. 'When you went out on the balcony of the flat, you saw the Museum of London. I held a couple of parties, and we invited anybody we considered to be on the left and who might make a GLC candidate. We got to know each other.' After the parties, Livingstone wrote to every possible left-wing candidate and included a list of GLC constituencies, in order of winnability.

A year before the 1981 GLC elections, the elderly leader of the Labour opposition on the council, Sir Reg Goodwin, suddenly resigned. Livingstone, attending for once to his cosmopolitan rather than workaholic side, was on holiday in Italy; he did not hear the news until the two-week competition to replace Goodwin was already three days old. The electorate consisted of Labour's twenty-nine GLC councillors; even though none of his protégés such as Wise and Ward had yet been elected to join them, Livingstone decided to run. After some tricksy manoeuvring by him during the multi-stage secret ballot, including voting for one of his opponents, in order to knock out the other, whom he considered more dangerous, he lost by a single vote.

Livingstone was only fleetingly discouraged. The new Labour leader was Andrew McIntosh, an affable but politically insensitive Labour right-winger who had been to private school – Livingstone himself had sometimes qualified for free school meals. McIntosh lived in prosperous Highgate in north London, was a personal friend of Michael Foot and his family, and fitted in running his own market-research firm alongside his GLC duties. Livingstone regarded him much as one of the salamanders he had kept since childhood might regard a plump and dawdling piece of prey.

Until the GLC elections in May 1981, Livingstone held back. He continued to orchestrate the selection of left-wingers as GLC candidates. He watched an overconfident McIntosh make almost no effort to expand his own power base by buttering up existing councillors, despite the fact that another leadership contest was widely expected to follow the elections. And he worked with Ward and other allies to cram Labour's 1981 GLC manifesto, which grew almost as long as a novel, with new ideas that would spread through British politics for decades to come:

> We promise ... a new partnership with the many voluntary bodies, charities, and pressure groups that can do much to help achieve Labour's objectives ... Public involvement in GLC policy-making will be encouraged ... The needs of public transport will have priority over private cars ... [We] will concentrate on the 'recycling' of materials such as glass, paper and metal ... [We] will introduce 'positive discrimination' ...

Some of Livingstone's preparations to take control of the GLC were blatant. One of his biographers, Andrew Hosken, records how in the run-up to the 1981 elections Livingstone told McIntosh, with a typically disarming combination of bluntness, casualness and menace, 'Look, Andrew, I am going to beat you, however many seats we win; if there is a Labour administration, it will elect me leader.' Yet at this stage Livingstone and his ambitions went largely unnoticed by a national media obsessed by Tony Benn and his bid for the Labour deputy leadership. During the GLC election campaign, the council's unpopular Conservative leader Horace Cutler tried strenuously to interest voters and the press in the 'Marxist' beliefs of Livingstone and his left-wing allies, and in their plans to overthrow McIntosh and run the capital. 'Keep London Out Of The Red,' urged Cutler's manifesto, which mentioned Marxism seventeen times.

In fact, Livingstone had never read Marx. His influences – as much as he had any fixed ones – were more eclectic: Tony Crosland and Roy Jenkins in their 1960s heyday as Labour politicians who believed that socialism should involve hedonism and freedom as well as greater equality; the same decade's anti-racist American attorney general Robert Kennedy; and the innovative, undogmatic communist city governments of 1970s Italy, most notably in Bologna. 'There was a book about it, *Red Bologna* [published in 1977] – we all read it,' Livingstone remembered. 'I have to say, it's a bit leaden. But it was about a council that was not tankie [slavishly pro-Soviet], which said to people, "You don't have to give up your whole life for politics. Just turn up and have a say about how your neighbourhood runs."'

Yet about Livingstone's less inclusive, more scheming side, Cutler was right. On 7 May 1981, as anticipated, Labour took the GLC from the Tories. It was not a landslide: thanks to the first GLC electioneering by activists aligned with the Social Democrats, and also perhaps to Cutler's red-scare tactics, Labour won only fifty of the ninety-two constituencies. By Livingstone's own reckoning, fewer than half – twenty-two – of the victorious Labour candidates were left-wingers; eighteen were right-wingers; and ten were centrists. Many people quickly concluded that the left's plotting had failed. On 8 May the front page of the right-leaning London *Evening Standard* carried a photograph of a grinning and seemingly relaxed McIntosh, jacket slung over one shoulder, like a businessman out for a riverside stroll, under the headline, 'THE LEFT LOSE OUT . . . Moderates "in control"'. So routine was this apparent outcome, and so likely to keep the GLC as a political backwater, the *Standard* had not even bothered to photograph McIntosh in front of County Hall, the GLC's headquarters. Instead, he was shown beside the much more newsworthy Houses of Parliament, directly across the water.

Livingstone himself posed for other press photos with McIntosh: hands behind his back, a half-smile beneath the thin moustache that made him look a little like a South American revolutionary. But off-camera he was busy. First, he persuaded the Greater London Labour Party, where the left was strong, to postpone a meeting of all the Labour GLC councillors, which was needed to confirm McIntosh as GLC leader, from 9 a.m. that day – the time McIntosh had scheduled it, to minimize Livingstone's time for mischief – to 5 p.m. Then Livingstone and his allies used the extra time to lobby the ten centrist Labour councillors, some of whom had been underwhelmed so far by McIntosh's leadership. At 3 p.m. Livingstone invited the converts, the likely converts, and the twenty-two left-wing councillors into one of many committee rooms in the immense, coiling interior of County Hall. For the next hour and three-quarters, unknown to McIntosh and most of the Labour right, Livingstone made a leadership pitch; then he suggested that those present make their own pitches for posts in his GLC administration.

At 4.45 the gathering broke up. Fifteen minutes later in another committee room, the meeting to confirm the Labour leader of the GLC, instead of being a formality, became the climax of a coup. By thirty votes to twenty, Livingstone deposed a startled McIntosh. Then Livingstone's supporters were elected to every key GLC post. On the front page of the next edition of *London Labour Briefing*, amid the usual inky earnestness and bargain-basement typography, there was an unusually snappy headline: 'London's Ours!'

But what exactly had they won? In 1981 the GLC was only sixteen years old. It seemed like an awkward and under-muscled adolescent when compared to its many predecessors and rivals in the messy, millennia-old, never properly resolved business of governing Britain's oversized capital: the City of London Corporation, founded in the early Middle Ages; the dozens of independent-minded London boroughs; the revered 1889–1965 London County Council.

Westminster governments had always been reluctant to grant the capital's administrative bodies too much power. London's unruliness and sheer size, its large number of left-wing voters, the fact that it surrounded Parliament – all these had long made national politicians, especially Tory politicians, nervous. In 1894 the Conservative leader Lord Salisbury described the London County Council, then impregnably Liberal and building much of Britain's first social housing, as 'the place where collectivist and socialistic experiments are tried ... where a new revolutionary spirit finds its instruments'. Five years later his government created the London boroughs to weaken the council's hold over the capital. In the early 1960s, during another extended period of left-of-centre LCC rule, this time by Labour, another Conservative government abolished the council altogether.

The GLC was put in its place. Unlike the LCC, the GLC was responsible not only for inner London but also the more Conservative suburbs and semi-countryside of the outer capital. This wider electorate, it was assumed, would make 'socialistic experiments' less politically possible. So too would the GLC's reduced range of powers: unlike the LCC, which had run everything from schools to hospitals, the new body, wrote the historians of London government Ben Pimlott and Nirmala Rao later, 'was intended as a slim ... strategic authority for the coordination of land-use planning and transport', often in complicated cooperation with the boroughs. It did not sound like a recipe for exciting city government. In 1967, two years into the GLC's existence and just after its second set of elections, the *Observer* published a cartoon of two women walking past a newspaper hoarding that was bellowing, 'Tories Win GLC'. 'I know what Tories are,' said one of the women. 'But what's GLC?'

Yet bureaucracies are cunning and resilient things. During the four GLC administrations that preceded Livingstone's – two Labour, two Tory – a GLC culture established itself that was more self-confident and cannily expansive than the outside world realized. Much of this culture was formed by County Hall itself. Built over a decade by the Edwardians, designed for the LCC when it was the biggest local authority in Europe, County Hall was a massive reef of bleached grey stone, thrown up on the south bank of the Thames, with dim inner courtyards like bottomless rockpools, deep attics and basements like grottoes, rows upon rows of windows, from grand fanlights to tight portholes, and an archipelago of satellite office buildings along the riverside and across the damp centre of the capital. Inside, County Hall was even more pointedly elaborate: almost as big as the Houses of Parliament, an empire-era, Escher-like world of marble and oak panelling that was regarded by the GLC's 37,000 staff and ninety-two councillors with a mixture of exasperation and awe. Livingstone writes in his autobiography:

> The longest corridor stretched for more than a quarter of a mile and some mornings the fog would leak in from the windows and obscure the end of it . . . By 1973 [when he arrived at County Hall] members of the GLC were looked after better than MPs . . . Committee chairs had . . . chauffeur-driven cars, constantly restocked drinks cupboards and access to the royal box at the Royal Festival Hall. Proceedings in the chamber mimicked those of Parliament and we were 'Honourable Members' rather than mere councillors.

As GLC leader, Livingstone would get rid of many of County Hall's rules and hierarchies, such as the requirement that staff wear a suit and tie whenever they visited the councillors' 'principal floor'. But he retained a sense that, despite the GLC's limited official role, County Hall was actually far more important than the average city hall. 'I got there and thought, "This is amazing. I must spend the rest of my life here,"' he told me. 'Incredible building, incredible history . . . And you could *do* things . . . It was the LCC that largely rebuilt London after the [Second World] War.'

Many of the GLC's self-consciously elite senior staff had been at County Hall since the LCC days, and shared with Livingstone an encyclopedic knowledge of London and the tricks and loopholes for governing it – if not much else. 'It was like Whitehall bureaucracy,' he recalled, saying the phrase as impatiently and contemptuously as John Hoskyns. 'A valuers' department; the largest law department, public or private, anywhere in Britain . . . I'm sure many of them voted Labour, but they were implacably conservative. If we'd got 60 councillors' – instead of the fifty Labour won in 1981 – 'I'd have taken over the machine. But I had to work through the bureaucracy.' A few of its officers, such as Maurice Stonefrost, the head of finance or 'Comptroller of Financial Services', who liked unexpected ideas and drove fast cars, were receptive to new ways of doing things that might energize the council. Others were keenly aware that Livingstone's political vulnerabilities could be exploited to obstruct him: 'There were eight members of the Labour group [of councillors] that wanted me to drop dead.' Either way, in County Hall's thousand offices, subdivided and confusingly renumbered over the decades, all sorts of schemes, conservative, radical, or ridiculous, could be discreetly initiated. During the Cutler administration, for some of the GLC's most high-status social functions, the parks department used to obtain penguins and let them loose in the committee rooms.

GLC leaders tended to be showmen. Londoners often like a bit of flash; it was also a way of compensating for the council's lack of formal powers. Desmond Plummer, who led it for the Tories from 1967 to 1973, drove a gold-coloured Mini Cooper and was an enthusiast of urban motorways, for which he flattened congested but characterful parts of west London. Cutler wore bow ties and a goatee beard, like a devilish theatre impresario. He publicly considered bidding for the 1988 Olympics, which he envisaged being staged in the ailing London docks; pioneered the sale of council housing, half a dozen years before Thatcher; and talked to a picture of her that he kept above the fireplace in his County Hall office. Livingstone derided Cutler's 'pretension' and 'overbearing confidence'. Yet, from the start, his own style as leader was just as loud.

'The thing about the GLC in '81 was,' he said, 'it was the first time my generation had got its hands on anything.' Thirty-two years later, we were in his spruce but narrow kitchen in Cricklewood, a modest, terraced part of northwest London. The tiny, hard flakes of a grudging late-winter blizzard were scouring the windows. Livingstone, now sixty-seven, was semi-retired from politics, at least for the time being, a 'house husband' wearing slippers and a fleece zipped right up: 'I hate the cold. I've got my usual dry cough.' His sense of youthful vindication and optimism in the spring of 1981 sometimes seemed very distant. But he kept returning to it. 'If you'd been interviewing me then,' he said, 'I'd have assumed that we'd be in a socialist society by now. You assumed things were going to always get better. You might have temporary setbacks like Thatcher. Or Reagan. But we were on an onward' – the word was lost to his cough – 'because we had been in America since Roosevelt [in the 1940s], and with us from Attlee. All the way through the 1970s, and into the 1980s, you assumed that one day there would be a Labour government that would not repeat the mistakes of Wilson and Callaghan.'

In the early 1980s Livingstone and his closest allies expected that his GLC would be a model for such a government. Michael Ward recalled how in 1981 'we came in with incredible confidence. We thought Thatcher was on the skids. We thought there would be a Labour government within two or three years, and that the ideas and policies we developed would have a major influence.' Livingstone's own ambitions went further. In his autobiography he quotes at length a 1982 portrait of himself, unpublished at the time, by Hugo Young, a widely read and judicious political editor and commentator at the *Sunday Times*. Young had just met the GLC leader for the first time. He found him

> Humorous, decent, open, extraordinarily detached, very committed of course. A good political analyst. Very adept and knowledgeable with electoral figures. Also young. One remembers that he can afford to wait, unlike Benn. I think he will be leader of the Labour party before the end of the century.

More immediately, Livingstone intended that his GLC should avoid the mistakes of its Labour predecessors. In particular, he looked back at the Goodwin administration of the mid-1970s, in which he had played several minor roles, including vice-chairman of the Film Viewing Board, one of the GLC's many little tentacles into the life of the capital. 'As I loved film I was disappointed with the rubbish we had to see' – during the 1970s much of the struggling British film industry had settled for making soft porn – but he had 'opposed censorship on principle'. More formatively, he had watched Goodwin's GLC go badly wrong. It had been elected on a brave manifesto, promising to expand London council housing significantly, and slash fares for public transport with the aim of ultimately abolishing them altogether. But when the mid-1970s recession hit, Goodwin's administration ran short of money. 'Big promises were not kept,' as Livingstone saw it;

panicky and politically divisive cuts were made in public spending, and Goodwin lost power in 1977. The conclusions Livingstone drew were the same as Thatcher did about the Heath government: be an authentic radical, not a fair-weather one; push through your reforms quickly; keep an eye on the money; and above all, don't make U-turns – or at least don't be seen to.

Livingstone also shared Thatcher's flair for political symbolism. On the day of his first full council meeting as leader, a march organized by the Trades Union Congress to draw attention to unemployment, the People's March for Jobs, which had set off from Liverpool a week before the GLC elections, and had attracted marchers and press attention from all over the country, finally reached London. That day, the national unemployment total passed 2,500,000. The core of a few hundred demonstrators, many of them exhausted-looking, jobless young men, were carrying a banner, with potent symbolism, from the famous north-to-London 'Jarrow March' against unemployment in the 1930s. They were surrounded by thousands of supporters.

Livingstone met the marchers on the outskirts of London, and announced that they would be fed and accommodated at County Hall for the next two days and nights. The food and drink would be paid for out of a budget previously used by Cutler's GLC for more exclusive civic receptions. And the demonstrators would sleep on camp beds that had been stockpiled by the council, before Livingstone's time, for use during or after a nuclear war. The practicalities had all been worked out by Valerie Wise, who had been a GLC councillor for only a few days but was already becoming one of Livingstone's most trusted County Hall lieutenants. The whole stunt was at once ingenious, outrageous and shrewdly populist – in the middle of an awful recession, why shouldn't the unemployed as well as London's great and good enjoy the generous hospitality of County Hall? It was also a small but vivid demonstration that the established order of things in London, and by implication Britain, could be overturned surprisingly quickly – that another radicalism beside Thatcherism was possible.

Livingstone had a provocatively tenuous GLC mandate. Would Labour have won a workable majority there in 1981, or even won at all, with such an inexperienced left-winger as their frontman? Was a

GLC leadership secured by an internal party coup, immediately after an election, actually legitimate? Yet during 1981 and 1982 Livingstone used his position as leader to poke the British establishment in one sensitive area after another. In July 1981 he declined an invitation to attend Diana Spencer and Prince Charles's wedding. Instead, he showily went to work as usual at County Hall, which had been semi-officially rebranded as 'the People's Palace'. He told the *Observer*, 'I would like to see the abolition of the monarchy.' The same month, as riots burst out across England, he attributed much of the disorder to 'gung-ho' policing and 'government-induced mass unemployment'. On 13 July *The Times*, then more than now the establishment's paper and usually calm and fair in its news reporting, announced on its front page with heavy innuendo that Livingstone 'was on the streets of Brixton at the height of the rioting'. The paper reported that the GLC leader had twice told policemen there that 'he understood now why the people of Brixton had rioted', that his 'remarks were immediately the centre of a vigorous surge in the crowd', and that 'there were shouts of approval from perhaps a dozen youths'.

Livingstone also took on the nuclear-weapons lobby. His GLC hired the anti-nuclear journalist Duncan Campbell to help track down and publicize long-buried official documents detailing government preparations for a nuclear attack on London. Some of the capital's official nuclear bunkers were then shut down by the GLC, their intended government inhabitants named, and CND and the public invited to inspect them. In 1982, along with nineteen other local authorities, the GLC refused to take part in what was planned as the biggest government civil-defence exercise since the 1960s, Operation Hard Rock, and the exercise had to be cancelled. The following year, the council declared London a nuclear-free zone. Billboards were plastered with GLC posters showing an enormous lawn, filled to the horizon with rows of wooden crosses. 'Don't litter London's parks,' went the nicely typeset, sans-serif slogan. 'Make London nuclear free. Not home to mass graveyards.'

But it was over Ulster that Livingstone the controversialist truly excelled. In 1981 the number of deaths caused by the twelve-year-old war there rose by almost half on the previous year. After a slackening in the violence for much of the late 1970s, 1981 brought other related horrors. On 5 May, three days before Livingstone took office at the GLC, the Provisional IRA hunger striker Bobby Sands died after more than two months of fasting. As often with Ulster in the early 1980s, his death prompted an implacable response from Margaret Thatcher – 'Mr Sands was a convicted criminal. He chose to take his own life' – and condemnation of that implacability from the United States to Iran. In October 1981 the IRA planted two fatal bombs in London, the first such attack for two and a half years. In 1982 they detonated a nail bomb in Hyde Park, as soldiers of the Queen's official bodyguard rode past, and another device under a bandstand in Regent's Park, as army musicians played songs from *Oliver!* to a lunch-hour audience of office workers and tourists.

With London a front in the Irish war once more, and also home to hundreds of thousands of Irish immigrants, it was not unreasonable for the leader of the GLC to make an intervention on Ulster. And by 1981 Livingstone, like many London left-wingers, considered himself well briefed on the conflict. Always a keen autodidact, he had 'learned a lot about Ireland from my reading', from 'contact with Irish people', and from 'involvement in the Troops Out movement', an Anglo-Irish campaign begun in London in 1974 against the British military presence in Ulster and for a united Ireland. His autobiography continues mildly, 'I believed that violence would continue until there was a political settlement, and that inevitably meant negotiation with the IRA.'

Since the 1970s all these stances have at times attracted wide support among the public and in Whitehall. But 1981 and 1982 were not very accommodating years in British politics for uncomfortable truths or nuanced arguments. When Livingstone welcomed Alice McElwee, the mother of another IRA hunger striker, Thomas McElwee, on the stately steps of County Hall; or, two days after a deadly IRA bomb in London, told a gathering of Tory students in Cambridge that the IRA 'believe they have strong political motives' and were not 'psychopaths'; or when he invited the newly elected Sinn Fein politicians Gerry Adams and Danny Morrison to London, despite opposition from Michael Foot as well as the Thatcher government – the response made the monstering of Tony Benn by the press seem like a rehearsal. 'The leader of Britain's capital city,' frothed the *Daily Express* on 22 July 1981, was 'giving encouragement . . . to the enemies of this country.' On 13 October the *Sun* described Livingstone as 'the most odious man in Britain'. The paper went on, 'Since he appeared on the national scene, he has quickly become a joke. Now . . . the joke has turned sour, sick and obscene. For Mr Livingstone steps forward as the defender and the apologist of the criminal, murderous activities of the IRA.'

In response to these sledgehammer lunges, Livingstone tried lawyerly precision: 'I at no time said that people who set off a bomb aren't criminals,' he told the BBC news programme *Nationwide* on the day of the *Sun* article. And also dry wit: 'Quite frankly, I wouldn't agree with what I was quoted as saying.' He tried clear statements of principle: 'I've never supported violence as a means to a political end,' he said in a statement on 21 August 1981 after meeting the children of a woman whom McElwee had burned to death. 'I want all sides to sit round a table.'

But these points were not widely reported or heard. The British press rarely wrote about Ulster in shades of grey. And Livingstone had created an expectation that he would be politically outrageous. He insisted to me that this had happened partly by accident. 'In the run-up to the '81 elections, it never occurred to me that we would become the centre of all this media attention. Because in the previous ten years I'd been in local government, it was desperately trying to get *any* media attention.' So at the beginning of his administration, he went on, his small, nasal voice just as impregnably even as in 1981, and just as effortlessly and manipulatively mixing attention-getting frankness with something more selective, 'Nothing prepared us for this complete *wall* of media interest. It just knocked us over. The first few weeks, I kept saying, "It'll stop soon. They'll lose interest and go away." So we had no strategy for dealing with it.'

County Hall was a short walk from Westminster and from the offices of most national newspapers. So 'Red Ken' was an easy story – especially as during 1981 Livingstone, keenly aware of his own quotability and charm, and bursting with radical policies and stances, seemed to find it impossible to say no to interviewers. On his second day as leader, he gave an audience to the well-known Tory journalist Max Hastings that established a tone for even the more fair-minded Livingstone coverage. With either naivete or calculation or both, perhaps hoping to undercut his growing reputation as County Hall's socialist ogre, Livingstone invited Hastings to his home in safely bourgeois Maida Vale in north London. Afterwards Hastings wrote:

> He is separated from his wife and says that everything he owns is in the bedsit: a portable snooker table, a tank of salamanders, a wardrobe, a bed, a suitcase, a couple of chairs and a portable TV. He has spent the afternoon doing the ironing, with which he persisted through the early stages of our interview.

A few of these details – the snooker, the unusual pets – would usefully serve to soften the public Livingstone during the strident GLC years to come, and beyond. And the fact that Hastings seemed to find a man ironing rather strange said much about Tory male traditionalism, and its ignorance of the feminism-influenced masculinity that was slowly challenging it. But the overall portrait was powerfully negative: at best, of someone 'consumingly dedicated to politics' and eccentric in his personal habits; at worst, of an utterly self-contained fanatic. Even leftish newspapers quickly decided that Livingstone was a slightly alien presence in British politics: a 1982 *Observer* profile called him 'the demon king of County Hall'.

His working habits there did not help to dispel this obsessive aura. 'I started my day reading reports on the way to work,' he writes in his autobiography. 'The rest of the day was spent on paperwork, and popping into committees and meetings where I was needed. I always had lunch in the members' restaurant to keep in touch with [GLC] backbenchers.' In an earlier memoir of his GLC years, Livingstone says he worked a '70 to 74-hour week' during his first two years as leader, and up to '84 hours' after that. 'I just staggered through,' he said to me. 'I was doing perhaps four [public] meetings on a Saturday. A GLC car driving me round London from meeting to meeting to meeting. I can't remember what I did on Sundays.' He paused. 'Sometimes I had meetings on Sundays too.'

Livingstone was much more youthful than previous GLC leaders. He did not turn forty until 1985; Goodwin had left office at sixty-one, and Cutler at sixty-eight. Livingstone did not become a father until 1990, and spent some of his time as GLC leader single, after separating from his first wife – as Hastings had tut-tuttingly noted. The separation led to a divorce in 1982 that Livingstone attributed to 'my workaholic commitment to politics'. Like his fellow workaholic and rebel Margaret Thatcher, the 1980s Livingstone was good at sleep management and had strong health – certainly better than that of the other great hope of the left, twenty years his senior, Tony Benn.

And yet, like Thatcher, Livingstone seemed in 1981 and early 1982 to have taken on far too much. This applied not just to his gesture politics but to his administration's meatier policies.

Almost half the mammoth 1981 Labour GLC manifesto had consisted of ideas for revitalizing the London economy. Large parts of the capital had been troubled for decades: from the oily, increasingly hemmed-in engineering workshops of the northwest; to the unlovely, half-empty office blocks built by 1960s and 1970s speculators in the West End, their tenants slipping away to the Home Counties; to the increasingly deserted, empire-sized docks in the east. This decay accelerated sharply under the first Thatcher government. Between 1979 and 1982 unemployment in London trebled. Contrary to the conventional wisdom then and since, that Thatcherism was a relentlessly pro-London project, joblessness rose faster in the capital from 1980 to 1982 than the national average. Even tourism, long the great hope for a post-industrial London, suddenly seemed vulnerable. After booming for much of the 1970s, the number of overseas visitors to London fell by 6 per cent in 1979, another 6 per cent in 1980, and – despite the royal wedding – 7 per cent in 1981.

'We didn't want to see London continue to decline,' Livingstone told me. 'I don't think we saw it challenging New York, in the way that it eventually did. But basically we were looking at creating a city where everybody could get a job and a home.' Quite a task. Yet, he 'assumed that by demonstrating we were taking on all these things, we would get re-elected'.

The great hope of the new GLC's economic policy was the Greater London Enterprise Board. Michael Ward set it up. Like Valerie Wise, he was a new GLC councillor and an inexperienced politician. But he was also an inquisitive economic thinker, interested in the successful, socially responsible capitalist economies that were being overseen by left-wing councils in northern Italian cities such as Bologna; and in the debates about whether workers should own or manage businesses, debates that had been taking place in the more forward-looking parts of the British left since the early 1970s. Ward also understood more conventional approaches to the economy: his father had worked for decades as a civil servant in the Department of Trade.

In 2013 Ward was still living near Tooting. His house was more suburban than Livingstone's, broad and bay-windowed, facing a park. Since the 1980s Ward had had a successful career as a consultant and chief executive, for both public- and private-sector organizations, in the increasingly fashionable and lucrative field of urban regeneration. I had occasionally heard him on the radio being interviewed about the state of British cities and sounding slick and politically pragmatic. But in person he was less corporate: a moon-faced man of sixty-three in brown shoes, no tie, and a professorial grey jumper. Books and pamphlets, many of them about the Labour Party, covered every wall of his large study. High up on one shelf sat the slightly squashed, well-worn box of a board game called Class Struggle. Elsewhere in the house, Ward had carefully stashed Livingstone-era GLC brochures and policy documents. He still had twenty copies of the council's industrial strategy. As he talked, a little jumpily at first, in a precise, high voice that lacked Livingstone's droll calmness, Ward kept getting up from his crowded desk and leaving the room to fetch supporting evidence for his memories and arguments. The policy papers were generally glossy and well designed, in the Livingstone GLC style. They were also still pristine – as if they could be implemented now.

The administration's economic rescue plan was in part reactive. 'We thought, "Some manufacturing jobs have gone. Others must replace them,"' he remembered. But the means to this traditional Labour end of protecting industry, where the party still found many of its most loyal supporters, were more modern and iconoclastic. At the Enterprise Board, said Ward, 'I was very clear that we would fund cooperatives, but we would also fund small businesses. At the London Labour Party conference in 1980, when the [1981 GLC] manifesto was agreed, there was a man who produced a leaflet saying this was disgraceful, that the GLC should only fund cooperatives, and that what I was proposing was "capitalism on the rates".' Ward grinned for the first time: 'Nice slogan.'

In a broader sense, too, he went on, 'arguing that the London economy was a major concern of London government was novel and contentious in 1981. We were right out on the frontiers of local government. Whereas by the late 90s an economic role was fully built into the structure of London government.' Shortly after that, the Blair administration created the current London mayoralty, and Livingstone again outmanoeuvred the Labour hierarchy to snatch control of the capital. For all Ward's mildness, like the other veterans of the Livingstone GLC I met, he gave off a strong air of vindication.

Yet in 1981 the work of the Enterprise Board, or GLEB for short, did not always live up to the official pamphlets. Ward, who like Livingstone had no children at the time, often spent his Saturdays at County Hall, reading endless requests from would-be entrepreneurs for GLC funding. One day, 'A very nice proposal, very well presented, came in from a man who wanted to revive eel-fishing on the Thames.' Ward grimaced. 'I didn't know even whether there were eels in the Thames, but the proposal was full of detail about how eel-fishing had been a traditional activity etc, and the letter had been forwarded to me by Tony Banks,' the late Labour left-winger and man-of-the-people London politician, who was then GLC councillor for Tooting. The historical claims in the proposal about Thames eel-fishing were true. Ward wrote back to the applicant: 'I must pass your request on to my officials for assessment. It's been a great pleasure to read.' A few weeks later, 'Tony started badgering me for a substantive answer. I saw the official who was investigating it. And he said, "We can't do this! This bloke's a crook!"'

Other setbacks were more subtle. Behind his desk Ward folded his arms. 'We did a lot of work sponsoring local cooperative development agencies. They were good, honest people. They did some good stuff. But the problem with cooperatives was this: you would get six dedicated people with an idea for a business, who with a little bit of pump-priming money [from GLEB] would get it going. But at the end of five years there would still be those six people, working all hours of the day and the night . . . They were not a solution to mass unemployment. We would ask ourselves, "Why don't cooperatives grow?"' His voice trailed off: 'I don't think they did.' By its own estimate, the GLC 'contributed' to an increase in employment in cooperatives, across the whole of London between 1981 and 1986, of under a thousand jobs.

Meanwhile some of GLEB's larger projects encountered even harder economic truths. 'Almost the first case we dealt with in 1981,' said Ward, 'was the Callard & Bowser toffee factory in west London.' This was threatened with closure by the famous confectionery firm, founded in London 144 years earlier. 'We met the trade unions. We met the management. We funded quite a professional management consultant to do a study . . . on the confectionery industry, and how this was a viable plant.' But the firm shut it anyway. 'What I realized terribly quickly,' continued Ward, beginning to sound more like his pragmatic modern self, 'was that any manufacturing company that had several plants in the UK was *adjusting* – to the way that the retail market was changing, the distribution market was changing, and they were trying to go from six sites to three . . . At GLEB, you could say what you liked about the skill and quality of the London workforce . . . The fact was, the surviving factories in London' – many of which dated back to the capital's last peacetime manufacturing boom, during the 30s – 'were not state of the art by the 80s. And companies could sell their London sites for housing.'

Another time, GLEB tried to work solely with unions to save a factory. In the early 1980s the industrialist Lord Weinstock, admired by Thatcher then for his unsentimental cost-cutting, decided to close a London plant that made parts for telephone exchanges. Shop stewards at the plant argued that they could run it themselves, and asked GLEB for help. Ward went with them to see Weinstock, persuaded him to let the stewards take over the factory, and provided it with a GLEB subsidy. 'But,' Ward continued evenly, 'the exchanges were moving from one technology to another. The products the plant was making were finished. And the skills of the workforce, and the machines, were not adjusted to making the products that would be needed in the future.' The factory made a persistent loss. 'We had to pull the plug after a year or two.' Ward went back into idealistic mode: 'It was *very* painful.'

He looked up from the pile of impressive GLC brochures that had been accumulating on his desk throughout the interview. 'I don't think we understood what was happening,' he said. 'I think the whole left, the whole Labour movement, even the Tories, didn't understand what they'd got into – the kind of change that was on the cusp of happening in the economy. There was this long-term decline of the London manufacturing sector.' And there was also the rise of another economic sector in the capital that the left – even the most exploratory minds at GLEB – knew far less well. 'Between 1981 and 1986,' said Ward, 'I never once met the City of London Corporation officially. I hardly went into the Square Mile.'

'If I'd had any idea what was coming, I wouldn't have taken these issues on all at once,' Livingstone said to me. 'Everything was just driven through so rapidly. On every front we advanced! There was real indigestion for people.' Zipped up in his fleece in his warm kitchen, he chuckled drily over the mug of coffee he had been unhurriedly sipping. 'Most commanders would say, "Better to advance in stages."'

In October 1981, under the neat, populist slogan 'Fares Fair', his GLC cut the price of London bus and Underground tickets by between a third and a quarter. The policy was partly Livingstone's own idea. He had been Labour transport spokesman before the GLC elections, and he used public transport himself, even as council leader, with a trainspottery relish. He knew that the Underground, where fares had risen fast since the late 1970s despite the declining incomes of many recession-squeezed Londoners, was relatively underused. Fares Fair was to be funded by a new London tax, a 'supplementary rate' paid mostly by businesses and collected by the boroughs – some of which were Conservative-controlled, or had no Underground stations, or both.

The policy lasted four months. Public transport usage soared: 'An additional half a million people switched to using buses and tubes,' according to Livingstone, usually accurate, if selectively so, with his figures. 'Car use in London was down by 4 per cent, with less congestion and ... fewer accidents.' After decades of underfunding, diminishing passenger numbers and creeping shabbiness, the capital's public transport began its slow modern climb back to relative prestige and functionality. But then Fares Fair was stopped by the courts. The outer London borough of Bromley – Conservative, Tubeless, self-consciously respectable, many of its councillors already irritated by Livingstone's noisy inner-city leftism – found a forgotten clause in the twelve-year-old legislation covering the financial management of the capital's public transport, which could be interpreted as making the fare cuts illegal. After hearings at the High Court, the Court of Appeal and finally the House of Lords, 'to our utter amazement,' writes Livingstone, Bromley won.

Afterwards Livingstone was attacked by the Labour right on the GLC for having a naive and reckless transport policy, and by the Labour left for failing to defend it to the death. Faced with possible disqualification from office and being 'surcharged' – under local government law, councillors could be made personally financially liable for voting to spend money illegally – Livingstone voted once to defy the Lords, then backed down. 'When faced with a real challenge from the capitalist establishment,' wrote Paula Watson, an old ally, in *London Labour Briefing*, 'our representatives on the GLC surrendered.'

In other ways too, during the second half of 1981 and early 1982 the reign of 'Red Ken' seemed to be rapidly unravelling. In August 1981 his personal approval rating was 11 per cent, and Labour were in third place in the London opinion polls, behind both the Conservatives and the Social Democrats. During the autumn two Labour GLC councillors defected to the SDP, and the Labour majority on the council shrank accordingly from a manageable eight to a vulnerable four. Meanwhile Livingstone was effectively cut adrift by the national Labour Party. Its right-wingers saw his outspoken radicalism, justifiably, as aiding the Tories and SDP, while the party leader Michael Foot remained close to the man Livingstone had deposed, Andrew McIntosh. Only the sheer complexity of the Labour divisions at the GLC prevented Livingstone becoming a coup victim himself: 'I've no doubt that the majority of the Labour group would have liked to have seen the back of me,' he wrote afterwards, 'but couldn't agree on a replacement.'

'The demon king' received hate mail, obscene phone calls, an assessment by three psychologists in the *Daily Mail* as 'a fanatic' and an attention-seeking 'hysteric', and a faceful of red paint from a member of the racist National Front. He even suffered an attempted assault, by a gang shouting 'commie bastard', outside a pub in leftish, gentle Hampstead. His usually equable political adviser and confidant Bill Bush, Livingstone wrote, 'became worried about my personal safety and . . . urged me to [use] the leader's car'. Livingstone refused. He liked the bus too much; more importantly, like Thatcher, he knew the political value of defiance: 'If I showed the slightest sign of weakness I'd be gone, so I had to project confidence in our ability to turn things round before the next election'.

But thirty-two years later, he could be more honest about his initial performance as GLC leader. 'Politics is so much about odd chances,' Livingstone said, ruminatively. 'That's the weakness of the Marxist ideology about inevitable historic shifts.' He began to drift off into London Labour history: 'I became the leader of the GLC partly because I was the only left-winger who survived the '77 election.' Then, like a salamander striking, he suddenly got to the point: 'I really wasn't ready for it.'

8
Are You the Cleaners?

In 1980 Ann Pettitt was an impatient but dreamy thirty-three-year-old with a stubborn blue gaze, living in a half-renovated wreck of a farmhouse outside Carmarthen. She had two untidy sons, aged two and four, and a partner, Barry, who had recently been a teacher and was now trying to become a builder. She was busy and also lonely, a recent arrival in southwest Wales from London, with no relations nearby, not many friends yet, and 'a vast vegetable garden and small field of unruly animals we were meant to be eating'. Her days were dominated by mud, hanging out nappies to dry against a huge hillside sky, and finding spare moments to read about the outside world. Increasingly, the topic that most interested her was radiation sickness.

'I was reading in the paper about nuclear power,' she wrote later, 'and how radiation affects the youngest most ... because their cells are dividing the fastest, and I was reading about the cover-ups of leaks.' In 1979 a partial meltdown had occurred at the Three Mile Island nuclear reactor in America. There had been a botched attempt to conceal the accident's seriousness. By mid-1980 Pettitt had absorbed so much about such subjects that she 'sort of ... blew a fuse'.

Among the construction debris and toddler clutter of the farmhouse, she pulled out some rolls of white wallpaper from an understairs cupboard. Then she took a black felt tip and covered them in thick, angry words. Some were her own amateur slogans – 'Nuclear Power – Poisoning Our Environment', 'Nuclear Weapons – More And More Built Every Year – This Cannot Go On'; and some were quotations from a 1979 article by Lord Mountbatten, Prince Charles's late mentor, who had increasingly turned against nuclear weapons while serving as Britain's most senior naval commander.

Pettitt took her furious scrolls to a wholefood shop in Carmarthen. Its owner, like her, was a *Guardian* reader and an incomer, part of the left-leaning, environmentally conscious, ex-urban diaspora that had been straggling into Wales since the 1960s, in search of rural utopia and cheap property. She asked if he would display her polemics. He agreed; better than that, he offered to help her organize a meeting.

Thirty people came to the first gathering of the Carmarthen Anti-Nuclear Campaign. Many were alarmed by a recent announcement that the Thatcher government planned to survey a site in north Wales for a nuclear waste dump. Yet the meeting did not go quite as they expected. 'A young scientist came,' Pettitt remembered when we met, 'and he said, "I don't know why you're all so worried about nuclear power. Nuclear weapons are going to get us a lot quicker." And I thought, "My god, he's right. It could happen. They – politicians – could be that stupid. Or a terrible accident could set off a nuclear war."'

After the meeting, during the second half of 1980 and into 1981, Pettitt and her fellow apprentice campaigners shifted their attention almost entirely to nuclear weapons. She read E. P. Thompson's 'Protest and Survive', and found it 'one of the most stirring pieces of polemic ever written in the English language. People rang each other up and said, "Have you read it?" and passed it from one to the other.'

But then the Carmarthen group seemed to get bogged down. In the spring of 1981, wrote Pettitt, 'I was trying to help write a leaflet in someone's house in Kidwelly, about nuclear-free zones. I was feeling bored and stuck generally with the way we seemed to be creating a re-run of the CND campaigns of the Sixties.' Her father had been in CND then, and as a teenager she had been on some of its famous cross-country marches, enjoying their mild anarchy and opportunities to meet boys. But the more indoor, incremental side of anti-nuclear activism, in either its 1960s or 1980s versions, did not excite her: 'The usual suspects doing the usual thing in greater or lesser numbers,' she wrote. 'We were another item of conventional furnishing in the political room.' Then, in the house in Kidwelly, 'My eye caught an item in a *Peace News* magazine that was lying open on the floor, about a group of women walking from Copenhagen to Paris to protest . . . I no longer felt bored or stuck, I felt terribly excited.'

Through the spring and summer of 1981, sometimes while she was alone in a wet field trying to round up her cow for milking, sometimes in meetings and conversations with a handful of other women from the Carmarthen campaign and other tiny anti-nuclear cells across Wales and southern England, Pettitt conceived a plan. A new group, called Women for Life on Earth, would undertake a ten-day 'Peace March' – starting in Cardiff in late August and heading eastwards across the west of England.

Pettitt was small and wiry, with strong calves: a good walker. But at first she found it hard to recruit other marchers. She decided she would walk alone if necessary. 'If you have an idea and you want to make it happen,' she wrote afterwards, in a rather Thatcherite tone, 'you have to take responsibility for it yourself.' But gradually a few dozen women came together, mobilized by letters from Pettitt, and ads in obvious places (the *Guardian*) and not so obvious ones (*Cosmopolitan*). Media interest, Pettitt assumed, would be attracted by the women's relative ordinariness – none were well-known activists – by the length of the march, and by its novel target, one rarely selected so far by anti-nuclear activists: cruise missiles.

These stubby-winged cylinders, bulbous, blind-looking and long as a minibus, were slow-flying but low-flying and therefore hard for radar to detect. Designed and made in America, they were descendents of the German V-1 flying bomb that had devastated parts of east London during the Second World War. Yet each missile was infinitely more destructive, with a warhead sixteen times as powerful as the nuclear bomb dropped on Hiroshima. Cruise was also more accurate than traditional nuclear missiles, thanks to a computer guidance system; less vulnerable to pre-emptive attack, because it could be fired from a mobile launcher as well as a fixed silo; and comparatively cheap – $1 million (then just over £500,000) per missile. The weapon could be presented to the public as a shrewd upgrade in austere times.

Right through the 1970s, British defence ministers and officials had repeatedly insisted that they had 'no plans to develop or acquire such missiles'. Then in December 1979, a few months after Thatcher took office, her government and its NATO counterparts abruptly announced that the United States would station 464 cruise missiles in Western Europe, including Britain. As with previous transformations of the British, or British-based, nuclear arsenal, further information was held back: Whitehall habitually keeps its decisions on nuclear weapons as secret as possible for as long as possible, and then presents them as a fait accompli. It was not until June 1980 that the defence secretary, Francis Pym, deigned to tell the House of Commons that the 160 missiles to be deployed in Britain would be based at

> the United States Air Force standby base at Greenham Common … and RAF Molesworth, a disused airfield in Cambridgeshire, currently used by the United States Air Force for storage purposes. Greenham Common will be the main operating base … It is planned that the first units will deploy at Greenham Common in 1983.

Pym did not mention that the missiles' ability to be launched from almost any piece of flat ground would make most of the country into a Russian target. Instead, he stressed that Britain's share of the cost would be relatively small – 'about £16m' – and that with the two bases requiring major refurbishment to house the missiles, 'quite a lot of work … will be available to local contractors'. The missile-launch personnel would be American, but '[any] decision to fire will be a joint political decision … between ourselves and the United States'. Yet, pressed by MPs about exactly what this meant, Pym conceded that, unlike many other NATO missiles, cruise would not have a 'dual key' – a firing system and protocol that required British as well as American involvement.

> We could have a dual key if we shared in the cost and the ownership of the weapon, but we do not; it is a United States weapon … It is neither necessary nor a very sensible use of our very limited resources to have joint ownership … There is, as there has been for years, a very close alliance between ourselves … and our American allies. We are entirely confident and content with the present arrangements. They are working mutually to our advantage …

The blatant power imbalances in the cruise scheme, made worse by its likely part in an American plan to fight a 'limited' nuclear war in Europe, outraged some British patriots. 'A manifest symbol of subjection,' thundered E. P. Thompson in the May 1980 issue of the bracing Marxist journal *New Left Review*. Although Pettitt was actually half-French, she told me that in the aftermath of the cruise announcement, she thought, 'What kind of ally are we? We are the floating aircraft carrier. So we die, in order to save you.' But she also had another thought: 'Cruise are on the ground . . . You can get at them. You can go there. You can protest there. That's where we should go. The fools – they've stuck them on the ground!'

'Before Greenham,' Pettitt told me, 'marching and occupation were already part of my history. I'd been involved in student sit-ins at Bristol University. I'd been on the London squatting scene in the 1970s.' She also knew the airbase at Greenham in Berkshire and how to get there: she used to hitchhike to university along the road that ran right past it. So walking the hundred-odd miles from Cardiff to the suddenly high-profile future missile base was in some ways a simple and practical political gesture. The marchers planned to cover a manageable dozen miles a day. It would be summer. And they would be crossing some of south Wales and southern England's gentlest, most photogenic, most symbolically peaceful landscapes, the water meadows and grassy valleys of Wiltshire and west Berkshire.

Yet in the weeks leading up to the walk's start date of 27 August, complexities also arose. 'I was absolutely convinced it had to be a march by women,' Pettitt wrote afterwards. 'We felt that women felt differently about war and violence than did men, and that these feelings . . . came from the fact that so many of us were mothers and carers for others.'

This version of pacifism had a long pedigree. In *The Long Road to Greenham: Feminism & Anti-Militarism in Britain since 1820*, Jill Liddington writes of a 'maternalist' tradition within the British peace movement: 'It was thought appropriate for Victorian women to undertake quiet peace propaganda . . . By 1914 this maternalist thinking had been broadened by Olive Schreiner, a feminist who argued . . . that women as mothers "pay the first cost on all human life" . . . In the 1930s the Women's Co-operative Guild mounted a poignant "never again" campaign against any return to military conscription of their sons.'

Liddington's book, published in 1989 by Virago, the influential British women's press, identified two other forms of feminism that had long played an important part in pacifism: 'equal-rights feminism . . . rooted in a recognition of women's traditional exclusion from political power and in the optimistic belief that once this was rectified war would cease – or at least become less likely'; and a 'radical feminist strand [which] stresses . . . male violence . . . [and] links military aggression with domestic and sexual violence'. She quotes the early American feminist Charlotte Perkins Gilman, writing in 1911: in war, 'We find maleness in its absurdest extremes.'

Yet Pettitt herself was not keen on sweeping condemnations based on gender. She had sons and a male partner. She had been active in the women's liberation movement in London during the 1970s, and had grown hostile to what she called 'the simplistic, anti-men style of feminism'. While devising and publicizing the Greenham march, she wrote, 'We were worried we might be . . . alienating men', many of whom – such as E. P. Thompson – also opposed cruise missiles. There were also practical considerations: 'We would need the cooperation of friendly groups along the route to find us accommodation and food. These groups would have men all inconveniently mixed up with their women. Moreover, we wanted people to accompany us along our route [by coming] out of the towns.' So Pettitt and the other organizers came up with a delicate, not necessarily durable, compromise. 'The marchers themselves would be women and the pre-publicity would make that clear, but men . . . would be welcome to show support by walking with us for part of the day as long as they accepted that . . . it was a women's march, women in front, literally, women as spokespersons, women taking the decisions.'

During August they hurriedly made the final arrangements. A blunt explanatory leaflet was produced for the marchers to hand out, its message deliberately kept to a few words on one side – CND leaflets usually rambled for paragraphs – and a picture of a Hiroshima baby deformed by radiation on the other. A leaflet for the marchers themselves to read recommended bringing two pairs of walking shoes and lots of socks, and explained that a hired van and back-up car, paid for by the marchers and by donations, would accompany the march to carry luggage and any children who had been brought along and needed transport. For snacks and road soreness, the organizers provided plasters, sunblock, lemonade and biscuits. They made a banner out of an old sheet, dyed pink and covered in peace symbols.

A mention of the march in the *Sunday Times* produced further recruits.

On 26 August 1981 the participants gathered in Cardiff. 'There didn't seem very many of us,' Pettitt wrote: thirty-six women, four men and three children. Apart from the organizers and a few other activists from Wales, they had never met and did not know each other. 'We felt uncomfortable and apprehensive.' Pettitt describes the group as 'all ages and accents'; Liddington goes into more detail:

> A 58 year-old grandmother and market gardener from Fishguard; a 15 year-old from Luton . . . Eunice Stallard, another grandmother, from the Swansea valley; Helen John, a forthright nurse, Labour Party supporter and mother of five from Llanwrtyd Wells; Denise Aaron, a mother of four young children from Chester, who felt she was very unpolitical.

Helen John had only found out about the march a week before. A precise woman with strong forearms and a formidably level voice, originally from Essex, she was older than Pettitt and, at this stage, much more traditional in her politics: 'I had missed the entire consciousness-raising movement,' she told me. 'I'd been having five children and being a nurse and a midwife. I didn't know what feminism was.' At first, it barely occurred to her that the gender make-up of the march might be an issue: 'I couldn't see anything wrong with men being there.' Yet she quickly sensed the march's potential, not just for protest but for personal transformation. She left her husband, Douglas, and four of her children at home, and turned up in Cardiff with a single son in a pushchair. Two days into the march, one of her older children met them and took him home. 'It was quite amazing. For the first time, I could think for myself, without thinking of someone else first.'

The marchers set out on a brilliant Thursday morning, just before the Bank Holiday weekend. They wore sunhats and sundresses, shorts and sandals, T-shirts with more peace symbols, even flip-flops. A young mother called Thalia Campbell wore a purple jumpsuit, with ribbons in the other suffragette colours attached, and performed cartwheels while they walked as close to the middle of the road as passing traffic and the police would allow. Pettitt was worried that her footwear advice had not been followed. 'I feared . . . we would all succumb to blisters by the end of the day, and have to complete the journey by coach, looking ridiculous.' Helen John intervened: as a medical professional, she offered to perform twice-daily, semi-compulsory foot inspections. Her new comrades agreed.

Otherwise, 'By [the first] lunchtime a kind of irrepressible mirth had set in,' wrote Pettitt. Nearing Bath the next day, the protesters were joined by The Fall Out Marching Band, a group of anti-nuclear street musicians with a carnival of saxophones and trumpets: 'They were playing in a festival that weekend. They had heard about us and had come to accompany us into the city.' Afterwards,

> On the way to Batheaston we ransacked the hedgerows for wild hops and arrived covered in green garlands . . . The sun still shone out of a cloudless sky and the roads were long, shadeless and bounded by chalky banksides . . . The police car with us broke down on a lonely stretch across the Wiltshire Downs, so the women at the front held the banner with one hand while pushing the car along with the other.

It was all very exhilarating, and possibly life-changing. But was it having any wider effect? Pettitt increasingly doubted it. Sympathizers along the route offered beds and food, or thickened the tiny marching column for a few miles. Yet when the marchers strode into towns and villages, slightly wild from outdoor living, singing 'Take the toys from the boys' and thrusting out their anti-cruise leaflets, many people just stared at them as if they were harmless eccentrics. Even in Bristol, a city with a strong left-wing and anti-nuclear scene and Tony Benn as an MP, the marchers found themselves greeted at a specially arranged rally by 'three bemused punks', a 'handful of significantly older CND members', and no one else.

Part of the problem was the march's double identity as both a feminist and anti-nuclear project. Only a little later in the decade such hybrids would become commonplace, indeed almost compulsory, on the British left; but in 1981, at least away from London's promiscuous radical politics, many activists were still wedded to single causes. At first, some feminists saw the Greenham march as too nuclear-fixated, while some CND members saw it as too feminist. Another problem was the press. Every morning during the march Pettitt rang the newspapers. Peace activism, they would patronizingly explain to her, was 'last year's story'. Local television took a little more notice. Tanned women with toddlers and a cause marching through a sweeping, usually politically sleepy landscape could be turned into a nice news item. But the TV reporters made little effort to find out exactly why the women objected to cruise missiles. Only East German TV paid the protest sustained attention: 'They turned up to film us every day.'

Just over half way through the march, a few days from Greenham, the protesters stayed the night in the Wiltshire market town of Melksham. The evening was stuffy, and an earnest folk concert had been put on for them in one of the old houses on the main square. Bored and restless, Pettitt sneaked out. On a bench in the square she noticed two of the other marchers, Liney Seward and Lynne Whittemore, whom she knew well from Wales, furtively smoking home-grown marijuana. They called her over, passed the joint, and said they'd had an idea.

Like her, they felt the march was turning out to be ineffectual. As things were going, they would get to Greenham almost unnoticed except by the peace movement, and then just go home. So why not do something more lasting and eye-catching? All three women knew from their 1970s adventures the benefits that direct-action politics could bring. They also knew a bit about the suffragettes, and their successful tactic of chaining themselves to railings at potent locations such as 10 Downing Street. Seward and Whittemore suggested the marchers do something similar at Greenham.

Pettitt was both thrilled and thrown by the idea – by the open-ended commitment and potential for law-breaking it involved. When the hazy plan was put to the marchers as a whole, she remembered, 'There was massive disagreement. Most of the women were not used to protest. They were saying, "I came on a march. I didn't come on something that might turn violent." It required a lot of talking through. There were two women who were from a feminist consciousness-raising group, and they introduced that approach.' On two different days during the march, the women stopped and sat in a circle, while the men looked after the children, and took turns to speak. There was no vote – 'We'd have split the group' – but a loose consensus eventually formed in the plan's favour. Four women would chain themselves to the Greenham fence on behalf of all of them. The volunteers were

Seward, Whittemore, the grandmother Eunice Stallard, and Helen John.

In Marlborough, a public-school town in Wiltshire that had been breeding conformists and rebels for two centuries, Pettitt and Seward visited an ironmonger. 'We couldn't stop ourselves from giggling,' Pettitt wrote, 'as we surreptitiously measured how much [chain] was needed to go round waists.' After all the discussion, and with Greenham now close at hand, the marchers were paranoid that the authorities would find out or work out what they had in mind. The marchers were also running short of money: Pettitt and Seward could only afford 'four of the smallest padlocks'.

At 7.30 a.m. on 5 September, a Saturday, before the sun got too hot and USAF Greenham Common properly woke up, two cars stopped outside the main gates of the future cruise-missile base. The entrance was set back from the busy A339, with lawns sloping down in front and a policeman scrutinizing visitors. For days, anyone following the steady advance from Wales of Women for Life on Earth knew that the march was due to reach the airbase later that morning. The marchers expected to be met by extra police, and so had decided that the 'chain gang', as Pettitt called it, would arrive ahead of the rest of the protesters in borrowed cars, sprint to the fence, chains already around their waists and concealed under skirts, and lock on in seconds, before they could be apprehended. Partly as a diversion, another of the marchers, Karmen Cutler, would simultaneously arrive by car at the gates. She would read out an open letter addressed to the base commander, written by Pettitt in a pub the night before.

But there were no extra policemen at the airbase that Saturday morning. Instead, the chain gang ran from one of the cars to the fence and locked on, unobstructed. The lone policeman watched from a distance, uncomprehending. When Cutler approached him seconds later and began reading out the open letter, he mistook her and the other protesters – as if playing his part in an unsubtle feminist satire – for the base's cleaners.

The policeman was corrected. He radioed the airbase, and was joined by a man in military uniform; Cutler then read out the letter to both of them. Meanwhile the four chained women sat against the fence, Helen John squinting in the sun but otherwise almost lolling, as if she could sit there all day. Over the previous twelve hours, she and the others had deliberately drunk little and eaten nothing.

Later that morning, the rest of the marchers arrived on foot. Supporters joined them from Newbury, a comfortable, Conservative-voting commuter town a couple of miles away, and from elsewhere in southeast England. A few journalists turned up. When one of them called the Ministry of Defence for a reaction to the protest, according to Pettitt the MOD said it had no plans to move any of the women on. That evening, with a slight autumn chill creeping in, Pettitt gathered branches from a nearby wood and lit a campfire on a patch of concrete beside the gates, a few dozen yards from the women who were still chained on. Discreetly, the protesters then began to take turns in the chains, so that the original four could pee and eat. Pettitt did a stint: 'That night I lay in my sleeping bag . . . propped against the fence, and couldn't sleep,' she wrote. 'We had done it, whatever it was.'

The women did not yet fully realize it, but Greenham Common was one of the best places imaginable to stage a confrontation with the overmighty, transatlantic power structures that had grown up around British-based nuclear weapons. A great sweeping tabletop of gorse heath and grassland, fringed with deep-green stands of birch and bracken, in 1981 it was one of the few charismatic landscapes left in an increasingly suburbanized southeast England. The common had hosted Bronze Age earthworks, Edwardian picnickers, centuries of poachers, cowherds, botanists and cloud-spotters. For some visitors it was symbolic and precious territory. 'When our march got there, I thought, "My God, it's the Forest of Arden [in *As You Like It*],"' Pettitt said to me. 'Somewhere to take to the woods and uphold better values than the corrupt court values.'

From the seventeenth century onwards, Greenham's open spaces had been occasionally used by the army for manoeuvres or marshalling troops, but more bucolic activities always resumed, and with them the right of public access. Then in 1940 the British wartime government requisitioned the heathland and built the longest military runway in Europe. Initially, the airbase was used by the RAF for training, but in 1943 it was loaned to the Americans as a base for fighters and transport planes, and it played a central role in the D-Day landings. At the end of the war the Americans left, the airbase closed, and plans were made to reopen the common to the public. Then the nuclear-weapons complex intervened. In 1951, with the Cold War deepening, the Americans were looking for European bases for their atom-bomb-carrying aircraft. The British government, eager for American protection against the Russians and for American help with Britain's own nuclear weapons, again handed over Greenham's English Arcadia to its domineering foreign ally. There were protests: a meeting of the usually placid Newbury public and local business figures condemned 'the loss . . . of ancient common lands and liberties'. But the British government again requisitioned the land, using emergency powers left over from the war. From 1956 to 1964 noisy, nuclear-armed American bombers flew from Greenham, ready to launch an apocalypse at a few minutes' notice.

Similar instances of American military expansion, Whitehall acquiescence, and British national sovereignty compromised, with the minimum of debate and legal justification, happened all over the country from the 1940s onwards. In *The Unsinkable Aircraft Carrier: American Military Power in Britain* (1984), another unsettling book by the investigative reporter Duncan Campbell about a subject Whitehall would prefer the public not to think too hard about, 135 US military bases and facilities in Britain were listed. As today, this presence ebbed and flowed with America's strategic needs; and in theory at least, with the needs of its NATO allies. In 1964 the American bombers left Greenham. Before they did so, the British government persuaded Newbury Borough Council, since the 1940s the official owners of the common, to sell it the land inside the airbase perimeter. The part of the common outside the fence, where Pettitt and the others would turn up seventeen years later, remained the property of the council, beyond military control.

During the Détente era of the 1960s and 1970s the giant airbase was little used. Its long perimeter, meandering and dipping for miles through woodland, made it hard to guard. In 1966 Greenham was lent back to the Americans as a 'standby base', after the French government, more independent-minded than the British, ended American use of French airbases. In 1972–3 the Heath administration temporarily housed refugees from Uganda at Greenham: a rare instance of benign Whitehall behaviour there. In 1978 the Ministry of Defence announced that huge American military tanker aircraft would be based at the airbase. But it was dissuaded by local campaigners, who objected to the racket the planes would make.

When the deployment of cruise missiles was announced two years later, these campaigners did not stir. 'We are pro-NATO, pro-defence,' one told the *Guardian*. 'Cruise missiles are supposed to be nice and quiet.' One of the town's main employers was the Atomic Weapons Research Establishment at Aldermaston, a dozen miles away.

Yet a few locals were anti-nuclear. Joan Ruddock was in her mid-thirties and lived near Aldermaston. An able and ambitious Labour Party and peace activist, she worked in a Citizen's Advice Bureau, had smart, shortish hair, and none of the hippy aura of some of the Welsh-based peace campaigners. In June 1980, within hours of the cruise announcement, she had co-founded the Newbury Campaign Against Cruise Missiles. At first it was small, just thirty members, but by the time the marchers got to Greenham a year later, it had five times that. The Newbury group quickly provided the marchers, who had arrived with hardly any food or camping equipment, with a scattering of local allies and vital practical assistance. 'They brought blankets, cooking stuff, food,' Pettitt remembered. 'People took us back for baths. Or they'd just come and talk to us.' The Greenham Common peace camp was under way.

At first, it seemed as unexpectedly easy as the chaining on. 'Every day more supplies arrived,' record Barbara Harford and Sarah Hopkins, both active supporters of the peace camp, in their 1984 book *Women at the Wire*, part of what became a rapidly expanding Greenham literature. 'A frame tent . . . chemical toilets, calor gas burners . . . their first post – a telegram from Bradford Women's Liberation Group.' In the early days, surprisingly, 'Relations with the [service] men on the base were pleasant and polite. They even helped the marchers fix up a standpipe to the water supply on the road opposite the main gate.'

The camp established itself to the immediate southeast of the airbase gates and the chained women. The site was quite exposed, with a few slender trees, sloping, gravelly soil, the base immediately behind and the A339 in front, only a few dozen yards away and carrying much of the Newbury rush hour. 'I sat there attached to the fence on and off for about three weeks, with people whizzing by at 60 miles an hour,' remembered Helen John. 'One person out of every several thousand waved.' At night, the protesters were kept awake by the airbase floodlights, and by military vehicles rattling in and out of the gates.

But the site was sunny, and through September the weather stayed good. More tents were acquired. John donated a caravan 'from an abortive French holiday – my sons had hated it'. Postal donations paid for the hire of a portakabin. Meanwhile some of the dozen peace-camp residents constructed 'benders', igloo-shaped structures of arched young branches covered in plastic sheeting, which would become a Greenham trademark. The camp began to look like a cross between a self-built 1960s commune and a small free festival, the anarchic outdoor music events that had sprouted illicitly across southern England during the 1970s.

In other ways, too, the camp became a continuation – sometimes a culmination – of the experiments of those decades in alternative ways of living and thinking. This was partly due to the feminist, pacifist and environmentalist ideas that the marchers brought with them to Greenham; and partly due to the life of the camp itself. 'You did sit around talking,' remembered Pettitt. 'There wasn't much else to do, at first, except for survival: cooking, washing. And sitting round a fire is a better space for ideas than some smoke-filled room.'

Helen John told me when we met, 'The consciousness-raising-style meetings – I'd never seen anything like it in my life. I thought they were insane, at first. But then I could see the changes in the women.' She herself changed. Early on, she drove a van from the camp back to Wales without insurance, 'my first-ever bit of law-breaking'. Near the border, 'I met [my husband] Douglas, collected some duvets from him, and went straight back to Greenham.' She had never slept in a tent before: 'I like my home comforts. I'm impractical. I don't like getting my hands dirty.' Yet, 'When I was at Greenham, I didn't catch a cold. You did smell of campfire smoke, but once you start living outdoors, as people all over the world know, you adapt. You just dress differently. Your body adapts. Your mind adapts.'

Douglas worked on oil rigs, and was on shore leave during the march and her first three weeks at Greenham, so he looked after their children. 'During those three weeks, I made up my mind,' Helen John said. She had no job to go back to. At the end of the period, 'Douglas popped up at Greenham and told me I had to come home, because I had five children. I said he had five children, and if anyone was going to give anything up, it was going to be him: I was going to stay at Greenham. He thought I was insane.'

Helen was forty-four. At the camp, 'I was cut adrift from everything that I knew.' More and more, this became a deliberate act on her part: 'My children came down to Greenham. I quickly discovered that it was a place I wasn't madly keen on my kids being around. It wasn't the right environment . . . I had no idea what tomorrow was going to bring. But I felt as if I had discovered another brain.'

'That first November, I fell in love with a woman [at the camp]. Much younger. She was 18 – nine months older than my daughter. I was streetwise, but not educated. She was very well educated. She'd just turned down a scholarship to Oxford – she was going to study Arabic. Her father couldn't believe it. She said, "Why would I want to go to that *dump*?" At Greenham, every syllable she said, everyone listened. She didn't rant and rave.' Back in Wales, 'Douglas was devastated. It was a terrible shock. Leaving him was a terrible shock for me, too.' They divorced, and her new relationship lasted until 1984. Since then, 'We've always kept in contact: she's a lawyer now. Medical negligence.'

After Greenham, Helen John's own life altered much less. When we spoke in 2011 she was seventy-four, but she looked younger, her face almost unlined, the slightly faraway grey-blue gaze I had seen in photos of her at Greenham exactly the same. She was on her way to RAF Waddington in Lincolnshire, where she was attempting to establish a peace camp to protest against the airbase's use for remote-controlled drone warfare in Afghanistan. It was November, and she had been camping on and off through the autumn on the windy flatlands outside the base, in a small tent on her own. Only a handful of local activists were offering support, but she seemed calm rather than frustrated, dressed in a thin green cagoule, voice measured as ever, like a religious person who believes that setbacks are simply tests of resolve and patience.

'Because nobody has been nuked for a long time, people have fallen asleep – they think it's not going to happen,' she said, as we skirted the vast base in her tiny car. But the weapons were just as terrifying a threat as in 1981, she pointed out: that morning the papers were full of stories about their possible production in Iran. She nodded at the airbase fence, and expertly switched the subject to drone warfare: 'Look at this beautiful countryside. They'll have young men sitting in there who'll be killing people 12,000 miles away. Cruise was the first of these stealth weapons.' Only twice did her almost mask-like face show feeling: when she talked about her Greenham relationship; and when she talked about the US. 'America, to me, is a vile and horrible military insanity. Decency – they have none. The Americans are the only people who've used nuclear weapons. And they have never removed themselves from one square inch of military land in Britain.'

In 1981, as winter approached at Greenham, Helen John's fierceness and obduracy, however simplistic – the Americans did occasionally relinquish their British bases – became increasingly central to the peace camp. Some of the women left after the first weekend. No timescale had been fixed for the protest, and few clear goals, except a demand that the new defence secretary John Nott take part in a televised debate with them about the cruise deployment – a demand which was ignored. Many of the protesters had lives outside Greenham to attend to. Pettitt herself was torn: 'I couldn't commit myself to staying,' she wrote, 'but I couldn't just walk away and say, "Oh well, we tried", either.' Like most of the other camp residents, she came and went.

Pettitt spent some of her time away talking to the press, trying to capitalize on their initial Greenham interest. As during the march, it was not an encouraging experience. In London she 'literally knocked on the plate-glass doors' of Fleet Street: 'Not one news editor would deign to send anyone down to Greenham.' Britain was a politically hectic place in 1981, jostling with protests and new and old interest groups trying to get attention. 'These things always fizzle out,' a world-weary young *Sun* reporter told Pettitt, after agreeing to talk to her in his newspaper's lobby. The journalists who did go to Greenham were mostly photographers, just wanting a snap of the chained-up women, not an explanation of the peace camp. After a week, the protesters mockingly acknowledged the limits of the chain stunt, replacing the tethered women with home-made dummies.

In October the weather turned. There was rain, wind, cold, mud. 'Helen remained indomitably cheerful, but some of the others fell out with her,' wrote Pettitt. 'She had an intense dislike of work rotas and would destroy these as fast as anyone . . . would devise them. She regarded people who talked about "taking decisions democratically" as fuss-pots who would never get anything done.' I asked Helen John whether she agreed with this portrayal. 'There were lots of people I couldn't get on with,' she said calmly. 'And lots of people who couldn't get on with me.'

By late October there were only two or three people living at the camp during the week. 'Sometimes I was the only one who was there,' John told me. Soon afterwards Pettitt began 'thinking [how] to persuade Helen to make some kind of dignified tactical retreat', such as 'hold a demonstration, block all the gates to the base, and then leave'.

There were also problems at the camp over the men. The few who had arrived as part of the march were intermittently joined by others, not all of them committed to world peace – 'undesirables from the town' in Pettitt's words. Helen John remembered, 'They stumbled in. To them it was a bit of a lark. Some of the lads wanted to buy a load of dope and cosy down for the winter.' In 1981 even well-heeled Newbury had an unemployment rate of 8 per cent and plenty of jobless escapists and drifters. Pettitt thought that all the men spent too much time strumming guitars and not enough contributing to the camp's domestic tasks. It was also increasingly felt by feminists at Greenham and beyond that the presence of men muddied the message. The protest had started billing itself as a 'Women's Peace Camp'. Finally, there was a growing feeling among the Greenham women that the phoney-war phase of relations with the authorities would soon end, and that men might be a liability in any confrontations, which the women were determined to keep non-violent. In February 1982, after days of meetings, to which several furious male peace activists contributed, the men living at Greenham were asked to leave. They did so. Outside male supporters of the camp were told that, while their donations were still welcome, they should not make any extended visits.

The same month, construction of the Greenham cruise-missile silos started. There would eventually be six, clustered in two rows of three at the southwestern end of the airbase, over a mile from the peace camp. From a distance, they were long and low, with shallow sloping sides covered in grass, like ziggurats or burial mounds: malign-looking, monumental, even a little beautiful. Beneath the grass were layers of clay, sand, concrete and titanium, designed to survive a nuclear detonation in the air above the base, or a direct hit by a 2,500-pound non-nuclear bomb. Inside each of these six shells was a series of rooms, the biggest the size of a bus garage, housing the twelve-wheeled juggernauts from which the missiles were fired, their ready-to-rise launch tubes as ribbed and phallic as any feminist peace propagandist could have hoped for. Each silo, manned by the 501st Tactical Missile Wing of the United States Air Force, also contained bedrooms, a loo, a lounge, and a communications room linked to NATO headquarters. One silo, write Wayne D. Cocroft and Roger J. C. Thomas in *Cold War: Building for Nuclear Confrontation*, 'was manned around the clock against the threat of pre-emptive nuclear attack. On warning of such attack, the vehicles within would have driven onto the airfield from where the missiles could be launched.'

The missiles themselves did not arrive at Greenham until November 1983. But well before then several other things about the silos became apparent. Their blank immensity and seeming impregnability made the peace camp look, by comparison, even more like the work of naive amateurs or heroic underdogs, depending on your political perspective. And while the silos were surrounded by a triple-layered fence, ten feet high and topped with razor wire, with strips of open land between the layers, a little like the killing zones along the Berlin Wall, the rest of the exposed airbase perimeter was much flimsier: a lower, single-layer fence of thin metal chainlink covered in plastic, which could easily be cut. Finally, the silos themselves, which had been erected on the site of an old American nuclear bomb store, situated as far as possible from the main airbase buildings, were in places only 20 or 30 yards from public land. That land was wooded, with plenty of cover for potential intruders.

At first, the silo construction was more of a problem than an opportunity for the protesters. Over a hundred British labourers, carpenters and steel specialists worked on the project. Further jobs and profit for the Newbury area came from a wider upgrade of the base, including extra sewerage to accommodate the thousand Americans of the 501st

Tactical Missile Wing. The town was not fussy about where its business came from: in 1982 a local firm designed and made £20 million of equipment for Russia's main gas pipeline.

The creation and early days of the peace camp were greeted locally with a mixture of curiosity and indifference. There were readers' letters in the *Newbury Weekly News* about nuclear weapons, yet most did not even mention the protest. The camp was only yards from the airbase's miniature American settlement, complete with Main Street, numbered streets from First to Sixth, and a military PX shop loaded with Midwestern treats; but otherwise the protesters had few immediate neighbours. The area fringing the common was more countryside than suburb.

Yet from late 1981 relations between the camp and the town began to worsen. On 1 October the *Newbury Weekly News* reported euphemistically that the district council had 'had numerous telephone calls and conversations' about the protest, and quoted the council chairman Frank Osgood: 'It would be nice if they were moved.' On 19 November, Helen John told the paper with typical frankness that in her experience local people found the protest 'rather strange and irresponsible'. In short, 'They think we are mad.'

On 21 January 1982 a spokesman from Newbury District Council told the *News*, 'We have given the women a reasonable amount of time to make their protest, but they are trespassing and must go.' He cited the council's previous removal of gypsy encampments from the common as a precedent. Soon afterwards the peace camp received its first eviction notice from the council. The protesters ignored it.

On 4 February the *News* printed its first reader's letter about Greenham, from one Julian Bridger:

> I drive past . . . [and] am fed up with seeing these women insulting our American friends and allies . . . Living off social security payments financed by over-burdened taxpayers like myself. When this 'fifth column' in our midst is eventually moved on I trust the council will make them pay for all the road traffic signs defaced with their slogans . . . I am all in favour of cruise missiles being based at the base. I only wish someone would drop one on the women's peace camp.

Bridger's views were a little extreme by local standards. But over the spring other letters to the *News* added further crude but potent brushstrokes to an emerging Greenham caricature. The women were 'squalid', 'outsiders', 'playing right into the hands of the international communist regime'. When they ventured into Newbury to mark the anniversary of the atom-bomb attack on Nagasaki (9 August 1982), and attempted to lay 100,000 stones on a war memorial to represent those killed, 'Housewives and war veterans . . . complained,' the *News* reported. 'A crowd gathered and the police feared a disturbance.' That did not happen – the Greenham women retreated – but 'a group of housewives and youths began sweeping [the stones] away with their bare hands'.

Back at the camp, after dark, the few remaining protesters sometimes received unwelcome visitors. 'They threw maggots onto our tents,' remembered Helen John, narrowing her eyes. 'And bags of pigs' blood. Tents got trampled. One sleeper got kicked in the face.'

Yet from late 1981 the positive response to Greenham strengthened too. In November, Pettitt arrived back at Greenham from Wales, expecting to have to persuade Helen John to wind up the peace camp, to find the protesters' portakabin crammed with sacks of mail from supporters. A few days later the left-wing press finally woke up to the camp's significance. The *Guardian* columnist Jill Tweedie, a fixture on the paper's widely read Women's Page since the 1960s, visited Greenham. Tweedie called herself 'a faint-hearted feminist', and the piece she produced began with characteristic ambivalence. 'It is a slight but definite shock to hear of women, mothers, who cut such atavistic bonds [at home], even for a short time, in the name of a greater good.' A less-than-flattering digression followed about other British women who had left their families, to follow the cultish, Rolls-Royce-driving Indian mystic Bhagwan Shree Rajneesh. But then the column gradually turned into an endorsement and an advertisement for Greenham: 'If you'd like to join them, bring [a] tent . . . and be prepared to contribute 50p a day. If you'd like to help, send donations . . . Urge those with caravans parked for the winter to park them at Greenham . . . They will be cherished.'

Newbury was an easy place for supporters and reporters to get to: right in the middle of southern England, close to several motorways, only three-quarters of an hour from London on a fast train. Even some journalists on right-wing papers now caught the Greenham bug. In December the London *Evening Standard* published 'Suppertime with Mrs Pettitt's Pickets', a faintly patronizing but sympathetic feature including a thought-provoking quote from Pettitt herself. Greenham, she said, 'wouldn't take on the male idea of a battle which could be "won" or "lost". Changing the situation will be a much more gradual process.'

In February 1982 the Labour leader Michael Foot visited the camp for the first time. Twenty-four years earlier he had been one of CND's founders; now, after many contortions, his party was in favour of unilateral nuclear disarmament. What this meant would be spelled out by the next Labour general-election manifesto, in 1983: 'Cancel the Trident programme, refuse to deploy cruise missiles and begin discussions for the removal of nuclear bases from Britain, which is to be completed within the lifetime of the Labour government.' Behind this iconoclastic stance were several forces: Foot's own beliefs; a shift against America within his party; and a transformation of the British peace movement itself.

For years the movement had seemed close to moribund. British anti-nuclear activism had first boomed in the late 1950s and early 1960s – the era of the Cuban Missile Crisis and other Cold War panics. But starting in the late 1960s, non-nuclear causes such as the Vietnam War drew away volunteers and energy. During the 1970s better relations between the superpowers, including some agreement to limit their nuclear arsenals, seemed to undermine CND's *raison d'être*. In 1972 even the *Guardian* mocked its annual London rally in Trafalgar Square as 'pitifully small': by this time CND had fewer than 2,000 members. In 1976 the peace movement's concerns had receded so far from the collective radical consciousness that a rare article in the feminist magazine *Spare Rib* mentioning 'nuclear war' turned out to be about conflict in nuclear families.

British women had been prominent in 1950s peace campaigning, often outnumbering men, but had been gradually pushed aside in the early CND hierarchy. Many then found 1960s and 1970s feminism of more relevance to their lives. In the late 1970s, as Pettitt's experiences in Wales demonstrated, it was anxiety about nuclear power, not nuclear weapons, that first began to attract women, and men, back to the anti-nuclear cause. Much of this happened through groups like hers that formed outside CND, which was widely – and often correctly – regarded as bureaucratic, stale and cautious in its tactics, and living off former glories. When Pettitt contacted CND about her planned anti-cruise march, hoping to get financial support, 'We were ignored, patronized, rebuffed. The general attitude was, "Who the hell are you?"' When she persisted, and secured a hearing at CND headquarters in London, the official she saw constantly interrupted their meeting to answer the phone.

But during 1980 and 1981 CND revived. Thanks to the renewed East–West confrontation, the publication of E. P. Thompson's 'Protest and Survive', and the controversy over cruise, membership began growing again. Younger, fresher activists rose rapidly through the hierarchy, such as the anti-cruise organizer Joan Ruddock, who was elected CND chair in November 1981. For the first time since the 1960s, public events put on by CND were dynamic occasions, and of interest to the outside world. In October 1980 its annual rally drew 80,000 people: a crowd many times its membership, and the first big attendance for a decade and a half. Fashionable rock bands such as the Pop Group and Killing Joke played clanging, thrillingly apocalyptic songs to a Trafalgar Square thick with young faces – the rally was a site of political possibility again, rather than somewhere for melancholy old peaceniks to go through the motions. The following year, CND seized an opportunity to stitch itself into British youth culture: Glastonbury.

Like CND, the festival had had a bad 1970s. The idyllic first gatherings at Michael Eavis's lush Somerset farm in 1970 and 1971 had been followed by a long hiatus, partly down to the difficulties of staging a growing event, and also to Eavis's ambivalence about some of the freaks and wanderers that adventurous 1970s festivals attracted. In 1978 a bedraggled convoy from a washed-out Summer Solstice celebration at nearby Stonehenge arrived at his farm, and Eavis was arm-twisted by the police and others into putting on an impromptu festival remembered mainly for its grey skies and sense of the British counter-culture treading water.

In 1979 a more elaborate festival was held regardless, in aid of the

United Nations' Year of the Child, and it was an almost unqualified disaster. In keeping with Margaret Thatcher's election that year, Eavis formed a company to run the event. Festival-goers were charged £5, Glastonbury's first substantial entry fee. Yet the long weekend made a loss of £49,000, according to the historians of the festival Crispin Aubrey and John Shearlaw, thanks to a fatal combination of organizational 'airy-fairyness' and 'gangster types' getting involved in running the entrance gates. The company collapsed soon afterwards.

In 1980 there was no festival. Instead Eavis helped set up a Somerset CND group, partly because of the cruise issue. He decided to try again with the festival the following year, to professionalize it once and for all, and to offer CND the profits. This was not pure altruism: 'With CND on board, there [would be] a huge source of willing volunteers to man the pay-lanes and to do the stewarding and the car-parking,' wrote Andrew Kerr, a long-standing Glastonbury organizer. The CND bureaucracy would provide an administrative machine the festival lacked, and the anti-nuclear cause would give Glastonbury a sense of purpose and a sharper public image. Younger, more politicized bands – of which there was a rare glut in 1980 and 1981 – would be keen to come and play. Finally, the festival would gain access to CND's fast-growing mailing list, and be able to advertise to a new generation: less tie-dyed, more engaged, more youthful. In short, working with CND would enable Glastonbury to modernize and become a proper business, albeit a charitable one. 'In a way, CND made Glastonbury,' writes George McKay in the most official of the festival's histories.

In October 1980 Eavis went to the CND rally in London and then straight to CND headquarters with his proposal. A deal was concluded: the 1981 event was officially named the Glastonbury CND Festival. Even more musicians than usual wanted to play: the CND official who kept interrupting Pettitt was fielding their calls.

In the end, she had winkled a £250 cheque for her march out of an old contact at CND headquarters. Meanwhile in Somerset that spring, Eavis formed a construction crew out of the local jobless. 'A good thing to get people off the streets,' he announced, with puritanical vigour – his father, like Margaret Thatcher's, was a Methodist preacher. Then Eavis had them build a new version of the Pyramid

Stage, Glastonbury's traditional centrepiece, out of old telegraph poles and corrugated metal sheeting. Perhaps a little insensitively for a peace festival, he had bought the sheeting from the Ministry of Defence, which had been using it as reinforcing material for ammunition depots. But he also agreed to have the new stage topped with a mighty CND logo, 9 feet in diameter, each of its ribs as thick as a person. It proved too heavy to lift, and was left onstage for the festival performances, dwarfing the musicians.

Some of the Glastonbury old guard disliked the festival's politicization. What had been a hazily defined free-for-all, escapist, hedonistic, psychedelic, New Agey, its original Pyramid Stage carefully sited near a ley line, now had a specific and forbidding issue looming over it that not all the festival-goers wanted to be reminded about. But Eavis persisted. At the 1981 festival, among the sun-scorched fields and the craft stalls, the self-probing singer-songwriters and the cosmic rock veterans, there was a CND marquee. It showed a continuous loop of the *The War Game* (not to be confused with the 1983 anti-nuclear movie *WarGames*), a terrifyingly realistic television drama about a nuclear attack on Kent, which had been made in 1965 but never broadcast in Britain on account of its rawness. On the Pyramid Stage, the CND general secretary Bruce Kent spoke for half an hour one evening. The Thompson Twins, then a clattery, earnest young band, played what was billed as 'No Nukes Music!' E. P. Thompson also spoke. 'The whole festival had this CND bit speckled through it,' remembered Mark Hollingsworth, a precocious twenty-four-year-old management graduate whom Eavis had hired to help make the sprawling hybrid work. Mixing music and leftish politics had already been successfully tried in Britain during the late 1970s by the Rock Against Racism campaign, but its events had been briefer and more one-dimensional – bands and little else. Hollingsworth, a friend and distant relation of Eavis, had seen the chaos of the old Glastonbury at first hand, and choreographed the festival as precisely and subtly as he could. 'CND got what Mercedes and Coca-Cola would now call good brand associations from the event,' he told me, 'although we didn't have those words then.' For the first time, Glastonbury made a profit. '1981 was our breakthrough,' Eavis told McKay. Afterwards the festival gave CND £14,000.

For the next six years Glastonbury happened every summer without fail. Each time the attendance was bigger, the bands' hair shorter, the CND branding more ubiquitous – badges, car stickers, festival programme inserts – and the donation to CND larger. The festival quickly became the organization's most lucrative fund-raising event. Beyond Glastonbury, throughout these years, CND and peace activism grew into a kind of 1980s counter-culture. It had its own national network – a teeming 1987 CND Scrapbook featured anti-nuclear groups from Shetland to Windsor; its own celebrity supporters – U2, Susannah York, Harold Pinter; its own, ever vaster public gatherings – CND's 1981 London rally attracted 250,000 people and had to be moved to Hyde Park; its own conventional wisdoms – the malignancy of Thatcher and America as well as of nuclear weapons; and its own converts in unlikely places, including one of the chancellor's children.

In his memoirs, Geoffrey Howe recalls that his son Alec was a CND member while at York University. For a protest in December 1980, Alec 'was to have dressed up as US President-elect Ronald Reagan, and to have led through the streets of York, by a noose tied around her neck, a female student dressed and made up as Margaret Thatcher'. The browbeaten chancellor might have had similar feelings towards the prime minister, somewhere deep down, but when news of the planned demonstration and his son's CND membership got out, Howe was publicly embarrassed and Alec had to be dissuaded. Later he took part in a toned-down version of the march anyway.

Anti-nuclear ideas seeped into other unlikely parts of the British establishment. By the mid-1980s even the public school in Marlborough, the prim town where the Greenham women had surreptitiously bought their chains and padlocks in the late summer of 1981, had a Peace Society. As a sixth-former there, on a scholarship, with my minor social and material resentments towards richer peers beginning to turn into an interest in left-wing politics, I went to a few meetings. The society was run by 'Miss Russell', a rare female teacher at the school, slightly austere and androgynous in appearance, with John Lennon glasses and short hair and a faintly disapproving air towards the institution around her. We mocked her behind her back, but were also intrigued: '*She's* been to Greenham Common.'

*

In 1987 the left-wing feminist Beatrix Campbell published a characteristically stern book about the readiness of women to vote for the right in Britain, a phenomenon that was more marked than in comparable countries. Its one more upbeat section was about Greenham and the peace movement. 'Nuclear politics were possibly the only aspect of the national agenda not defined by Thatcherism,' wrote Campbell. She interviewed well-off Tory women about the peace camp and found, as well as horror at its muddle and earnestness and subordination of family life, a degree of admiration – even jealousy.

In October 1981 Ann Pettitt addressed the quarter of a million people at the CND rally in Hyde Park. 'I never wrote anything down,' she recollected later about this and many subsequent speeches. 'I thought about what I wanted to say . . . [before] memorizing the beginning and the end and leaving the middle to whatever came into my head.'

The Greenham women took bigger and bigger risks over the following year. In August 1982 they invaded the airbase for the first time. At the main gates, in brazen mid-morning sunshine, 'We ran in, all very nervous,' Helen John remembered. 'We ran at the sentry box. He ran out . . . with his arms out to stop us, like a goalkeeper. I just fell about laughing. I couldn't run any more. He grabbed me by the scruff of the neck and said, "Come on, Mrs John, you don't want to be ridiculous." I said, "I do want to be ridiculous!" Meanwhile the others occupied the sentry box. That was the first time we were arrested.'

A very public cycle was now set in motion, involving dozens of further incursions and hundreds more arrests; dozens of court appearances and failed peace-camp evictions; mass convictions and dozens of brief imprisonments; feelings of martyrdom and defiant returns to Greenham; followed by more incursions. 'The escalation was completely haphazard,' Helen John told me. 'It was improvisation. People would have an idea, and act on it. As long as you were completely non-violent, and took full responsibility for your actions, you could do it.'

On 5 October twenty women got into ditches that had been dug just outside the base to hold new sewage pipes for the coming American garrison. They wove a vast spider's web of wool and string across the ditches, entangled themselves in it, and lay down. 'While I was being dragged off' by the police, wrote one of the participants, Jane Lockwood, in her diary, 'I [deliberately] went completely limp . . . We were all cautioned . . . Workmen appeared and began hammering wooden posts into the ground to line up the trench. Action again! A group of women ran back on to the site and removed the posts . . . and a hammer, which was lobbed into the bushes.'

That winter the peace camp's cleverness and cheek, and the authorities' apparent helplessness before it, reached a peak. First, on 12 December, the protesters managed to encircle their massive neighbour by mobilizing 30,000 women to hold hands around the airbase perimeter. Then, on 1 January 1983, the peace camp filled the usual festive-season news vacuum by getting four dozen women into the silo complex itself. Hiding ladders and bolt cutters in the woods beside its supposedly unscalable fence, they waited until just before dawn. Then they scrambled over before the base security could spot them. Raissa Page, a sympathetic freelance photographer, accompanied them. A deftly composed picture of a ring of women, holding hands on top of a silo, their silhouettes tauntingly triumphant in the airbase's lights, police cars slewed to a stop impotently below them, appeared in newspapers around the world. For sixteen months at Greenham, a small group of rebellious citizens had made fools of the state. It was an achievement any true Tory libertarian ought to have appreciated.

PART FOUR

Revolution in the Head

9
Secret Thatcherites

Between 1980 and early 1982 so many politicians and economists, patriotic film-makers and admen, peace activists and royalists, businessmen and rioters were groping towards their own new versions of Britain. But in some other areas of British life, ignored or little noticed by Westminster and by state-of-the-nation columnists, the change had gone much further: a different country, the one we inhabit now, was already fast coming into being. One such area was music.

In late 1980, a couple of weeks before Christmas, as the then profitable and powerful music press was about to settle back into its customary semi-holiday of end-of-year charts and self-congratulatory retrospectives on the rise of acts that it had championed, Paul Morley of the *New Musical Express* went to a pub in the scuffed north London suburb of Kilburn to interview a band from Sheffield. Vice Versa had been around for almost three years: angular young men playing fast, severe, slightly studenty songs. 'Artist at War' and 'Trapped in Celluloid' were typical titles. Their sound was bolted together from buzzing early synthesizers, thudding basic drum machines and even stiffer chanted vocals. Since the late 1970s this sort of skeletal, often portentous, sometimes beautiful music, frequently from the increasingly hollowed-out cities of the north of England, and labelled industrial or postpunk by trendsetting music journalists who had tired of the cartoonish roar of the mid-1970s punk movement, had been a hip, if minority, taste in British pop.

Vice Versa had made a modest name for themselves, in Sheffield and beyond. They had released a cassette and two singles. None had got anywhere near the Top 40, but postpunk and industrial bands were not generally interested in mass sales, or at least claimed not to be; innovation and critical acclaim were more important currencies. Some of Vice Versa's songs had been played by John Peel, BBC Radio 1's great validator and popularizer of adventurous music. Meanwhile the group had done brief shows at cultish venues in Sheffield and London, and Rotterdam in Holland, dressed in close-fitting grey and black, clustered tightly behind their keyboards and microphones, their body language a mixture of the statuesque and the manic. Morley came to one performance. Vice Versa's 'stage presence was volatile, music excitable and intentions dramatic,' he wrote approvingly in the *NME* afterwards.

During the late 1970s and early 1980s the *NME* sold almost as many copies as *The Times*: between 200,000 and 270,000 weekly. And such was the cachet of the *NME* and music journalism generally, and the scarcity of other sources of proper discussion and information about pop music and wider pop culture, it was estimated by the music paper that each of its wordy A3 copies was devoured by ten people – I was one of them – perhaps a majority of the entire population of earnest Britons in their teens and twenties.

Morley was one of the paper's most important writers. In 1980 he was a garrulous, young-looking twenty-three-year-old, but he had already been writing for the *NME* for four years, and for his own self-published music magazine, or fanzine, *Out There*, for several years before that. His prose had an intoxicating fizz – adjectives and assertions bubbling through alliterative, multi-clause sentences, with shoals of commas barely keeping order; and a precocious authority, based on a teenage immersion in cultural and media theorists such as Marshall McLuhan, while working in a bookshop instead of going to university. There was also, sometimes, a darkness just below the surface. Morley's father had killed himself in 1977. Some of Morley's best-known writing had been about Joy Division, the most gorgeous and successful, but also the bleakest, of all the postpunk bands. Their singer Ian Curtis had committed suicide in May 1980.

Seven months later, when he went to meet Vice Versa in Kilburn, Morley was even hungrier than usual for the fresh emotions and ideas that he believed pop music was uniquely able to convey. For one thing, the postpunk trend was now three years old – a near-eternity in the fast-moving, fickle world of British music at the time. 'There was a sense that something had failed in the air by 1980,' as Morley put it to me. 'There had been an incredible eruption in '76, '77, '78' – he meant punk and early postpunk – 'that seemed to be changing everything. And then [in 1980] we were kind of back to where we were.' In the *NME* that December he was more explicit: 'While the pop charts have been smoothed down, and have become harder to penetrate, at the other extreme the new underground has settled in place. A stern circuit of protest and featureless tenacity . . . It has given groups a false sense of security, a low sight to aim for.' He derided 'the hippies in the [music] establishment . . . so deeply rooted and so widespread', and the whole 'rock'n'roll way of working: the futile toiling, the dirty gigs, the crippling routines, the weak style, the limited language, that whole senseless draft and duty.' Finally, he had tired of the pessimistic, usually left-wing sentiments of punk and postpunk: 'You can't moan all the time.'

But when he met Vice Versa that month, Morley got a small shock regardless. 'I sat down,' he told me, 'and they said, "Oh by the way, we're called ABC."' Fairly established three-year-old bands didn't change their names very often. And, as the rest of the interview quickly made obvious, the band had changed a lot more than just its name. Martin Fry had been one of Vice Versa's keyboardists: tall, acne-scarred, and slightly wooden onstage, where he would stoop concentratedly over his instrument, repeatedly push back his curtain of hair, or sometimes let his hands hang limp by his sides, all the while wearing a slightly uptight polo neck under a V-neck jumper. Now he was ABC's singer and joint spokesman. His hair had been trimmed: a debonair blond diagonal fell across his forehead, emphasizing the jut of his jaw. And he was suddenly full of swaggering talk. 'I want the music to be more sex, more exertion on the part of both parties – player and listener. The death of . . . that dreary attitude,' he began, in a sort of declamatory shorthand, eerily similar to Morley's own writing at its bossiest. 'We want . . . five singles in the Top Ten,' explained ABC's saxophone player Stephen Singleton, more concretely.

With Vice Versa, Fry went on, 'We were not achieving what we wanted to . . . We were not . . . progressing. We were frustrating ourselves.' He dismissed his old band's austere aesthetic and reputation: 'Words like "artistic integrity" are meaningless these days. It's got to be colour, dance, excitement.' Changing from Vice Versa into ABC, he and Singleton summed up, was going 'from Matt to Gloss'. They extended the consumerist, leftie-baiting analogy: ABC was 'a new brand name'. They even proposed that their band was part of a bigger cultural and social trend. They called it 'the new optimism'.

Amid all this rather cryptic bravado were a few airy generalizations about what ABC would actually sound like. They would be less abstract than Vice Versa, less European, less influenced by icy continental electronic artists such as Kraftwerk; and more American instead, informed by earthier musics such as soul and funk. Fry and Singleton would not, and probably could not, be any more specific: ABC hadn't yet recorded anything.

In the pub in Kilburn, Morley took some minutes to take it all in. 'I could tell he was like, "What's this?"' Fry remembered. But then it dawned on Morley that ABC might be part of the new thing he was looking for, an alternative to both 'smoothed down' mainstream pop – in 1980 Olivia Newton-John and ABBA had British number ones – and the increasingly ghettoized 'moan' of punk and postpunk; or rather, a new music that would somehow combine the best qualities of all of them; and that, to his excitable, culture-saturated, twenty-three-year-old mind at least, would have major social consequences. 'My attitude was, if we want to change the world, let's have every song in the Top 40 with real intelligence – because that will influence people to think differently.'

Morley combined his ABC material with interviews with two other mouthy newish bands, Essential Bop and Restricted Code – both as badly named as Vice Versa and now even more forgotten – and expanded it all into a staccato 4,000-word essay-cum-manifesto, which the *NME* published on 20 December 1980. 'There is definitely a new mood spreading,' he wrote. 'Towards an overground brightness . . . Modern excitement . . . choice and value.' In increasingly Thatcherite-sounding language, highly provocative in the context – the *NME* had an overwhelmingly Labour-voting staff and readership – Morley praised ABC for 'getting stuck in' and 'getting on with the job'. The band were 'highly organized'. They 'know that image . . . is all important'. They 'want a big display in the supermarkets, not to be stuck on a high shelf in the corner shop'. Morley conceded, 'ABC talk too much. But . . . something can happen in 1981.'

His piece did not change pop music overnight. The *NME* half-buried it on pages 26 to 28, and gave it the bland contents-page billing of 'Three For '81?' Fry and Singleton went back to Sheffield, and started turning ABC into more than rhetoric.

In 1981 this alternately hard-edged and leafy south Yorkshire city, with its muscular skyline of Victorian spikes and municipal slabs, its green hills and strangling ring road, was a surprisingly good place to hothouse an exotic new avant-pop hybrid. Fry had moved to Sheffield five years before to study English literature at the university. Graduating in 1979, he had thought about becoming a journalist – 'I went to the *Guardian* office in Manchester, and did a little tour' – but had settled instead for life on the dole in Sheffield, 'daydreaming about forming a band', and setting up a short-lived fanzine, *Modern Drugs*, in which he cast a sometimes harsh eye over those who already had. The local economy was beginning to struggle badly as the city's famous steel industry contracted, squeezed by foreign competition. By the early 1980s, frightening new social problems such as mass joblessness and – not unrelated – heroin addiction coexisted in the city with old-fashioned provincial rigidities. 'If you sat in some guy's [habitual] seat in a pub,' Fry told me, 'when he came in, he'd expect you to get up – because he was going to play dominos there that night.' Yet in other ways Sheffield was good for would-be bohemians. 'The buses were only 10p. Distances are short. There were loads of music venues, and loads of empty workshops left over from the cutlery business. Bands used them as really cheap rehearsal space.'

The Human League, Heaven 17, Cabaret Voltaire, Clock DVA: Sheffield was buzzing with futuristic new groups, some following the same dystopian path as Vice Versa, others, like ABC, wandering off it in search of warmer territories. The latter approach was a risk. 'What if nobody likes what you're doing?' Fry remembered thinking. 'John Peel was going to play the next Vice Versa record . . . But we locked ourselves away in a terraced house in a derelict crescent, where you could make as much noise as you wanted. We rehearsed day and night, wrote songs . . . And we bought cycling tops. They were the brightest things we could find. It was to get away from the black, the long grey raincoats, the whole style of the times.' For an *NME* photo shoot, the band posed in a Sheffield gym. Still talking in upbeat sound-bites three decades later, Fry explained the symbolism to me: 'We're not in a nightclub, we're not in a bar. It's not sleazy. The drugs' – punk and postpunk had been awash with them – 'are over. This is much more . . . optimistic. And a sign that ABC are going to physically move around, on the dance floor. And try to *compete*. Trying to compete was an old showbusiness idea; but I think it was also a prevailing mood. In Britain in '81, it was just there.'

In October, ABC released their first single. 'Tears Are Not Enough' certainly sounded like the product of hard graft. Gone was all Vice Versa's aggression and distortion; in its place was a clean, choppy, completely different sound, with non-electronic instruments – guitar, bass and drums – striving to be as slick as the American funk and disco bands such as the Jackson 5 that Fry idolized. Over this calculatedly commercial backing he sang in a highly stylized, theatrical voice: sometimes deep and almost spoken, sometimes a slightly strained falsetto. The lyrics, which he had co-written after being dropped by a girlfriend, were an intriguing mixture of malice, hurt and self-consciousness – 'Excuses had their uses/But now they're all used up' – as if Fry was an old-fashioned, world-weary romantic who had also read Roland Barthes, in particular the French semiotician's voguish 1977 book *A Lover's Discourse*.

On *Top of the Pops*, Fry wore a white evening shirt with a dark but spangly suit – again the feel was traditional glamour in quotation marks – and danced in a cautious, heavy-shouldered sway. Filmed mostly from below, he looked handsome and commanding, even faintly aristocratic, with his flicked blond fringe and a stage sneer, but not yet completely fluent in his new role. The song, for all its energy, sounded similarly undercooked. It got to number nineteen in the charts: respectable but not quite one of the big hits Singleton had promised *NME* readers almost a year before.

Despite all their rehearsing, ABC were never, realistically, going to match the decades-drilled grooves of their American heroes. 'Our musicianship was OK,' said Fry. 'We got by.' So instead they further played up ABC's theatricality and knowingness. Fry loved old Hollywood films, and the band decided to present themselves as 'almost from the 30s, the 40s. I'm there as the crooner . . . the matinee idol. People wanted that in Britain in the early 80s. They wanted a strong figure. They wanted individuals. They wanted heroes.'

On the sleeve of ABC's 1982 debut album, *The Lexicon of Love* – a distinctly Barthesian title – Fry held a gun and a girl, while dressed like a 1930s private eye in waistcoat and tie. His sense of cultural timing was good: the big film of the previous year, in both Britain and America, had been *Raiders of the Lost Ark*, an equally knowing homage to the adventure fictions of the 1930s. Dashing male characters were back in fashion, after the doubting, mumbling anti-heroes of 1970s movies.

For most of the album, ABC changed their sound again. In late 1981, despite their stop-start development, they had been signed up by a major record company, Phonogram. After responding too slowly to punk and postpunk, such conglomerates were now desperately eager to catch the next British pop wave, whatever it was. ABC used their new status and budget to hire a rising English record producer, Trevor Horn, who was known for the intricacy and lavishness of his productions. Horn did not disappoint them. He helped conjure a quick succession of singles: 'Poison Arrow', released in February 1982, 'The Look of Love', in May, and 'All of My Heart', in August. The songs swooned and thundered with a drama rarely heard in pop since the heyday of the great American orchestral alchemist Phil Spector in the 1960s. They were concise, no more than four minutes long, but the songs moved quickly and smoothly between sparseness and overripeness, between sly, riddling verses and addictive choruses, between desolation and euphoria. Lonely keyboard notes acted as curtain-raisers, guitars echoed in the distance, the bass prowled; then drums crashed, horns surged, and strings rose in humming clouds. Above it all, Fry sang with a new conviction, domineering and loud. He remembered, 'We used to say to each other, "If people listen to the songs on rollerskates on a Walkman, they'll just shit themselves and fall over." That was our dream.'

In 1982 I didn't have a Walkman yet, even though Sony's individualistic electronic miracle had been on sale in Britain since 1980, but I got my first radio just before 'Poison Arrow' came out. Listening to pop music quickly became important, and not just because I was twelve. My family had recently moved to a new, much smaller army house, a semi on a dull, deserted-seeming military estate in Surrey, just outside London, so that my father could commute to a new job in equipment procurement at the Ministry of Defence, which in peace-time seemed a bit bureaucratic and banal. He left early, returned late, and didn't like London; I spent a lot of hours in my bedroom with Radio 1. 'Poison Arrow' was one of the first pop songs I fell in love with: its rich sound, but also its romantic but arch words, which were appealing to an almost-teenager who did not yet want to deal too directly with girls.

All three singles made the Top 10. Yet ABC's rush of success was not just down to radio. It was also down to a fresh medium, the pop video. Films to promote songs and bands had been around for decades – the Beatles' *A Hard Day's Night* in 1964 had been one of the first – yet they had generally been one-offs or novelties, rarely central to the workings of the pop marketplace. Then *Top of the Pops* began showing videos more regularly in the late 1970s, bands began making them more often and more inventively, and in August 1981 a whole American channel devoted to the form was launched: Music Television, MTV for short.

ABC's interest in the visual, and films in particular, made them enthusiastic participants. For *The Look of Love*, 'We went to the meeting where the director made his pitch to us, and he said something like, "I want to film a lizard with a gold chain and a diamond-encrusted bracelet,"' Fry remembered. 'And we went, "No. We want it to be like *An American in Paris* [the 1951 Hollywood musical]. And Benny Hill. And that's it – whatever you say." If I'd said, "I want to be covered in ice cream," they wouldn't have said no, because we were on a roll.'

The resulting video was a riotous, cartoonish carousel of images: a clown, a juggler, a muscleman, funhouse mirrors, multiple femmes fatale, a Punch and Judy show, a pair of naughty boys in lederhosen, a singing, levitating nun, and the band dressed in straw boaters and striped blazers, like characters from the American musical – or like Etonians at their annual Fourth of June carnival. Paul Morley even appeared. 'I was probably doing an interview with him,' Fry half-remembered, 'and said, "We're doing a video tomorrow, why don't you come down?"' Morley played a foxy-looking youth wearing a gold lamé suit, the same kind of suit that Fry had worn in ABC's previous video. The whole thing was intoxicatingly self-referential and clever and, if you saw it too often, verging on claustrophobic and smug. 'We didn't want it to look like real life,' said Fry. 'We wanted visual gag after visual gag. We wanted to have a party. To show people having fun.' He paused. 'MTV *hammered* it.' The single got to number eighteen in the American charts, thrillingly high for a little-known and brainy British band. Shortly afterwards, in 1983, ABC toured the United States. In New York, Fry was told, 'Andy Warhol wants to meet you. Come round to the Factory.'

That same year Morley left the *NME*. Bullishly switching from participant-observer to proper pop player, he set up a record company with Trevor Horn and Horn's wife and manager, Jill Sinclair. Zang Tuum Tumb – the spelling varied – was named after a seventy-year-old avant-garde poem by Filippo Tommaso Marinetti, the Italian Futurist and, later, Fascist. But the project quickly became known as ZTT. 'All company names were initials then,' Morley explained to me. The enterprise had other orthodox business influences: 'I was inspired by entrepreneurs. I thought they were showmen, just like writers and artists were – people who created events and performances. And I worked very closely at ZTT with Jill, who was a proper entrepreneur. I remember we were filmed once for a BBC Newsnight special, and I was talking about a black and white video I wanted to make, and she said in the background, "We're not the Arts Council, you know." It was about making money.'

During the early 1980s such talk went from heresy to orthodoxy for a startling number of arty British pop musicians. 'I want success,' Adam Ant – once an obscure punk singer, now a teenage pin-up – told his instant biographers Fred and Judy Vermorel in 1981. 'Cult is just a safe word meaning "loser".' Boy George, once a squatter and night-club adventurer, now a mainstream star with his sugary band Culture Club, told Morley in May 1982: 'With the punk thing everyone was making impractical attacks on being rich . . . But they all wanted to be rich. You have to be. I've got plenty of money . . . And I worked for it, really hard.'

In June 1981 the shrewd journalist Mark Ellen wrote in *Smash Hits*, an unashamedly commercial pop magazine founded in 1978 that was now beginning to erode the *NME*'s dominance:

> Even two years ago, the notion of an 'artist' being a businessman was considered almost immoral and only associated with balding, middle-aged supergroups who spent more time making investments than making albums . . . [But now] Adam Ant admires [his fellow star] Gary Numan . . . for the simple reason that, 'business-wise, he's one of the forerunners in being in control of your own destiny.' Adam extends the idea of being in control as far as designing (or at least, approving) every Ants record sleeve, T-shirt, badge, poster and sticker. And he never drinks . . . 'In my business you have to have a very clear mind.'

In August 1982, in *The Face*, another newish, shiny, successful magazine with few hang-ups about the increasingly mercantile quality of British pop, Culture Club's drummer Jon Moss extrapolated from the state of music into the state of the nation.

'I think that people feel that despite the economic situation they're more than capable of doing things,' he said. 'People are digging in and working harder.'

'Do you approve?' asked his interviewer.

'Yes, very much so! Last year it was nightclubbing, staying out all night, drugs, sex, general decadence and "fuck it, enjoy yourself, bollocks to everything." This year people are . . . watering down their attitudes. They're taking a clearer look at themselves and what's going on.'

Moss and Numan were openly Conservative voters and relatively mainstream musicians. But more daring, politically ambiguous pop figures had developed a fascination with the corporate world too. John Lydon, previously Johnny Rotten, the ragged, nihilistic singer of the Sex Pistols, named his next band Public Image Ltd as early as 1978. For their first album cover, despite the ferocious music inside, they wore not shredded punk clothes but boardroom-ready suits. They were not a band, announced Lydon, but a communications company. In 1979 they began using a logo – the letters PiL, cleanly typeset and placed carefully on a slant across a black and white circle – that would have been crisp and memorable enough to sell soap.

Heaven 17, ABC's Sheffield peers and rivals, went further, filling the record sleeves and videos for their swaggering funk tunes with executive jets, office towers, secretaries and sales charts, and pin-striped band members sporting briefcases and oiled-back banker haircuts. The band insisted that the imagery was meant to be ambiguous rather than celebratory: founder member Martyn Ware said he was a Benn supporter. But in the *NME* in March 1982 he dismissed the 'antique image of rock musicians as . . . tortured artists . . . If you work with a record company, you create music to make a living . . . The best and least hypocritical way of doing that is to act as a business.' When recording a song, he went on, it was up to 'the individual' to 'excel themselves and surpass' others. 'They can't sit back.'

Bands who did not get with the programme suddenly found the music press's favour withdrawn. Gang of Four were an astringent quartet from Leeds, named after the infamous 1960s and 1970s Chinese Communist Party faction and not the SDP's rather less ruthless founders. From 1978 to 1980 they had been one of the hippest bands in Britain, honing a highly original version of rock music that combined a brittle, tense sound with lyrics that managed to critique modern consumer capitalism and how it poisoned personal relationships, without being either dull or simplistic. Gang of Four were stars of Rock Against Racism in the late 1970s, and their politically committed music seemed perfectly attuned to the period's wider concerns. But by 1982 the cultural climate, and the once-adoring *NME*, had shifted. 'As an ideological rock band, the Gang are by definition in trouble,' began an interview with them in the paper that May, written by the pragmatic music-press veteran Charles Shaar Murray. 'Rock and ideology both being more than a little out of favour at the moment . . .'

A week earlier the band's latest single, a lecture on the dangerous attractions of militarism titled 'I Love a Man in Uniform' – which, in Britain in the spring of 1982, would turn out to be rather timely – had been reviewed contemptuously by Murray's *NME* colleague Gavin Martin: 'So what is the purpose of bringing political discussion into pop music? Does anyone still listen to this . . . for pleasure, or is it more out of a sense of duty?' Martin made the escapist whirl of 'The Look of Love' his Single of the Week instead.

Thirty years later, I asked Morley whether something had been lost when British pop turned glossy in the early 1980s. We were in a north London pub, only a few miles from the one where he had gone to meet Vice Versa in December 1980. We had already been talking for an hour. Morley, still a prolific pop writer, still stubbly and mischievous-looking, still having ideas slightly quicker than even his fast mouth could carry them, had been carving and massaging the air above our table with his pale hands, as if he could pull some perfect pop genre out of thin air.

But at my question he became stiller and graver. 'I always took it for granted,' he said, 'that anyone who was doing anything interesting in that world was going to be of what we call the left . . . But we were living in a time when the left, obviously in a way, had failed. Political campaigns seemed to me fraught with problems. I was committed to ultimately the same ends as those who were more directly politically involved on the left. But I was more interested in the politics of the imagination . . . in trying to keep alive the spirit of the left through the art . . . through the way that a record sleeve was [designed] . . . The better works were going to encourage people to think about better things, to . . . want a better world.'

It seemed a very vague sort of leftism. And wasn't setting up a company, especially in early Thatcherite England, a vaguely political act of a different sort? 'No, no,' Morley said immediately. 'I wouldn't say I went into ZTT with a hardcore political understanding of what it was to be an entrepreneur.' At the time, he insisted, he had seen the company more as a continuation of the 1960s counterculture, as a naughty cultural experiment. He cited ZTT's biggest success, the outrageous *Frankie Goes To Hollywood*, and in particular their second single, 'Two Tribes', in 1984: 'I loaded it with iconography about nuclear war. I even put a colour ad for it in *Smash Hits*, and all it did was tell you how many nuclear warheads America and Russia had. And it was Number One for nine weeks, and there was part of me that thought, "Yes, this is it: provocative entertainment."' He stopped. 'And then the Number One after that? George Michael. Soft sentimental ballad. It hit me between the eyes, winded me. I realized that people just buy records, of all sorts.' He grinned. 'I was probably a bit over-involved in the state of pop music.'

When I saw Martin Fry a few weeks later, he was more forthcoming about the implications of his early 1980s activities. Like Morley, he was still making a good living from pop music. With neat symmetry, his house was in Kilburn. The area was a little less scuffed these days, and Fry's Edwardian terrace, on a long, dappled side street, was broad-shouldered and discreetly plush, with perfect paintwork and floors. We met in the middle of a Friday morning, and Fry was padding around, shoeless, a trim middle-aged man in Prada jeans with a pop-festival performance that weekend to save his energy for. 'I'm making more money now than in the 80s,' he said. 'Then, I was endlessly paying back record company advances.' ABC, and *The Lexicon of Love* in particular, remained a big live draw.

At first, Fry insisted – like Morley – that his early 1980s adventures had nothing to do with Thatcherism. 'When Thatcher was elected in '79 . . . I just thought it meant reactionary times. Those [fears] were my politics.' Yet, unprompted, he kept coming back to the topic. 'A lot of the things that were happening in the 1980s were benefiting me,' he said a few minutes later. 'People were spending more money, more people were buying records after the dark end of the 70s. Our audience was changing, getting wealthier. British pop went around the world.'

He paused. 'I didn't know what to think. I was ambivalent about it. Sheff was hurting, still. When I got back there from America, it was really depressing. Part of it was exhaustion – I'd been the little gold lamé puppet everybody wanted to meet. But also I didn't understand why life was still so hard in Sheff. They weren't going punting or drinking cocktails. You'd drive down the motorway near Sheff in 1984, and the police would stop you, because they were battling the miners. That was why we didn't follow *The Lexicon of Love* with *The Lexicon of Love Part Two*, which ABC's record company wanted. It felt wrong to do another glossy, escapist kind of record.'

Instead the band's second album, *Beauty Stab*, released in late 1983, was pared back to a plain rock sound and self-consciously crammed with songs about greed and unemployment. In places, it even sounded faintly like Gang of Four. But it lacked their fire and precision, and sold only moderately. 'I can understand how with the suits and the whole thing,' Fry went on, 'that people would think we were yuppies.' The acronym for young upwardly mobile professional had been coined in America in the early 1980s and, like so much else then, quickly spread across the Atlantic. Fry returned one more time to ABC's complicity or otherwise with this new Britain. 'Politically ... we felt guilty,' he said. 'I felt uncomfortable. I didn't buy stocks and shares or wear red braces.' Another pause. 'But then again, if you're a songwriter, you've got to document your time.'

Pop musicians were not the only trend-conscious Britons who sensed a subterranean shift in their country, and in themselves, at the start of the 1980s. In the January 1981 issue of *The Face*, the journalist Jon Savage interviewed the fashion designer Vivienne Westwood about her latest collection. Both had been important protagonists in punk, Savage as a keen-eyed combiner of music journalism and doomy social commentary, Westwood as the maker of many of the Sex Pistols' glamorously wrecked outfits. Her 1981 collection had an apocalyptic-sounding name – World's End – but there its connection with 1970s darkness ended. World's End was actually the name of the area of London where Westwood had done much of her work. More importantly, the clothes were startlingly luxurious: big, confident silhouettes in lustrous fabrics, gold, royal blue and deep red, voluminous and extravagant whereas punk fashion had been tight and frugal.

'To look rich is *great*,' Westwood explained. 'Golden girls with wonderful bodies on the beach ... that's who I want to wear [these clothes]. I don't want people to think, "Gosh ... if I wear these clothes I've got to be part of the underground." These are definitely overground clothes. They're for chatting in aeroplanes in ... You have to ... strut around. They give you a great lift.' Savage did his best to present her collection and comments as typical Westwood rebelliousness, a reaction against the recession, 'a blast of defiance, colour splashed onto a canvas of drab'. Helpfully, she also told him, 'Margaret Thatcher's an idiot ... destroying people's lives.' But it was impossible to avoid the feeling that Westwood had absorbed some of Thatcherism's social aspiration and materialism. The designer was now 'aiming upmarket', wrote Savage. 'Times have changed.' Weren't her clothes now too expensive, he asked her, for 'most kids'?

Westwood began talking in general terms about a possible, cheaper diffusion line. Then she lost patience: 'You can't always put yourself into the role of . . . a social service.'

If dressing rich was one way to break with the egalitarian, proletarian 1970s, there was another way, even more taboo-breaking and irresistible to the early 1980s fashion-conscious: dressing posh. The trend, like so many then, started with musicians. In 1979 half a dozen working-class north Londoners with good media and clubbing connections formed a rock band called The Gentry. 'The name was meant to be ironic, an anti-punk statement,' wrote their guitarist Gary Kemp later. 'We were mostly Labour voters.' But, he went on, the name also suited how they dressed: 'browns and beiges . . . waistcoats . . . wing collars . . . green velvet slippers . . . small bow ties'. By 1980 The Gentry had renamed themselves Spandau Ballet, switched to funk and soul, and grown from an exhaustively hyped nightclub act into a proper pop band; yet their appetite for aristocratic, backward-looking clothes remained. They wore spats and sashes, capes and neckerchiefs, tweed jackets, even monocles.

During 1981 the pop fascination with poshness spread beyond London. The cheeky Glasgow guitar band Orange Juice had 'lately taken to pretending to be tweedy Scottish gentry', *The Face* reported in July. In August, Orchestral Manoeuvres in the Dark, a bright, urban-sounding synthpop group from the Wirral, released a video for their hit single 'Souvenir' entirely filmed in the landscaped grounds of the public school Stowe. The band gazed into the green distance like melancholy eighteenth-century patricians, rather than grammar-school boys from near Liverpool.

That same month *The Face* devoted an admiring double-page spread to some actual toffs: a fleetingly hot eight-piece band from various smart areas of west London, called Funkapolitan: 'Toby . . . [has] been making a living in the antiques trade – Christies . . . as do his parents . . . Nick is wearing paisley carpet slippers and a terribly smart blazer . . . Kadir, one of the two White Russian Prince brothers in the band, [is] the diminutive centre frontman.'

That *The Face* should be one of the main chroniclers of this shift was no coincidence. The vibrant, picture-heavy magazine was minutely sensitive to fashions; more than that, it had been founded in

1980 partly to treat pop and street style in the same lavish way that posh monthlies such as *Tatler* and *Vogue* had long treated high fashion and high society. The founder of *The Face* was a Labour-voting ex-mod from unaristocratic Lincoln, Nick Logan. He told me, 'I felt, "Why should the devil have the best tunes?" I want to give my people the good stuff, the glossiness, take it away from being the exclusive property of the nobs.'

But the line between stealing from and subverting upper-class culture, and validating, even celebrating it, was not always easy to draw, especially in a country like Britain, where that upper-class culture remained so large and deep-rooted; and especially in the worlds of pop and fashion, where elites and snobbery were almost as ingrained as they were on the grouse moor. In January 1981 a *Face* contributor, Geoffrey Deane, nicely summed up the abrupt switch of hipster focus from punk and postpunk darkness to guilt-free hedonism and poshness: 'Taffeta,' he wrote, was 'rapidly replacing Kafka in the hearts of the well-informed.'

By the end of 1981 the trend had gone mainstream. Every week from October to December, ITV broadcast an hour-long instalment of *Brideshead Revisited*, a languorous, panoramic adaptation of Evelyn Waugh's 1945 novel about a declining English aristocratic family in the 1920s, 1930s and 1940s. The series was often dark – the family tormented by alcoholism, stunted relationships, existential doubt – but it was also full of champagne and picnics, charming men with white trousers and floppy fringes, perfect Oxford quadrangles and country-house vistas. In the grimy, volatile Britain of 1981, *Brideshead* was escapist, aspirational viewing – after all, its narrator Charles Ryder was a middle-class man intoxicated by the upper classes – and the ratings were enormous for such a slow and involved drama: over ten million viewers for the final episode. The near-simultaneous success of *Chariots of Fire*, also full of well-spoken chaps in rose-tinted settings, reinforced the sense that Britain was falling in love again with its upper classes, or at least with some of their past incarnations. Membership of the National Trust, with its emphasis on reverential visits to ancestral piles, had been a mere 226,000 in 1970 – the era of a strong left, working-class heroes and weakening social deference. By 1981 membership had more than quadrupled.

The following year, even a bitter London play about public-school cruelty, homophobia and traitors, *Another Country*, was taken by some of its audience as principally an exercise in style and glamour. 'When we transferred to the West End,' remembered its writer Julian Mitchell in the *Guardian* in 2014, 'people came again and again, dressed in blazers and boaters.'

Subtly, and sometimes not so subtly, connected to all this was a change in the fortunes of the posh themselves. Perhaps the most obvious indication was the performance and contents of one of Logan's models, *Tatler*. Various incarnations had been published intermittently since 1709; but by 1979 the latest was a doddery seventy-eight-year-old monthly: inward-looking, stiff with dull gossip, bruised by the bad surgery and botched relaunches of successive owners, and left with a frail circulation of 12,000. Then Tina Brown became editor. Twenty-five, prosperous middle class rather than posh, the daughter of a successful British film producer, she was a precocious networker and journalist who had written widely noticed, waspish pieces for national magazines while still an undergraduate at Oxford. She quickly turned *Tatler* into a clever new hybrid: part-glitz, part-amateur sociology, which traced in entertaining and inquisitive detail the ups and downs of the British aristocracy, as it emerged from the challenging post-war decades of redistributive taxation and dropped h's into the more promising, less egalitarian environment of the Thatcher era.

At first, this promise was more theoretical than real. For its February 1981 issue, *Tatler* despatched Andrew Osmond, 'former officer with the Gurkhas, former diplomat', from his Oxfordshire home to Piccadilly, to see how the citadels of upper-class London were faring in the recession. '"Business is still very bad," said the taxi-driver,' Osmond's piece began. 'In fact it has never been worse. "If you ask me, it's the crunch, mate. This is the beginning of the end."' Osmond then walks west along bone-grey Piccadilly:

> ... in the dark afternoon, uncertain where to go ... looking in shop windows and trying not to think about money, of which we have not much left ... I am not doing well at my job yet continue to send my children to expensive public schools to make sure they grow up like me: a predicament not exactly rare among the English.

> Ah, here is Fortnum & Mason ... My wife [is] American. But she knows the form ... that in the restaurant at Fortnum & Mason a grilled cheese on toast, with tomatoes and bacon, is called a Blushing Bunny ... Our table turns out to be next to the Duchess of Kent's ... We grab the menu in excitement, but some tinkering bastard has killed off the Bunnies ... We eavesdrop on the Kents. This is not an easy thing to do, because they murmur to each other ... hardly moving their lips, like people on the run in an enemy country ... After the royals have gone I lean across the table and take my wife's hand. 'I have just had an idea,' I say ... 'Let's emigrate.'

A dozen pages later in the same *Tatler*, there was an article about young British expats in Hong Kong. 'More and more boys from good British stock are rushing ... to find gold in one of capitalism's last frontier towns,' it started. 'The gloomier the economic climate in Britain, the more attractive seem the hit-and-run profits in Hong Kong.' Those recruited by the residual colony's lingering cluster of British-run businesses, venerable but hard-nosed institutions such as the Hong Kong and Shanghai Bank (now HSBC), were 'Oxbridge graduates with goodish degrees or hereditary Johnnies from Dumfriesshire'.

The reporter was Nicholas Coleridge, one of several sharp writers Brown had recruited to *Tatler*. In Hong Kong he interviewed and eavesdropped on a selection of cocky young Britons in striped shirts who worked long hours, watched their investments race upwards in the booming local stock market, performed drunken pranks and drove flash cars. Coleridge did not quite realize it, but in Hong Kong a brash new British lifestyle was being pioneered, which by the end of the decade would become the norm in the City of London.

By mid-1981, *Tatler* was beginning to notice that even back in Britain the upper-class mood was lifting. 'The rebound has begun,' wrote Emma Soames in a piece about a revival of masqued balls that May, 'The first whiff of a move away from austerity.' In November a magazine largely and unashamedly focused on the homes of the landed classes was launched: *Interiors*, later *The World of Interiors*, with spread after beautiful spread of gilded, heirloom-stacked photographs. And then there was the royal wedding. 'The season's surprise fashion success is the Lady Di look,' declared *Tatler* in May 1981, introducing a drooling picture special about her, headlined 'Royal Tease'. 'Girls all over the country are frenziedly cloning themselves: Lady Di hairstyles, Lady Di hacking jackets, Ladi Di knickerbockers, and the quintessential Lady Di blouses with the pie-crust frilled necks.'

By 1982 the aristocratic revival was in full cry. In April another *Tatler* writer, Nicholas Hill, discovered that at Cambridge University, 'Undergraduates are no longer hankering for the obscure charms of the hoi-polloi.' He went on:

> Charm, style and nostalgia have now replaced the aggressive arrogant Sixties and the dull uncertain Seventies. This romantic mood is evident in all aspects of undergraduate life ... Anoraks and patched jeans have been replaced by jackets, ties and skirts ... Ex-public-school boys wear cords and brogues ... Only the outdated trendy Lefties and an occasional football rowdie can be seen scuttling about in baggy Seventies sweaters and evil-smelling socks. The girls are refreshingly feminine in their prettily-coloured pedal-pushers or knickerbockers. Once again it is possible to distinguish between the sexes.

Hill continued approvingly: 'Elegantly served dinner parties lit by candles are commonplace. Cocktails have been revived ... Current status symbols: your own house (£20,000 to £30,000 is sufficient for a small one); a Range Rover ... a battered teddy bear' – the doomed Lord Sebastian Flyte had clutched one in *Brideshead Revisited* – '... Academic achievement is admired but it is unfashionable to work ... Junk food, smoking and the Blue Boar Hotel (Trust House Forte) are out.' In an accompanying photograph, four members of the True Blue Club, 'the oldest dining club in the world (founded 1756)', including 'the dashing Earl of MacDuff, heir to the Duke of Fife', stood clinking glasses, dressed in long and dandyish eighteenth-century jackets with lacy shirt cuffs poking out. They looked like Adam Ant. Or was it the other way round?

That there were toffs at Oxbridge was not news. But their renewed brazenness signified something larger. The social commentator Peter York called it 'Reactionary Chic'. In his 1984 book *Modern Times* he wrote: 'There's been this box opened, and ... out have come the most incredible sentiments ... the most insensitive language, the most extraordinary symbols of . . . what? Forward into the past, backward into the future . . . Out have come basically all those things that no one would have given house-room to – not publicly anyway – in the early seventies.'

Even more than Tina Brown and *Tatler*, York understood this counter-revolution. Like her, he was middle class not patrician. Born as the less grand-sounding Peter Wallis, he grew up in leftie, bourgeois north London, at a fascinated distance from the stucco labyrinth of the posh west. Under his original name, he co-founded (and still works for) a cryptically named market-research company, SRU, discreetly advising media companies and other clients. As Peter York, he wrote (and still writes) insidery journalism, both barbed and celebratory, about London and its hinterland's ever-shifting elite.

In 1975, writing for *Harpers & Queen*, he discovered – or helped discover; the scoop's origins are disputed – 'Sloane Rangers'. As York described them then, they were unambitious, quietly snobbish, formal upper-class young women living in a small area around Sloane Square in west London, 'sweet girls, if a little . . . predictable'. They were a highly distinct tribe – 'they come from manor-houses, farms, and Army and Navy backgrounds' – but in some ways a secret and beleaguered one. 'Employers [are] galled by the Rangers' British amateurism . . . There are other attacks on the nice Sloane girl . . . higher education, and T-shirts and *Time Out* and Chou en-Lai.' York concluded, 'You will never get anyone to *admit* belonging to the Sloanes.'

Seven years and a royal wedding later, their status was rather different. In 1982, with his old *Harpers* editor Ann Barr, York co-authored *The Official Sloane Ranger Handbook*, an expanded, unisex and much more bullish version of his original article, as much a how-to guide as satire. 'Who Sloanes Wins', bragged a rosette on the back cover. 'Diana,' the book continued inside, 'pepped up the Ranger wardrobe and boosted morale.' These more confident 1980s Sloanes 'often start up their own little businesses . . . particularly telephone-and-we'll-bike-it-over'. Or they commodified their ease with playing roles and dressing up: 'Acting didn't use to be a Sloane profession, but now public-school boys people all the television dramas of high life.' Barr and York naturally cited *Brideshead Revisited*. Their *Sloane Ranger Handbook* sold a million copies.

Meanwhile another quieter but equally telling literary craze spread through bookshops. For much of the post-war period, travel writing had been quite unfashionable in Britain. As the country shed its empire, and its self-image as an expansive, exploratory power, as more sophisticated ideas about the foreign spread from anthropology and sociology, as international travel became a mass pastime, so books about intrepid men traversing exotic lands – and they were almost always men – became more marginal. 'The travelogue,' wrote one of its lonely post-war masters, Colin Thubron, in 2011, was 'charged with cultural colonialism and heroic self-posturing.' By the 1970s, Britain's future seemed to be in the European Union, and among many liberal or left-leaning Britons, who made up much of the book-buying public, travel writing about faraway places had become either irrelevant or, to use Peter York's words, one of the 'reactionary' things 'that no one [gave] house-room'.

But, given time, cultural and political trends usually generate their opposites. In 1977 the blue-eyed, blond Bruce Chatwin published *In Patagonia*. He was thirty-seven years old, an ex-director of the auction house Sotheby's who had turned himself into an elegant, eagerly commissioned journalist for smart magazines. He was as tanned and handsome as the most romanticized colonial officer, and in some ways his book was an anachronism: an account of a journey to one of the wildest, remotest, most obscure places a Briton could imagine, the windswept far south of Argentina, its only neighbours the frigid tip of Chile and one of Britain's last and saddest colonial backwaters, the Falkland Islands. Yet Chatwin dealt with his subject in a pithy, contemporary, multi-dimensional style, breaking up his material into jewel-like fragments of history, memoir and anecdote. His book appealed to fans of derring-do and postmodern literary games alike.

After *In Patagonia* came a whole caravan of travel books by Britons. 'Travel writing is undergoing a revival: not since the 1920s and 1930s has it been so popular or so important,' wrote Bill Buford, editor of the then equally fashionable literary magazine *Granta*, which devoted a special issue to the genre in 1983. Some of the books, such as Jonathan Raban's *Arabia* (1979) echoed Chatwin's self-awareness; others, such as Redmond O'Hanlon's *Into the Heart of Borneo* (1984), were essentially excellent boys' adventure stories, untroubled by much, if any, guilt about Britain's past adventures abroad. 'The author wishes to thank 22 SAS,' wrote O'Hanlon, going on to include a gleeful description of all the 'kit' he had been allowed to borrow from the British army regiment most involved in the vicious end-of-empire wars of the 1960s and 1970s, and involved in one still in Northern Ireland.

During the late 1970s and early 1980s, British imperialism became steadily less an object of embarrassment or condemnation in Britain – as much as it ever was – and more one of fascination. In February 1981 a new London-based fashion designer, Willie Brown, had a collection called 'Clothes for Colonial Man' featured in *The Face*. The magazine explained neutrally that the outfits 'combine a classically Highland feel with that of "early settlers"'. In 1982 the lauded travel writer and historian Jan Morris published *The Spectacle of Empire*, a book that examined British imperialism as 'a theatrical spectacle with all the world our stage', rather than as a system of racial and economic domination. 'With the admirable there came the rotten,' Morris conceded. But 'violence was seldom a tool of imperial policy'.

In 1977 the British novelist Paul Scott, whose *Raj Quartet* of novels set in colonial and postcolonial India had been published in the 1960s and early 1970s to little acclaim, won the Booker Prize for another novel with the same setting, *Staying On*. In 1980 a television adaptation was broadcast by ITV; four years later, the *Raj Quartet* received the same treatment, as the fourteen-part series *The Jewel in the Crown*. Another novel about the Raj, M. M. Kaye's *The Far Pavilions*, became a best-seller in 1978; and also a television series in 1984, broadcast by the supposedly left-wing Channel 4. There was a sudden rush of films about colonial India: *Gandhi* (1982) *Heat and Dust* (1983) and *A Passage to India* (1984). In 1981 came another Booker winner about the Raj and its aftermath, *Midnight's Children* by Salman Rushdie. That May the usually sceptical journalist Ian Jack, long interested in India, wrote a piece for *Tatler* suggesting that in 1980 he had considered giving up reporting and instead renting out ex-colonial bungalows to British tourists in the Indian hill station of Simla, complete with Victorian novels and cooks offering 'mulligatawny, roast mutton etc'. It was not clear whether he was joking. In 1982 the ever trend-conscious *Tatler* commented, 'A reappraisal of the Raj has spread like a contagion.'

It is risky to read too much about the direction of a country from its culture. The Raj revival, the return of poshness, the renewed interest of British pop and fashion in conventional success and glamour and making money: all these early 1980s crazes had their contradictory elements. The Indian dramas, for example, were often full of ambiguity or hostility towards empire as well as imperial nostalgia. One of the central scenes in *Gandhi* was the infamous machine-gunning of unarmed Indian protesters by British soldiers at Amritsar.

Creations such as films or novels can also have long and complicated gestations – something that those who attribute clear-cut political or social meanings to culture prefer not to dwell on. Evelyn Waugh's *Brideshead Revisited* was written during 1943 and 1944, under a wartime Labour-Conservative coalition. Its televised adaptation was partly filmed in 1979, during the relatively calm, unformed first phase of the Thatcher government. The TV series that was broadcast two years later should not be interpreted too single-mindedly as a Thatcher-era artefact, whether escapist or celebratory.

And yet, at the start of the 1980s, British culture, and how Britons responded to it, *was* sending important signals. Alfred Sherman, a key Thatcher adviser and speechwriter during the 1970s and early 1980s, perhaps the cleverest and prickliest of them all, perceptively summed up her governing project afterwards: 'accommodating changes which had already been generated in the bowels of British society'.

Few other leading figures in her administration noticed the hints that popular culture was giving. Thatcher herself was not an avid consumer of it. Right through the 1980s one of her favourite pop songs remained 'Telstar' by The Tornados, a galloping instrumental – perhaps it spoke to her self-sufficiency – inspired by the early space race and released in 1962. But even she experienced culture's ability to shape people's deepest thoughts and assumptions. During the famously hot, listless parliamentary recess of the summer of 1976, she kept herself busy by reading all 845 pages of the collected poems of

Rudyard Kipling, the great articulator of British imperialism and what drove it. From then on, wrote Thatcher's official biographer Charles Moore in the *Daily Telegraph* in April 2013, these poems about patriotism and foreign adventures, about duty and doggedness, and above all about the sacrifices and glories of war, 'echoed constantly in her mind'.

10
Scams

In early 1982 the sun came out. Britons shop more in good weather. Yet the chainstores that increasingly studded the otherwise grey-brown, slightly fusty high streets, and dominated the country's cautious scattering of new, American-style malls, began to notice something odd about their sales patterns, which the end of 1981's near-incessant cloud and rain could not fully account for. Where unemployment was deepest, the chainstores 'were not selling noticeably fewer goods' than elsewhere, reported the watchful social analyst Anthony Sampson in his 1982 book *The Changing Anatomy of Britain*. More broadly, 'MPs for those [jobless] areas were struck by signs of unusual activity and lack of leisure.'

Sampson had one straightforward explanation: 'Redundancy money ... the first major source of new capital for ordinary people since the [servicemen's] postwar gratuities in the forties.' He also had a more speculative one: moonlighting.

In April 2013, the week after Margaret Thatcher's funeral, I went to see her employment secretary from 1981 to 1983, Norman Tebbit. Now eighty-two, he was living in a typical retired English politician's house, handsome and old, in a typical retired English politician's town, polite and full of tea shops: Bury St Edmunds in Suffolk. 'The Chingford skinhead', as he was once known, came to the door in slippers. Over his short, bony frame he wore soft cords, a shirt in a country check, and a green jumper with elbow patches – the off-duty uniform of the cosier sort of rural Tory. He smiled warmly and made me a cafetiere of coffee. He referred to 1980s union leaders by their first names. Except as a demonstration of his often forgotten ability to switch from political thuggishness to charm – days before, he had smeared the perfectly justified protesters at Thatcher's funeral as 'brain-dead bigots' in the *Daily Telegraph* – some of the interview was rather anodyne. Sitting almost slouchily in his small study, with its volumes of the Benn *Diaries* as well as books by Tories, Tebbit was low-key and genial, his infamous Essex drone less cutting than usual, as if he was holding fire until his next column.

But when I asked about moonlighting, or illegally taking paid work while drawing the dole, the former employment secretary became more animated. 'It was always going to happen in the early 80s,' he said baldly. 'Wherever the welfare claimant levels were high.' He shifted to less Whitehall language: 'Of course there were blokes working down the market . . . But they were actually contributing to GNP. I still get letters from people now, writing to me about something or other, and at the end they say, "I got on my bike . . ." I know guys who just got themselves a ladder, and a wash flannel, and a bucket – and then they were *doing better*.' His thin face suddenly split in a wolfish grin: 'It was wonderfully unregulated.'

At the Conservative Party conference in October 1981, dominated by the recession and the summer's riots, which had not finally stopped in Toxteth until the end of July, the chairman of the Young Conservatives, Iain Picton, made a short speech. Picton was a Tory moderate who had lived in Liverpool and felt the government was not doing enough about youth unemployment. According to Tebbit's combative memoirs, *Upwardly Mobile* (1989), Picton's speech implied that 'rioting was a natural reaction to unemployment'.

Tebbit had just been made employment secretary. But his response seemed emotional as much as ministerial. Sitting onstage in a row of cabinet ministers, wearing a dead-toned suit, shirt and tie that accentuated the dark ledges of his eyebrows, the sallow skin over his skull, he blinked slowly and, barely moving his head or thin lips, said to the audience with exaggerated calmness: 'I grew up in the 30s with an unemployed father.' He paused heavily. There was near-silence in the cavernous Blackpool Winter Gardens. 'He didn't *ri-ot*' – Tebbit drew out the syllables disgustedly. He paused again. 'He got on his bike and looked for work, and he kept looking 'til he found it.' Applause burst around the last dozen words like fireworks.

Along with Thatcher's 'not for turning' soundbite at the previous year's party conference, Tebbit's 'on yer bike' speech, as it quickly and widely became known, was a rare moment of successful rhetoric for a government that was struggling to make itself understood. And unlike Thatcher's soundbite, Tebbit's was not just a general statement of defiance; it suggested a specific way forward.

Officially, moonlighting was not part of the government's plan for greater labour mobility. But in private many senior Tories acknowledged moonlighting's importance to getting the economy going – or at least to stopping it getting worse. In July 1980 Thatcher attended an off-the-record lunch for *Sunday Times* journalists. One of them, Hugo Young, recorded afterwards in his meticulous private journal that she was 'a great proponent, it seems, of the black economy . . . the cushioning effect this was having on unemployment'. In 1981 her vital intellectual ally, Patrick Minford, wrote in his pamphlet 'The Problem of Unemployment', with a mixture of frankness and coyness: 'There are apparently opportunities for unrecorded part-time work in the shadow economy which . . . ameliorate unemployment.'

As a rule-bending port city with deep-rooted poverty, Liverpool had always had an individualistic, ducking-and-diving side to its economy. In 1982 one aspect of the city's portrayal in *Boys from the Blackstuff* noticed less by commentators, perhaps because it was less completely despairing and more politically ambiguous, involved the main characters in the series sneaking off to work illicitly while also signing on; and the efforts of the benefits bureaucracy to catch them. There was slapstick and satire in this subplot. The benefits-fraud officers drove a knackered van – thanks to the Thatcher government's public-spending cuts, it seemed fair to assume. In the first episode the officials were given a speeding ticket by a policeman. He disliked benefits snoopers because he used to be unemployed himself.

There was bitterness, too, in the drama's portrayal of the unemployed effectively being forbidden to work. 'I want,' said Chrissie, the show's shambling, tormented Everyman, already close to tears in the opening instalment, 'to come home with dirt on me hands, and not have to hide it.' Yet the show also vividly dramatized how expectations about work were being recalibrated in the early 1980s. Cash in hand, irregular hours, no loyalty, every man for himself: these were becoming workplace norms, the series suggested. Not just in Liverpool, but across all the desperate job markets of urban Britain, the ground was being prepared for the modern indignities and cruelties of the zero-hours contract. As Chrissie put it to Snowy, a left-wing plasterer who still thought work should be skilled and regular and about taking 'pride': 'When you're scared . . . you think about yourself . . . about feeding the kids and paying the rent . . . Your beliefs go right out the window.' Or you acquire new ones without quite realizing. In Bury St Edmunds, I asked Tebbit, who had seen *Boys from the Blackstuff* (he did not say when), if he thought its characters had actually been Thatcherites, rather than, as commonly assumed at the time and ever since, purely Thatcherism's victims. 'In many ways, yes,' he said, grinning again. 'They're in a deregulated bit of the economy.'

Moonlighting, 'doing a job on the side', 'doing a foreigner' – a strong British xenophobia lingered in the early 1980s – these side-of-the-mouth euphemisms littered the dialogue of the period's many socially conscious dramas, such as Mike Leigh's 1983 film *Meantime*, set in a threadbare east London and a gaudier Essex; and Phil Redmond's soap opera *Brookside*, set in an aspiring but fragile new Liverpool suburb, and first broadcast in 1982. But even for a government that idealized the free market, the black economy had its drawbacks. It generated no tax revenue. It sometimes intersected with more serious criminality. It was, after all, illegal – awkward for a Tory Party that since the early 1970s had claimed insistently that it was uniquely tough on law and order. And it made no contribution to the official economic statistics, which well into 1982 remained dire in most instances.

Could moonlighting somehow be legitimized? In 1981 the Centre for Policy Studies, a right-wing think tank that had been crucial to Thatcher's capture of the party leadership, both as an organizing base and a source of ideas, offered the government a solution to the conundrum: the Enterprise Allowance Scheme, or EAS for short. One of its architects was a drawling Oxford-educated venture capitalist called David Cooksey. 'What we were trying to do at the CPS,' he remembered, when I saw him at his sleek offices near Sloane Square, 'was come up with a whole series of schemes that enabled people to take more risk . . . to think entrepreneurially. There were three million unemployed, and moonlighting was absolutely rampant. Our scheme, to a certain extent, was meant to lead those people down the path to righteousness – and make them into VAT payers.'

'In essence,' said an official report on the Enterprise Allowance Scheme in 1986, 'the EAS represents an open invitation to Britain's unemployed to create their own jobs.' The terms of the invitation were fairly simple and attractive. If you were between eighteen and sixty-five, on the dole, and had been jobless for at least thirteen weeks; if you could 'demonstrate' to the government that you had 'a valid business proposal' and 'access to £1,000 to invest in that proposed business'; and if you could 'undertake to work solely for the business' for 'a minimum of 36 hours a week'; then the government would pay you £40 a week, for a year, to help get that business started. That wage would replace your unemployment benefit. Depending on which of the fiddly variety of dole rates you had previously been on, your income would increase by between almost a quarter and almost half. Less measurably, but more importantly to the scheme's devisers, your self-esteem would rise, your dependency on the state would shrink, and, in the long term, assuming a decent proportion of the new businesses succeeded, the government's finances would benefit. During 1981, Cooksey recalled, 'It took a *huge* effort to get the Treasury to realize that they should give a little to the scheme, and then they would be much better off.'

In January 1982 pilot schemes were launched in Coventry, north Kent, Wrexham in north Wales, north Ayrshire in Scotland, and north-east Lancashire. They were all areas chosen, said the 1986 report, for their 'high unemployment due to . . . structural changes taking place in the national economy' – or as opponents of the government might have put it, the sort of places where its economic policies had done the most damage. From an undeclared number of applicants, the government selected 3,331 would-be entrepreneurs. They were a youthful but rather traditional social cross section. Nine-tenths were men. Almost three-quarters were married. Over half were in their early thirties or younger. But the pilot offered some hope to Thatcherites who aimed to create a new kind of Briton: 50 per cent of those surveyed for the 1986 report about their reasons for applying cited 'independence', 'self-actualization' or the 'desire for control' – a greater proportion than those who simply wanted to use the scheme to get a job or make money.

Most of the participants proposed 'businesses that could become cashflow-positive pretty quickly,' as Cooksey put it. A quarter became builders. 'You'd get restaurants, people setting up as painters and decorators – to be a plumber or a heating engineer you obviously had to have qualifications, but you didn't for those; and also a lot of sort of' – a faintly baffled note entered his creamy metropolitan voice – '*craft* and small retail.' People making and selling things from their homes? 'Exactly.'

These enterprising Britons were largely left to their own devices by the government. The 1986 report explained:

> [They] were obliged to attend a one-day induction seminar where the government's Small Firms Service . . . outlined the rudiments of business practice and offered some subsequent counselling. No training was offered . . . and, apart from a possible three-monthly follow-up visit – the Manpower Services Commission [the state body overseeing the scheme] reserved the right to visit the business and inspect the accounts – and a fortnightly cheque for £80, many entrants [to the scheme] had no further formal contact with the MSC.

The Enterprise Allowance Scheme was an ambitious blend: of state subsidy and lightly regulated, sink-or-swim, semi-anarchy; of panic about unemployment and optimism about capitalism; of noisily idealistic social reform and a simultaneous, quieter acceptance of hierarchy and privilege. The requirement that participants in the scheme come up with £1,000 of private investment to match the government's contribution – around £3,500 in today's money – heavily favoured applicants 'with a bit of family capital', as Cooksey put it.

After the pilot had been running a year, the government contacted a sample of its guinea pigs to see if they were still in business. One in eight had given up. These failed enterprises had lasted 'an average of five months'. Once the pilot had been going for a year and a half, which meant its initial participants had had twelve months of state subsidy followed by six months standing on their own feet, the government conducted another survey. It found that just over half the original businesses were still trading.

Did Cooksey think that was a high casualty rate? For a moment, in his crisp white shirt, he looked out of our meeting-room window, at a perfect blue sky over the luxury boutiques of Sloane Street. 'It's natural,' he said calmly. 'People *try* to set up on their own. Some people can do it. Some people can't. Losing companies like that is not very damaging to the economy. It's a lot less damaging than subsidizing them to continue. What you want is the winners flowering, and so on.'

One of the Enterprise Allowance's other devisers was not so sanguine. Nigel Vinson was a successful plastics entrepreneur with a slightly loose tongue, less urbane and less detached than Cooksey from the daily struggle of starting a business. Energetic, engaging, an enthusiast for small-firm rather than corporate capitalism, and not automatically loyal to what he coolly called 'the Tory party', Vinson was an important behind-the-scenes figure in the right-wing London think tanks from the mid-1970s onwards.

He was eighty when we met at the Centre for Policy Studies in Westminster in 2011. All pinstripe and rebellious grey curls, in an otherwise hushed and spotless grand meeting room, he was scathing about how the Thatcher government initially treated the Enterprise Allowance Scheme and entrepreneurs in general. Geoffrey Howe was 'a good chancellor in some respects,' he conceded, 'but he got it wrong in so many ways. On the one hand, the government were creating entrepreneurs. On the other hand, Geoffrey Howe handicapped himself by this passionate, overdone commitment to monetarism.' Vinson cited the policy's insistence on crushingly high interest rates, and what these did to necessarily indebted new businesses: 'It bankrupted swathes,' he said. 'But if you started out as a barrister' – as Howe had – 'with the best will in the world, you've not come up the hard way, knowing that if you can't sell something you might starve.' He concluded with a snort: 'The Tories did immense harm to new businesses, while wanting to encourage them. That's the paradox.' Thatcher set ordinary people free, but into a landscape that her other policies had already shaped to suit other, more powerful interests, such as large corporations or Britons with inherited wealth. The results sometimes disappointed Thatcherism's idealists.

In August 1983, regardless, the pilot Enterprise Allowance Scheme was expanded into a national programme. Participation grew almost tenfold. During 1984–5 it almost doubled again, to over 46,000 new government-backed businesses a year. Even the proportion of female-run ones slowly picked up, to almost a quarter by April 1985. Stars of the scheme emerged, such as Julian Dunkerton, who used it to help him found the street-fashion empire Superdry, and Alan McGee, a hedonistic Scottish socialist who used it to establish the riotous indie pop label Creation Records. Neither were businesses you could exactly envisage Margaret Thatcher patronizing. But the Enterprise Allowance Scheme remained true to its permissive vision.

Yet one thing about the scheme did trouble Cooksey a little, in retrospect. 'The truth of the matter is,' he said, 'virtually all the businesses that were set up, I think, didn't go on to employ a lot of people. It was self-employment, really.' The 1986 report discovered that even firms which survived for three years created an average of one job each. It was the same lesson that Ken Livingstone's Greater London Enterprise Board – which in its optimism as well as its name had a telling amount in common with the Enterprise Allowance – was receiving at the same time, when it backed small workers' cooperatives. Britons might learn to become more entrepreneurial. But the easy wins of the post-war era, when white-collar work was expanding worldwide and British industry still seemed strong, were gone.

One country's politicians can alter a complex, internationally connected modern economy less than they, and the public, often think. Yet there were a few signs in 1981, and a greater number in early 1982, that Britain's economy was more alive than the many pessimists on both left and right believed.

Some of the good economic news had little or nothing to do with the Thatcher government. 'In 1981 there was a worldwide fall in agricultural prices, and the cost of food dropped dramatically,' pointed out Vinson, who was a farmer's son and owned an estate in rural Northumberland. 'There had been huge improvements in farming technology, and there was a drop in demand for food because of the world recession. Food is such a multiplier [of prices in general] when its cost goes up, and the opposite happens when it goes down.' The British inflation rate fell from an excruciating 22 per cent in mid-1980 to a painful 12 per cent by the end of 1981 – still little better than the Conservatives had inherited from Callaghan's supposedly spendthrift government – to a merely uncomfortable 8 per cent by mid-1982. Vinson's expression changed from explanatory earnestness to mischief: 'Margaret Thatcher and her whole government were luckier than is often said.'

And then there was North Sea oil. Discovered in the late 1960s, first extracted from these difficult waters in the mid-1970s, it had tantalized four successive, cash-hungry governments before Thatcher's, with the seemingly ever-receding promise of extra tax revenue. In the early 1980s, oil and its revenues finally arrived in sufficient quantities to make a politically important difference to the public finances – £3.8 billion in 1980–81, £6.1 billion in 1981–2, equivalent respectively to over 3 per cent and nearly 5 per cent of total state spending. Here again, the Thatcher administration was lucky. North Sea oil was a huge new industry that it had not created; and, for reasons which had nothing to do with the British government, the global price of that industry's product had just soared, thanks to the 1979–80 oil crisis. Thatcher would become infamous for her harshness towards heavy industry, especially when it was sited in northern Britain. But it was just such an enterprise, largely hidden from public view over the North Sea's blurred horizon, that would help sustain her.

Another fortunate inheritance was the Austin Metro. The delicate British car industry's long-trumpeted new model went on sale on 14 October 1980. British Leyland's head of sales and marketing, Tony Ball, with his background running car showrooms, made sure that every single BL dealership had at least six Metros in stock that day. The company's previous, faintly complacent policy had been to make customers place orders for brand-new models, and then wait gratefully for them to be delivered. But the strength of demand for the cute, frugal Metro overwhelmed Ball's preparations. In Manchester a thousand people converged on a single showroom that was holding a Metro launch party. Those who couldn't get in banged on the doors and windows. Police had to clear the streets. Across the country more than 20,000 Metros were reportedly sold by lunchtime. Or at least ordered: stocks frequently ran out. 'Quite suddenly, a new Metro became *the* car to have,' wrote the automotive historian Graham Robson afterwards, 'to show that one was economy-conscious, [and] that one was also patriotic.' Between October 1980 and April 1981, 56,000 Metros were bought, a rate of sale 'almost unprecedented in BL's history' for a new car.

Meanwhile, in the City of London, a related, but more abstract and risky form of British capitalism established its first modern outposts. In April 1981 the International Petroleum Exchange opened. After two oil crises in less than a decade, oil had been transformed from a stable into a volatile commodity, and the exchange aimed to take advantage. The energy minister Hamish Gray explained to the House of Commons in May that it would offer 'trading in gas and oil futures contracts ... The market provides hedging facilities against future price movements for both oil traders and consumers,' he continued – sounding more like a PR man for the City than an elected politician who might keep an eye on it. 'I understand that the exchange organizers have been encouraged by the high volume of trading.'

The same month, in *Tatler*, Nicholas Coleridge wrote a prophetic piece about London commodity traders. Interviewing three, he found the sort of reckless City swagger that would later fascinate 1980s novelists and, later still – too late – horrify regulators and economists and the rest of us. 'Commodity broking has become the front-line playground for money-minded City swains,' Coleridge discovered. His interviewees wore 'wide-boy suits' and worked twelve-hour days, tethered to other exchanges in New York and Hong Kong, perpetually shouting into phones. One unusually reflective broker confessed to Coleridge that trading-floor behaviour was based not on the real strengths and weaknesses of the commodities involved, but on 'psychology ... on the artificial machinations of the market – the bluffs, double bluffs ... Brokers are like fish. They want to be with the crowd and yet one step ahead ... Suddenly one fish moves ... and the whole shoal darts after him ... It *is* like a casino.'

While much of the City in 1981 retained a post-war starchiness, weighed down like other parts of establishment Britain by heavy lunches and over-promoted public schoolboys, commodity broking, Coleridge found, had an 'aggressively classless ambience ... trading floors where scores of Kevin Keegan lookalikes [took part in] some of the sharpest, least contemplative bidding in the Square Mile'. Quick-witted lads from Essex competed with Oxbridge graduates.

Coleridge's most outspoken interviewee was a twenty-six-year-old working for an American firm. The brokers, he said, were 'the sort of people who advertised electronic equipment at grossly inflated prices on the noticeboards at school, capitalizing on a situation ... Commodities still haven't caught on here anything like as much as they're going to.'

It was an unsteady base on which to build a renewed British economy. But in 1981, as often in modern Britain, the government was happy to take growth wherever it could find it. A major preoccupation in Downing Street and the Treasury during 1981 and 1982 was the minutely shifting graph of national productivity, or the average output by Britons for every hour worked. After falling and then flatlining in 1980, as the recession set in, the graph tilted slightly upwards in early 1981 and then steepened. By the spring of 1982, the national productivity rate was close to a tenth above its pre-recession peak – twice as strong a recovery as after the previous recession in the mid-1970s. Some Thatcherite economists and politicians called this a 'productivity miracle'; they took it as evidence that monetarism, and the convulsive job cull that came with it, was bringing decisive benefits. But the upturn in the graph was no sharper than in the short-lived economic boom under Heath in the early 1970s. The graph flattened again in 1983.

During 1982 parts of the original monetarist strategy were quietly abandoned. In March, Howe produced a far less severe budget than the previous year, effectively cutting rather than raising taxes. He also sidestepped the ongoing Whitehall row about exactly which measure of the money supply should be the basis for economic policy, by saying that the government would now be guided by a 'diversity of [monetary] targets' – a classic piece of Howe phraseology, half numbing bureaucrat's jargon, half wily euphemism. He claimed credit, too, for the fact that high interest rates, previously a favourite monetarist tool, had fallen by a fifth since the autumn. In his own mind at least, the chancellor was a moderate and flexible man, not an ideologue, so he could change course without tormenting himself too much about U-turns. At least one more rigid Thatcherite was initially disappointed by the budget. Thatcher's chief economic adviser Alan Walters told Howe, 'I would have preferred it somewhat tighter.'

But the return of economic growth eased even Walters' doubts. In the second quarter of 1981, after shrinking for the five previous quarters, the British Gross Domestic Product expanded by an inglorious 0.2 per cent. For the next year, like a bad British Leyland car on a wet morning, the recovery stopped and started, quarter by quarter: GDP rose by 1.3 per cent, 0 per cent, 0.4 per cent, 1.3 per cent. Yet, according to this politically potent if always approximate statistic, it did not go into reverse. And by the start of 1982 some of the public were beginning to notice. In a chewy but much-cited essay in the July 1987 edition of the *British Journal of Political Science*, the respected academics David Sanders, Hugh Ward, David Marsh and Tony Fletcher noted that 'personal economic expectations', the percentage of people expecting their economic circumstances to get better minus the percentage expecting them to get worse, improved from -25 in December 1981 to -19 in January 1982, -17 in February and -16 in March.

Thatcher's inner circle found their own more anecdotal grounds for hope. John Hoskyns told me in 2012: 'One of my City contacts – one of the top brokers – told me in the summer of '81, when I went to the Irish Guards' annual parade, "We're all saying in the City that the government has got it right." It was very reassuring. I told Margaret straightaway.'

Yet Hoskyns remained anxious through the rest of 1981 and into 1982. 'The real question was,' he continued, 'would things in the shops, so to speak, be sufficiently better by the time she called an election?' In early 1982 the SDP were still advancing: Roy Jenkins won the Glasgow Hillhead by-election that March. And Michael Foot's Labour Party were not yet disastrously unpopular. In both January and February the Conservatives came third in MORI's reliable monthly opinion poll. I asked Hoskyns whether, looking back, he felt that the haltingly improving economy of 1981 and 1982 would have been enough in itself to get Thatcher re-elected. He paused for much longer than usual. Beyond the picture window of his living room, rain darkened the small lake at the end of his long garden. Eventually he said: 'I'm thinking aloud . . . I suspect . . . No.'

But in Britain, which for a democracy grants unusually large powers to premiers and their ministers, even one-term governments can change society, if not the economy, for decades to come. In August 1980 Margaret Thatcher's increasingly bogged-down administration produced a Housing Act. Even more than most legislation it was prolix and repetitive, but its ambitious intention stood out: 'to give ... the right to buy their homes ... to tenants of local authorities'.

The Act continued determinedly, 'Where it appears to the Secretary of State that tenants ... have or may have difficulty in exercising the right to buy effectively and expeditiously, he may ... do all such things as appear necessary or expedient to enable ... tenants ... to exercise the right to buy.' The Act envisaged a revolution in how a large minority of Britons lived. The government was not going to allow that revolution to be obstructed by Thatcherism's many enemies.

That revolution had been an awfully long time coming. Contrary to the conventional wisdom, cleverly sown by the Conservatives in 1980 and doggedly cultivated by right-wing Britain ever since, selling off council homes was not a sudden stroke of genius by the Thatcher government. The idea was as old as council housing itself. 'Nineteenth-century housing legislation required that council-built dwellings in redevelopment areas should be sold within ten years of completion,' point out the historians Colin Jones and Alan Murie in their revelatory 2006 book *The Right to Buy*. During the 1920s council homes were sold 'on a small scale'. During the 1950s sales accelerated: 5,825 in May 1956 alone. By 1972 even a distinctly leftish Tory environment secretary, Peter Walker, could declare to his party conference that the ability of council tenants to buy their homes was a 'very basic right', and that they should be offered a 20 per cent discount on the market price. Later in the 1970s, now a backbencher, Walker went further, suggesting that municipal properties should simply be given to their tenants. Michael Heseltine, the Conservative shadow environment secretary from 1976, who was close to Walker and like him had a populist side, agreed.

Many Conservatives had long seen property ownership as self-improving, socially and morally as well as materially. 'A wide distribution of property ... makes for a sound community,' declared Harold Macmillan as minister of housing in 1951. He and other Tories also considered it increasingly vital to their party's electoral chances, a means of winning the increasingly numerous votes of the upper working class and lower middle class. Although post-war Tory governments built plenty of council housing, including more in 1953 and 1954 than in any year under Labour, this construction programme was more pragmatic than ideological, a response to war damage. Once this housing emergency had passed, Tory enthusiasm for municipal homes soon declined. 'The council house system today is morally and socially damaging,' said Enoch Powell in 1962, then minister of health and pioneering a new, more hard-edged form of British right-wing politics over a decade before the Thatcherites. 'I think we ought to do something about this nuisance.'

Most of the Labour Party felt very differently. Labour councils, responding to the squalor and overcrowding of Victorian and Edwardian cities, and the graphic failure of private landlords and developers to deal with it – indeed the glee with which some of them exploited it – had constructed much of Britain's early municipal housing in the 1900s. Labour councils and governments carried on building it in large quantities for the next seven decades. By the early 1970s some Labour local authorities were even buying up whole streets of decaying inner-city properties from private landlords, and turning them into council homes – a tangible and potent demonstration of state power making up for market failure. By 1980 the proportion of all British housing in state hands was 'large ... by international standards,' write Jones and Murie, 'almost one in three households'. Most Labour politicians believed that there were few reasons, electoral or moral, to risk unravelling the housing safety net that made a congested country habitable for tens of millions.

Yet during the mid- and late 1970s some influential Labour figures, such as Harold Wilson's press secretary Joe Haines and Jim Callaghan's economic adviser Gavyn Davies, began to wonder whether renting from the council, often for life, was a satisfying way for such Britons to be living, and also whether governments could afford to keep building the necessary properties. By the late 1970s, the Wilson and then Callaghan administrations were increasingly short of money; and their more forward-thinking members were increasingly interested in the growth of consumerism and private property, and how Labour might adjust to it, before the other parties could take full advantage. Both Labour governments built progressively fewer council homes. In 1977 a high-profile housing study by the Callaghan administration accepted that 'for most people, owning one's house is a basic and natural desire'. The language used by Labour and the Conservatives to talk about the issue was beginning to converge.

The proportion of Britons who were homeowners had already been rising steadily for decades, and in 1970 it had passed 50 per cent. From the mid-1970s to the mid-1980s this was a trend driven as much by anxiety as home-making or materialism. In what seemed like a perpetual rollercoaster economy, with inflation frequently climbing and wages and stock markets frequently plunging, owning a property felt reassuring, and a rare safe bet financially. Yet the same economic volatility meant that homebuilding by private developers stopped and started. If owner-occupancy was going to carry on growing, then the country's near-ubiquitous council estates seemed to provide the obvious solution.

Again contrary to right-wing myth – and melodramatic punk lyricists – British municipal housing by the end of the 1970s was not simply a concrete dystopia of stained towers and windswept post-war courtyards. Jones and Murie write, 'It consisted mainly of houses with gardens, built to high specifications' – often better than in the private sector – 'over the previous 60 years.' Less than a tenth of homes were high-rise flats. Across much of Britain the typical council property was a spacious 1930s or 1940s semi with rosebeds, on the edge of a small town or village, slightly isolated and lacking in local services, but cheap. The average English council rent in 1981 absorbed less than 7 per cent of the average income.

However, even tenants in the best properties were increasingly dissatisfied. 'The quality of service in terms of rights, representation . . . advice, repairs and maintenance,' write Jones and Murie, 'was generally poor . . . If council housing was regarded as a flow of services, rather than just a physical entity, the "delegitimation" of council housing was endemic.' By the early 1980s many residents wanted a change of status.

Even in a recession a surprising proportion could afford it. The sheer extent of municipal housing meant that it accommodated millions of skilled and white-collar workers as well as the poor. There had been a long post-war increase in mass living standards, which slumps had interrupted but not yet decisively reversed. And many older council tenants had built up large savings, not least because of their low rents. A huge new class of potential property owners had been created; it just needed a government to legislate that class into existence.

It would not be Callaghan's. Lobbied by Labour councils still fiercely attached to municipal housing, and swamped by other problems, the instinctively cautious Callaghan simply parked a detailed plan worked out by Davies and others that would have let tenants buy their homes with state-subsidized mortgages, and would have put the proceeds back into building more council properties. 'It was a monumental own goal,' Davies told me in 2006. 'There is still bitterness over it.'

At the 1979 general election, council-home sales featured prominently in the Conservative manifesto. In this slim, seductive pamphlet, otherwise heavy on rhetoric and light on detail even by manifesto standards, the Right to Buy was given as much space as enormous issues such as education and health, and explained right down to the precise discounts to be offered to tenants. These were to start at 33 per cent off their home's market value, and were to rise, according to how long they had rented it, to a maximum of 50 per cent for tenants of twenty years' standing or longer. 'We shall also ensure,' promised the manifesto, 'that 100 per cent mortgages are available.' For any purchaser, and particularly for people in late middle age or older, the British age group most likely to vote Conservative, these were extremely generous terms; or as Davies put it to me, half-impressed and half-horrified, 'You were insane if you didn't buy.'

Whether these terms represented a good deal for the state, which had after all built these homes and would lose the rental income from them, was not something the manifesto explored. Nor were related, even more fundamental, questions. Would the country be left with enough cheap homes after the sell-off? And would the policy backfire if the population, and therefore the demand for housing, rose? The population of the UK had stagnated throughout the 1970s, but that situation might well end if the national revival promised by the Conservatives occurred. Even without such a miracle, given that the UK was part of the European Union, and also linked by other busy immigration routes to its vast former empire, and to the United States, a stable or falling population in the long term could hardly be assumed. But effectively it was. The Right to Buy, say Jones and Murie, 'was introduced at a time of some complacency in British housing policy . . . For the first time in over a century there was not a shortage of housing, at least in numerical terms.'

On winning power, Thatcher made the forceful Michael Heseltine environment secretary. She and the Treasury quickly squashed his notion about giving away council homes. The Treasury needed the money from sales. The prime minister, with her acute sensitivity and loyalty to Tory-inclined social groups, believed, probably with good reason, that a giveaway would enrage homeowners who had painstakingly saved for deposits and paid off mortgages.

Instead, within a fortnight of taking up his post, Heseltine issued an official circular recommending council-home sales. To his frustration the legislation took almost eighteen months to draft and push through, with obstinate resistance coming from Labour councils and the House of Lords. But by August 1980 the Act was passed. Thatcher herself introduced the policy in a special television broadcast. 'If you have been a council tenant for at least three years,' she began, enunciating her words even more slowly and carefully than usual, as if addressing a slightly dim child, 'you will have the right, *by law*, to buy your house.' She gave a couple of firm, no-going-back nods: 'And that's that.'

'The Right to Buy': it was a clever slogan, clear, quick to say, easy to remember, and combining two of modern Britain's favourite preoccupations, personal freedom and purchasing, while also encapsulating the more seductive side of what the Thatcher government was offering the country. Her use of the word 'house' in the broadcast, when millions of council tenants actually lived in flats, was also significant. It gave the policy an aspirational flavour: reassuringly suburban rather than proletarian and urban.

The Right to Buy TV ad that soon followed gave further, less subtle, hints that the government's intended housing transformation would reinforce rather than upset the existing social hierarchy. In a generous, tidy semi without a tower block in sight, like the setting for a middle-class sitcom, an envelope containing a Right to Buy leaflet dropped onto the front doormat. A small tousled boy, wearing dungarees, white-skinned, picked it up. He ran eagerly to the breakfast table. There, his mother, in her mid-thirties, dressed in a spotless white blouse, and with a Diana-like haircut, was reading a newspaper and sipping from a genteel white teacup. The old-fashioned implication seemed to be that Father was out at work. The camera moved closer to the table, revealing that Mother was poring over a print ad, headlined 'How to go about buying your council house'. The TV commercial revealed itself as an ad for a government information campaign, as much as for the Right to Buy itself. Then a voiceover began in a chirpy Cockney accent – the ad's one concession to the existence of a working class – informing viewers that, 'There are nearly five million council tenants in England and Wales, many with families like yours . . . *You* can decide whether to turn *your* home into *your* house.'

Sales started slowly. During the remaining four months of 1980, fifty-five council homes were bought in England under the new legislation. Some Labour local authorities were deliberately sluggish in dealing with would-be buyers. In the London borough of Greenwich, council staff refused to give out application forms, and sometimes denied that a Right to Buy existed at all. But Heseltine, empowered almost without limit by the 1980 Housing Act, beat his municipal opponents in court. Then came the sales surge: in 1981, 66,321 English Right to Buy purchases; in 1982, 174,697 – almost as many dwellings as in the whole of Liverpool, a sales peak that would be repeatedly approached again during the rest of the 1980s but never exceeded. In Wales, too, sales peaked early, in 1982. In Scotland, people were more cautious, the highest annual figure not reached until 1989. There were also regional variations: in England, sales were fastest in London, the southeast and the southwest; and slowest in the industrial, or increasingly ex-industrial, north.

But certain patterns were universal. Semis sold better than terraces. Houses sold better than flats – at first by almost fifty to one. Low-rise flats sold better than high-rise ones. Properties with gardens, or with garages, were strongly in demand. Rural and suburban properties sold better than urban ones. Homes on small estates sold better than homes on large ones. Homes with non-council neighbours were the most sought after of all.

Similar subtle and not so subtle social gradations defined the buyers. A thorough, politically neutral national survey conducted by the Department of the Environment in 1985–6 and published in 1988, looking back at the first five years of the Right to Buy, found that:

> [Purchasers] were a highly diverse group but . . . clearly not representative of [council] tenants as a whole. Buyers were disproportionately drawn from the middle aged and the better off, many with adult children sharing the home and the expenses. Most were in full-time work, usually manual skilled or white-collar occupations, and with more than one wage-earner in the household. Buyer incomes were on average about double tenant incomes.

Buyers were ten times less likely to be unemployed than non-buyers. And they were twice as likely to know existing homeowners. In fact, 'Two thirds of buyers reported that all or most of their family or friends were owner-occupiers.' In all these regards, the survey quietly concluded, council-home buyers in the first half of the 1980s showed a strong 'continuance' with those who had bought council properties during the decades before the Right to Buy became law.

Thatcherism, in some ways, was a highly skilful exercise in feigned egalitarianism – as indeed is capitalism itself. Just as the enthusiasm of some Thatcherites for moonlighting tacitly favoured those with the confidence and ability to play the benefits system – moonlighting was not an option for the old or infirm – and just as the Enterprise Allowance Scheme was open only to those with access to private loans or savings, so the Right to Buy, for all its appealingly inclusive rhetoric, was not a right available to all.

Those who could not afford to exercise it tended to be lone parents, younger tenants, people living on their own, or Thatcherism's economic losers: the unemployed or low-skilled. There were also psychological barriers. Some had been erected by the government's own Right to Buy advertising, with its emphasis on houses and families; others were more ancient, to do with class assumptions and ignorance and caution. Non-buyers tended to be afraid of mortgage debt, or of taking responsibility for repairs. Or they didn't think property ownership was for the likes of them. Or they simply didn't like their home enough to buy it: during the 1970s, more vulnerable tenants had become increasingly concentrated in the worst council properties. Often, non-buyers were simply too overwhelmed by the rest of their lives. Even after five years of the Right to Buy, the 1988 report found, almost a tenth of council tenants were completely unaware of the scheme at all. Among the remaining nine-tenths, the vast majority of whom qualified for it, 'knowledge of the Right to Buy was found to be sparse and often inaccurate ... 45% did not know whether they would qualify ... and a further 14% believed they would not ... In all, only two out of five tenants believed they were eligible and only 15% claimed to know their discount entitlement ... [such] estimates of discount entitlement were, moreover, usually inaccurate.'

The government and its press allies presented the Right to Buy as a triumph regardless. Either way, the scheme did succeed in altering how many Britons thought. The 1988 survey asked 1,230 buyers why they had bought, and received the same kind of hard-headed, individualistic, essentially Thatcherite responses as participants in the Enterprise Allowance pilot had provided when they had been surveyed two years earlier: 'good financial investment ... the "bargain" which discounts on sales provided ... the sense of security ... of pride ... the freedom to repair or improve ... the desire to have something to leave the family ... to move up the housing ladder ... to increase mobility'. Two-thirds of those questioned said they had not expected to become homeowners until the Right to Buy legislation. As in all successful capitalism, a new demand had been created and then satisfied.

The discounts were pivotal to the process. The official prices of the state assets being sold off were respectably high: in southern England in 1981 the average valuation of a Right to Buy property was £19,557, a tenth more than the average price paid for a private-sector home by an English first-time buyer. Yet most Right to Buy purchasers actually paid much closer to £10,000: 'The average discount obtained' nationally, reported the 1988 survey, 'was 44%.'

Buyers typically borrowed almost the entire cost of their property. Pension lump sums and personal savings, sometimes built up from redundancy payments, covered the rest. 'Contrary to a common belief,' the 1988 survey continued, 'there was little evidence of children or other younger relatives buying on behalf of an elderly parent';

and only '2% of buyers had borrowed money from parents and other family members'. The Right to Buy, like many of the rights created by the Thatcher government, was exercised individually or by the nuclear family, not more communally.

Meanwhile the government received a financial windfall, not as juicy as North Sea oil, but substantial: £692 million from council-home sales in 1980–81, £1394 million in 1981–2, £1981 million in 1982–3. Thatcherism liked to present itself as a rejection of the post-war, state-driven, more profligate way of doing things. But in housing, her administration was actually the post-war state's beneficiary, selling off the assets that it had built up. A similar dependency lay, almost never acknowledged, behind her social and economic reforms generally. Her freedom to make Britain more risk-taking and individualistic in some ways only existed because the country she had inherited, for all its flaws and tensions, was a relatively stable, unified place underneath: more equal in the late 1970s than it had ever been, still permeated by shared class assumptions, largely at peace – there had been few riots in Jim Callaghan's Britain. Her administration, supposedly dynamic and new, in fact partly lived off this social capital that stodgy old social democracy had produced. What would happen when that social capital began to run out, like what would happen when Britain ran out of cheap housing, was, in the early 1980s, a question for another day.

The Treasury intended to use the Right to Buy income to help pay off the stubbornly large public debt. Yet Heseltine wished local government to retain some financial independence. Unusually among Thatcher's ministers, he also had some sensitivity to the wider consequences for housing of Right to Buy. He successfully argued that councils should be allowed to keep three-quarters of the income from sales, in order to replace the homes sold. Contrary to Right to Buy's small but growing number of critics since the 1980s, the policy did not kill council home building overnight: over 250,000 state-owned dwellings were completed between 1980 and 1985.

But the rate of construction did slow, year by year. The share of the income from sales that went to councils was gradually eroded, against Heseltine's wishes. In 1983 Thatcher moved him to the Ministry of

Defence, in large part to use his bulldozing charisma against CND and the women of Greenham. Once he settled into the task, debating with them in public – his predecessors had been too anxious or disdainful to do so – while privately encouraging the press to present them as dupes of the Soviet Union, they never quite held the initiative again as they had in the early 1980s.

Meanwhile rents for remaining council tenants rose with a new alacrity from then on. By 1991 they were 55 per cent higher, relative to average earnings, than they had been ten years earlier. 'If it were not for the Right to Buy,' conclude Jones and Murie, 'the council housing sector as a whole would have generated huge surpluses [from rental income] and the rise in real rents . . . would not have been necessary. It is therefore questionable who has subsidized the Right to Buy.' Or to put it more directly: home ownership was made possible for wealthier council tenants through discounts paid for by their poorer neighbours.

Yet in the early 1980s, the full cost of the Right to Buy was less apparent than the new front doors, new kitchens and bathrooms, new paint jobs and fireplaces, new pebbledash and stonecladding, new garden balustrades and double glazing, new porches, conservatories and mock-Tudor panels that began to appear across the previously muted and communal landscape of British municipal housing. The prime minister posed regularly with new owners, in their lovingly arranged kitchens, on their swept-clean doorsteps, in their trimmed front gardens; the owners usually a little younger than the average buyer, and dressed up for the occasion, with photogenic children at hand. Thatcher herself looked genuinely fascinated and delighted, sometimes even sitting on a garden wall – winning one of her battles to reshape the country, for once. Until the spring of 1982 it did not seem likely that she would win many more.

11
Our Friends in the South

For most of the twentieth century, the SS *Great Britain* slowly rotted in the freezing blue waters of the Falkland Islands. Designed by Isambard Kingdom Brunel near the height of the Industrial Revolution and the British Empire, shortly after Britain had established its questionable modern hold over the Falklands, on its launch in Bristol in 1843 the sleek passenger steamer was the biggest and most advanced in the world. For the next forty years she sliced back and forth across British-dominated oceans, to Australia, India, and North and South America, sometimes as a civilian vessel, sometimes as a troopship. In the 1880s, finally approaching obsolescence and damaged by a storm, she was dumped in the choppy harbour at Port Stanley, the Falklands' capital and only substantial settlement. There she was converted by the Falkland Islands Company, the colony's only substantial business, into a floating storage hulk for wood and coal.

In December 1914, early in the First World War, a German fleet approached Port Stanley, aiming to destroy its coal stocks and wireless station, both essential to the Royal Navy's ability to patrol the vast and empty South Atlantic. The *Great Britain* was hurriedly used to refuel a squadron of British warships. At the subsequent Battle of the Falkland Islands, the overconfident German fleet was decisively defeated.

But that was seemingly the last of the *Great Britain*'s glory. In 1937, leaking, pitted with rust, stripped by the relentless Falklands wind, she was towed a few miles north to Sparrow Cove, an unpopulated, even more exposed inlet. Holes were blasted in her sides, so that she would not shift with the tide, and she was beached upright in shallow water: a skeleton of Victorian greatness, surrounded by penguins.

The Falklands are a surprisingly spacious place – a tattered archipelago the size of Wales with the population of a large village. There is no pressing need for tidiness. Instead, the soaked and sun-bleached junk of centuries lies scattered around, as if the islands were a giant farmyard or a rambling open-air museum: Victorian agricultural tools, boxy 1940s vehicles, and above all, battered vessels and shipwrecks left by the mountainous South Atlantic. The best wrecks become landmarks, and until the 1960s the *Great Britain* attracted local walkers and scavengers for timber and metal parts. In the Falklands of the mid-twentieth century, denuded of much of their purpose by cuts to the Royal Navy and the opening of the Panama Canal, which meant that merchant ships could avoid the South Atlantic, there was not much else for the dwindling population to do.

Back in Britain, even those with official Falklands responsibilities focused less and less on this unproductive, hard-to-defend imperial remnant, 8,000 miles distant, and twenty times closer to Argentina. 'I thought the Falklands was an absolutely terrible place,' John Nott, Margaret Thatcher's defence secretary in the early 1980s, told me. 'I'd seen quite a lot of photographs of it. Port Stanley was a dump. The rest of the Falklands . . . I mean, it's Salisbury Plain' – the famously bald and comfortless plateau used by the British army for training – 'but worse.'

Occasionally someone in England took a more careful look at the archipelago. In 1967 Dr Ewan Corlett, a naval architect and maritime-history enthusiast, wrote a letter to *The Times* pointing out that the *Great Britain* was still beached in the islands. He urged that she be repaired and sailed home. A salvage operation was organized, partly funded by the property developer and patriotic philanthropist 'Union Jack' Hayward, and also involving the Duke of Edinburgh, the Royal Marines, and the then governor of the Falklands, Sir Cosmo Haskard. In early 1970 a tiny task force, a tugboat and giant floating pontoon, sailed from the English Channel to the islands. The disintegrating *Great Britain* was gently raised off the seabed. A large crack in her hull was stuffed with mattresses donated by Falklanders. Then she was lashed onto the pontoon for the risky voyage back to Britain.

On 22 June 1970, three days after the election of a new Conservative prime minister with ambitions to be a national saviour, Edward

Heath, the task force made it back to Britain. On 5 July the inert, drab-looking *Great Britain*, like the wingless carcass of some giant insect, was towed up the River Avon towards the Bristol dock where she had been built. A hundred thousand people, the equivalent of a quarter of the city's population, jammed the riverbanks to watch – cheering, blowing horns and hooters, throwing petals. They also waved Union Jacks. From the South Atlantic, a British nationalism had been reawakened.

During the 1970s, the age-old British appetite for foreign adventures was smaller than usual, but it never completely went away. The empire had been largely dismantled. Britain stayed out of the war in Vietnam. Soldiery in far-off lands was replaced by the grim precautionary routines of the Cold War and the containment action in Northern Ireland. My father was part of a generation of British servicemen, the first since the 1920s, who did not expect to be involved in many wars during their careers, and possibly none at all.

A few opportunities for exotic deployments remained. A British garrison lingered in sticky Belize in Central America, to prevent an invasion by neighbouring Guatemala, which for decades had claimed the former British colony as its territory. In what was then Rhodesia, now Zimbabwe, another former British colony, a British force helped police a delicate 1979 peace agreement between the white supremacist government and black guerrilla groups – an agreement negotiated in London under the supervision of Thatcher's conciliatory first foreign secretary, Lord Carrington. In the British-influenced Sultanate of Oman in the Middle East, detachments of Royal Marines, SAS men and regular British soldiers spent the first half dozen years of the 1970s helping to smother a protracted left-wing rebellion.

Unlike the seemingly endless and unwinnable Cold War and the conflict in Ulster, these relatively deft and successful operations helped sustain a belief in British military prowess. In a country losing confidence in so many other ways, justifiably or not, this idea was especially appealing. Meanwhile a certain glamour still attached itself to military clothes and military history: from the combat fatigues and flying jackets worn by posey British bands such as The Teardrop Explodes and The Clash – who released an album in May 1982 called *Combat*

Rock – to the name and decor of London's most-hyped nightclub, The Blitz.

But this militarism remained low-key by British standards. The feats of our boys in Oman or Belize were drawn-out and often clandestine; they rarely appeared on newspaper front pages. It would take an operation much closer to home, and seemingly much easier to understand, to revive British jingoism.

On 30 April 1980, among the usually quiet wedding-cake terraces south of Hyde Park in central London, six heavily armed men entered the Iranian Embassy and took everyone they could hostage, including two visiting BBC journalists and a British policeman. The embassy occupiers belonged to a group seeking self-determination for part of western Iran. They demanded the release of comrades held in Iranian jails, and their own safe passage out of England.

For almost a week TV crews from around the world gathered in front of the perfect stage set of the building's colonnaded white facade. The Thatcher government followed what her principal private secretary Clive Whitmore called a 'strategy of patience', granting minor concessions such as the broadcast of the occupiers' demands on television, while preparing a more confrontational alternative for if or when negotiations failed. Unseen by the cameras or the hostage-takers, SAS men entered buildings around the embassy and installed viewing and listening devices. To hide the sound of the drilling, the government instructed the British Airports Authority to direct planes lower than usual over central London.

On the sixth day of the crisis, a Bank Holiday, the embassy occupiers, frustrated at the progress of the negotiations, killed a hostage with little warning; and threatened that they would soon kill the others. Shortly after 7 p.m., as a still spring evening began to settle over the terraces, reporters spotted a cluster of bulky men in black on the embassy roof. The BBC and ITN replaced their normal evening schedules with a live broadcast of what followed.

Wearing balaclavas and gas masks, the SAS men began to abseil swiftly down the back of the building. Meanwhile at the front, other black-clad figures suddenly materialized on balconies next to the embassy. Silhouetted against the stucco, submachine guns jutting, they moved fast across the facade like climbing gorillas. There was a camera-juddering explosion: orange, purple and oily grey. A cacophony of dog barks began in the near distance. The men in black all disappeared into the building.

As smoke from the blast ghosted slowly along the sealed-off street, dusting the frozen lines of expensive cars, reporters and policemen scrambled to take cover behind them. From the now inscrutable embassy facade came muffled shots in quick, controlled bursts, and a woman's scream. After less than a minute, the first rescued hostage was conjured from the building. Seconds later a piece of white material was frantically waved from a window. Flames appeared in another. In the deep blue evening sky above, a khaki-coloured helicopter with a bulbous protusion on one side – 'what appears to be a gun pod', said the ITN reporter, Paul Tilsley, with terse excitement – came swooping in over Hyde Park. Less than two minutes later, figures in civilian clothes, some of them still in spotless, smart skirts, were escorted gently but firmly by policemen out of the front door of the embassy. 'After six days and almost eleven hours exactly,' announced Tilsley, 'the hostages reach safety.'

All but one were brought out alive. Of their six captors, only one survived. The *Boy's Own* drama of the television footage, quick and conclusive as a cartoon, obscured the fact that viewers learned little else about how the raid had actually gone. Thirty-two years later, two of the SAS men involved belatedly and improbably approached the dry public-policy magazine *Prospect* and offered their accounts. One of the men, interviewed under the pseudonym Pete Winner, revealed that from the beginning of the raid:

> Things started to go wrong . . . We recommended using ladders, but they wanted abseiling because it was much more glamorous . . . One of the abseilers put his foot through a window [prematurely] and the head terrorist heard the noise . . . The leader of [one SAS] team, a Fijian guy, who carried too much ammo . . . [his] abseil equipment jammed and he [was] swinging in the flames . . . The guy was badly burned because he didn't have flameproof overalls. We told them we should have flameproof overalls and we were told to use bog standard black overalls . . . We couldn't use a charge to blow in the back door because the blast would have sent shrapnel up to the guys on the balcony. So we had to

> use a sledge hammer ... that held up the speed of entry ... [Another] guy ... his gas mask burned off ... [and his] gun jammed ...

Yet in 1980 what mattered was the raid's outcome; and the sudden, graphic impression it gave of renewed British resolve and military vigour. More than six months afterwards, in November 1980, *Harpers & Queen* carried an item about a ball for an SAS benevolent fund, to be held at Annabel's, the favourite nightclub of rich right-wing Londoners. 'Every ticket had been sold ages before, and all week Annabel's had been besieged by telephone calls from members desperate to come and gawp at the gallant heroes of the Princes Gate siege.' During January and February 1982 a British movie based on the siege was filmed with the cooperation of the SAS, including meetings with some of the soldiers involved and use of the regiment's motto for the title, *Who Dares Wins*. The film gave its version of the siege a crude and implausible political twist by moving the setting to the American Embassy, and making anti-nuclear activists the villains. But it was pacy and stirringly patriotic. I saw the film as soon as it came out.

Margaret Thatcher herself was 'elated' for days following the storming, writes her official biographer Charles Moore. Only hours after the operation, according to the historian of the SAS Tony Geraghty, she visited the victorious soldiers at their temporary base near the embassy. Sitting cross-legged on the floor, with uncharacteristic humility, the prime minister watched the TV footage of the hostage rescue with them. She also posed for a private photograph with three of the SAS men, standing against a wall, looking slightly stiff and star-struck, wearing pearls and a pale suit while they flanked her with their black uniforms, their gas masks and submachine guns. 'Maggie loved us,' Pete Winner recalled. 'After the siege we had an open cheque book.'

The unpopular prime minister received a rare rush of praise from around the world. 'The superb demonstration of British guts and British efficiency ... is an inspiring example to free people,' telegrammed Richard Nixon. 'Congratulations on marking your first year of government with [a] magnificent operation,' wrote Lord Chalfont, an excitable former Labour minister. 'It again means something to be a British citizen abroad.'

*

The only problem with this new militarism, at least from a jingoistic perspective, was that Thatcher did not really seem willing to pay for it. The SAS might have been offered a better budget, but it was a single regiment; the rest of the armed forces found her government much less generous. In June 1981, barely a year after the embassy raid, the government published a White Paper setting out its intended approach to defence over the next half-decade. 'Britain already spends 5.2% of its gross domestic product on defence – one of the highest figures anywhere in the [NATO] Alliance,' the frank document pointed out early on, 'even though we are not among the wealthiest members and continue to face sharp economic difficulties.'

The government planned to permit a slower than usual increase in military spending. Given the perpetually rocketing costs of defence equipment, this would mean drastic cuts to parts of the armed forces. With much of the army and air force committed to defending Britain and Germany from the anticipated Soviet hordes, and Britain committed to modernizing its nuclear weapons for the same reason, the obvious thing to cut was the Royal Navy. Unlike the army and air force, it was still one of the largest in the world – it had sixty destroyers and frigates alone – and its usefulness in protecting Western Europe against a Soviet assault expected to come by land and air was not immediately obvious. To the defence secretary John Nott, whose thinking shaped the White Paper, the navy's *raison d'être* was, he told me, more 'emotional and psychological – the great Nelsonian tradition . . . to be the blue-water navy that polices the seas. There was a huge snobbery in the Royal Navy that only they could do it.' Or to put it more provocatively: 'They were always looking for missions to keep the chaps happy.'

Nott had done his military service in the army. During the 1950s he had been a lieutenant in the Gurkhas, confronting communist guerrillas in the nasty end-of-empire war in Malaya. Another formative influence was his great-great-great-grandfather, General Sir William Nott, a successful commander during the otherwise often disastrous and overstretched British campaigns in Afghanistan a century earlier. Nott junior had been left sceptical about the idea of British military omnipotence. 'When I was in Malaya,' he remembered, 'the navy had ships in [nearby] Singapore, looking for something to do, looking to give us a hand. They used to come along and shell the jungle. It was a completely pointless exercise. Because the jungle muffled the blast. We all used to laugh.'

In 2012, as in the early 1980s, Nott did not look or sound like most people's idea of an ex-soldier. Bespectacled, professorially balding, narrow-shouldered verging on weedy, he had a downbeat, metallic, slightly grating voice that switched barely perceptibly between seriousness and man-of-the-world mockery. He might have been a retired senior civil servant or an ex-undertaker – except that he had a large house in Chelsea, with a downstairs toilet full of framed cartoons of him with Margaret Thatcher. Across the antique-filled living room, cast into gloom by a wild, drenching day worthy of the Falklands, Nott's little eyes radiated occasional mischief and continual self-assurance. 'The memoirs are rather good,' he said, 'don't you think?'

In *Here Today, Gone Tomorrow: Memoirs of an Errant Politician* (2002), Nott carefully set out his credentials as one of the modern Conservative Party's bolshier and more intriguing right-wingers. He had joined their state-shrinking crusade in the 1950s, well before Margaret Thatcher did. In the early 1970s he set up a free-market dining club with another prickly right-winger, Nicholas Ridley. 'We discussed whether we should ask Margaret Thatcher to join us. But we were uncertain . . . whether she was "one of us".'

To Nott and Ridley, and other iconoclastic British free-marketeers such as Alan Walters, transforming British civilian life was the priority. 'The radical right,' said Nott, 'were more concerned with economic policy than defence policy.' Besides, to them government spending on defence was just as questionable as in any other area. 'The waste at the Ministry of Defence is absolutely phenomenal,' Nott told me. Despite his awkward, unbiddable quality – or perhaps because of it – Thatcher appointed him defence secretary in January 1981, when her government's finances were at their thinnest. 'I really did want to get a grip on that damned defence budget,' Nott told me. He proposed cuts including the loss of a dozen frigates and destroyers, an aircraft carrier and two assault ships. The navy's capacity to operate beyond Europe, which it had long clung to, would be greatly reduced. In response, Nott continued, 'The navy were just completely obtuse. I could not have a sensible intellectual discussion with them.'

Of all the naval enemies he made, none was more implacable than the First Sea Lord, Admiral Sir Henry Leach. The head of the service since just after Thatcher's election, Leach had a stare like a searchlight and a mouth like a torpedo slit. He had decided to join the navy by the age of ten, with the tacit encouragement of his naval officer father, whom he adored. Leach made it onto his first ship in 1941. The same year, his father was killed in one of the great humiliations of British naval history, when the supposedly state-of-the-art battleship he was commanding, HMS *Prince of Wales*, overconfidently deployed without airborne protection near Singapore, was sunk by half a dozen small Japanese torpedo bombers. Leach junior was himself in Singapore at the time; on hearing of the sinking, he undertook an agonizing search for news of his father, who had refused to leave his stricken ship. Like Thatcher's equally driven strategist John Hoskyns, who also lost a heroic father in a famous defeat in the Second World War, Leach was affected for good. 'All of us in the MOD were always conscious of Henry's father,' Nott recalled. Did he think Leach spent his naval career wanting to avenge his father and the *Prince of Wales* disaster? 'Entirely right.'

From 1941 Leach sailed in everything from Arctic convoys to the shrinking British fleet in the post-imperial Far East, and maintained a belief in the sacredness of the Royal Navy throughout. Opposite the title page of his memoirs, published in 1993 and grandly titled *Endure No Makeshifts*, he quoted the writer and imperialist John Buchan: 'The sea has formed the English character and the essential England is to be found in those who follow it.'

Like many senior British military men who watched their country's superpower status steadily evaporate during the post-war era, Leach regarded Britain as a place of posturing left-wing politicians and trains that no longer ran on time, and preferred the Conservatives to Labour. But Nott's proposed naval cuts predictably enraged him. When I first picked up Leach's memoirs in the British Library, I found a handwritten letter, apparently untouched and inadvertently left between the endpapers. Dated 16 December 1982, soon after he finally retired from the navy, it had been written by the admiral himself to a friend, in a neat hand full of forward-sloping, impatient diagonals. Its tone was valedictory and calm except for one sentence:

'After a bitter final four months' battle with that creep Nott we have managed to claw back just about everything.'

Shortly after the publication of the 1981 defence White Paper, Nott visited the centuries-old naval dockyard at Portsmouth. It had been singled out for 'a lot of redundancies', as he put it to me. His memoirs record:

> I was on the dockyard premises talking to the unions. I noticed hundreds of menacing-looking dockyard workers converging on the glass-covered headquarters building where my meetings were taking place. Gradually the yelling from the assembled men grew in intensity ... I asked the admiral commanding the dockyard if he had sufficient Ministry of Defence police on duty:
>
> 'No, they are all at the International Defence Equipment Exhibition in Southampton ...'
>
> 'Well, I think we are about to have a violent riot ... You had better call in Hampshire police ...'
>
> 'We can't do that. We never invite civilian police on to dockyard premises.'

Instead, Nott was advised by another naval officer and by union officials to go outside and address the crowd:

> A soapbox was erected ... As soon as I opened my mouth a hail of metal bolts and other dangerous missiles were hurled in my direction and the glass of several windows and doors was shattered. Amazingly nothing struck me, and I was hustled back into the building and the doors were locked. This time the Hampshire police were called in plus two coaches ... we were ushered into the coaches and led by a police car towards the exit. However, the men had not dispersed and hurled their missiles at the coaches. Several naval and civilian officials were covered in shattered glass, but we escaped ... None of this appeared in the press.

*

By the early 1980s a similar mix of cost-cutting and panicky miscalculation characterized Britain's dealings with the Falklands. These stony, thinly grassed, sometimes beautifully sun-streaked islands – the same distance from the equator as southern England but much more elemental, their treeless hills exposed to sea weather from all directions – had been a headache for distant governments, territorial adjudicators and historians for five centuries.

In the 1500s Dutch, Florentine, Spanish, Portuguese and English navigators exploring the near-landless South Atlantic sighted the islands for the first time with varying degrees of certainty. The Englishman Richard Hawkins mapped a little of their misty, treacherous coast. A lost ship from a Spanish expedition may have spent a winter sheltering among the islands. Otherwise, they had always been uninhabited, except for probably brief occupations by pre-colonial peoples from the South American mainland, 400 miles away.

In 1690 an English naval captain, John Strong, made the first confirmed landing on the archipelago, and named the sound between the main islands after Lord Falkland, the Treasurer to the navy. During the eighteenth century, first France, then Britain, then Spain established tiny Falklands settlements, and with them competing territorial claims. In 1770 a Spanish fleet and invasion force made the British abandon their toehold after a token show of resistance. Enraged MPs forced the Westminster government to begin preparing for a war to reinstate the British settlement. Spain backed down, and the British returned to the islands. In 1776 they left again: Westminster was no longer willing to pay to protect the Falklands. But the British left a plaque in their evacuated compound restating their original claim.

In 1790 the two countries signed a sprawling and ambiguous treaty, the Nootka Sound Convention, by which Britain promised to end its 'colonial ambition' in 'South America and the islands adjacent', while not explicitly giving up all its interest in the Falklands. During the first third of the nineteenth century, the Spanish empire in South America slowly collapsed, and Argentina came into being as an independent country, inheriting the Spanish claim to the Falklands. The islands themselves descended into a semi-anarchy of multinational whale- and seal-hunting and violent criminality. Britain, now in its most insatiable empire-building phase, opportunistically revived its involvement in the archipelago. In 1833 and 1834 British warships expelled the few Argentinians still there and took control of all the islands. In 1841 the Falklands became a functioning British colony, complete with governor and settlers.

For the next hundred years, the sour, yellowish landscape was determinedly seeded with scattered sheep farms and huddles of houses, often built of corrugated iron, known locally as 'wriggly tin'. A hard-working, hard-drinking, inward-looking, sometimes lonely population of a couple of thousand established itself, drawn mainly from Scotland and the south coast of England. Argentina pursued its claim to the islands, which it called Las Islas Malvinas, only intermittently. Then, in 1948, the ambitious nationalist government of Juan Perón hinted heavily that it might seize the islands. In London the Labour foreign secretary Ernest Bevin told his Argentinian counterpart, 'If any attack is made on the Falkland Islands we will defend ourselves and there will be hostilities.' No invasion occurred.

In the twentieth century, as previously, there was a big element of bluff to Britain's Falklands stance. Except during the First and Second World Wars, the British garrison in the islands was small: often only a few dozen soldiers, occasionally as few as half a dozen, supposedly defending hundreds of miles of coastline and dozens of islands. Many of these were scarcely inhabited, and all were extremely hard to travel across, as the only proper roads were in Port Stanley. From 1945 onwards, as Britain began paring back its navy and its once-extensive network of South Atlantic naval facilities, so the Falklands garrison became more and more isolated. Steadily fewer British warships visited. The reinforcements the islands might need in a hurry were now based in Britain, three weeks' sailing away. Flying in soldiers instead was effectively impossible, with Argentinian airspace to the north and west, the Antarctic to the south, and thousands of miles of ocean to the east, devoid of British airbases. Until 1979 the Falklands had no runway suitable for long-distance aircraft.

In the mid-1960s Argentina began a sustained effort to acquire the islands that would last almost two decades. One level of this campaign was relatively subtle and diplomatic. Argentina used the United Nations' official opposition to colonialism, first to start discrediting the British occupation internationally, and then to force London to begin negotiating with Buenos Aires about how the long-contentious colonial situation in the South Atlantic could be resolved. The British government quickly accepted that the talks could be wide-ranging.

This was not as surprising as it now seems. By the mid-1960s

Britain had been giving up bits of its empire, many of them much bigger and more useful than the Falklands, for almost two decades. Dignified retreats, recognizing economic and military realities, selling out British settlers, accepting foreign claims to sovereignty: however you described these manoeuvres, they were one of the main things the post-war Foreign Office did. Also, Britain had been busily trading commodities and immigrants with Argentina ever since the country's creation. In 1914 the only ever overseas branch of Harrods opened in Buenos Aires. Half a century on, Britain was now an economically fragile ex-superpower, and it needed such trading relationships more than ever.

The negotiators met, sporadically but persistently, between January 1966 and February 1982: sometimes in public and sometimes in secret, sometimes under Labour governments and sometimes under Tory ones, sometimes in Buenos Aires and sometimes in London, sometimes in neutral locations and sometimes in unlikely ones, sometimes pointlessly and irritably, sometimes cordially and constructively. One of the warmest meetings occurred in September 1980. Nicholas Ridley, recently appointed as a Foreign Office minister by Margaret Thatcher, covertly saw his Argentinian counterpart, Carlos Cavandoli, at the 'Hotel de Lac in the picturesque lakeside village of Coppet, ten miles or so from Geneva', according to an anonymous Whitehall figure in the official history of the Falklands War by Sir Lawrence Freedman. 'Mr Ridley's visit to Geneva with his wife is . . . for a short holiday break,' the official cover story went. 'He hopes to do a little water colour painting.'

In fact, Ridley was offering the Argentinians a proposal:

> 1. Titular sovereignty over the Falkland Islands (Islas Malvinas) . . . would be transferred to Argentina, with effect from the date of signature of the Agreement.
>
> 2. Continued British administration of the Islands . . . would be simultaneously assured by means of a lease-back to the United Kingdom for a period of 99 years . . .
>
> 3. The British and Argentine flags would be flown side by side on public buildings on the Islands.
>
> 4. The British Government would be represented by a Governor . . .

5. The Argentine Government would be represented by a Commissioner-General.

6. There would be a Joint [Anglo-Argentine] Council to arrange cooperation over the economic development of the Islands and their maritime zone.

'The Argentine reaction was positive,' writes Freedman. 'Cavandoli claimed to have been thinking along the same lines and would have been ready to put forward a similar proposal.'

Britain had already long accepted that Argentina had a role in the life of the islands. In 1971 the two governments signed a Communications Agreement, arranging for LADE, an airline operated by the Argentinian air force, to provide flights to and from the archipelago. All passengers were required to carry a special identity card issued by Buenos Aires. In 1972 Argentina laid down the islands' first proper airstrip, on rare flat land east of Stanley. In 1974 Britain granted the state-owned Argentinian oil and gas companies a monopoly of petrol and gas sales on the islands. In 1980 a house was built in Stanley to accommodate the local LADE commander. A few other Argentinians settled in the close little town. Increasingly, Falklanders went to Argentina for holidays, and education and medical treatment, rather than distant Britain. The Argentinian navy even gave Port Stanley two yachts, although these remained pointedly unused.

Meanwhile the wider web of Anglo-Argentinian connections continued to grow. British bank loans to Argentina had reached almost £2 billion by 1982. Britain trained Argentinian military officers and pilots. Britain began buying Argentinian footballers: the nimble, mesmerizing midfielders Osvaldo 'Ossie' Ardiles and Ricardo 'Ricky' Villa both began feted careers for Tottenham in 1978. The same year, more improbably, a hit British musical opened in the West End of London about Perón's wife and political comrade, Evita, who had died a quarter of a century earlier.

Britain also made missiles and warships for Argentina. Despite the potential for a naval confrontation over the Falklands, the ever-pragmatic British defence industry was quite happy to supply the same types of vessel to both countries. In 1971 two examples of a new, supposedly economical but powerful destroyer, the Type 42, were being discreetly and simultaneously constructed for the two navies at the famous old shipyard in remote Barrow-in-Furness in Cumbria. On the British ship, HMS *Sheffield*, welding gear set off an explosion, killing two workers, tearing open a 25-foot split in the stern, and threatening to delay the already troubled Type 42 programme. As a solution, Argentina allowed the whole prefabricated stern section of its destroyer to be attached to the British vessel. In the Falklands eleven years later the *Sheffield* would again have dealings with the Argentinian navy, but they would be less collaborative.

During 1981, as part of Nott's cuts, the Ministry of Defence even considered selling Argentina one of the Royal Navy's aircraft carriers, HMS *Hermes* or HMS *Invincible*, and the ship's complement of potent Sea Harrier jet fighters. According to Freedman, arrangements were made for an Argentinian admiral, Jorge Allara, to inspect *Invincible*. Only anxieties from the Foreign Office that the aircraft carrier might be used against the Falklands held up, but did not yet terminate, the idea of a sale.

By the early 1980s Argentina, previously a brittle democracy, had an entrenched military dictatorship. It threw supposed subversives out of helicopters into the South Atlantic, took away newborn babies and 'disappeared' their mothers, and acquired international notoriety for its internal 'Dirty War'. Yet the Thatcher government found some of its less brutal policies of considerable interest. On 11 June 1980 Nicholas Ridley wrote to her private secretary Ian Gow:

> Last week, after I brought the Argentine Minister of Economy to see the Prime Minister, she asked if I would prepare a short note setting out the salient features of what has been achieved in Argentina . . .
>
> 1. Main Features of Policy
>
> Money Supply: Kept under tight control . . .
>
> [State-owned] Monopolies: Exposed to competition wherever possible, denationalized [privatized] wherever possible . . .
>
> Subsidies: To all enterprises reduced to very small levels . . .

2. Main Results

... Unemployment: Down to 2%.

Economic Growth: After a fall, growth resumed ...

Inflation Rate: Brought down ...

3. Points of Interest to UK Recovery Programme

(A) Time Scale: The first year was quite easy, years two and three the most difficult, year four the first when really impressive results became apparent. The slowest element to come right was industrial production, because of the time it takes to re-equip and modernize plant and human attitudes. It is vital not to change course or let up ...

(E) The pressure on industry ... had to be harsh and real, and closures and bankruptcies allowed to proceed ...

The two governments' approaches to the economic and psychological remaking of their countries were almost identical. But Argentina's reform programme fascinated senior Thatcherites because it had been going for longer. In August 1980 another rising Tory radical, the trade minister Cecil Parkinson, flew to Argentina for a week-long official visit. Ridley had been there the previous year, within two months of Thatcher's election, and other Tory ministers would visit in September 1980 and September 1981. But Parkinson, suave in a tennis-club way and a favourite of Thatcher, felt a particular kinship with Argentina: 'My wife's grandmother was Anglo-Argentine,' he wrote afterwards. 'Her family had settled in Argentina in the 1860s and owned and farmed substantial estates. The men had returned to England to fight in the British forces in the two world wars.'

Parkinson waved away the issue of Argentina's human-rights record. When his visit 'caused an uproar amongst the [British] left, I pointed out that they [the junta] were no more repressive than the hard-line Communist countries which I visited with the approval of the TUC'. On 12 August the *Financial Times* reported: 'Parkinson Foresees Rise In UK-Argentine Sales . . . Following talks with Argentine leaders, Mr Parkinson said the two countries are approaching their economic problems in similar ways.'

Yet for all the links between the two countries and governments, the Argentinian hunger for the Malvinas remained. In 1964 an Argentinian pilot landed a light aircraft on the scruffy little racecourse near the governor's residence in Port Stanley, planted an Argentinian flag, and handed over a letter to a bemused passer-by declaring Argentinian sovereignty. Two years later twenty armed Argentinian nationalists hijacked an Argentinian airliner and forced it to fly to the Falklands. Again, the plane landed on Stanley racecourse. The hijackers took four islanders prisoner, spent the night on the racecourse, and then surrendered. 'The Argentine Government publicly dissociated themselves from the incident,' the British government noted afterwards, 'but there were demonstrations throughout Argentina in support . . . and shots were fired at the British Embassy in Buenos Aires while the Duke of Edinburgh was on an official visit there.' The following month an Argentinian submarine secretly landed soldiers by night on the coast near Stanley. They surveyed the locality for suitable invasion beaches, then slipped away.

In 1974 the brash, large-circulation Buenos Aires newspaper *Crónica* launched a campaign for the islands to be invaded. Again, the Argentinian government denied involvement, but the British ambassador was suspicious enough to warn them that any attack on the archipelago would be met with force. Two years on, amid more Buenos Aires press agitation for an invasion, an Argentinian destroyer fired shots across the bows of a British Antarctic Survey ship near the Falklands. The same year, an armed group from the Argentinian air force secretly occupied the unpopulated island of Thule, one of several tiny, icy British territories between the Falklands and the Antarctic that were claimed by Argentina. In the snow the Argentinians provocatively erected a bright red, tubular, moonbase-like barracks, a helipad and a fluttering flagpole. Then they established a garrison the same size as the British one on the Falklands, 1,200 miles to the northwest.

It took the British a month to realize what had happened. When they finally did so, the Callaghan government protested to Argentina, which insisted the base was for scientific purposes and refused to dismantle it. The British, afraid that a confrontation over Thule might have disastrous consequences for the Falklands, allowed themselves to be persuaded that their sovereignty had not been seriously compromised. They made no further effort to remove the Argentinians, and no mention of this humiliating mini-invasion to Parliament or the press.

A year later, in early 1977, British intelligence learned that the Argentinian navy had drawn up a contingency plan for an invasion of the Falklands. Seaborne and airborne forces would seize the islands; simultaneously, the Argentinian government would ask the United Nations to send peacekeeping troops, whose arrival in the Falklands, it was anticipated, would make British military retaliation impossible. That autumn the Callaghan administration became anxious that Argentina might implement this plan if the next round of Falklands negotiations, due to start in December, got bogged down. So the British government launched a military initiative of its own.

Callaghan was the son of a naval officer, and took a strong interest in naval matters: as prime minister, he liked to know the daily location of every British warship. In November 1977, in complete secrecy, he ordered two Royal Navy frigates and a naval tanker and supply ship to leave Britain for the South Atlantic. A nuclear-powered attack submarine was also sent there from Gibraltar. The largely old-fashioned Argentinian navy had no effective means of defending itself against a nuclear submarine. The British task force was ordered to 'establish a presence in the area of the Falkland Islands . . . to protect British lives and property . . . by deterring or countering Argentine aggression'. Argentina was not told of the warships' presence, but its close ally the United States was; historians and politicians have argued ever since about what, if anything, Buenos Aires learned. Either way, no Argentinian invasion fleet sailed. In late December the British vessels were withdrawn, as covertly as they had been despatched.

Callaghan's successor as premier was, at first, much less alert to the military side of the Falklands situation. Usually intimidatingly good on detail, Margaret Thatcher did not know, even roughly, how long it took a warship to steam from Britain to the islands. When she was told by Admiral Leach in March 1982 that it was three weeks, she was baffled and tried to correct him: 'Three days, you mean?'

When I visited the Falklands in 2012 the thing that surprised me most about the islands, after the brash, jeeps-and-sunglasses wealth from sea fishing and oil exploration which had fattened Port Stanley since the 1980s, was that many older locals talked about Thatcher more with bitterness than with reverence. 'There has been a huge cleansing of the public memory about her,' said John Fowler, the deputy editor of the *Penguin News*, the Falklands' only newspaper. He was a white-bearded, tanned man in his mid-sixties, wearing a denim shirt and with a quietly bruised air. He had emigrated to the islands from Yorkshire in 1971, recruited by the British government to help solve the Falklands' perennial shortage of teachers. At various times he had also been the islands' director of education and manager of its tourist board, and he had acquired some of the born Falklander's reserve and watchfulness towards outsiders. We met in a back room at the newspaper's minuscule offices on the Stanley waterfront, a ragged, atmospheric strip of ancient storage sheds and jetties that the oil and fishing boom had yet to prettify. The surprisingly strong Falklands sun thrust through the windows; on metal shelves around us, cuttings from the islands' ambiguous, often-forgotten history dried and crumbled.

In the 1970s and at the start of the 1980s, Fowler continued, in a quiet, reined-back voice, 'I used to think of her as Margaret Thatcher, Milk Snatcher. Her end of the political spectrum was not mine.' He had been even more repelled by her government's friendliness towards Argentina: 'Most of us knew what the Argentinians were capable of doing, to their own people. But in 1980 and 1981 we were being given away to them.'

In November 1980 Nicholas Ridley arrived in Stanley to try to steer local opinion towards the compromise he had secretly devised with the Argentinians in Switzerland a few weeks earlier. It was a large task. Like Ulster Unionists, many Falklanders combine an unshakeable attachment to Britain with a suspicion that all British governments may sell them out. And like Unionists, Falklanders have formidable and unforgiving memories. Before my 2012 visit I had contacted an elderly, well-connected Port Stanley businessman to ask if he would show me round. When I said I wrote for the *Guardian*, he immediately started talking about Richard Gott, a respected former South American correspondent for the paper who had occasionally written sceptical pieces about the British claim to the Falklands. 'We call him Chalfont's poodle,' said the businessman – referring to a trip to the islands Gott had made with Lord Chalfont, when the latter had been a mildly pro-Argentinian British minister. The trip had happened forty-four years earlier.

Ridley was a less engaging character than Gott or Chalfont. Blunt, sharp-faced, sometimes haughty and impatient – at the Oxfordshire station he used to get from his Cotswold mansion to London, he was known as a great barger-in and slammer of train doors – he also considered the Falklands conundrum somewhat beneath him. 'I confess to being bitterly disappointed at finding myself dealing with the problems of Latin America,' he wrote later. Already fifty-one in 1980, almost the same age as Geoffrey Howe or Thatcher herself, he felt he should be a Cabinet minister, helping to save Britain.

In 1980 the Falklands had a total population of 1,813. It had fallen relentlessly since a modest peak half a century earlier. It was so normal for islanders to emigrate to England, either for several years at a time or permanently, that Southampton was known in the Falklands as 'Stanley North'.

Many of those who remained were not the sort of people to impress go-getting Thatcherites like Ridley. 'It wasn't a hugely ambitious place,' said Nancy Poole, a farmer I met at a little racecourse in the bleached hills above the hamlet of Goose Green. We were 50 miles, several hours and several worlds away from Stanley. Diminutive and in her sixties, with gappy teeth and mellow eyes, Poole was wearing a thickly padded boiler suit, still the national costume outside the capital. All around her, in the icy summer wind, men in the same garb drained cans of beer at high speed, while others wobbled or hurtled past on horseback. A whooshing, fizzing PA system, between announcing the winners, played near-indecipherable fragments of live commentary from a football final back in distant England, as if we were still in the 1930s. 'I came to the Falklands aged three months,' said Poole. 'But someone will say at my funeral, "She wasn't a local."'

Yet until the 1980s she found the islands 'a lovely place to live'. Even in Stanley there was almost no advertising. In its small grid of streets that sloped prettily down to the harbour, people grew their own vegetables in large cottage gardens, blocking out the wind with hedges that they had raised inch by determined inch. On the edge of town, peat for heating could be dug up for free. Out in the sparsely farmed wilds beyond, known as Camp – from the Spanish *campo*, for countryside – free milk and mutton were customarily given to farm employees.

'The whole population was the same,' said Poole, 'earned similar, did similar.' The islands were more heavily unionized than Britain, with a single General Employees Union negotiating a 'basic minimum monthly wage' with the equally ubiquitous Falkland Islands Company, as well as 'long-service awards', 'extra payments', and 'the automatic adjustment of wages and salaries to the cost of living'. A painstaking 1976 survey of the islands by the Labour peer Lord Shackleton found this system conducive to 'industrial peace', and 'a highly-regarded means of protecting most of the population . . . It has, however, had the subsidiary effect of substantially reducing skills differentials, possibly [because] there is insufficient monetary inducement to acquire a skill.' Shackleton concluded that 'most native born islanders . . . live in conditions of dependence'. They relied on the paternalistic Falkland Islands Company, and on subsidies from the British government when times were hard, which they increasingly were during the 1970s and early 1980s as the international price of wool, the islands' main export, went into steep decline. The enterprise society this was not.

In November 1980 Ridley spent less than a week meeting Falklanders and their elected councillors. 'Some' of the councillors, recorded the islands' more powerful, Whitehall-appointed governor, Sir Rex Hunt, 'appear prepared to see talks [with Argentina] on lease-back' – London's euphemistic shorthand for handing over sovereignty. But there was 'no support' for any 'joint [Anglo-Argentinian] administration' of the islands.

The councillors asked Ridley to address a public meeting in Stanley. It was held in the boxy little town hall and 400 people squeezed in, about half the town's entire adult population. John Fowler was one of them. 'It was fairly late in the evening,' he remembered. 'I suspect Ridley had had a couple of G&Ts. He was being heckled, and he got cross. And he said something along the lines of, "If you continue with this intransigence [towards a deal with Argentina], on your own heads be it. We will not be sending a gunboat to save you." And sitting in the town hall, bottom right, were three or four Argentinian air force officers. I'm sure they shot out of the town hall and got on the phone.'

According to Freedman, Ridley was not quite that foolish. When an unnamed islander in the audience told him that transferring sovereignty to Argentina would mean 'giving up' the Falklanders' 'birthright', Ridley replied: 'Well then you take the consequences, not me.' The islander asked incredulously, 'Doesn't Britain own the Falklands any more?' 'Indeed we do,' said Ridley. Then more airily: 'We'll help you any way we can.'

Thatcher's emissary was asked what Britain would do if the Argentinians invaded. 'Kick them out!' he said. The audience laughed. Ridley shouted over the derision: 'Of course we will! Goodness me – that's not the problem. The problem is do you *want* the Argentinians invading you and us kicking them out in a state of perpetual war. That's what you've got to think about. I mean it's all very well sitting here saying someone else must come and kick the Argentinians out... But is that good... for all your futures? Is that the way you want to live?'

Ridley's performance, however you precisely recalled it, suggested a British government whose Falklands policy was unravelling. Vague one minute and definite the next; alternating between threats against Argentina and the implication that a deal with them was unavoidable, and between professions of undying loyalty to the islands and expired patience – Ridley did not seem to know his own mind, let alone Whitehall's. He omitted the disastrous Falklands trip from his memoirs.

But when he got back to Britain, he could not avoid giving an account of it to the House of Commons. It was 2 December, shortly before Parliament stood down for Christmas, and the fate of the

Falklands was still assumed by the Foreign Office to be of minor interest in Britain. Again, Ridley made a statement that tried to face in several directions at once. 'We have no doubt about our sovereignty over the islands,' he began. 'The Argentines, however, continue to press their claim. The dispute is causing continuing uncertainty, emigration and economic stagnation in the islands. Following my exploratory talks with the Argentines ... the Government have been considering possible ways of achieving a solution.'

A sudden clamour of MPs jumped up to respond. The thundering Tory patriot Sir Bernard Braine declared: 'The islanders are wholly British in blood and sentiment.' The thoughtful Labour left-winger Peter Shore urged the government to 'uphold the rights of the islanders'. The Liberal Russell Johnston, who represented some of the faintly Falklands-like Hebrides, demanded that Ridley 'disown ... the shameful schemes for getting rid of these [Falkland] islands which have been festering in the Foreign Office for years'.

Ridley had been ambushed by yet another protagonist in the ever more intricate, now accelerating Falklands crisis: the British Falklands lobby. Like one of the grey-brown squid found in huge numbers off the islands, the lobby had been quietly reaching its tentacles into Parliament and the London media for a decade and a half. The lobby's main instrument was the Falkland Islands Emergency Committee, set up in London in 1968, just as it began to seem that the British and Argentinian governments might do a deal over the archipelago. Partly funded by the Falkland Islands Company, which might have much to lose if Argentina became more involved in the islands and ended the company's local monopoly, the committee quickly became a highly effective cross between an unofficial embassy and a campaign office for the islands' overwhelming anti-Argentinian majority. The committee harried the Foreign Office whenever there was the slightest whiff of a Falklands sell-out, coordinated its activities with and encouraged all the diehards back in the islands, recruited MPs to the cause, and briefed sympathetic newspaper journalists.

Right-wing British tabloids that mourned the empire and distrusted foreigners, such as the *Daily Express*, were particularly drawn to the committee's defiant arguments. Meanwhile the Falklands, which were endlessly photogenic, beleaguered, and both a novelty and reassuringly familiar – a sort of South Atlantic Gibraltar – made good copy for newspapers of all kinds. The islands got regular and generous full-colour spreads in the Sunday magazines of even the more liberal broadsheets. British reporters relished visiting the Falklands – I did – rather more than, say, parts of northern England that were suffering similar depopulation and economic decline.

The notoriety of the Argentinian regime also helped the cause. Ridley and Parkinson may have been unsqueamish about the junta, but opposition to South American dictatorships ran strongly through the Labour Party. Thus support for the Falklands status quo became a cross-party campaign with a progressive tinge, rather than simply something for Tory nationalists and nostalgists. Finally, starting in the 1970s, a realization slowly dawned in Britain that the sea around the islands contained rich fishing grounds and possibly large oil deposits as well, neither of which had been properly explored, let alone exploited. Long before the South Atlantic rivalry finally reached a climax in the spring of 1982, the islands had acquired an unacknowledged power in British politics and culture. Any confrontation with Argentina in the Falklands could massively magnify that power. And a sufficiently bold – or desperate – British leader could exploit the crisis.

Margaret Thatcher was made 'anxious' by Ridley's Commons statement and the fury it provoked, Freedman records. Over the winter of 1980–81 her administration effectively abandoned its idea of a Falklands lease-back. Yet the government put almost nothing in its place. The British negotiators carried on sporadically talking to the Argentinians, but now offering them no meaningful concessions. In October 1981 the islanders elected a new set of even more anti-Argentinian councillors. Privately, frustration at such stubbornness persisted in Whitehall, all the way up to 10 Downing Street. In October 1982 Thatcher told the Franks Inquiry, an official investigation chaired by the flexible grandee Lord Franks into Britain's Falklands policy up until that spring: 'The islanders ... I do not think they understood ... the full significance of the position ... After all, they had lived quite sheltered lives.'

In June 1981, as part of its defence cuts, her government announced that the only Royal Navy vessel assigned to the islands, HMS *Endurance*, would be withdrawn from service in April 1982. The *Endurance* was a stubby former Danish merchant ship that had been converted to carry two military helicopters and two small-calibre guns, and less publicly, extensive surveillance equipment. The ship was expensive to run for its modest size; and it attempted to patrol the territory between the Falklands, Argentina and the Antarctic only from November to April, the South Atlantic's brief spring, summer and autumn, when the seas were relatively calm. The vessel had been repeatedly picked out for culling by Ministry of Defence cost-cutters since the mid-1970s, but the Thatcher government's Labour predecessors had always eventually decided against it. In October 1977 the foreign secretary David Owen, like Callaghan a keen armchair admiral, explained that, 'For us to announce ... the paying off of the *Endurance* would be seen by the Argentines ... as a clear admission of weakness on our part and a lack of determination to defend our interests ... [and] would also have a serious effect on the morale of the islanders themselves.'

Yet, in this as in many areas, the Tory government was not interested in following the advice of the 1970s governments it despised. Instead Mrs Thatcher's Falklands policy took its own path through 1981 and early 1982: neither compromising with Argentina, nor deploying the forces to the islands necessary to dissuade the Argentinians from responding militarily to the diplomatic stalemate that resulted. It was a risky, barely coherent approach. There was a chance that it could work: the islanders might get scared and soften their stance; or the Argentinians might get distracted by other issues – such as their extremely tense relations with their neighbour Chile. The latter also involved an Argentinian territorial claim, over long-disputed islands nearer the South American mainland. Argentina had come close to invading them in December 1978. In February 1982 there was almost a battle over the islands between the Argentinian and Chilean navies.

But the new British Falklands policy felt most of all like an act of procrastination: by an over-committed, domestically focused, not wholly competent government that was short of money. It became obvious to some of those charged with implementing the policy that it would probably not work for long. 'In the summer of 1981,' wrote Thatcher's seasoned foreign secretary Lord Carrington in his memoirs, *Reflect On Things Past*, 'Argentine impatience was visibly mounting . . . We had a certain sense of sands running out.'

12
We Won

On the calm moonlit evening of April Fool's Day 1982, a sharkish Argentinian Type 42 destroyer, the *Santísima Trinidad*, whose design, sea trials and crew training had all been carried out in England, appeared undetected off the southeast coastline of the Falklands, half a dozen miles from Port Stanley. Ninety Argentinian marines clambered down into small inflatable boats. Bulkily dressed in neoprene suits over their uniforms, with their weapons and other equipment also cocooned in waterproofs, they took over an hour to disembark. Then they puttered off towards the shore, engines down low.

This stretch of coast, almost uninhabited, screened from Stanley and its tiny garrison by a line of hills, seemed ideal for a landing. It may have been one of the invasion sites Argentina had secretly surveyed in the 1960s. But in the darkness – it was now almost 11 p.m. – the inflatables missed their planned route and ran into a floating maze of seaweed. Propellers snarled in the fronds. The marines revved their engines. Some of the boats remained stuck. Some of the engines burnt out. Oars were used instead, but rowing out of the seaweed took too long. In the end some boats had to be towed to the shore by others. The marines hurriedly disembarked at the first beach they saw, a mile from where they had intended to land.

But no one had spotted them. The soldiers split into two groups: one to march to Stanley by the shortest possible route – less than three miles – and capture Government House, the faintly Scottish mansion, full of fireplaces and defiant conservatory plants, where the governor of the islands lived and worked; and one to attack a barracks just beyond Stanley, where most of the British garrison was expected to be asleep.

Yet, as the Argentinians belatedly discovered, walking in the Falklands is difficult. Away from the rare roads and pavements, the ground is lumpy: hard tussocks of long grass with sudden, squelching dips in between; or endless fields of boulders, where close-packed rocks slope randomly up and down, the smaller ones slipping under your feet as you scramble over, or clanking against each other, like old bones. In daylight it is easy enough to twist an ankle, or worse; in darkness, with military rucksacks tugging on their backs, loaded rifles occupying their hands, and their eyes groping around for the enemy rather than focused on the ground, even elite soldiers, Argentinian and British alike, stumbled along in 1982 at less than a mile an hour. 'We were very surprised by the difficulty of the ground . . . [by] what the reconnaissance photographs showed as "grass",' one of the commanders of the Argentinian landing party told the well-informed British military historian Martin Middlebrook. The first casualty of the glorious invasion of the Malvinas was an Argentinian officer who broke his ankle before a shot was fired.

At around 5.30 a.m. on 2 April the marines finally surrounded the barracks and threw in tear-gas grenades. The buildings were empty. About an hour later, having waited for their comrades to deal with the barracks, the other Argentinian force entered the grounds of Government House. Lovingly framed by glasshouses, perfect lawns and low, cottagey stone walls – as if one of the main reasons for Britain to keep the Falklands was to publicize British gardening – the complex looked hard to defend. A few weeks before, an Argentinian 'tourist', claiming to be an architect, had visited the governor Sir Rex Hunt and successfully requested a copy of the building's plans. As a microcosm of Britain's misreading of Argentina's intentions in the early 1980s, it was hard to better.

Yet when the first five Argentinian soldiers approached the rear of the building in the slow, cloudy dawn, confidently expecting to break down a door, surprise everyone inside, and demand that the governor surrender, they strode into an ambush. Thirty-one Royal Marines, who had been redeployed from the barracks, and a dozen other assorted armed personnel, including Hunt himself with a pistol and his driver with a shotgun – all of them belatedly alerted to the invasion – had arranged themselves at good vantage points in the chilly corridors and upstairs billiard room of Government House. For the next three hours, until almost 9.30 a.m., they fired and threw grenades, wounded three Argentinians, one fatally, took three prisoner, and kept the others pinned down in the gardens and outbuildings. Although there had been no declaration of war, the fighting was unrestrained: an Argentinian medic was mistakenly injured by the British; a wounded Argentinian officer slowly bled to death because he was holding a grenade and the British refused to believe it was safe to treat him.

While the unexpected siege dragged on, a much more formidable Argentinian force started to come ashore on one of the lovely white sand beaches near Stanley airport. Twenty amphibious armoured personnel carriers, American-made Amtraks, with towering sides and headlights like huge eyes as if they were sea monsters emerging from the waters, ground their way up the beach. They swiftly captured the airport, which like the barracks had been left undefended. Then they roared towards Stanley itself, engines running as loud as possible to intimidate the British soldiers, and perhaps the stubborn Falklanders themselves. The invasion force had over a thousand troops available if required: more than fifteen times the size of the whole British garrison.

At the edge of town a few British troops hidden in a house fired rockets and machine guns at one of the personnel carriers. But the vehicle survived with only one crewman hurt. The British soldiers scattered. By 8 a.m. the armoured vehicles were in among the flimsy wooden houses. For some Falklanders, there was confusion and a sense of ancient nightmares coming true. 'My little sister actually thought it was the Germans,' I was told by a freckly sunburnt man, a 'ninth generation' islander who lived on Pioneer Row, one of Stanley's oldest and most fragile streets. 'She kept saying, "The Germanys are coming! The Germanys are coming!"'

He was ten at the time, a fan of Argentinian footballers – 'Ricky Villa was one of my heroes' – but he soon worked out what was really going on. 'I remember putting on a Union Jack T-shirt, and standing by the window as the Amtraks went past.' As he talked, he pointed across the narrow road as if it had happened that morning: 'They gouged the top of the wall opposite our house.'

Whale-like Argentinian transport planes disgorged troops at the airport. Argentinian artillery, far more powerful than anything the British garrison had, were unloaded on the beach. At Government House, with more and more Argentinian bullets flying in through the windows, Hunt was advised by the officer in charge of the increasingly outnumbered British force that he had three options: to order a break-out, and try to set up an alternative seat of government somewhere else in the islands; to let the garrison fight to the end; or to surrender. Fearing the first two would mean awful military and civilian casualties, Hunt contacted the commander of the Argentinian marines and proposed a ceasefire. At 9.20 a.m. the commander arrived at Government House, which his country had coveted since its construction in 1845. Five minutes later Hunt ordered the British troops to put down their guns.

On the front page of the *Daily Mail* on 3 April 1982 the main headline was a single word: 'SURRENDER'. Underneath was a large photo, variations of which appeared all over the British and international media during the first week of April. In slightly dim and fuzzy silhouette, giving the scene a distant, unreal, almost underwater feel, a dozen live British soldiers lay on a road in an orderly, submissive row. Disarmed, their uniforms rumpled, their faces were pressed into the gutter, or twisted up awkwardly and helplessly towards the edge of the pavement, like fish out of water. Over them stood several armed men in darker, less bashed-about uniforms, looking relaxed and proprietorial. Beyond these guards was a military vehicle, foreign-looking and modern, and beyond it, a patch of neat grass and a small hillside of gorse. Except for the soldiers and the milky South Atlantic sea-light, it could have been the golf-course belt of Surrey.

For a country that thought it was good at war, and whose defeats and capitulations, such as the early calamities of the Second World War, were safely back in the past, if they were remembered at all; for a country whose soldiers were almost always portrayed by the media as dignified and in control; and for a country that had not been invaded for centuries, but profoundly feared invasion, the starkness, swiftness and improbability of what had happened in Port Stanley was an enormous jolt. The British press tried desperately to soften the news, by emphasizing how long and how strongly the defenders of Government House had resisted against overwhelming odds, and by pointing out that, unlike the Argentinians, they had suffered no casualties. If you tried hard enough – and as a patriotic twelve-year-old I tried – the battle of Government House could be interpreted as another example of heroic British soldiery. But this feeling of pride did not last long. Within a few days an Argentinian administration was operating in Stanley, Argentinian troops had control of every significant settlement in the archipelago, and Falklanders had been ordered to drive on the right from now on. 'It's all over,' wrote the naughty but intensely nationalistic Tory MP Alan Clark in his diary on 2 April. 'We're a Third World country.'

That afternoon he left Westminster early – 'no point in hanging about' – and went back to his country residence, Saltwood, a medieval castle in Kent, a county more haunted than most by past English military glories:

> I ate some brown toast and crab apple jelly and, it being such a lovely evening, went for a meander down the valley. I am so depressed by what I heard today [from a Foreign Office spokesman in the Commons] – the shuffling and fudging, the overpowering impression of timidity and incompetence. Can it have felt like this in the Thirties . . . on those fine weekends when the dictators, Hitler and Musso, decided to help themselves to something – Durazzo . . . Prague – and all we could do was wring our hands . . . ? I have a terrible feeling that this is a step change, down, for England. Humiliation for sure and . . . military defeat. An apparition that must have been stalking us . . . I suppose, for the last sixty-five years.

For any British prime minister, having British territory taken by surprise and by force, by a supposed military inferior, and while Britain was not even officially at war, was a disaster from which it would be hard to recover. The last comparable foreign-policy meltdown, the abortive Anglo-French attack on Suez twenty-six years earlier, without even being a failure in military terms, had destroyed the

Conservative premiership of Anthony Eden – until then popular, and widely seen as charming and economically competent – in less than three months.

Margaret Thatcher was neither popular nor charming. Nor, in the spring of 1982, did her government yet seem economically successful. She had been in office for nearly three years, and Conservative leader for more than seven. In both roles she had repeatedly promised to restore Britain to greatness. As prime minister, her foreign-policy rhetoric had often been aggressive, her remarks on defence even more so, and her broader sales pitch to voters had frequently boiled down to little more than her own toughness – 'the lady's not for turning'. To lose the Falklands to modestly armed Argentina made a mockery of all this. As the still-influential right-wing maverick Enoch Powell put it on 3 April in the House of Commons, with an elaborate courtesy that only drew attention to the glint of the knife within:

> The Prime Minister, shortly after she came into office, received a sobriquet as the 'Iron Lady' ... in the context of remarks she made about defence against the Soviet Union ... There was no reason to suppose that the Right Honourable Lady did not ... take pride in that description. In the next week or two this House, the nation and the Right Honourable Lady herself, will learn of what metal she is made.

In the spring of 1982, moreover, Powell was hardly the only Tory MP that Thatcher needed to worry about. Ever since she had snatched the Tory leadership, by unexpectedly challenging and narrowly defeating Edward Heath in 1975, presenting herself to most of the parliamentary party as a vehicle for protest rather than a serious candidate, her position had been secure only for brief periods. Sexism played a part – 'My god! The bitch has won!' – but her contentious beliefs were more responsible. Deep into the 1980s, only a minority of Tories, from the cabinet downwards, believed as she did in a profound remaking of Britain. She knew this and, being 'cautious Margaret', moved only incrementally to marginalize her party opponents and promote her supporters. By April 1982 only eight cabinet members, well under half the total, were Thatcherites in even the broadest sense: Howe, Nott, Tebbit, Parkinson, Nigel Lawson, now energy secretary, the education secretary Keith Joseph, the trade secretary John Biffen, and Thatcher herself.

The other senior ministers were a different breed of Conservative: more gradualist, less confrontational, more centrist, less ideological, often less intellectual – the latest products of a famously flexible and ruthless tradition that went back at least two centuries. In the late 1970s and early 1980s journalists and more informed voters began categorizing these Tories, with encouragement from Thatcher's sometimes venomous press operatives, as 'wet'. Yet the clever insinuation that the wets were a weak and cowardly upper-class elite – the term 'wet' was an old public-school taunt – understated their threat. Some wets, such as the Leader of the Commons, Francis Pym, and the Lord Privy Seal, Ian Gilmour, certainly had posh backgrounds, but they were also sharp operators, expert briefers of journalists and leakers of details of the Thatcher government's many bitter cabinet arguments. They quickly caricatured the Thatcherites in turn as 'the dries': unfeeling, too cerebral. Meanwhile other wets, such as the minister of agriculture Peter Walker, a union shop steward's son who had made a fortune performing ruthless corporate takeovers, knew more about the realities of business and social mobility than most of the dries. Thatcher did not dare sack Walker until 1990.

All prime ministers have internal enemies. Some premiers deliberately define themselves against their own parties, as Tony Blair did in the 1990s. Both scenarios only become perilous when a premiership is seen to be failing. During the months leading up to the invasion of the Falklands, the wets attracted a dangerous number of recruits and defectors. In February 1981 Alan Clark, who was closer to the dries, wrote in his diary: 'Party is in poor shape. Wets want to go back to full Heathism.' In July, Nott and Biffen, always the most independent-minded of the dries, unexpectedly joined forces with the wets and opposed a deepening of the government's spending cuts. In August the Tory Party chairman Lord Thorneycroft told *The Times*, in the sort of unsubtle code Westminster politicians favour when publicly manoeuvring, that he was suffering from 'a little rising damp'. In November 1981 Thatcher received a letter signed by twenty-one Conservative backbenchers, 'writing collectively to warn you' of their 'fundamental disagreement with the government's economic analysis'. Nine days later, Thatcher was alerted by her private secretary Ian Gow, one of whose most valued roles was to gauge the mood of the parliamentary party, that the backbench wets were 'now 45 people' – one more than her Commons majority.

The Conservative Party mutinies against struggling leaders with infamous ease. Throughout 1981 there were regular reports in the Tory press of plots to depose Thatcher. Many of these stories, and much Westminster gossip, presented Pym as her most likely replacement. He was a decorated Second World War hero, more consensual in his Toryism, a deft political player in private, and a man. On the downside, he had a sometimes glum public manner, and a slightly furtive, rodent-like look to him. He still wore his hair slicked back, in the manner of a 1950s grandee, and he had been to Eton. Compared to Thatcher, and every other British prime minister since the early 1960s, none of whom had come from privileged backgrounds, Pym looked a little like a throwback.

Paradoxically, Thatcher was also protected, to a degree, by the weakness of her position: it encouraged many wets, Pym included, to believe that they should simply wait for her to fall, rather than topple her and risk a Tory civil war. 'They didn't think she would last,' Tebbit told me. 'They thought events would be on their side.' And they didn't want blood on their hands? A contemptuous look came over his hard face: 'Yes.'

But with the Falklands crisis it seemed that the wets' desired 'events' had finally materialized. On 7 April Clark saw unnamed senior Tories 'striding up and down the Smoking Room Corridor' in the Commons, 'telling anyone whom they can apprehend' that Thatcher was unlikely to be able to retrieve the situation. 'It is only on occasions such as this that the implacable hatred in which certain established figures hold the Prime Minister can be detected,' he wrote. 'They are within an ace, they think, of bringing her Government down.'

The Falklands disaster had already brought down her foreign secretary two days earlier. Lord Carrington was hardly the most culpable person in Whitehall. As his memoirs point out, when the decision had been taken to withdraw HMS *Endurance* from the South Atlantic, he 'wrote on several occasions to the Defence Secretary, John Nott, to ask that the Ministry of Defence should reconsider'. Yet Carrington was also, his memoirs admit, 'the minister in charge' of the increasingly threadbare and contradictory pre-invasion Falklands policy. He personified its shortcomings vividly by travelling on official business to Brussels and then Israel in late March, during the very days when the Argentinian invasion fleet, completely unknown to the British, was being provisioned and then heading for the islands. In some ways Carrington was a politician from another age: a hereditary peer, he spoke and voted in the Lords rather than the Commons, and had first been a minister under Winston Churchill. He also had a rather old-fashioned sense of political responsibility. 'With people very naturally turning on the Government and accusing it of mismanagement,' he writes about the Falklands invasion, 'it [was] right, in my judgement, that there must be a resignation. The nation feels that there has been a disgrace. Someone must have been to blame. The disgrace must be purged.' He resigned on 5 April.

Carrington was a wet, part of the compromising Whitehall and Foreign Office establishment that Thatcherites disliked. And besides, he was approaching the end of his career. He was seemingly the perfect Falklands scapegoat. But for precisely that reason his resignation was not enough to satisfy the government's critics. Nott was also pressured to resign. As the minister responsible for the withdrawal of the *Endurance* and the chief advocate of naval cuts, he was arguably more directly to blame than Carrington for the invasion. But Thatcher believed she could not afford to lose another senior cabinet minister, especially not the defence secretary, with Britain effectively at war. Nott survived.

In another sign of her weakness, she felt obliged to replace Carrington with Pym, who had been shadow foreign secretary and was a respected Commons presence. The promotion turned him into a much more high-profile figure. If the Falklands situation continued as it was, or worsened, or was resolved by him rather than any other means, he would be perfectly positioned to replace her as prime minister.

Yet for the first few days of April neither Pym nor Thatcher nor any other senior Conservative seemed on top of the crisis. During the night and morning of the Argentinian invasion, Port Stanley's patchy radio communications with Britain had stopped working. So, on the morning of 2 April, despite the shoot-out at Government House, despite the Argentinian press reporting triumphantly that their forces had landed in the Falklands, the British government did not know what was happening. The Foreign Office minister Humphrey Atkins insisted to the Commons: 'No invasion has taken place.' That afternoon, two hours after the British troops in the islands had surrendered, and with Westminster and the British media frantic with Falklands rumours, but with the Stanley–London radio link still down, Pym told the Commons, with what was either laughable ignorance or the most short-sighted evasiveness, 'There is no confirmation of any change in the position in relation to the Falkland Islands.' David Owen was one of the MPs present. 'In our heart of hearts most of us knew that the Falklands had been invaded,' he told me. 'We were totally misled.'

The next day, when reality could be held back no longer, the government permitted the House of Commons to sit on a Saturday for the first time since the Second World War. As Thatcher left Downing Street to attend, a crowd booed and hissed her. She then made an alternately ponderous and nervous speech before the packed House. Perhaps its worst moment was an admission that on 31 March the government had 'received information which led us to believe' – like Pym's, her language was face-savingly pedantic – 'that a large number of Argentine ships . . . were heading for Port Stanley'. Yet her government had decided 'to take no action to escalate the dispute,' she went on, 'for fear of precipitating the very event that our efforts were directed to avoid'. To the bitter end her Falklands policy seemed to have been based on self-delusion and weakness. As Thatcher spoke, 'far too fast', wrote Clark – usually one of her admirers – 'The whole Opposition started laughing and sneering.'

Labour had almost limitless ammunition to use against her. There was the party's now demonstrably better record at deterring the Argentinians. 'We did not lose the Falklands,' as the Labour MP Jeff Rooker put it, crushingly interrupting her in the Saturday debate when she unwisely tried to compare the invasion to the Argentinian occupation of Thule in 1976. Then there were the many recent Commons warnings about the Falklands from senior Labour figures: on 9 February 1982, from Jim Callaghan: 'Is the Prime Minister aware that the Government's decisions to withdraw HMS *Endurance* ... is an error that could have serious consequences?'; on 23 March, from Denis Healey: 'Surely ... the only option is to allow [the aircraft carrier] HMS *Invincible* to spend some time around the Falkland Islands'; on 30 March, from Healey again: 'The Argentine Government are reported to be sending ... five or six warships ... towards the islands ... [But] the Government have left Britain in a position of extreme weakness as a direct result of their defence priorities. That is why we face a damaging humiliation.'

There had been other signs over the winter and spring that a Falklands invasion was imminent. Thatcher herself admitted to Parliament on 3 April that 'There was a good deal of bellicose comment in the Argentine press in late February and early March.' The military regime in Buenos Aires was going through a particularly combative and erratic phase. General Leopoldo Galtieri, a right-winger whose ferocious anti-communism had won him powerful allies in the Reagan administration – such as Jeane Kirkpatrick, US ambassador to the United Nations – had seized power in December 1981. Yet under Galtieri the Argentinian economic experiment so admired by Thatcherites had begun to misfire spectacularly. Just as in Britain, cuts in public spending, including cuts in defence spending, produced a spiral of recession and government unpopularity.

On 25 February 1982 the *Guardian*, which was well informed about South America, carried a short report on Argentina's 'continuing economic crisis' alongside a longer one on the Galtieri regime's determination to 'seek big concessions from Britain' over the Falklands. 'If these were not forthcoming,' the paper went on, 'sources within the military ... confirm that at least some senior officers are prepared to consider military action. The Government is unpopular because of its economic policies ... On this argument, the invasion of the "Malvinas" ... would rally patriotic sentiment for the regime. The generals in question are reported to believe that an operation to take over [the] islands ... would be logistically simple.'

On 2 March the defence attaché at the British Embassy in Buenos Aires had sent a memo to the governor of the Falklands, Sir Rex Hunt, entitled 'The Argentine Military Threat to The Falklands'. 'Those I have talked to in the [Argentinian] military recently,' it warned, 'stress that this year is an important one indeed for Anglo-Argentine relations. Putting the worst possible interpretation on things this could mean an Army President . . . giving orders to the military to solve the Malvinas problem once and for all . . . at a time when it may . . . seem most attractive to him to do something popular.' Galtieri had already presided over Argentina's latest inconclusive military stand-off with Chile.

The memo was received in Port Stanley and London with something close to a yawn. 'It says nothing which we don't already know,' a civil servant wrote across the top in a lazy hand. A fortnight later came the final heavy, insufficiently heeded hint from Argentina. On 18 March a transport ship belonging to the Argentinian navy landed forty-one Argentinian scrap-metal workers on South Georgia. Once a prized whaling centre, 900 miles east of the Falklands, it was now an island of seals and rust, but still a British territory and used by British scientists. The Argentinian workers had a legitimate commercial contract to dismantle and remove old whaling gear and anything else that could be salvaged from the disintegrating buildings. Yet from the moment they arrived on South Georgia, it was almost comically obvious that their presence also had other purposes. They ran up an Argentinian flag; some of them wore camouflage clothing and carried guns; and after a few days they were joined by a dozen Argentinian marines. At the least an Argentinian foothold was being established, as on Thule in 1976. This was the Thatcher government's interpretation of events; it protested ineffectually to Buenos Aires and despatched two dozen soldiers from Stanley to end the occupation. But a shrewder British government would have understood that the ever-escalating South Georgia incident was part of a bigger game. As some graffiti added to a wall on the island by the scrap-metal workers made clear: '*Las Malvinas son Argentinas*.'

The Argentinian seizure of the Falklands, you could say, was one of the least surprising surprise attacks in modern military history. Yet Margaret Thatcher was emphatic, in 1982 and ever after, that she did not see it coming. 'I never never expected the Argentines to invade the Falklands head-on,' she told the Franks Inquiry, when it investigated whether her government and its predecessors had misread years of warnings.

On 5 April 1982, hours after hurriedly replacing Carrington with Pym, she appeared on the evening news bulletins. She looked pale and jumpy. Her usually immensely steady eyes flicked from side to side under the camera lights. Her voice was even slower and deeper and more mannered than usual, as if she were trying to calm herself down, and her answers were uncharacteristically verbose, foggy and repetitive, as if she were playing for time. She told ITN: 'We have to try to recover what is our sovereign territory, we have to recover what is our sovereign territory, that is our problem . . . and we will tackle it ourselves, we hope diplomatically, to have the support of everyone else and so many other people have openly condemned aggression and this is why I say to you it is important that aggression does not succeed.'

Yet the destruction of her reputation anticipated by so many, possibly including Thatcher herself, never happened. The first indication that she might survive and even feed off the energies of the great Falklands storm came in the emergency Commons debate on 3 April. Near the end of her garbled speech came a brief cloud-break of decisiveness and clarity: 'The Government have now decided that a large task force will sail as soon as all preparations are complete. HMS *Invincible* will be in the lead and will leave port on Monday.' Then she concluded with some pompous but equally potent generalities: 'The people of the Falkland Islands, like the people of the United Kingdom, are an island race. Their way of life is British.' The echo of Winston Churchill's 1964 best-seller *The Island Race* was probably not a coincidence.

Thatcher had never been to the Falklands. She had never experienced their extremely un-British isolation and emptiness; their almost Soviet absence of modern commerce; their dusty ranch-style farms that could have been in Texas. But nor had most MPs and voters. The islands were a blank slate on which all manner of patriotic myths could be written.

The Labour leader Michael Foot spoke next. As elegant and confident an orator as he was inelegant in other contexts, his speech was much better than hers – 'an excellent performance', Clark judged. But Foot spent his first ten ringing paragraphs talking about everything but her government's Falklands failures. The invasion was 'an act of naked, unqualified aggression, carried out in the most shameful and disreputable of circumstances'. Its perpetrators were vicious authoritarians: 'Thousands of innocent people fighting for their rights in Argentina are in prison and have been tortured and debased. We cannot forget that fact when our friends and fellow citizens in the Falkland Islands are suffering.' Parliament had 'a moral duty' and 'a political duty' to 'ensure that [the Falklanders'] . . . association with this country . . . is sustained'.

During the Suez crisis of 1956, Labour and Foot in particular had eloquently opposed the British military expedition and tellingly undermined its domestic credibility. But the Falklands task force was launched with cross-party approval. All the dogged work by the Falklands lobby over the previous decade and a half had paid off. Even the mild-mannered SDP backed the task force. The party's one relatively macho figure, David Owen, told the Commons he hoped that 'peaceful military action', in the form of 'a naval blockade' of the islands plus 'firm diplomacy', would be enough, but went on, tellingly shifting into the future tense, 'We all know that there will be great difficulties in a resisted [British] offence against the Falkland Islands . . . But nothing said in the House should exclude any possibility of repossessing them.'

Thirty years later Owen explained his stance to me. He said he had hated the political discord over Suez: 'My brother-in-law was [there] on HMS *Theseus* in '56. I was angry at seeing the House of Commons split. War does require from the politician the discipline of support.' When I looked slightly startled, he qualified himself: 'Or outright opposition. There isn't a halfway house in war.' The nature of the Argentinian regime and its summary occupation of the Falklands suppressed such 'outright opposition' to a British military response, at least in the Commons, already not the most pacifist of democratic parliaments. On 20 May, just before the task force began landing thousands of British troops on the islands, thirty-three MPs, only a twentieth of the total, voted against the use of force.

But there was another, deeper, more primal reason for the fierceness of so many British politicians over the Falklands. 'I did believe,' said Owen, 'that it was one of those moments when the whole way that a country sees itself can be changed. If we'd scuttled out of the Falklands ... I think a defeat there would have been a huge defeat. These are the fundamental questions for a country. You have to decide: "Is this country still capable? Is this country played out?" This was Thatcher's call. And she called it correctly.'

With a strong steer from Admiral Sir Henry Leach. On 31 March, when parts of Whitehall including the prime minister finally began to realize that an invasion might be coming, the First Sea Lord was the most senior naval officer present in Britain. His superior, Admiral Sir Terence Lewin, the Chief of Defence Staff, was on an official visit to New Zealand. Early that evening, Leach read the latest Ministry of Defence briefings on the situation in the South Atlantic and was astonished to find that, even now, the ministry's advice to the government was that a fleet should not be sent, since the Royal Navy had so many other commitments and the Argentinian manoeuvres might be a bluff. Leach sensed both an outrage and an opportunity. 'What the hell was the point of having a Navy if it was not used for this sort of thing?' he wrote afterwards. He went looking for Nott, his great adversary and one of the leading task-force sceptics.

The defence secretary was not in his office at the MOD. Leach was told that he had gone to the Commons. Leach was driven there at high speed. Then, in his full uniform, tall and still slim at fifty-eight, the admiral strode into the Central Lobby. He was kept waiting for ten endless minutes while Nott was located. The minister, it turned out, was in Thatcher's Commons office. Leach burst in, to find the two of them holding a frantic, but directionless and despairing meeting about the Falklands situation with an assortment of senior civil servants.

'We were discussing ... an appalling piece of information' – the probable invasion – Thatcher recalled at the Franks Inquiry. 'It was the worst, I think, moment of my life ... And then the First Sea Lord just appeared ... He just came in and was absolutely marvellous.' According to Leach, after listening to the civilians for a while longer, as they argued about whether or not to send a submarine to the Falklands, the prime minister asked him, 'Admiral, what do you think?'

Leach writes: 'I had my chance ... "I would strongly advise that we [send] a very considerable Naval Task Force with strong amphibious elements."' For the next few minutes, as if enacting his deepest fantasy of British naval greatness restored, Leach ran through a list of aircraft carriers, amphibious assault ships, destroyers and submarines, recommended the requisitioning of civilian merchant ships, the mobilization of thousands of Royal Marines 'supplemented by at least one additional Army Unit', and the deployment of 'every single [Sea Harrier] aircraft that can be made operational, including those normally used for training'.

The prime minister mostly listened in deferential silence. 'We wanted to know exactly how much he could send,' she told Franks. 'He just went over it one after another, and it was the biggest armada I think he told us that had ever set sail from here for a very very long time. All of a sudden we realized that there was something we could do.' Occasionally she interrupted with a sharp question, such as: 'Shall we have enough air cover?' Leach replied that he could only offer 'local air superiority before the [British] landing. I won't pretend that it will not be an operation involving considerable risk.'

Most of the task force, he went on, could be assembled in '48 hours', but the operation would be too big to be carried out in secret. Such a fleet would take 'about three weeks' to reach the Falklands. Thatcher then asked the essential question:

> 'Could we really recapture the islands . . .?'
>
> 'Yes, we *could* and in my judgement (though it is not my business to say so) we *should*.'
>
> 'Why do you say that?' snapped the Prime Minister.
>
> 'Because if we do not, or if we pussyfoot in our actions and do not achieve complete success, in another few months we shall be living in a different country whose word counts for little.'
>
> The Prime Minister looked relieved and nodded . . . Well into the night, when the meeting finally broke up, I left with full authority . . . to assemble and prepare the Task Force on the lines proposed.

For the previous two decades, on the wilder fringes of British right-wing politics, where the most choleric newspaper columnists and disillusioned ex-servicemen lurked, there had been a dream that one day the military, and perhaps a military strongman, would step in during an emergency and rescue the country. In the 1970s these hopes had coalesced around the recently retired General Sir Walter Walker, like Leach an austere figure with a distinguished service record and stronger political opinions than servicemen were supposed to have in Britain's civilian-dominated democracy – we were not supposed to be Argentina, after all. During 1974 and 1975 Walker excited right-wing newspapers and alarmed left-wing politicians by leading a paramilitary volunteer network, set up to 'act', as he vaguely but ominously put it, 'if there was a collapse of essential services' or 'a breakdown of law and order'. Walker's private army, as some of his critics and admirers referred to it, quickly wilted, one of 1970s Britain's many exotic but failed political seedlings, longer on rhetoric than organizational strength or public appeal. But Leach's decisive Falklands advice to Thatcher half a dozen years later, with its crucial, illicitly political element – 'if we pussyfoot . . . we shall be living in a different country' – was military influence over British politics finally achieved by other means.

In the days after the admiral's meeting with the prime minister, the readying and departure of the task force was turned into an epic, brilliantly manipulative piece of public theatre. It formed the opening scenes of a panoramic Whitehall production, combining the traditional British expertise at improvised military operations and at war propaganda, that would run, to credulous rave reviews in most of the British media, for the rest of the Falklands conflict, and indeed for over a year afterwards – right up until the next general election.

At the legendary old naval ports of southern England – Portsmouth, Poole, Southampton, Plymouth (where Owen's constituency was) – there were suddenly telegenic long quaysides of pale grey warships. Spotless from years of prosaic peacetime service, they had not been seen en masse by the public for years. Now they were loaded with helicopters and armoured vehicles, ammunition and rations, including pallets of Argentinian corned beef, at apparently miraculous speed. Britain's supposedly dying docks were suddenly whirring and clanking with life again, the veteran cranes beside the ships swivelling, lifting, dipping, lit after dark by floodlights. Checking on progress in Portsmouth, Nott encountered some of the dockers who had thrown bolts at him the year before. They proudly told him they were now working almost around the clock. 'What a wonderful country we live in,' the usually cynical Nott gushed afterwards.

The requisitioning of civilian ships, the first since the Second World War, included not just everyday, anonymous-seeming vessels such as the tubby container ship *Atlantic Conveyor*, but also towering, charismatic liners such as the *QE2* and the *Canberra*, widely regarded as some of the last great products of Britain's disappearing shipyards. And to see these luxurious craft being ingeniously converted for military use – the *Canberra*'s sun deck and swimming pool became a flight deck for helicopters – was to see, if you were so minded, a warrior nation toughening up again after the peacetime decadence of the 1960s and 1970s.

Inland, for the first time since Suez, the last British wartime amphibious operation, the main roads to and from the south coast were green with military vehicles. During the first four frantic days of provisioning, 3,000 lorryloads of equipment passed through Hampshire alone. The logistical challenge was one of the reasons Nott had initially questioned sending a fleet to the Falklands. A student of military history, he was conscious of his great-great-great-grandfather's perpetual difficulties with supplies during the nineteenth-century British campaigns in Afghanistan – like the Falklands, stony and barren and thousands of miles away. But in early April 1982 the energy and apparent efficiency of the British military surprised Nott and changed his mind.

Looking back from 2012, he suspected that some of this logistical miracle was a sleight of hand: 'I think in fact they'd done a hell of a lot of work the week before.' After all, Denis Healey, who had been a more assured defence secretary in the 1960s, and was still unusually respected by the armed forces, had warned the Commons on 30 March that an Argentinian fleet was 'reported to be' steaming towards the Falklands. 'So Henry [Leach],' Nott continued, 'could come to that meeting with Thatcher and say with great confidence that he could put the fleet together by Tuesday.' Nott unzipped a knowing Whitehall smile. 'I didn't realize it at the time. I just assumed that the task force was another off-the-cuff Nelsonian action.'

Either way, to Nott and the other Thatcherites, the British state certainly felt different in wartime from the cautious and, in their view, obstructive bureaucracy they had dealt with in government so far. 'One of the good things about the invasion happening so suddenly was that the Whitehall machine was completely poleaxed. We didn't have all its committees breathing down our necks. The shackles of bureaucracy just fell off. There was no Treasury meddling.' Significantly, the chancellor Geoffrey Howe was not appointed to the war cabinet. For Falklands purposes, the government's usual austerity no longer applied. According to Sir Lawrence Freedman, the final cost of the conflict to Britain was £1.8 billion: exactly £1 million per Falklander.

Despite her tendency to turn every crisis she faced as premier into a personal drama, Thatcher herself was energized by the war as never before – and as she probably never was again. On 14 May, midway through the conflict, she spoke at the Scottish Conservative conference. After finishing her speech, she spontaneously returned to the microphone and spoke unscripted about the conflict:

> What really thrilled me, having spent so much of my life in Parliament, and talking about things like inflation, Social Security benefits, housing problems . . . and so on, is that when it really came to the test, what's thrilled people wasn't those things, what thrilled people was once again being able to serve a great cause.

The task force left Britain in a week-long parade: sailors lined up on decks, their families thronging quaysides and medieval port battlements, patriotic civilians squeezed in beside them with Union Jacks, as if Diana's wedding in 1981 had been a rehearsal for all this. More patriots formed impromptu harbour escorts, their yachts and motorboats dwarfed by the warships, as if replaying the miraculous 1940 retreat from Dunkirk in reverse. The spectacle, televised worldwide, stirred more than the usual suspects. In Washington DC, Amy Wilentz of the peaceable American liberal magazine *The Nation* was astonished to find her colleague Christopher Hitchens, then one of Britain's most internationally renowned left-wing journalists, 'gathering himself up grandly in the Café Loup . . . and telling me he would happily serve on one of her majesty's ships that were at that moment steaming . . . to keep the sheep and shepherds under British rule'.

In fact, Hitchens personified the mix of feelings that made the Falklands War far more popular in Britain than later, much less militarily risky operations such as the 2003 invasion of Iraq. He was a long-standing foe of the South American dictatorships, his father had been a naval officer, and he had a concealed but deepening admiration for Margaret Thatcher: in 1979, he confessed much later in his autobiography, 'I deliberately did not vote to keep Labour in office . . . I was guiltily, secretly glad to see her terminating the long reign of mediocrity and torpor.'

Yet this war in particular was not going to be won by patriotic yearnings and stage management alone. An attempt to recapture the Falklands, fiercely opposed by Argentina, was always the most likely climax to the crisis – given the sheer scale and visibility of the task force, the Thatcher government's vulnerability and stubbornness, and the Galtieri government's similar qualities. But such an operation would involve defying the conventional wisdom of modern warfare in multiple ways, as many MPs and servicemen muttered to each other and to the less jingoistic journalists while the British fleet spent most of April chugging south. 'For the first time probably since Gallipoli in 1915, an amphibious operation was to be mounted with no air photographs of the enemy,' wrote Brigadier Julian Thompson, commander of much of the task force's modest and hastily assembled land army. The Gallipoli expedition, largely devised by Thatcher's idol Winston Churchill, had been notoriously overconfident and disastrous: the British troops and their allies had barely made it beyond their invasion beaches despite months of fighting. With casualties at appalling levels, winter closing in and support at home weakening, they had been humiliatingly evacuated.

Some pessimists imagined a similar scenario in the Falklands. Others feared the Argentinian air force, which had far more planes than the task force. Without full control of the air, the British fleet could meet the same fate as Leach's father's ship in 1941. Other doubters feared the South Atlantic, and the effect it would have on the British vessels and their crews if they were forced to maintain a blockade of the islands for months on end with no friendly harbour for thousands of miles (Thatcher herself thought the sea conditions would make a blockade impossible). Others still feared Galtieri's closeness to the Americans: the most widely drawn lesson from Suez had been that Britain should not launch wars without Washington's support.

My father was one of the worriers. When Argentina invaded the Falklands, he was still working in equipment procurement at the MOD. With the war, the usual patient rhythms of his work – overseeing, say, the development and purchase of a new army rucksack – became more tense and frantic. He spent much of early April helping to arrange for the *Atlantic Conveyor* to carry the task force's tents and helicopters, so that the British soldiers would not freeze or get stuck in the Falklands' boggy expanses. He came home even later than usual to our sparse army semi in temperate Surrey. We watched the Falklands-dominated *Nine O'clock News* as a family: my father mostly silent, knowing more than the melodramatic but MOD-steered South Atlantic reporters; my mother, an SDP supporter, in another stiff armchair, objecting softly to the war in general and Margaret Thatcher's noisy leadership of it in particular. Occasionally my father would let out a burst of bottled-up words about the awfulness of Galtieri or the Britishness of the Falklanders. He had been brought up in colonial India, where his father was a senior policeman during the Raj's final years: my father understood the appeal of holding onto imperial ways in faraway places. Yet he also understood that Britain's days as a military superpower were gone. 'I'm not sure,' he said to me on a walk as the task force headed south, 'that we can do it without the Americans.'

In late April and early May the task force finally reached the South Atlantic. The progress of most of the ships had been slowed by a lengthy stopover halfway, at the British territory of Ascension Island, a sort of desert Falklands in the mid-Atlantic, so that their hastily loaded cargoes could be rearranged and replenished. Contrary to appearances, the task force had not left Britain in a fit state for war. Even the identification papers issued to the few, solely British journalists permitted to travel with the fleet were not in order: left over from Suez, parts of them were written in Arabic.

Yet when the fighting resumed in the South Atlantic, it was at first deceptively one-sided. On 25 April a combined British air, sea and land force including members of the SAS swiftly recaptured South Georgia. 'Just. Rejoice. At. That. News,' Thatcher commanded reporters, and by implication the public, as she stood outside

Downing Street, eyes blazing. But her overly emphatic told-you-so tone conveyed vulnerability as much as vindication.

On 2 May a British nuclear submarine sank one of the Argentinian navy's most important ships, the cruiser *General Belgrano*, which had been built before the Second World War. Three hundred and twenty-three Argentinians died. The conflict seemed a mismatch. 'We are going to war as if to the manner born,' wrote Hugo Young in the *Sunday Times* just before the Belgrano story broke. 'More than 80 per cent of the electorate, according to the opinion polls, back the operation . . . This war, instead of being strange and improbable and not a little mad, is made to sound normal and well within our competence.'

That impression lasted two days more. On 4 May an Argentinian Exocet missile, one of the most feared and destructive naval weapons of the time, hit the British destroyer HMS *Sheffield*. The missile struck the ship just above the waterline, midway along her starboard side, not far from where the section of her Argentinian sister ship had been welded on in the Barrow-in-Furness shipyard; more importantly, it struck close to some of her most important and heavily manned rooms. The subsequent fire was made more lethal by inflammable foam mattresses – a sign of a navy that had got used to peacetime – which had been earmarked for replacement by more fire-resistant ones ever since the early 1970s; and also by the *Sheffield*'s single, sealed ventilation system, which had been designed to keep out radio-active dust in a nuclear war, and which instead spread toxic smoke throughout the vessel. Twenty sailors were killed, and the destroyer was fatally damaged. It was the first Royal Navy vessel lost in action since the Second World War. 'The waves of emotion that spread through Whitehall were almost tangible,' Leach wrote afterwards. 'Ministers and officials were deeply shocked and indeed it seemed that for many [Britons] this was the first real comprehension that the country was *at war*.' Or as Thatcher put it, in a private memoir of the conflict, fragmentary but sometimes candid, which she wrote in secret in 1983 and was released in 2015: 'With the tragic sinking of the *Sheffield* and the realization that other ships . . . could be damaged by Exocets – we had a real public-relations problem on our hands.'

*

David Rhodes was one of the millions jolted back in Britain. 'I'll always remember, it was a Tuesday night, I was watching News At Ten, and all of a sudden they said HMS *Sheffield* had been hit by an Exocet missile.' But the consequences for him were more significant than for most British civilians. 'Eight o'clock the following morning, there's a call for me from John Nott's office, from his PA: "We were wondering if you could help us?" I said: "I've already worked your problem out."'

Rhodes was an entrepreneur and a Yorkshireman, and direct and self-confident even by those standards. During the 1960s and 1970s, while working at the strong electrical engineering department of Leeds University, he had been one of the first in Britain to take technological breakthroughs from academia and turn them into products. In 1977 he had set up his own electronics company, Filtronic Components Ltd. 'I was fed up,' he told me, 'with having to put all my effort into getting research grants, which were given out by *committees*, by people who didn't know what you were talking about. And I thought, "I might as well make some money."'

When we met, at a flimsy-looking industrial estate on the outskirts of Leeds, Rhodes was driving a new Jaguar. He strode into the tiny, cold lobby of his latest company, sixty-nine years old, big-shouldered, with a white goatee, ushered me immediately to the car, steered it fast up a steep hill with strong, fidgety hands, and pulled up a minute later outside an Italian restaurant. He asked for his usual table, ordered his usual pizza – 'extra cheese, lots of chillis' – then cut it up methodically and started gobbling it down. Between bites, sometimes during bites, with bits of blood-red pizza shrapnel flying around, he explained how he had helped save the task force.

One of Filtronic's early products was a piece of equipment for the RAF's Tornado fighter jet, 'which, basically, electronically deflected missiles' away from the aircraft. 'You see,' said Rhodes, rocking back and forth on his chair, 'the missile's got a radar, and our product in effect grabbed that radar's signal, distorted it, delayed it . . . and created a phantom target.' He paused and chewed. 'Now, ships are much more vulnerable than planes to missile attack. By the late 70s, the electronic countermeasures systems on British warships [against missiles] were quite sophisticated, and ran on the same basic principles as the Tornado's. But the ships were also getting a new communications system called a SCOT [Satellite Communications Onboard Terminal]. And the SCOT was so high-power that, when it was in use, it . . . blinded the receiver system for the electronic countermeasures [warning of incoming enemy missiles].' Rhodes shook his large head. 'Unbelievable.'

During the late 1970s Filtronic began developing a gadget to stop this happening. Called a waveguide bandstop filter, it was 'like a little rectangular piece of metal, with little rectangular tubes coming out'. The whole device was about 8 inches long by 4 inches wide, and weighed barely a pound. A price was envisaged of around £5,000; the cost of each warship it could shield was over £20 million. In 1980 a prototype of the bandstop filter was given a trial by the Royal Navy. 'It was successful, very successful,' said Rhodes. 'But then they were stopped from buying any more, because *someone* in the government decided that everything the Ministry of Defence bought had to be subject to competitive tender. And this equipment couldn't be competitively tendered – because nobody else could make it!'

Two years later this typical piece of defence cost-cutting by the first Thatcher government helped sink the *Sheffield*. The destroyer was using its SCOT system until just before it was attacked; not being fitted with a bandstop filter, it learned of the incoming Exocet only a few seconds before impact. Even before the MOD phoned him, said Rhodes, 'I knew *exactly* what had happened.' The next morning, Nott's office said to him, 'We want filter sets for 19 ships.'

Rhodes agreed. Despite his earlier dealings with Whitehall, he retained a grudging admiration for Thatcher – 'on the things she knew about, she was quite good. The problem was her advisers' – and he felt Britain had 'an obligation' to liberate the Falklanders. As a three-year-old start-up with annual sales of only £300,000 (£1 million today), his company also needed the money. It employed forty people and occupied two anonymous industrial units, just off a main road, in a valley outside the little town of Shipley in west Yorkshire. Here, over the next three weeks, from early to late May, while the British warships in the South Atlantic were being attacked by the Argentinians with mounting ferocity, Filtronic manufactured its vital filters for the task force at the excruciating rate of one a day.

Rhodes didn't have enough employees or milling machines to make them any faster. 'We worked 19 days straight. We started at two o'clock in the morning, and people had rests at about eight o'clock at night. Then we started at 2 am again.' The reasons for this unusual double shift were disclosed to as few people as possible. 'My family knew, because I was going out in the middle of the night. My technical people knew, because they had to work out what to do.' Early each evening, an unmarked chauffeur-driven car from the MOD parked near the industrial units, and waited discreetly until the day's product was ready for collection. 'We had problems and setbacks. The filter was just pure copper. And machining copper's not easy. Then it had to be welded and soldered together. That's not always a precise science, and if the filter wasn't quite right, you would see that in its performance when we tested it. Then we would have to bend the metal, lever it. We didn't start again from scratch – there wasn't the time or the materials to do that. So we couldn't say to the MOD, "The filter will be ready at six every evening." Sometimes it was nine. The car just had to wait.' Then each filter, about the size of a gold bar, was driven to an RAF base – Rhodes was not told which; Yorkshire had half a dozen – and flown individually and immediately to the South Atlantic. There it was delivered by parachute to the task force, and installed on one of the nineteen ships deemed most worthy of protection against Exocets. 'It could be fitted in an hour. The sailors didn't need to know what it was. It was just bolted on. They used to fix it behind one of the ships' antennae. It was weatherproof, sealed from the outside world.'

The Argentinian Exocet attacks continued. The final one came two days before the end of the war. But, said Rhodes, none of the British ships fitted with his filters were struck by the missiles: their anti-missile systems now worked. After the war, he received letters of thanks from Nott and from Admiral Sandy Woodward, the commander of the task force. Filtronic was paid £100,000 for its work. 'We actually made money on it,' said Rhodes. 'But not that much.'

Yet Rhodes's gadget hardly made the task force impregnable. After the *Sheffield*, Woodward recorded, 'We lost ... *Coventry*, *Ardent*, *Antelope*, *Atlantic Conveyor*, and *Sir Galahad*. If the Args' bombs had been properly fused for low-level air raids' – many hit British ships but did not explode – 'we would surely have lost *Antrim*, *Plymouth*, *Argonaut*, *Broadsword* and *Glasgow*. And we were very lucky indeed that

Glamorgan and *Brilliant* were still floating in mid-June.' He feared even more for his unscathed larger vessels: 'One major mishap, a mine, an explosion, a fire . . . in either of our two aircraft carriers would almost certainly have proved fatal to the whole operation.' Without the partial protection the carriers' jets provided, the task force, and the British troops that landed on the islands' utterly exposed, treeless slopes in mid-May, would have been a simple target. Margaret Thatcher knew this too. During the war a memo from her circulated in the MOD. Its key sentence read: 'What if we lose a capital ship?'

Losing the *Atlantic Conveyor* was disastrous enough. Struck by two Exocets that had been aimed in the direction of the nearby aircraft carriers, the container ship, with a hold half-full of fuel and cluster bombs, burned and then exploded so quickly that the rest of its supplies for the British land forces were also destroyed, except for two helicopters. Thatcher wrote in her war memoir, 'I knew *also* that aboard the Atlantic Conveyor had been 19 Harriers – [aircraft] reinforcements that were sorely needed.' After the assault, she went to bed not knowing 'if . . . we had lost them . . . Perhaps that was the worst night of all.' The next day, she was told the jets had been flown off the ship before the attack: 'Relief flooded on [*sic*] me . . . We were *not fatally* wounded.'

Woodward wrote less ecstatically in his diary: 'Down goes another £100 million worth.' My father came home from the MOD just as terse and gloomy. The British plan for recapturing the Falklands involved landing troops well away from Port Stanley, where most of the Argentinian forces were concentrated, to minimize the chances of a Gallipoli-style stalemate on the beach or an immediate enemy counter-attack, and then advancing swiftly across the islands' mountainous interior towards the capital. Without the *Atlantic Conveyor*'s tents, and without most of its helicopters, the bulk of the British troops would now have to walk the 60 rocky, boggy miles, carrying most of their ammunition and provisions, sleeping in the open with the Falklands winter approaching, and fighting their way through, rather than leapfrogging, any Argentinian defences that were in the way.

The land campaign that followed lasted only three and a half weeks, from 21 May to 14 June. But the British advance was so fraught and photogenic, so doggedly step-by-step and hard-fought, so dramatically but uncritically reported, so risky and bloody-minded – the British troops were outnumbered almost throughout – and so in keeping with the self-image of the British army, and of many Britons, and of Thatcher herself, as resourceful and determined underdogs, that it became legendary in Britain even as it was happening. Thirty years later, with the Falklands War undergoing one of its regular anniversary gildings in the British press, I went to the most iconic and pivotal battlefields.

At San Carlos, the minuscule coastal settlement where the British soldiers landed on 21 May, at first miraculously unopposed, the slopes leading up from the inlet were steep and utterly lacking in cover. Shreds of sun-bleached khaki tarpaulin still marked the shallow foxholes the British soldiers had scratched out, to defend themselves against a counter-attack by land that never came. Out on the water, where the stationary British transport ships and their escorts had been lethally attacked from the air instead, the waves of 'Bomb Alley' were tombstone-grey. But over the inlet sat a low, heavy, typically Falklands cloud lid – difficult for even the bravest pilots to fly through: on many days the task force's great friend.

Twenty miles closer to Stanley, above the scattered wooden and tin houses of another lonely settlement, Goose Green, was a wide-open and grassy isthmus. On 28 and 29 May, the 2nd Battalion of the Parachute Regiment, led by Colonel 'H' Jones, sought to seize it from a larger, more heavily armed Argentinian force, shortly after Thatcher's press secretary Bernard Ingham had promised reporters, impatient for a first British land victory, 'We're not going to fiddle around.' Thatcher recorded in her Falklands memoir: 'We were all concerned that there appeared to be little movement out of the [San Carlos] bridgehead.' At Goose Green in 2012, the treeless lumpy slopes where the paras were trapped by machine-gun fire, attacked from the air with napalm, lost Jones and fifteen others, and came close to losing the whole battle, were still ragged with craters and large metal fragments driven into the ground. At times during Goose Green, only the damp, dense, peaty soil, which absorbed much of the blast of the Argentinian artillery shells, kept the British casualties down.

At Bluff Cove, 30 miles further forward in the advance on Stanley, the British luck with the landscape and weather finally ran out. On 8 June, a showery day but just good enough for flying, two British landing ships were spotted by the Argentinians on an exposed stretch of coastal water framed by low headlands. After confusion and arguments among the increasingly jumbled and tired British command hierarchy, the ships were laden with soldiers and equipment for disembarking, yet almost undefended. They were bombed. Forty-nine people died, including thirty-nine members of the Welsh Guards.

At a commemoration yards from where the catastrophe happened, I met a former Welsh Guards sergeant, a slow-moving, middle-aged man of few words in an official Falklands veteran's sweatshirt. 'I got off the ship right before it was attacked,' he said. He indicated the pebbly shoreline where he had been disembarked, and then swung his gaze out over the water. 'We saw the planes coming over. I lost a lot of friends. My best friend died.' He paused. 'Wars are bloody.' He had been in Northern Ireland before the Falklands. I asked how the two conflicts compared. 'It was easier here,' he said. 'Because you knew who the enemy were.'

Finally I went to Mount Tumbledown, one of the grey line of peaks that overlook Stanley. The British took Tumbledown during the last night of the war. From a distance it wasn't much, just a steady incline of brown grass with a pile of rocks on top. But up close, the rocks were a fortress: soldier-sized clefts, bigger natural bunkers, blind corners, lookouts with views for miles, unscalable overhangs, sheer drops. It took the 2nd Battalion of the Scots Guards eight hours of near-chaotic night-fighting with grenades and bayonets to capture Tumbledown, which was blasted all night by a freezing 50-mile-an hour gale. 'Contrary to expectations,' wrote their commander Major John Kiszley afterwards, 'the enemy were standing and fighting.' By the end so many Scots Guards had been killed or wounded, or had got lost in the darkness and the rocks, that Kiszley reached the summit with only three men.

Tumbledown was finally captured by 9 a.m. During the rest of the morning of 14 June, Argentinian soldiers in the surrounding hills and in Stanley began to lay down their guns. During the afternoon dirty, grinning columns of victorious British soldiers marched into the tiny town, accompanied by a group of British reporters almost as jubilant. They walked past enormous piles of discarded Argentinian rifles, entire roadsides of barely used Argentinian armoured vehicles, and clots of Argentinian prisoners-in-waiting, looking miserably cold despite their elaborate, puffy battle uniforms – the whole panorama an almost precise, shame-erasing reversal of the scenes of British capitulation in Stanley seventy-four days earlier.

Just before midnight the Argentinians formally surrendered. 'They are reported to be flying white flags over Port Stanley,' Margaret Thatcher announced to the House of Commons, with an enormous emphasis on each word, savouring the moment, or unable to quite believe it. 'What happened . . . that day,' she wrote in her memoir, 'seemed like a miracle.'

In the rush and relief of victory, many people in Britain forgot what a modest enemy Argentina had been – had they ever known it. Argentina had not fought, let alone defeated, a foreign power for over a century. Its invasion of the islands, while long planned, had been launched at barely a week's notice: when the erratic politics of the junta in Buenos Aires, the deadlock in the negotiations with Britain over the islands, and the confrontation over the scrap-metal workers on South Georgia came into sudden alignment. The invasion force and army of occupation had been thrown together. It had muddled-up units, thousands of new conscripts, and too many troops from hot rather than cold parts of Argentina. Cooking equipment for the conquerors of the Malvinas took a fortnight to arrive, and rarely even reached those sent out of Stanley to occupy the wind-blasted hills. There, and along the less bitter but less defensible coastline of the islands, the Argentinian troops waited fearfully for weeks for the ever more certain counter-invasion by the much more experienced British army – an attack that their superiors 1,200 miles away in balmy Buenos Aires, echoing the pre-war complacency of the Thatcher government, had confidently predicted would never come. Even in mid-April, with the task force well on its way, Galtieri insisted to the American government's South American fixer Dick Walters: 'The British won't fight.'

When the British did, the increasingly miserable Argentinian garrison was passive, never launching a significant counter-attack. Intimidated by the alien Falklands terrain, worried about British air attacks if they were caught in the open, and still hoping for a negotiated settlement, most of the Argentinian troops stayed uselessly concentrated in Stanley. There and across the archipelago, divisions opened up between the officers and men, between the conscripts and regular soldiers, and between the hungry soldiers in the hills and the relatively comfortable ones in the capital. Meanwhile in Buenos Aires, age-old rivalries and tactical disagreements between the army, navy and air force steadily worsened, as each came to believe it was making the greatest sacrifice in the increasingly disastrous war against the British.

In the end, the Argentinian strategy for defending the Malvinas came down to little more than holding the hills for as long as possible, and hoping that mounting casualties and the arrival of winter would make a British victory politically and physically impossible. Two hundred and fifty-five British service personnel were killed in the war: roughly one for every seven Falklanders, a fact that hangs, almost too enormous to be mentioned, over the life of the islands to this day, like one of the South Atlantic's limitless-seeming clouds. But more than a hundred times as many people had sailed with the task force. The unspoken fear that ran through the crowds seeing the ships off, through Downing Street and Whitehall and the House of Commons – of a bloodbath in the Falklands – was not realized.

Winter came closer to beating the British. In the Falklands it usually starts in mid-May and lasts for at least four months. In 1982 it came late: '13 June brought beautiful, sunny, almost springlike weather,' wrote Brigadier Julian Thompson, commander of the task force's 3 Commando brigade. But the last battles of the war were still fought in snow and freezing mud. Despite having trained in the Norwegian Arctic, in preparation for an invasion by the Russians, nine of Thompson's men got frostbite. As Thatcher put it in her memoir, 'It was essential to repossess [the islands] with all possible speed and to wait for nothing.'

Had Argentina invaded the Falklands in mid-May or later, as it had originally planned, rather than at the very start of April, then the weather on the archipelago and in the South Atlantic might well have made their position impregnable. By the time spring came to the Malvinas, the passage of time, the ever-shifting priorities of international relations, and the fickleness of British public and political opinion might well have sunk Britain's chances of recapturing the islands, and Margaret Thatcher with them.

Even with the timing of the war in her favour, the Thatcher government considered making peace with Argentina for much longer than the British public realized, at the time or afterwards. 'Looking back,' wrote Thatcher in her memoir, 'it was easy to forget what a large part the attempts to negotiate played in the Falklands story.' At least one minister who had been cordial towards the junta before the conflict, Cecil Parkinson, retained some of his Anglo-Argentinian connections once the fighting started, despite being a member of the war cabinet. 'Since telephone communications were not cut off during the conflict,' he wrote afterwards, 'I did, from time to time, receive messages from my wife's relations [in Argentina] . . . urging us to try to find a peaceful solution.'

The day after the sinking of the *Sheffield*, on 5 May, Thatcher summoned her entire cabinet – rather than the smaller war cabinet – to consider a peace plan that had been laboriously stitched together over the previous four weeks by Peru and America. The often vaguely worded document proposed that Argentina and Britain withdraw their forces, that an 'interim administration' of other countries govern the Falklands, and that the islanders' 'aspirations and interests' be 'taken into account' in any 'definitive settlement' of the islands' status. The scheme, Thatcher wrote later, did 'not provide unambiguously for a right to self-determination' for the Falklanders; but it was supported by her foreign secretary, and potential usurper, Francis Pym. To her frequent discomfort, he had spent much of April, and would spend much of May, criss-crossing the Atlantic, doggedly trying to negotiate an early end to the war.

More surprisingly, on 5 May the peace plan was backed by the cabinet – and, reluctantly, by Thatcher herself. 'The truth was that none of us liked the terms,' she confessed in her memoir, 'but if we could make them reasonable . . . and secure the withdrawal of Argentinian forces, and therefore avoid further loss of life – we would agree.' There were arguments for this huge U-turn: international opinion had shifted against Britain after the ruthless sinking of the *Belgrano*; the Thatcher government did not want to alienate the Americans in particular; and there was a strong chance Argentina would reject the plan anyway – which it did. But untidy, unheroic compromise was not how the Iron Lady approached the Falklands conflict in public.

*

During my interview with David Owen, in his peaceful living room beside the Thames, it was only when we got to the Falklands that his answers lost some of their magnanimity. 'Thatcher messed up over the Falklands, but she also reaped the rewards,' he said quietly. 'I felt it then. And I feel it to this day.'

In early 1983, Owen continued, shortly after the Franks Inquiry published its report on 'the period leading up to the Argentine invasion', as the potentially explosive terms of reference put it. 'I was talking to David Watt, a very good journalist and a very good friend of mine. And I was bemoaning the report not giving me the credit I was due, for spotting the threat to the Falklands when I was foreign secretary under Jim Callaghan, and bemoaning the report not saying how responsible the Thatcher government had been for ignoring that threat. And Watt said, "David, it's a simple thing. We won. That's all they're saying down the pub. We stuffed the Argies. The last thing they want to have is anyone arguing that it could have been done differently."'

On 3 July 1982, three weeks after the Argentinian surrender, Margaret Thatcher spoke at the handsome racecourse outside Cheltenham in Gloucestershire, one of the favourite retirement spots for former servants of the British Empire. The occasion was a Conservative rally, held in a safe Tory constituency. Her party was suddenly 20 per cent ahead of Labour and 25 per cent ahead of the SDP-Liberal Alliance in the national polls: 'Today we meet in the aftermath of the Falklands Battle,' Thatcher began:

> Things cannot be the same again, for we have learned something about ourselves . . . When we started out [in the war], there were the waverers and the fainthearts. The people who thought that Britain could no longer seize the initiative . . . The people who thought we could no longer do the great things which we once did. Those who believed our decline was irreversible . . . that Britain was no longer the nation that had built an Empire and ruled a quarter of the world. Well they were wrong. The lesson of the Falklands is that Britain has not changed . . . Britain found herself again in the South Atlantic and will not look back.

As Thatcher spoke, the scarred ships of the task force were still on their way back to Britain. Chris Caroe, a twenty-one-year-old Royal

Marine who had helped capture Two Sisters, an Argentinian mountain stronghold next to Tumbledown, was on one of the troopships. One night as it battered homewards through the wintry South Atlantic, he told the *Chester Chronicle* decades later, 'We went into the mess and someone put on the tape for *Chariots of Fire* . . . and the whole mess just sang and everybody was blubbing like a baby.'

For much of the rest of the summer, the ships straggled triumphantly into British ports, watched by crowds that outdid those which had seen the task force go: 50,000 people for the returning *Canberra* alone. In October an official Falklands victory parade took over the City of London, with jets from the campaign overhead and veterans lining the roads. Three hundred thousand civilians reportedly attended. In January 1983 Thatcher kept the great Falklands show rolling by visiting the islands herself. The same month, the Franks Inquiry concluded helpfully but improbably that the Argentinian invasion 'could not have been foreseen': 'We would not be justified in attaching any criticism or blame to the present Government.' Four months later, less than a year after the Argentinian surrender, and a year earlier than she had to, Thatcher called a general election, to take place on 9 June. Anyone who doubted that the Falklands conflict would feature in the campaign, overtly or otherwise, only had to be reminded that the war cabinet member Cecil Parkinson was the Conservatives' chief election strategist.

The Sunday before polling day, the *Observer* published a survey by Harris that asked voters to rate her government as a success or failure in eight fundamental areas. On education, only 9 per cent saw success. On the NHS and 'combating crime', only 11 per cent did. On the economy, 31 per cent did – exactly the same percentage as saw failure. Despite the recovery that had begun in 1982, despite all the ambition and energy of her administration, despite all the shifts in its favour in the cultural climate, most voters, on most issues, remained, at best, unconvinced. Only in two areas did the government's fans outnumber its critics: Thatcher's 'leadership', by 46 per cent to 19 per cent; and the Falklands War, by 51 per cent to 23 per cent.

Four days later the Conservatives were re-elected. Their total vote was down by 686,000 compared to 1979, and their vote share fell too: from 43.9 per cent to 42.4 per cent – a mediocre winning percentage by post-war standards, a reflection of the government's patchy record and general divisiveness. But the large anti-Thatcher vote was split almost evenly between Michael Foot's erratic Labour Party and the novel SDP-Liberal Alliance. The British electoral system, intolerant of such ambivalence, made the Conservatives the overwhelming victors, awarding them a Commons majority of 144, the biggest for almost forty years. The majority was so large, it almost guaranteed the Conservatives at least two more terms in office: the chance to embed Thatcherism in Britain.

PART FIVE

A New World

13
Cocaine and Glass

Many of the events that set Britain on a new course in the early 1980s happened in watery places: the announcement of the SDP breakaway from Labour in Limehouse; the coup by Ken Livingstone a few miles upriver in County Hall; the convulsive riots in the old seamen's quarter of Toxteth, in many ways the beginning of the end for northern Toryism; above all, the war in the South Atlantic. That seas and rivers and the historically charged streets that bordered them should act as backdrops for so much of the drama was not simply coincidence. In the early 1980s, more than now, Britain was still a self-consciously maritime nation. Its coast was thickly strung with the ports and shipyards which had made it a superpower, which had maintained it as such within living memory, and which in their shrinkage and decay showed the country's twentieth-century retreat more graphically than perhaps any other social symptom. In this rundown quayside Britain formed some of the 1980s' wildest hopes that the country's relative decline could be reversed. And some of the period's dreamers and schemers began, for good or ill, to build a new world.

In those days Peter Turlik drove to work in an Alfa Romeo coupé. The wedge-shaped little sports car was his one obvious indulgence. He was approaching forty, polite, fastidious, quietly ambitious, 'a technocrat' in his own mind; a Polish immigrant with kind eyes and strong forearms who had patiently spent the late 1960s and all of the 1970s in the slow, often futile business of urban regeneration, first for the London County Council and then for the GLC. Around 1980, Turlik told me later, 'I said to myself, if there isn't going to be a major change, a pretty dramatic transformation of ideas and funding, then

I'm off – to the private sector, possibly to the States. I had an aunt and an uncle who'd emigrated to Canada. On visits, I remember my uncle used to say, "Peter, Europe's finished! Toronto is growing. Come out to Toronto. You'll be wasting all your qualifications if you stay."'

Turlik's area of expertise was the London docks. From his sparse terraced house in Lambeth, with books about film in glass-fronted shelves, he would drive to the docks, right across the choked sprawl of inner south London. It took less than twenty minutes:

> Everyone was heading the other way. I'd cross the river through the Rotherhithe Tunnel, and quickly be at the top of the Isle of Dogs. There was a Port of London Authority gate there. There was one other entrance; otherwise the docks were completely fenced off. These gates had been locked for some time – the PLA did not make it easy to visit – but I had a key. You drove in . . . and it was like being on a private estate. It was about 5,000 acres. You drove east across the West India Docks, then there was a little swing bridge, that used to swing out when the last of the ships came in, and then you were on an estate road. There were no proper roads, no hierarchy of roads – the goods had been unloaded from the ships onto a railway – and the road was overgrown, because it hadn't been used for years. You easily got lost. The tarmac was patchy, and there was so much debris, stuff like nails, that you got punctures – I got terribly upset at what used to happen to my Alfa Romeo . . . And then you were in something like a ghost town. The buildings were there – enormous sheds made of corrugated iron, little brick ones – but they were empty. The quays were overgrown. There was a lot of timber lying all over the place. Bits of port machinery. All the cranes were still there, hanging. The railway tracks were there. There wasn't much vandalism; but it was pretty quiet, desolate. There was almost no activity whatsoever. There were a couple of pumping stations, as the docks were losing a lot of water through seepage. There was a core of PLA people still employed, with fairly esoteric titles: different harbourmasters for each part of the dock system, each with his little boat, whizzing around. But some of the dock gates had jammed shut. Instead of water flushing in and out, as it had when ships went in and out, now there was algae and other strange stuff floating around. There was a smell of pollution. In the winter, when the fog started to

come in from the river, you had to be very, very careful you didn't drive into the dock.

By the start of the 1980s, the London docks, and with them miles of riverfront and deep swathes of the city's poorer south and east that depended on the quaysides for jobs, were either dead, dying, or gasping for breath. The end of London as one of the world's great ports had come with both shocking speed and glacial inevitability. In 1966 the usually acute architectural critic and urban explorer Ian Nairn had written confidently in his book *Nairn's London* of 'the working river, sinuous loops of greasy water thick with boats'. The next year, the East India Docks closed. In 1968 the St Katharine Docks and London Docks followed; in 1969 the Limehouse Basin; in 1970 the Surrey Docks; in 1980 the West India and Millwall Docks; in 1981 the Royal Docks – the last significant docks left in the capital.

Almost 2,000 years earlier the Romans had selected these swampy riverbanks to found a major settlement in large part because of their suitability for sea trade: close to the continent, near enough to the Thames estuary to be easily navigable, yet far enough inland to deter seaborne attacks. 'London was a port before it was a city,' as the East End historian and activist David Widgery put it.

Yet in the long term it was always a port on borrowed time. The relative narrowness of the Thames for a busy trading river; the lack of room along its banks for loading and unloading as London thickened and took on other functions; the city's perennial road congestion, and pilfering from dock warehouses; the growth in the size of merchant ships and of their units of cargo – all these forced the docks gradually eastwards, away from the city centre and out towards the flat open spaces of East Anglia.

Between 1802 and 1921, the restless heyday of the British Empire, a sequence of ever larger and more impressive-looking docks were dug: from St Katharine Docks in the west, an elegantly enclosed series of basins right next to the City of London, to the Royal Docks in the east, then the biggest docks in the world, three immense windswept rectangles of water on the far edge of the imperial metropolis, framed by endless arching cranes and banks of warehouses and granaries. But the apparent orderliness and impregnability of this city-within-a-city, clanking and whirring behind miles of high dock walls, was as deceptive as Britain's economic supremacy. There were too many docks. Victorian speculators had built many of them in a competitive frenzy that did not consider their long-term profitability or efficiency. In 1909 the docks, now struggling commercially, were nationalized: the Port of London Authority (PLA) was set up to run and rationalize them. It spent the next half-century energetically, sometimes desperately, trying to maintain their international pre-eminence by building new harbour facilities and mechanizing the quaysides. With each modernization whole categories of dockworkers were made redundant.

Meanwhile, twenty miles away in Essex, on a wider, more flexible site, a rival port had already been established: Tilbury, also run by the PLA, quietly hedging its bets. Once the modern shipping container replaced less secure, more labour-intensive, more unionized methods of shipping cargo, in the 1950s and 1960s, the neatly stacked quays of Tilbury, and similar continental European ports, quickly took away London's sea traffic. Most of the city's Victorian and Edwardian docksides were simply too tight for manoeuvring these truck-sized metal boxes in large numbers, and too awkward for fleets of trucks to access quickly.

By the early 1980s, the PLA had lost interest in maintaining even a fraction of its East End empire as a viable port. The GLC's economic strategist Mike Ward told me: 'They were going to close the pumping station which stopped the Royal Docks from flooding. We voted to provide £200,000, or whatever it was, to keep the pumping station going. The PLA declined to accept it. I remember going to meet the chairman, and saying, "Look, you tell me that trade has moved to Felixstowe [another East Anglian port]. The public purse is having to meet the costs of building new dual carriageways to Felixstowe, which are more expensive than the cost of maintaining your pumping station." He said: "Nothing in my terms of reference makes me have to consider questions like that."'

During the 1960s the PLA started filling in its London docks. Those nearest the City, the authority shrewdly foresaw, might one day be profitably sold off as land for offices. But it treated docks with less development potential more casually. 'The PLA got a little bit of income from letting builders just chuck stuff in,' said Peter Turlik. Rubble, tyres, knackered doors, broken pipes, rotting boats, burnt-out cars: in an increasingly run-down east London, the filled-in docks became the most gothic landscape of all. 'There were problems, subsequently,' Turlik continued drily. 'Methane gas formed ... There were lots of little explosions. I used to be told, "There's something burning in Surrey Docks."'

The sense of London – and Britain – having drastically come down in the world was reinforced by a rash of scrap dealers, haulage yards and builders' merchants, renting slivers of the Isle of Dogs on short-term contracts, from the PLA in particular. 'There were a lot of rogues,' remembered a veteran of 'the island' in the 1970s and early 1980s, as locals called (and still call) the inward-looking peninsula. A gold chain swung beneath his open-necked shirt as he showed me around his still-extant riverside kingdom of corrugated sheds, so patched-up and ancient they could have been in the Falklands, while a single forklift poked fraying bales of recycled clothing.

'It was a beehive of activity,' he continued. 'A great community atmosphere. A lot of pubs. A couple of caffs.' The residential population across almost the whole docks area was shrinking fast – by over a quarter in some wards between 1971 and 1981. But in 1981 almost 40,000 people still lived in pockets of terraced houses or tower blocks between the expanses of waste ground and water. Few were wealthy – on the Isle of Dogs 86 per cent were council tenants – and while some neighbourhoods were close-knit, bonded by generations of rough dock work and their isolation from the rest of London, with that work now gone there was a sense of people clinging on. 'There was a lot of trouble round the area: break-ins, vandalism, arson,' said the man with the gold chain, matter-of-factly. Did he find the disused docks spooky? 'Not at all. They were sad.'

The dereliction extended all the way to Tower Bridge and the beginning of central London: rust-brown and sun-bleached on the north bank, moss-green and dank on the shadier south. Unlike the post-industrial voids that had opened up in northern cities such as Manchester and Liverpool, London's were in the eyeline of Westminster politicians and metropolitan property developers and millions of foreign visitors. Yet until the early 1980s most politicians and developers paid the dereliction little or no attention. The capital had many other troubled areas. Sections of the riverfront had been decaying for so long, they had become part of the scenery. Besides, the worst of the desolation was hidden behind the high dock walls.

Michael Heseltine became an MP in 1966. He had both a property business and a long-standing interest, rare for a Tory, in the condition of London. But it took him until the 1970s to discover the docks problem. In 2012 I asked him why. In his sunny top-floor office in Hammersmith in west London, sitting with one leg draped over the side of an armchair, he snorted loudly. 'Why should I go to east London? East London was a *long*, *long* way away. There was no commercial reason for me to go. There had been virtually no private-sector housing construction there since the war. It was virtually all publicly owned land, so there was no development on it.' Turlik told me, 'I remember the fuss people at the GLC used to make about going out to Docklands. "Oh, can't we leave it 'til next week?"'

Yet in a city as restless as London, such incuriosity was never going to be universal. From the early 1960s, even before the ailing docks finally began expiring, their combination of emptying waterfront buildings, unusual atmospheres and vistas, and seemingly frozen-in-time East End communities, began to exert a fascination for some outsiders. In 1962 the well-known journalist, drinker and Soho bohemian Daniel Farson bought a large corner pub in the Isle of Dogs, the Waterman's Arms. For two years he ran it as a traditional but socially ambitious 'singing pub' that drew an eclectic crush of celebrities: Francis Bacon, Shirley Bassey, William Burroughs and Clint Eastwood. Eastwood wrote 'rowdy' in the visitors' book.

Soon afterwards artists, always gentrification's scouting party, knowingly or not, began moving into some of the dock warehouses. They were attracted by their space and river light, which was getting brighter as London deindustrialized and fogs of pollution became less common. In 1965 David Owen bought his Georgian terraced house in Limehouse. In Wapping, less intimidatingly remote from central London, more warehouses were converted into residences during the 1970s, this time for adventurous middle-class homebuyers. With most of the river traffic gone, a water view could now be as peaceful, and potentially marketable, as a country view in the most sanitized part of the Cotswolds.

In 1975, the prophetic British novelist J. G. Ballard published *High-Rise*, a typically black satire about a fictional, upmarket apartment complex newly planted in 'abandoned dockland . . . along the north bank of the river', in east London. The following year, an equally perceptive observer of the capital, Barrie Keefe, a young East End dramatist, began a film script about a local gangster who wants to expand his empire, and partly legitimize it, by building a whole new cityscape of towers and glassy blocks across the docks. *The Long Good Friday* was filmed on location in the summer of 1979. It presented a sunlit wasteland of quays and cranes that was both desolate and beautiful, raw and covetable. The film was released to thrilled reviews in February 1981.

In the late 1970s another unsqueamish businessman arrived in Docklands, as journalists and planners were beginning to name and thus commodify the area. In Wapping, Rupert Murdoch's press conglomerate News International quietly bought a disused Georgian warehouse complex and filled-in dock. The company's chief executive, Bert Hardy, envisaged eventually moving its British newspapers there, in order to transform their working practices and industrial relations, which were fractious even by Fleet Street standards.

In 1981 Wapping's potential as a Thatcherite stronghold became greater still. Her government, which Murdoch's tabloids had helped into office in 1979, allowed News International to buy *The Times* and *Sunday Times* – despite, or, perhaps more realistically, because of, a chorus of warnings about the unprecedented concentration of press ownership that would result. The intolerantly right-wing Australian, it was widely feared, would end the editorial independence of what had hitherto been only loosely Tory papers. Those fears were soon borne out. On 22 March 1982 Thatcher's private secretary Ian Gow wrote to her economic adviser Alan Walters: 'The new Editor of *The Times*, Charlie Douglas-Home' – whom Murdoch had appointed – 'is an old friend . . . instinctively sound as a bell about economic policy, and a staunch admirer of the Prime Minister.' The next day, Gow informed Thatcher that Douglas-Home had 'telephoned . . . and said that he was determined to reverse the increasingly hostile tone of Editorials [under his less biddable predecessor Harold Evans], so far as the Government's economic strategy was concerned. He asked whether we could let him have a critique of recent Leading Articles.'

The same year, to the horror of conservationists, News International demolished many of its Wapping warehouses and began building a hulking, impregnable-looking printing hall. For now, Murdoch, who like Thatcher had a cautious, power-respecting side as well as a gambling one, remained too wary of the potent print unions to install newspaper presses or facilities for journalists there. Hardy had left the company in 1979, and the unused Wapping compound became known at News International in the early 1980s as 'Hardy's folly'. But gradually Murdoch changed his mind. During 1985 all the hardware needed to produce newspapers – presses, paper, ink, computers – was smuggled into the complex in convoys of unmarked lorries. One January evening in 1986, editions of Murdoch's papers were suddenly conjured from the plant for the first time. Its Docklands site, relatively remote, with few residential neighbours, meant that the police protecting his delivery trucks from the inevitable ring of protesters could be helpfully robust. That night, Murdoch phoned Hardy about what soon became known as Fortress Wapping: 'Thank you, Bert. You were right and I was wrong.'

The state also moved slowly to exploit the seclusion and seeming blank slate offered by Docklands. Between 1971 and 1973 a typically elephantine planning study commissioned by the Heath government had produced an exhaustive list of proposals for reviving the area, including a safari park, a sailing lake, a museum, an exhibition centre, a polytechnic, 'a fun park' and 'a merchandise mart'. Versions of many of these would be realized in Docklands decades later – the O2 Arena, the ExCel convention centre – but during the 1970s they were widely regarded as castles in the sky, and nothing came of them. Peter Turlik had dealings with the planners: 'They had a very good team . . . But I don't think they ever went down there! They did their work in rooms off Charlotte Street' – a sheltered avenue in central London with plenty of restaurants.

Instead, from the early 1970s to the early 1980s Turlik and a few other determined people at the GLC, in Whitehall, in community groups and on east London councils, got a thin scatter of amenities built in Docklands: an improbably bucolic city farm on the Isle of Dogs, a small sports centre and huddles of cosy low-rise council housing in Wapping, the convex engineering miracle of the Thames Barrier in Silvertown, a lumpy hotel and flashy marina in St Katharine Docks. 'Dialogue was opened with some developers,' remembered Turlik, 'and we were able to persuade one or two people. In Beckton, they set up the first Docklands business units in an existing industrial park.' It was a decent vision of how the docks might be regenerated: socially inclusive, a mixture of public spaces, affordable housing and commerce. But its execution was too slow and small-scale for what was threatening to become southern England's Detroit: 'I think one realized that if one carried on at that sort of level, it wouldn't transform the area.'

Meanwhile the wider world was turning against such social democratic solutions. On 26 June 1978, ten months before Margaret Thatcher took power, her shadow chancellor turned up at Farson's old Isle of Dogs pub. The shy, sober-spirited Geoffrey Howe had not come to the Waterman's Arms for a pint and a singsong; but to address a meeting of the Bow Group, a network of Tory intellectuals he had helped found in east London in the 1950s. He started his speech by describing Docklands in the bleakest terms: it was 'an urban wilderness ... In almost every [British] city ... one can see similar devastation ... Seediness is the order of the day ... Whole communities have been virtually blitzed by "planning"' – by which he meant state bodies such as the PLA – 'Whole industries have fallen off the edge ... And the businesses and industries of the future have not sprung up in their place ... This is the key to understanding the developing sickness of our society ... Lack of economic success is breeding social tensions and threatening to destroy the framework of civilized existence.'

For the usually euphemistic Howe, this was unusually melodramatic language: something was exciting him. The answer came in the next passage. In Docklands, 'The dereliction is itself an opportunity.' Since there were few existing industries and interest groups in the way, 'highly unorthodox methods' could be used to get economic growth. The models should be Hong Kong and Singapore, with their 'absence of unnecessary regulations and of heavy social obligations on commerce', and their 'tax concessions for pioneer businesses' (significantly, Howe did not mention these cities' related lack of democratic structures). Docklands should become what he called an 'enterprise zone' – not just for its own sake but as a 'test market or laboratory', where a future Tory government could 'go further and more swiftly', and achieve a 'breakthrough to a more dynamic future for our society'. Docklands, in other words, was intended to become the most Thatcherite place on earth.

In November 1980 the Thatcher government pushed through legislation creating the London Docklands Development Corporation (LDDC). It would have the power to purchase land compulsorily, and to take over land already owned by state bodies. It would become the planning authority for a huge squiggle of territory from Wapping to the Royal Docks, an area as wide as the whole of central London. And it would be answerable only to the secretary of state for the environment. Nothing quite like it had been seen before in British city government.

The east London councils and the GLC, all of which from January 1981 were Labour-controlled, and all of which faced the prospect of ceding much of their power over Docklands to this untried, barely accountable bureaucratic monster, managed to prevent the LDDC's immediate official launch. Their objections to the body were patiently listened to by a select committee of the House of Lords for three months, until May 1981. The Lords then deliberated for a month more. But away from the fuggy rooms of Westminster, out in the wide open spaces of Docklands, where rules were bent and much went unobserved, the LDDC was already at work.

Its first employee was Reg Ward. 'I do remember sitting in a meeting at the GLC when it was announced that he would be the chief executive,' said Peter Turlik. 'My assistant director shouted' – Turlik switched to a perfect imitation of a posh, tight Whitehall accent – '"Not him! God! It's going to be impossible! I mean, it's going to be impossible!" This made me prick my ears up. I thought, maybe this was the kind of person who could actually change things.'

Ward was a miner's son from the Forest of Dean, the alternately bleak and idyllic, ex-industrial, faintly anarchic far corner of

Gloucestershire. He had studied architecture at university, but then spent three decades in slightly dry government jobs, first as a tax inspector, then in local councils. He rose steadily until he became chief executive of the relatively sedate west London borough of Hammersmith, and then of comfortable Hereford and Worcester county council. Yet along the way Ward had acquired a reputation. 'He was a bit of a scoundrel,' said Turlik. 'He didn't toe the council's line. They were always having problems with him.'

By the time he was appointed to run the LDDC in 1980, Ward was fifty-three, but he still looked a little like a naughty schoolboy, tie askew, shirt crumpled, curly hair slightly too long and messy. He also had the air of a salesman, a prophet, even: a gaze that was simultaneously compelling and detached, the gift of the gab, and the ability to make whatever he was working on seem the most important thing in the world. That summer and autumn, before the legislation for the LDDC had even been passed, he spent three months nosing around Docklands on foot, looking, thinking, imagining.

Later that year Turlik went to see him. 'Reg said, "Look, are you coming with me? We're sailing down to Docklands on Monday, and I don't know what we shall find there."' Turlik left the GLC, with its staff of 37,000, and joined the embryonic LDDC, with its staff of less than a dozen. 'Someone else asked Reg at their interview,' Turlik remembered, '"How many people will I have in my department?" And he said, "I don't even know how many departments I'll have. We'll see what happens, what we need." People said to him, "Where are you going to set up your offices?" They expected him to do it in the shelter of County Hall. He said, "No. I'm going to go out there." They said, "There's nothing out there, Reg. There's no offices." And he said, "Well, I'll find a building. We'll clean it out." That was his style. And a lot of people just couldn't go along with that style. He upset people straightaway.'

Ward did not actually sail to Docklands (he drove). But he did find the LDDC an office building. In the heart of the Isle of Dogs, on the deserted quayside next to one of the Millwall Docks, between two drab, disused sheds, there stood an incongruous gleaming glass box, like a remnant from a Docklands future that had never happened. And that was exactly what the building was. Norman Foster had designed it in the late 1960s for the Fred Olsen Line, a shipping company that was trying to find a way to cling on in London. At a time when the dockers were becoming more militant about their traditionally awful working conditions, the building had provided generous off-duty facilities for them – showers, table tennis, a TV lounge with tropical plants and even elegant Eames chairs. Briefly, the open-plan, widely praised building promised a world where dockers would become a valued and skilled workforce. But in 1976 Fred Olsen moved its operations to Southampton. The building was enjoyed by pigeons instead.

'Reg loved modern buildings,' said Turlik. 'The Fred Olsen Shipping building was in a very good state . . . except internally. When we opened the door, there was pigeon shit all over the floors. Reg said, "We'll get a bit of carpet." There was a little cubbyhole to the side of the open-plan – a janitor's cubbyhole – that he took for himself. He put a mattress in there. He was literally there day and night. It was tremendous: there was a real sense of excitement. We were all coming in on Saturday mornings, with sandwiches and thermos flasks, excited to be working, and we knew that after we went home, late at night in those first few weeks, Reg used to check out what we had been doing, and write little notes on it: "No, I think we ought to be more . . ."'

Turlik's first job at the LDDC was to acquire land for redevelopment. He did it with a bluntness and cockiness for which the corporation would quickly become infamous. Thirty years later, sitting lightly next to me on his delicate living-room sofa in Lambeth, his amiable interview tone gave way to something steelier – part legalistic precision, part wheeler-dealer machismo – as he explained how the corporation's powers worked:

> The PLA had a chunk of land. You put a circle round it. And you said, 'That land will now be transferred from your ownership into our ownership. We will agree a value with you. We know it's gonna take a long time, 'cos you're gonna argue this, that and the other. So what we'll do at the outset is pay you 10% of a notional value. The land will transfer to us straightaway. And we can argue until the cows come home about how much we owe you for the other 90%.'

But what if the PLA, which had ruled Docklands for the previous seventy-five years, didn't want to sell? Turlik grinned: 'Tough. It's a compulsory purchase.'

Once the LDDC had the land, it ejected any tenants on the deliberately vague grounds that they were 'eyesores' or 'ill-sited' or 'bad neighbours', and then brought in demolition crews. 'When we started knocking down the dock sheds,' said Turlik, 'it gave everybody else in Docklands a big shock. But it was an important statement to make . . . The reality was, the port wouldn't be coming back. All the talk of port-related activities that you heard from the GLC and the councils well into the 80s was just' – he said the word with contempt – 'a *pipedream* . . . We knocked down about a third of a million square feet.' The rarer nineteenth-century buildings, however, were retained. Britain was a society increasingly interested in its 'heritage', and the corporation could see the value in reminding people of the docks' glory days. But despite Ward's love of modern architecture, almost all of the twentieth-century dock buildings were erased. Most of them were plain, shoddy-looking, patched-up – the decline of the area expressed in corrugated iron and cheap concrete. The LDDC wanted to sweep away the memory. In one of its boldly designed early brochures, intended to attract new businesses to the Isle of Dogs, there was a full-page photograph of a great flatness of freshly churned-up, chocolate-brown soil, devoid even of fragments of warehouse rubble, with a single bright-yellow digger in the distance and a one-word caption: 'Progress'.

Some at the corporation were less confidently Year Zero about the social transformation that their land clearances were cementing. 'We knew that there'd be a whole generation of local people lost,' said Turlik. 'One could understand that there was a population – communities – who had been dependent for many, many years on port-related activities. Son followed father into the docks.' He began to look a bit troubled: 'I remember a docker saying to me, "I want a proper job" – he meant working with his hands, in the open air – "I don't want to work in an office." I felt sorry for him. But I couldn't give him any hope. I couldn't say, "We're working on that for you." I had to say, "It will be your children who benefit from what we're doing."'

Yet such encounters were rare in the LDDC's early years. 'There was very little dialogue with the local community,' Turlik admitted. 'The only formal contact was when we used to have public meetings, and they were quite . . . confrontational. But I felt myself, "There's a time when the consultation has to stop." I remember consulting on every detail on every draft plan for Docklands during the 1970s.'

Stuart Innes also worked at the LDDC from 1980, first as Ward's assistant, later in community relations. A raspy, barrel-chested south Londoner, he had been seconded from the Department of the Environment. He had been so understimulated there, he told me, that he had been making a model aeroplane in his office when his boss phoned to ask if he wanted to go to Docklands and work for 'this madman'.

Once there, Innes was less worried than Turlik about the LDDC making enemies. 'We used to listen to the locals. On occasion, we changed our minds. But to make things work, you had to be a bit dictatorial – not like a local authority. Local authorities pride themselves on being accountable to their electorate, and all that sort of stuff . . . yak, yak, yak. We made up our minds, and off we'd go.'

After a decision had been made, Innes went on, 'You would sometimes have a huge fight with the locals at a public meeting. The fur would fly. And afterwards, all the people you'd been fighting would say, "Are you coming for a drink?" I liked Ted Johns' – a semi-legendary Isle of Dogs activist and LDDC foe who died in 2004 – 'he was a straight-up local guy. But I never understood a lot of the opposition, what motivated them. It was *extraordinary* to see the way they would witter on. They were complete twerps.' Innes paused. 'Colenutt in particular.'

On Innes's recommendation, I met 'Colenutt' a few days later. Bob Colenutt was a neat skinny man with oval glasses and cropped white hair – in the austere proletarian style of early 1980s left-wing activists – and a small but penetrating voice. In 1975, before he became a Docklands campaigner, he co-wrote *The Property Machine*, a fierce and far-sighted Penguin paperback which argued that 'the city is a zone of conflict between competing claims for land', and that this conflict was 'profoundly political'. It should be resolved, he concluded, by 'the development system [being] taken over by the state' and 'organized around social needs'.

Like Innes, Colenutt was a Londoner from outside Docklands. Like the LDDC, he was drawn by the area's potential for transformation, but the one he had in mind was very different. From 1979, when he began working for a left-wing Docklands pressure group, until the mid-1980s, when he was recruited to run 'a little Docklands unit' at Ken Livingstone's GLC, Colenutt campaigned stubbornly for the area both to change and stay the same. Well into the 1980s, he insisted to me, 'It was potentially a working dock. At the Royals in particular, it was still all there.' Yet he also felt that other, genuinely doomed docks should be built on, to egalitarian ends: 'This was east London's last chance for more council housing – a docklands New Town.'

Colenutt and the other anti-LDDC activists who converged on Docklands were young and energetic. 'We organized campaigns. We lobbied local authorities. We got involved in public inquiries, presenting evidence, acting as lawyers at these inquiries on behalf of community groups. We wrote reports. We had a newsletter. We went to a lot of community meetings, trades councils . . . We saw the Docklands battle as increasingly' – Colenutt suddenly hit the café table between us with the side of a bony hand – 'a battle about national ideology.'

As an overwhelmingly working-class area with lots of elderly residents, Docklands seemed fertile territory for a left-wing campaign tinged with conservatism. 'The older residents did feel a sense of loss, of anger, from the closure of the docks,' said Colenutt. 'There was an increasing air of disapproval of the way the LDDC were doing things, the lack of involvement of the community.'

But the problem was, he went on, 'I don't think there was a huge existing groundswell of people locally saying, "No LDDC".' After the frightening, depressing entropy of the 1960s and 1970s, across so much of Docklands, many locals were prepared to wait and see what the corporation came up with. Meanwhile to others, Colenutt and his comrades were not so different from the LDDC anyway. 'There was quite a strong sense of insiders and outsiders. They were quite parochial. So although quite a lot of people did get involved with our campaign, it was not a huge number. I never felt they were as close to us as I would have wanted.'

The development corporation, by contrast, seemed sometimes not even to register that the Docklands residents existed. In its brochures, the plentiful, sweeping photos of the area were usually unpeopled. In LDDC employees' memoirs, and in my interviews with LDDC veterans, the isolation of their work was a constant theme. 'You were on your own,' said Innes. 'You could walk for hundreds and hundreds and hundreds of yards and not see anybody.' Yet when I went to look at the site of the LDDC headquarters – true to the unsentimental spirit of Docklands, Foster's visionary building had long been demolished – there was a large council estate right behind it. As Turlik put it, 'We insulated ourselves.'

For all the corporation's powers and self-belief, it also relied on bluff. Its unexpectedly cute, memorable logo was a silhouette of Tower Bridge with waves beneath. Yet the bridge was at the far western extremity of its territory; neither the area around the bridge, already regenerated by other bodies and quite prosperous, nor the homely, faux-medieval architecture of the bridge itself were remotely representative of the rest of Docklands. The abandoned waterscape of the latter did not even always have waves: on windless days, the lack of ships left the Thames slack.

But during 1981 and 1982 the LDDC needed to talk up every asset it had. Because, in terms of new buildings and businesses, said Turlik, 'We had almost nothing to show. We were cutting down the old buildings. We were landscaping like mad. Putting in trees. Putting up big "For Sale" signs. And building roads in red brick.' The red roads were a cheap attempt to cheer up and rebrand the area, and establish an LDDC trademark. Yet there was a terrible recession going on. Worse still, most London developers and entrepreneurs had an instinctive resistance to investing in Docklands. An anonymous businessman told the historian of the area Janet Foster:

> You don't spend money on the east side of London ... in Tower Hamlets ... in Newham ... Poplar, Stepney and Bow. The names, you've got to admit they all sound wrong ... they're all shady Dickens areas or immigrant areas ... from the Jews to the Asiatics.

Sometimes the LDDC simply exaggerated how well it was doing. 'I was quite shocked by the extent to which it happened,' said Turlik.

The corporation's vice-chairman, Bob Mellish, was one of the worst offenders. A Labour MP on the right of the party, with a Docklands constituency, he gave the LDDC rare and valuable cross-party credibility. 'I remember Bob Mellish asking me for some figures – job creation figures from the last five months,' said Turlik, 'because he'd been asked a question in the House. And I totted them all up, and it was 230. "Two hundred and thirty?" he said. "Surely we've done more than that? I'm going to tell the House we've created nearly 500 jobs."'

The LDDC's main Westminster overseer was the environment secretary, Michael Heseltine. The corporation had been partly his idea. His main point of contact at the LDDC was the chairman, Nigel Broackes, a well-connected property and construction tycoon who used to tour the corporation's bumpy empire in a Rolls-Royce. During 1981, Heseltine told me, 'I used to call Nigel Broackes and say, "Nigel, what the hell's happening? I've created this edifice. You're the great genius of the private sector. What the hell are you doing down there?"'

The government desperately needed visible successes before the next general election. And Heseltine himself needed successes: in a particularly competitive cabinet, he was one of the most ambitious ministers. That competitiveness became built into the government's plan for Docklands. Inside the corporation's territory, on the Isle of Dogs and on a snake of land to the east, an enterprise zone was established in April 1982, of the kind that Howe had advocated at the Waterman's Arms four years earlier. While the corporation broadly followed Heseltine's economic ideas, which were that the state should intervene in economically barren places and make them fertile for capitalists – by buying up vacant land and building roads, for example – the enterprise zone followed a less pragmatic, more libertarian philosophy. In the enterprise zone, companies building new premises did not have to seek planning permission. They could offset the cost of construction against tax. They paid no rates for the first ten years. And they were exempted from some building and health-and-safety regulations. The intention, Howe said in 1988, was to create 'a kind of government-free zone'.

Howe and Heseltine both regularly visited Docklands, to check on progress and to make subtly rivalrous speeches. When I asked Heseltine how the corporation and enterprise zone compared, his usual ageing-lion charm momentarily evaporated: 'They were totally different. Geoffrey wanted one. I wanted the other. So the obvious thing to do was to have both.'

In practice, the two understaffed projects shared personnel, promoted each other in their brochures, and had the same brash day-to-day approach. Both schemes were also underestimated for a long time by their opponents. People at the Port of London Authority who had watched Whitehall schemes for Docklands come and go during the 1970s looked at the LDDC and, as Turlik put it, said, 'Oh, here they go again, another government initiative' – much as many people who had lived through Britain's short-lived 1970s governments wrote off the Thatcher government itself. Meanwhile the seemingly doomed quality of the latter throughout 1981 and into 1982 meant, continued Turlik, that 'people were constantly saying to us, quite openly, in pubs, in the community, at public meetings, "Make the most of it. Because we're going to have you out after the general election."'

The corporation frenetically carried on. Its staff grew to several dozen. Reg Ward stopped sleeping in the office and moved into Bridge House, an imperious Georgian dockmaster's residence on the Isle of Dogs. It had been built in the port's heyday and had epic views in all directions, which reinforced his sense that the endless water could be an asset and not a problem. His wife joined him from their home in Cheltenham – although not for long. She found the island at night too frightening. 'The divorce rate among corporation staff was high,' Innes recalled. 'I was a victim of it myself.'

At the Fred Olsen building, Ward roamed the open-plan, buttonholing his subordinates with 'ten ideas an hour', one ex-staffer told Janet Foster. 'Some would be brilliant and some would be loony.' Innes remembered: 'Monday morning, you'd come into the office, he'd say, "I've been for a walk. I've been looking at the tracks of the old docks railway. I've got this idea to build a new railway."' In 1987 the Docklands Light Railway opened, and the area began for the first time to acquire proper public transport. On another occasion, Ward remembered Innes's interest in model aeroplanes. 'He said, "You know about things with wings." The two of us went to Plymouth and some other provincial airports. Took a week. When Reg got back to Docklands, he said, "It'll work." And that's why you've got London City Airport.' The runway made ingenious use of a dead strip of land between two of the Royal Docks, which was so gigantic and cut-off it would have taken decades, if not centuries, to fill with new buildings. Less successful was a LDDC plan in 1982 to use the land to tether airships.

In an era of supposed government austerity the corporation was funded almost as unquestioningly as the Falklands task force. Between 1981 and 1988 it received £443 million from Whitehall. From 1983, unlike local councils, it was allowed to keep all the money it made from selling land to developers. Despite the proud pro-business, anti-state rhetoric that Conservative politicians and newspapers were increasingly using to describe the revolution under way in Docklands, 'The state spent far more through the LDDC than it had in Docklands previously,' said Turlik.

Ward and Innes went on a research trip to America. Since the 1950s US cities such as Baltimore and Boston had been successfully regenerating derelict waterfronts into sanitized shopping, office and tourism districts. 'We were in Boston one morning,' Innes remembered, 'and we were meant to fly down to some seminar organized by the British Embassy in Washington. But beforehand Reg suddenly carted me off all the way to bloody Detroit, to look at this building covered in black reflective glass, which overlooked the Canadian border. Reg had a thing about black reflective glass. We went into the building – didn't ask anybody: typical Reg – and just wandered about in there. And then we flew to Washington – all in a day.'

Back in London, the corporation's Docklands pamphlets were almost manic with suggestions. A 1981 prospectus, written in short, hyperactive sentences, claimed that the Isle of Dogs was suitable for 'marinas' and 'pharmaceutical industries', 'import-export' and 'manufacturing', 'printing, broadcasting' and 'high technology industries', 'computer hardware and clerical facilities' and – most presciently – 'financial institutions' and 'merchant banks'. The Isle of Dogs was 'next door to the City', the pamphlet stated, a little creatively. Then presciently again: 'London must grow eastwards.'

The broad-brush nature of all this was intentional. Ward and his subordinates saw their task as presentational as much as physical. Even five years into the LDDC's existence, on 18 November 1986, Ward could baldly tell *The Times*, 'We have no land use plan or grand design; our plans are essentially marketing images.' According to Turlik, Ward was completely at home with this anarchic approach: 'People in the office would say to him, "Where's the plan for Docklands, Reg?" And he would say, "There is no plan. We'll see how it goes. If someone comes along and wants to build a hotel, we'll say OK, and we'll work around that." So it was really medieval, organic planning.'

Appropriately, the corporation's first success was not one of the mirror-glass monoliths of Ward's dreams. It was modest, built of brick, backward-looking in design, and on a site miles from his beloved Isle of Dogs, in the less historically charged suburb of Beckton. Here, inland from the Royal Docks, there was a large rectangle of marshy ground that a housing association had been planning to build on, until the recession and government cuts intervened. A less publicized part of the LDDC's remit was to prompt the construction of cheap homes for sale, which were scarce in east London, thanks to the prejudices of developers and the local dominance of council housing. The policy was also part of the government's broader campaign for mass property ownership. In 1981 the corporation acquired the Beckton site. 'We said to ourselves,' Turlik recalled, '"Why don't we, as a pilot, divide the land into portions and try to attract housebuilders?"' Through a combination of Ward's salesmanship and lavish discounting – according to the Docklands historian Sue Brownhill, the 22 acres were offered 'at around half the market price' – four housebuilding conglomerates, Wimpey, Barratt, Broseley and Comben, were persuaded to construct just over 600 homes. The development was named Savage Gardens, after J. P. Savage, a councillor and pioneering housing activist in Victorian Beckton.

Construction began in November 1981. The mud was awful – the marshland rebelling against the experiment – but residents from the neighbouring council estates were so fascinated they came to watch, right through the winter. By the spring of 1982 almost half the homes had been sold, before they had even been completed. Many were bought by local council tenants – taking the government's new Right to Buy one stage further by moving out of municipal housing altogether.

The properties started at £18,000, almost twice the price then being paid for the average council home but about a third cheaper than the average private sale. And the Savage Gardens properties were almost all houses with gardens, detached or in tiny clusters, cleverly arranged in a maze of greenery and cul-de-sacs and little squares that shielded the development from the winter easterly that cut across the exposed flatlands of Docklands more sharply than other parts of London. Some of the houses had built-in garages and many had short driveways – they acknowledged the rapidly rising importance of the car and of private space in British life since the 1960s. But the southern edge of Savage Gardens also faced a small park with playing fields, and the architecture was appealingly cottagey, with steeply pitched roofs and gabled windows, secluded back gardens and solid porches. The whole estate was so presentable, it was easy not to notice that some of the houses were only one small room across.

On 26 February 1982, Heseltine and Broackes officially opened the development. It was raining, and a hundred demonstrators arrived too, including the local Labour MP and a local anti-LDDC group. They shouted through Heseltine's speech, claiming that through the development the government and LDDC were 'stealing' land that was needed for council housing. But in 1982 the idea that London, or Britain, should be careful that it did not run out of affordable homes to rent was confined to a few housing activists and left-wingers such as Bob Colenutt. Heseltine seemed unfazed. After his speech he strode among the little houses of Savage Gardens in a dark suit, taller than the trailing crowd, without an umbrella, his famous prow of hair swept back, his smile controlled but constant, like a satisfied admiral inspecting a line of frigates.

The estate was a breakthrough, but Docklands also needed new employers. The first significant one did not arrive until early 1983, only months before the general election.

Limehouse Studios was the creation of Limehouse Productions, a company set up two years before by refugees from Southern Television, a British broadcasting institution that had imploded after unexpectedly losing its ITV franchise. Unable to afford studio space in west London, the traditional hub of British television, the refugees looked east, and discovered the accountants' paradise of the Docklands enterprise zone.

On the Isle of Dogs, on a quay between two of the West India Docks, there was a former rum and banana warehouse. It was exactly the sort of dour, architecturally undistinguished structure that the LDDC had been demolishing all over Docklands. Except that it was immensely strong: 'It was built to last a thousand years,' remembered David O'Keefe, who became manager of Limehouse Studios. 'It had two-foot-thick concrete floors, concrete columns holding up the ceilings, thick walls, and tiny windows' – to discourage rum and banana burglars. 'The structural surveyor told us, "You can do what the fuck you like in there!"'

'The LDDC wanted £1m for a 200-year lease,' O'Keefe continued. 'We suspected they had no other prospects. We got it for £465,000.' Turlik admitted, 'We got quite excited. Because (a) Limehouse was a large enterprise and (b) it was based at the time, as I recall, in Charlotte Street. For us to actually capture an enterprise from the West End, to get them to go down to Docklands, we thought that would reflect a great deal of confidence in the area. And it was also the kind of activity that we wanted, a TV studio, to change the image of Docklands.'

Limehouse commissioned the British architect Terry Farrell, then early in his career as a flashy transformer of unloved urban corners. For a modest fee, Farrell turned the timeworn, matt, grey-brown facade of the warehouse into a zigzagging cliff of different blues, in stripes and wedges as smooth and impermanent-looking as giant Lego blocks. 'The front, it was a statement, because our basic clientele expected to see something a bit glitzy,' said O'Keefe, a dapper, tanned man with a residual television smoothness about him, as we had lunch in a burbling west London restaurant from which the Isle of Dogs, even in 2012, seemed very distant.

There was another challenge to attracting customers to such an unfamiliar facility: 'We had to *get* people there: audiences for game-shows, guests for comedy and music shows.' Taxis, he soon discovered, would not drive to the Isle of Dogs from the City of London, let alone the West End, and the Docklands Light Railway was half a decade off. O'Keefe resorted to having cards printed with directions to the studios and giving them out at taxi ranks. The very name Limehouse Studios played down the trek required: Limehouse, the area, was actually a mile nearer to central London.

Yet by July 1983 there were enough intrigued clients for production to start. One draw was the studios' huge warehouse spaces, strikingly punctuated by concrete pillars, which made possible a new, more loosely structured kind of television. Limehouse-made youth shows such as *Network 7* featured roving cameras, a live audience divided and distributed around the studio in loose, giggly groups, and a sense that almost anything could happen. On one edition, gay audience members came out to startled, spot-lit friends. It was the shape of things to come for much of British television: an inventive raucousness that would be exported around the world; and a sign that the new Docklands, like the new British economy the Thatcher government was helping into being, would be trading in less tangible commodities than the old docks.

Another early user of the studios was Spitting Image Productions. The company had recently been set up to turn the cult broadsheet caricatures of Peter Fluck and Roger Law into a television satire. It created a puppet factory on a remote upper floor. 'We improvised the lease on a scrap of paper,' O'Keefe remembered, 'at Le Gavroche at two o'clock in the morning.' For much of 1983, while the more respectable *Spitting Image* personnel tried to persuade broadcasters that their proposed show was a satire for adults and not, as was widely believed, a bad idea for a children's programme, the puppeteers worked 'with these fantastically dangerous chemicals, trying to work out the right kind of latex,' the producer John Lloyd recalled. The enterprise zone's loosening of health and safety controls proved very helpful. 'There were some really quite serious lefties in the puppet workshop who thought they were supping with the devil by even going into a television studio.' But Law, at least, felt a kind of kinship with the presiding spirit of Docklands: 'I understood Thatcher ... [She was] so black and white, and so were we.'

The sheer isolation of Limehouse Studios, its crinkly cartoon facade flashing in the uninterrupted evening sun on a fenced-off section of an otherwise empty quay; and the sheer performance of getting out there – both of these led to frolics and camaraderie. 'We bought a boat called the *Sloop John B*,' said O'Keefe. 'It used to be a brothel, moored on the Thames at Battersea. It still had a punishment room, with those exact words on the door. We did all our catering and hospitality on board.' He winked. 'Being on a boat is always fun. I won't tell you how much cocaine was snorted in the bowels of that boat.' A pause. 'Not by Limehouse staff, of course.'

In 1985, and again in 1987, Margaret Thatcher inspected the studios. O'Keefe remembered the prime minister's first visit. 'She arrived late. We had a pop group in one of the studios, who regarded themselves as left-wing. "We'll give her hell," they said beforehand. She walked into the studio, and within two minutes they were eating out of her hand, calling her "Ma'am". Some of the Limehouse management were fans of hers.' Was he? 'I, by every instinct, didn't like Thatcherism. I thought, look at all the damage it's done.' So how had he reconciled that with working in the enterprise zone? 'It's pragmatism. And earning a living. I'd gone independent.' For the only time in our convivial lunch, he changed the subject.

During Thatcher's second visit to Limehouse Studios, on 29 January 1987, she gave a brief, revealingly stream-of-consciousness speech:

> I came here about 18 months ago when I was going round Dockland [*sic*]; I was absolutely thrilled and fascinated with [the area], we came to this warehouse – it had been restructured, the front, I thought they had done fantastic things, I went round the studio, they were full of vitality and enthusiasm because many of them were having opportunities to do things they had never had before – and it reminded me very forcefully of everything which we have tried to do, of my fundamental belief that if governments create the background and we free things up as much as possible – then the great talents of the British public and the British people will take over.

Yet as she spoke, the studios' end was already approaching. For the previous three years, since 1984, a plan had been forming in transatlantic banking and property circles for the City of London to establish an Isle of Dogs outpost. 'In 1985 we started hearing the first mutterings from the City about their lack of office space,' said O'Keefe. 'We did lots of American shows at Limehouse, and one of the people involved told us that an American plan involving building an office tower on the island was being talked about.' In October 1985 the LDDC accepted the Canary Wharf scheme in principle. It would be the largest office development in Europe, but three-quarters of it was inside the enterprise zone and therefore needed no planning permission.

As the scheme changed shape haphazardly over the next two years, with participating banks and developers coming and going, and Reg Ward and the LDDC liaising, trying to coax ashore a far bigger Docklands prize than they had ever imagined catching, it became clear that Limehouse Studios was inconveniently close to the base of the proposed Canary Wharf tower, like a garden shed getting under the feet of Godzilla. 'We went to the LDDC seeking assurances that they would never compulsorily purchase our site,' O'Keefe told me. 'We got assurances, but not in writing.'

In early 1988 the corporation issued a compulsory purchase order. 'I felt sorry for the individuals concerned,' Turlik told me, with uncharacteristic, bureaucratic stiffness. 'But it wasn't as if they were being swept away without recompense' – the studio site was bought for £25 million, almost fifty times what Limehouse Productions had paid for it. Turlik relaxed into frankness again: 'And I had hardened by then, unfortunately. Big fat towers employ a lot more people, and people who build a big fat tower give you a lot more money for the same piece of land than the guy who'll build a two-storey shed. And we needed that money. Because by the mid-80s the government was setting up other development corporations, and there was a lot less money around.'

In May 1988 Thatcher ceremonially sank the first pile of the tower's foundations. A year later, after a protracted paper struggle with the LDDC, Limehouse Studios closed and were demolished, and any remaining traces disappeared beneath the bland bankers' citadel of the Canary Wharf complex. Its developers were the Canadian conglomerate Olympia and York. In Docklands, it was becoming clear, 'the great talents of the British people', which Thatcher had so breathlessly invoked during her visit to Limehouse Studios the year before, were no longer the driving economic force. The prime minister was a patriot, but she was a capitalist first.

14
A Journey

In November 1986, a few months before Margaret Thatcher won her third general election in a row, a slim book appeared about the right-wing ideas that were remaking Britain, the United States, and increasingly the rest of the rich world. *The New Enlightenment* opened with a page of acknowledgements that were as unsubtle as its title. The authors David Graham and Peter Clarke, both British, thanked a global network of the radical right's increasingly famous think tanks and intellectuals: 'the Institute of Economic Affairs in London . . . the old battler, Frederick Hayek . . . Lord Harris of High Cross and Arthur Seldon [who] read parts of the manuscript . . . the Reason Foundation of Santa Monica [which] helped to raise funds'.

In the world-travelling chapters that followed, Graham and Clarke first quickly dismissed socialism – 'dead' – social democracy – 'stasis' – and the welfare state – 'leaves the poor stranded'. Then they lingered reverently, almost mystically, over the virtues of entrepreneurial capitalism: 'Entrepreneurs are the givers of the modern world . . . He or she responds to the needs of others . . . They create things that afford pleasure. They take leaps in the dark. The entrepreneur is motivated, like an artist, by the desire to create.'

Finally, the book claimed, either intoxicatingly or naively, depending on your view of politics or the power of governments, that there was a 'double magic' to the economic and social loosening that Thatcher and Reagan and their imitators were overseeing, to what the authors called 'the greatest political shift' of the twentieth century. 'Not only does it free us to live as we choose within the real limits that bound our lives,' Graham and Clarke wrote. 'It also releases the human energy and knowledge that pushes back those limits, better than any other idea we know. Who can say no to it?'

Such right-wing triumphalism was not exactly rare in Britain in 1986, with the recession now five years in the past, the Falklands victory still reverberating, the Labour Party shedding left-wing ideas but still groping for a new identity, and the Conservatives' House of Commons majority a seemingly unassailable three figures. But the book's provenance was unusual for a Thatcherite polemic. 'This book is based on the television series, *The New Enlightenment*,' said the copyright page in small print, 'produced for Channel Four Television by Diverse Production Limited.'

Channel 4 had been broadcasting for exactly four years. During that time it had acquired an enduring reputation as the most left-liberal, worthily herbivorous, smugly 'alternative', tabloid-maddening media organization in Britain. Jeremy Isaacs, the channel's founding chief executive and a lifelong Labour supporter, told me:

> In 1989 I went to a party given by a [Conservative] cabinet minister, Kenneth Baker. And he insisted on dragging me up to Maggie, who was the prize catch of the evening. And she looked at me, and said to the circle around her: 'Look at this man. Nine and a half years of doing absolutely everything right' – by which I understood that she meant she had done absolutely everything right – 'and he doesn't believe a word of it!'

Yet in fact, during the 1980s, Channel 4 and the new broadcasting ecology that formed it and grew up around it was one of the places where Thatcher's revolution most thoroughly changed how people thought and acted. The fact that many of these people were leftists, and continued to see themselves as such, even as they altered their ways of working, their attitudes to earning, their behaviour towards competitors and trade unions; the fact that this mass conversion to Thatcherism was not always noticed or acknowledged by many of those involved – this made it all the more pivotal to how Britain changed in the 1980s, and to how Britain is still behaving now.

I met David Graham in Taunton in 2012. He was wearing a tweed jacket, as you might expect of a man of sixty-nine in a town in rural Somerset, but he had a sharp striped jumper underneath, no tie, a little dagger of a beard, and a transatlantic lift to the end of his sentences. He drove me in an old Mercedes to a car park behind the main shopping street. Then he led me up a rusty fire escape, across the flat roof of Krazy Kurlz hair and beauty salon, and through the back entrance of his current TV business, Attentional Ltd. We walked through half a dozen cluttered rooms, from which Attentional conducts research on 'the science of entertainment' for clients including NBC and the BBC, and deals with another Attentional office in Los Angeles. We then settled in a long tunnel of a meeting room overlooking the salon roof.

Like many innovators in the early 1980s, Graham was a bit of an outsider to England. His father was South African. 'As a child I lived mainly outside the UK,' Graham said, skating over the details. 'I got the tail-end of empire. Then I was away in the US and Canada for six years. I got an English Speaking Union fellowship to Indiana University in 1965, then I went to Canada to avoid the draft. In 1971, I come back to Britain and find the place is a mess. And then I get a job at the BBC, which is a good way of entering into the detail of that mess.'

From 1973, the year of the oil crisis, until April 1981, Graham worked on *Nationwide*, *The Money Programme* and *Panorama*, three of BBC television's main vehicles for exploring the turbulent country Britain had become. 'I loved working for the BBC. I did really good programmes – probably the best ones I ever made. The resources that were available to you . . . the access you got to people. However, it wasn't an environment I was completely happy with. Yours was a sort of corporate creative role. And a lot of the journalism was quite lazy. The ritual balance of interviews: you, the journalist, heard both sides of an argument from the protagonists. You synthesized a result. But you did not inject much original work.'

Graham began to talk as if addressing a particularly earnest production meeting, back in the 1970s or early 1980s. 'If you became interested, as I quickly did, in the economic crisis of the nation, and if you get hold of some good numbers, and know how to work them, you don't have to have this ritualized debate. It's not good enough for a country that's in the kind of trouble we're in. We've got to do a better job of saying what's going on.' He tried early fly-on-the-wall techniques: 'I lived with a community on a scheme in Scotland for eight weeks, for a *Panorama* on "the real unemployed". We had some really good analysis of the unemployment data, but we also got to the bottom of the key issues: the problem of immobility, that industry was collapsing around you but you couldn't leave your council house, there was nowhere else for you to go; and the guys who were doing illegal paid work and getting the dole as well.' He suddenly giggled: 'I rather sympathized with them.' For another, even more ambitious *Panorama*, Graham helped organize 'a sort of encounter group' to explore how British industrial relations could be improved, with usually antagonistic trade unionists and managers 'addressing each other' for five days. This was supposedly neutral current-affairs television shading over into polemic, even activism. But he felt the BBC rules were worth bending: 'These were critical issues, and I found my niche there, because most of *Panorama* would still rather be in the Georgetown Inn in Washington.' To many BBC reporters, American politics was more interesting than Britain's problems.

Throughout his BBC years, Graham thought of himself as left-leaning, but he was beginning to have doubts. His Scottish *Panorama* 'was condemned on the left,' he wrote in *The New Enlightenment*, for attacking the benefits system. That criticism, and what he had seen on the housing scheme, 'sent me off to look for other ideas' besides socialist and social democratic ones. 'I was the only person on *Panorama* who knew about the emerging radical right. I knew about the Institute of Economic Affairs, knew my Hayek, so I was asked to start covering that. David Dimbleby and I went off and interviewed Milton Friedman. We looked at the right's arguments, and tried to figure them through. I felt the energy and promise.'

He also began to fall for computer technology. 'In the middle of the 70s, Apple came along, and I was enthralled . . . I got an Apple in about 1977 and I played with it. That year, I took a leave of absence from the BBC, after a really bad spell at *The Money Programme* when I didn't get on with the editor.' Graham was thirty-four and childless; he converted part of his bedroom into a studio, and for a year roamed around the bright infinities of the newly unfolding digital landscape: computer graphics, computerized statistics, colour synthesizers. 'It was a huge liberation: scaling down the costs of making television. It was halfway to being a personal creator.' Much earlier than most, he was seeing the faint outline of the multimedia blogger, the YouTube poster. 'I went off to America to look at the latest gear. After a year I ran out of money. But I learned quite a bit about audio-visual experimentation, and I made friends with other people who were doing it, with a lot of video artists who were around at the time. One of them was Peter Donebauer.'

I met Donebauer a fortnight later. He lived by the Thames in west London, in a 1980s-style apartment complex designed to resemble a row of waterfront warehouses. Other, similar complexes lined both riverbanks as far as you could see. Small private helicopters thundered self-importantly overhead, to and from a nearby heliport. The aesthetics and elitism of Docklands had spread miles upriver.

Donebauer wore black linen trousers and a satiny, open-necked shirt. Although it was only May, he already had a settled tan. His hair was longish and elaborately flicked back, and he was barefoot as he padded across his double-height living room – dense abstract paintings, squashy cream furniture – to show me onto his riverside balcony. Like Graham, he was still working in his sixties, but perhaps a little less concentratedly: 'I prefer to be called a media entrepreneur than tied down to TV. And I am trying to reconnect as an artist.'

He had studied film and television at the Royal College of Art in the early 1970s. His father, a Czech immigrant, was an estate agent and accountant, and Donebauer junior had inherited his purposefulness: 'The Royal College had a redundant colour TV studio, no one was using it, and it became a kind of painting studio for me. I experimented with film and video and music.' For his degree show in 1974 he made an abstract piece called *Entering*, a pulsing, blooping, roaring splurge of colour and sound that was groundbreaking in the way it made the two interact, and it was shown, rather astonishingly, on BBC2. Yet Donebauer found his first experience of mainstream broadcasting exasperating: 'The BBC studios . . . I couldn't do it there! Such segregation between the producer and the engineer and the visual controller!' In the end, *Entering* had to be treated as an outside broadcast.

After college, 'I was not taken seriously by the art world. Galleries weren't interested. I was excluded by the people who'd managed to colonize video. They were into a very dry form of video art.' Donebauer rolled his eyes: 'conceptualism, very long takes, very boring'. He spent a year on the dole. He taught freelance at art colleges. More promisingly, he designed a synthesizer, the Videokalos, that produced both colour and sound. He established a company to sell it: 'I kept the books myself, double-entry and all the rest of it.' But building the synthesizers himself was arduous and sales were tiny. By the end of the 1970s, 'I was really stuck.'

Since 1969 he had been living in the same partially squatted building in south London: '251 Brixton Road', he remembered proudly. Then Donebauer conceded, 'I wasn't in the squat. I had built a separate studio there.' He occasionally wrote about the Videokalos and his other experiments for grainy, small-circulation British technology magazines, and David Graham read one of his articles during his year away from the BBC. 'He [Graham] came to me in Brixton. There was immediate attraction.' Donebauer laughed: 'David's an *interesting* character . . . He'd stepped out of the system slightly, he had a radical edge. But he pulled up outside the squat in a new Saab. "He's doing alright," I thought. And he thought, "God, this guy's living well, in a squat, with all these women." He liked my freedom. And we were both interested in innovation. We were both sort of left-wing.' Donebauer paused. 'But really it was an attraction of opposites.'

When Graham went back to the BBC, 'He got me in there, with my synthesizer, and we graphic-linked a *Panorama* programme. They generated graphics, I coloured them. They paid me £1,000 – big money. I had got fifty quid for them showing *Entering*.' The two men stayed in touch. By 1981 Graham had finally had enough of the BBC. Early that year he resigned from *Panorama*, and he and Donebauer set up Diverse Production to make their own television programmes.

'At the BBC, it was made clear to me,' said Graham, 'that this was tantamount to professional suicide. But I'd got the entrepreneurial frame. I'd been reading about firms. I'd observed them for *The Money Programme*: working and not working. I'd thought about them. Peter was the most entrepreneurial of the video artists.' Graham slipped into a sort of Silicon Valley jargon: 'I totally felt, "We're setting up a company that's not going to be the old-model corporation. It's gonna be well managed. It's gonna be dynamic. It's gonna use technology.

It's gonna create new ways of doing things. It's gonna retrain people in the most efficient modes – it's gonna save money. At the same time, it's gonna generate profits."'

The creation of Channel 4 made some, if not all, of these dreams achievable. The channel was formally established by the Thatcher government in November 1980. That year's Broadcasting Act introduced it with Whitehall dryness as 'the Fourth Channel', but there the legislation's caution ended. The new channel was 'to encourage innovation and experiment in the form and content of programmes'; and to broadcast 'a suitable proportion of matter calculated to appeal to tastes and interests not generally catered for'. Just as radically, 'a substantial proportion' of Channel 4's output was to be 'supplied' by small independent production firms, such as Diverse Production, rather than, as with previous channels, by the broadcaster itself. 'It was probably the only television channel in the world' with such an adventurous brief, wrote the cultural historian Sylvia Harvey in 1994.

The origins of Channel 4, like those of other early 1980s experiments such as the Livingstone GLC, were not in the 1980s, or even the 1970s, but back in the 1960s. In 1962 a government inquiry into the state of British broadcasting, the Pilkington Committee, attacked ITV, established seven years earlier as the country's first commercial channel, for being too populist and predictable in its programmes. The committee suggested that another, bolder commercial broadcaster should be set up 'in due course'. From the mid-1960s television sets with an extra button for this fourth channel (which would also compete with BBC1, established in 1936, and BBC2, established in 1964) began to be manufactured and sold.

A few years later the rebelliousness of the 1960s belatedly reached the television industry, and programme-makers frustrated by the institutional caution of the BBC and ITV started to form pressure groups such as the Free Communications Group to campaign for a looser, more permissive broadcast media. From the late 1960s to the late 1970s these dissidents and would-be experimenters, Jeremy Isaacs and Graham among them, in between making noted careers as broadcasters and making programmes that pushed broadcasting's existing boundaries, wrote articles for newspapers and letters to ministers, paid for and placed advertisements, made speeches and submissions to further broadcasting inquiries, sat on further broadcasting committees, and spoke to prime ministers. All the while they refined in their minds what would become Channel 4. Like the Right to Buy, it was an idea that intrigued Labour governments during the 1970s. The 1977 Annan Report, commissioned by the Wilson government three years earlier, 'bought my whole bill of goods,' claimed Anthony Smith, conceptualizer-in-chief of the articulate Channel 4 lobby. But it was an idea that was acted on by the Thatcher government.

The Conservatives had always been keen on commercial television: as an example of free enterprise, and as a way of diminishing the BBC. A Tory government had legislated ITV into being. By the early 1980s, particularly after the Falklands War, when the BBC had occasionally interrupted its loyal coverage to broadcast politically inconvenient facts about British military setbacks, a conviction was taking hold in the party from Thatcher downwards that the BBC was a den of lefties. Isaacs and many of the Channel 4 lobby *were* lefties, at least at this stage; but they were also worldly and adaptable TV people who were used to getting on with, and getting their way with, people of differing political creeds.

Isaacs had grown up in Bearsden, a famously bourgeois commuter town outside Glasgow. His father 'kept a small jeweller's shop', read the *Guardian*, and sent his son to Glasgow Academy, a private school where he was 'the only boy in my class to support Labour', as Isaacs junior proudly recalled in one of his two expansive memoirs. His pre-Channel 4 career was characterized by shrewd but convivial networking and brave, liberal programme-making: at the ITV company Associated Rediffusion in the early 1960s, Isaacs edited two documentaries about gay men and lesbians when homosexuality was still illegal. He liked good lunches and good wine, and spoke in a soft west of Scotland voice, with a sharp or mocking edge that you did not always notice until afterwards.

He suggested we meet at his club, the Garrick in Covent Garden. It was a white, airless June day, the after-lunch lull, and we sat in claret-coloured armchairs beside an open window through which no breeze came. Behind us, a man in a spotted bow tie read *The Times*, as if placed there by a satirist. Isaacs held a whisky, and at first sat leaning so far back in his pinstripes that his body was almost horizontal.

He started by talking about Willie Whitelaw, Thatcher's first home secretary, and the minister charged with overseeing Channel 4's development from an idea to a legislative fact to an actual broadcaster. 'Willie was a gentleman,' said Isaacs with courtly reverence. 'He had been a Conservative candidate in the constituency in which I lived. For Channel 4, he introduced a bill which the broadcasters I spoke to in Europe at the time regarded as the most extraordinary measure they'd ever seen – a rubric that was a new channel's dream.'

During 1979, both just before and just after the general election, with the Tories at their keenest to acquire allies and at their most receptive to outside ideas, Isaacs and his fellow Channel 4 campaigners won over Whitelaw and other senior Conservatives by astutely emphasizing the entrepreneurial side of their project, the way it would create a new television market. 'At a reception at Downing Street before we launched,' said Isaacs, 'after I'd queued to shake hands with Margaret Thatcher, she called out after me, "Stand up for free enterprise, Mr Isaacs!" And I went back to her, and I said, "Of course, we'll stand up for free enterprise, Prime Minister"' – the edge came into his voice – '" . . . some of the time."'

Before Channel 4 there were few British independent production companies. The BBC made almost all its programmes in-house. Most of ITV's were supplied by the large, well-established companies that held its regional broadcasting franchises, such as Granada and London Weekend Television. Start ups were further deterred by the strong broadcasting unions, who helped maintain an elaborate and relatively generous system of pay rates and job demarcations for technical staff: the reason there was no British television after midnight, wrote John Ellis in *What Did Channel 4 Do for Us?* (2008), was 'to avoid huge payments to broadcast technicians'. The unions were swift to black out programmes whenever this system was threatened. Meanwhile technology and the sluggishness of some of British commerce imposed other limitations: 'Television production was still resolutely analogue,' recalled Ellis. 'Graphics were drawn or printed pictures that were put under a caption camera . . . A one-hour (broadcast standard) videotape in its plastic case was only just light enough to carry around . . . Independent production companies setting up in London's Soho were quoted a waiting time of three months for a phone line.'

In all these ways, the British television industry, excellent though much of its output was, revealed a country still shaped by mid-twentieth-century scarcities and rigidities. But the sociable, socially perceptive Isaacs saw that the status quo was vulnerable: 'I knew that there were people inside the ITV companies who wanted to make a different range of programmes. And I knew that there were an enormous number of other people, who thought of themselves as the media generation, who wanted to work in television, but had no way of either getting jobs at ITV or the BBC or of selling programmes – the BBC and ITV already employed more documentary-makers than they had room for – and so they were making little films on a shoestring, they were teaching media instead . . .'

In September 1980 the forty-eight-year-old Isaacs was picked as Channel 4's chief executive. He narrowly beat a thirty-six-year-old prodigy from London Weekend Television, who submitted a fifty-page application including a complete, intricately segmented, slightly fogeyish schedule for the channel, with slots for anglers, motorcyclists and birdwatchers: John Birt.

Channel 4 in its first weeks was little more than some newspaper publicity and a few employees having nervously excited meetings. It had no offices of its own, and it was not scheduled to start broadcasting for another two years, in November 1982. Yet Isaacs got dozens of phone calls every day from people calling themselves 'independent producers', a term that had scarcely been used before in Britain. He was frequently accosted in the street by people with programme proposals.

To widen and bring order to the process, he called a public meeting. He chose an ambitious venue: the Royal Institution, a colonnaded set of rooms off Piccadilly where famous scientific research and public lectures had taken place since the eighteenth century. During the Industrial Revolution, Michael Faraday had discovered electromagnetic induction and Humphry Davy had invented the miner's safety lamp here; now, in an increasingly post-industrial Britain, Isaacs booked the steeply raked, semicircular lecture theatre to talk about a TV channel. It was either progress, or something less edifying.

The meeting took place on 16 January 1981. So many would-be Channel 4 programme-makers turned up – between 450 and 600 – that an overspill room with a sound feed had to be hastily arranged. In the lecture theatre, before Isaacs spoke, 'It was like a great babble,' remembered Phil Redmond, then a scruffy young Liverpudlian TV writer with an idea for a 'snapshot of Britain' soap opera called *Meadowcroft*, which he soon renamed *Brookside*. 'It was like the Roman senate, and Jeremy was the emperor, and he walked across the senate floor.'

Isaacs spoke for fifty minutes. His tone was stern – at least to those expecting Channel 4 to be a free-for-all, a sort of televised 1960s happening. He said Channel 4 wanted 'programmes that show this country for what it is', that treated it as 'a multi-racial society – not very evident in this room', and that 'explain what is going on in the world'. With a hard-nosed patriotism that Thatcher would have been proud of, he also said the channel wanted 'programmes that show how this country can earn its living in the world. And programmes that help it to do so.'

Isaacs explained to me, 'I wanted to make this clear: this was not going to be a channel for anarchists. Some independent producers wanted to do absolutely everything anew. Others . . . didn't want to do anything original, they just wanted to do the programmes they were good at. I shook them rigid by saying, "I'm not going to have any furry beastie programmes, because we've got a lot of that in British television already. And don't take off the shelf something that's been stuck there for years. Give me something original and splendid."' Stretched out in his Garrick armchair, he switched in an instant from clubbable to cutting: 'Very few of them did.'

For its headquarters, Channel 4 rejected British television's traditional, slightly stuffy west London heartland and went further east, to Fitzrovia. On the northern fringe of central London, the area was a lattice of relatively cheap Georgian streets that for two centuries, wrote Nick Bailey in his 1981 book *Fitzrovia*, had housed 'a vast array of service industries and insecure tenancies . . . a complex warren of workrooms for craftsmen and artists' studios'. Fitzrovia was also full of pubs with bohemian pasts, and boisterous, cosmopolitan restaurants that were perfect for the lunching and drinking required by the rising, unbuttoned professions of an increasingly media-driven country. 'Charlotte Street,' noted Isaacs approvingly in his memoirs, was 'where I first saw Londoners eating out-of-doors.' During the 1970s advertising agencies began moving in, including Thatcher's attention-grabbing propagandists Saatchi & Saatchi. Film-screening and editing facilities set up shop. All were useful neighbours for a new commercial broadcaster.

Operating on a tight budget that was another harbinger of British television's future, Channel 4 took space in an awkwardly shaped, hard-to-let modern building midway up Charlotte Street. Its two stumpy towers stuck on top of a three-storey slab were part disused cinema, part offices and part flats. Channel 4 moved in in late 1981, over Christmas. Its first board meeting there took place in a half-built, unheated conference room the following month. The channel's launch night was now only ten months away. The participants sat with their coats on.

The new broadcaster's staff were a contradictory lot. In its recruiting, Channel 4 was self-consciously eclectic, even reckless. An advertisement for commissioning editors, the key link between the channel and the independent production companies, told anyone interested, 'You may work in broadcasting, journalism, the theatre, modern dance, rock, politics, philosophy, religion . . . Television production experience may be an advantage but is not essential.' When the women's editor of the *Guardian*, Liz Forgan, came to interview Isaacs about his plans to show unpatronizing programmes by and about women, he asked her spontaneously to be Channel 4's head of news and current affairs. 'Do you realize I don't like television?' a startled Forgan responded. 'I never watch it . . . I know nothing about it.' Isaacs was undaunted: 'Just what we want.' Forgan signed up.

Yet behind this open-mindedness lurked shared assumptions. All five of the channel's original independent directors, and its chairman and deputy chairman, joined the SDP early on. Despite Isaacs' Tory connections and the channel's creation through Tory legislation, actual Conservatives were rare among the early Charlotte Street staff. And in its financial structures and operations Channel 4 was in some ways more a hopeful SDP-style compromise between the market and the state than a truly Thatcherite experiment. The channel was state-owned, through the Independent Broadcasting Authority (IBA); it did not sell its own advertising until 1990, and it dealt with the independent production companies, when it came to paying them, less like a wheeler-dealer than a fastidious Whitehall department. 'The standard contract for C4 work,' wrote John Ellis, 'was [an] arrangement in which the actual costs of production were minutely inspected by C4 production accountants and a standard percentage fee was calculated.'

In its commissioning of programmes, however, the channel was much less cautious. By May 1982, less than a year and a half after Isaacs' appeal for ideas at the Royal Institution, the channel had given 'over 400 commissions to the independent sector', reported the trade magazine *Broadcast*. The channel anticipated that these would make up almost a third of its programmes – 'more than we dreamed possible', celebrated its programme controller Paul Bonner. Less inspiringly, the other two-thirds would be bought in from abroad and from the ITV companies. Meanwhile so many proposals were still arriving from independent producers, the report continued, that Isaacs 'has asked [them] to hold back from making new submissions until those presently in the pipeline are ready for broadcast'.

From the start, one of the independents most in favour at Charlotte Street was Diverse Production. David Graham knew Isaacs through the campaign for Channel 4. Graham's innovative late 1970s work for the BBC had also come to the attention of Anthony Smith, now a Channel 4 board member. And then there was the name and underlying concept of Graham's company: Diverse.

It began as something between a profundity and a banality. 'We were trying to think of a name,' remembered Donebauer, 'and one of our first employees said, "What sort of programmes are we gonna make?" And I said, "You know, a diverse range." And they said, "That's not a bad name."' Donebauer beamed on his apartment balcony: 'Actually, it became a brilliant, brilliant name. Because it was a brand. Diversity: lots of different programmes for different people. My dad was always very sensitive to language, because he was fluent in three, and he said to me, "I never used to hear the word diverse, people didn't use it . . . and then [in the early 1980s] it was suddenly out there a lot."' The company name also echoed exactly one of

Isaacs' favourite ideas about television and society. 'The most important thing I was trying to say with Channel 4,' Isaacs told me, 'was that broadcasters should no longer seek always to serve a mass audience. They should come to a realization that the days of an entire family sitting in a row watching television were behind us. Millions of people were living on their own. Attitudes were changing, tolerance was growing.' Or as he put it in less liberal, more Thatcherite terms in his 1989 memoirs, when she was still ruling and dominating Britain: 'Society is not a slab of solid feeling . . . We catered for the interests of individuals who could make viewing choices on their own, and for themselves.'

Channel 4 was both a symptom and a cause of a country becoming more free but also more lonely; more sensitive to difference but also more fragmented. For the British left and right alike, in these shifts there would be profound victories and profound defeats.

But the first Diverse proposals David Graham sent to Isaacs were a little less cosmic. 'I think we had a consumer programme called *Hard Pounds*,' remembered Graham. The clunky title, with its dour suggestions of austerity and recession, was deceptive: the show was meant to be for the politically pivotal 'C2 end of the working class: smart plumbers and taxi drivers, working class entrepreneurs. I wrote to Jeremy, "These social groups should be the benchmark audience for Channel 4." He liked the idea. He kept asking me who they were: "Do they go to boxing matches? Tell me more about them!"' A little closer to Isaacs' cultural comfort zone was a suggested Diverse arts programme 'that would have entirely used computer graphics', thus saving on presenters and performers. Both ideas struck him as 'original' and pithily expressed, but neither went any further; instead, Isaacs and Forgan contacted Diverse with an idea of their own. Against strong competition, it would grow into the early Channel 4's most notorious show.

Every weekday at 7 p.m. Isaacs intended to broadcast an extended programme of 'considered, serious news'. No independent production company had the expertise or resources to make it, so reluctantly Channel 4 awarded the contract to Independent Television News (ITN), which had been making bulletins for ITV since the 1950s. To salve their radical consciences, Forgan and Isaacs decided to subvert this orthodox news coverage by introducing a novel element: on Fridays, instead of the second half hour of Channel 4 News, there would be 'an alternative news'.

In Britain in the early 1980s 'alternative' was a loaded word. It was widely taken to mean left-wing, counter-cultural, rebellious, separate from the mainstream – sometimes smugly so. CND was alternative. Ken Livingstone's GLC was alternative. The new wave of non-sexist, non-racist comedians such as Alexei Sayle were alternative. The gobs of leftover punks you still saw stuck to city street corners were alternative. Wearing Doc Martens and a donkey jacket, the clothes of the militant coalminer, of the shrinking industrial proletariat, was alternative – especially if you were middle class and wanted to show solidarity with the Tory-oppressed workers. Even when I was at Marlborough in the mid-1980s, among the sons and daughters of Thatcherism's victors, 'You're so alternative!' was still a common taunt, a way of cutting the more questioning, priggish pupils like me down to size, but with a hint of curiosity underneath. The ubiquity of the word deep into the decade made it clear that Thatcherism had not, yet, completely won.

Successfully pitching her idea to the Channel 4 board, Forgan said: 'I would like to unsettle viewers . . . to disturb their notion that they know what is going on because they saw one television [news] programme . . . This may prove such an uncomfortable feeling that viewers turn away in droves . . . [But] if we can persuade them to stay and understand the [news] process I think we shall have rendered a real service to democracy.'

To Graham and Donebauer – smart, high-minded, impatient to make a mark as their thirties began to rush past, bursting with years of accumulated thoughts and dissatisfactions about the role and tone and look and structure and working practices and half-concealed ideologies of conventional television – it was a thrilling brief. The programme they proposed in response tried to yoke together a whole skittish stable of journalistic impulses. *Friday Perspective*, as they first named the show with deceptive blandness, would be unlike any previous news programme: both story-breaking and an exposé of how news worked; both left-wing and unsparing about all interest groups;

both grittily factual and highly visual; both iconoclastic and accessible; both expansive in its subject matter and economical to produce; both with its own point of view and responsive to the public.

'The briefing leapt off the page,' Isaacs remembered. 'It was brilliant.' With an initial one-year contract agreed, Diverse looked for premises. Other independent producers were working from home or from a couple of small rooms each in central London, but with a weekly show to make and dozens of employees required to make it, Diverse needed much more space. They considered Docklands, but Graham said it was too far from his home in less gritty southwest London. They settled on Barons Court in the more affordable, transient part of west London, where they found a small disused factory up a dead end. It had been used for making pub dishwashers, and there were still half-built machines lying about; but it had lots of whitewashed rooms of different sizes, perfect for TV production and all the meetings that went with it, and there was land around it for expansion. 'Peter [Donebauer] was very smart to spot it,' said Graham. 'He knew how to handle property.'

Diverse installed studio and editing facilities. Unusually, Channel 4 paid for a substantial proportion of the equipment. Diverse also brought in some of Donebauer's colour synthesizers and graphics gadgets. 'David was a visionary – or determined to be a visionary,' remembered Steve Hewlett, an early recruit, a bolshy twenty-four-year-old left-winger and former student activist whose BBC contract had not been renewed because he was considered a security risk. 'He was determined that we'd have a paperless office, so we had these BBC micros. But the computers never quite got networked. And we wrote so many versions of the scripts, colour-coded, that the building filled up with even more paper than a normal office.'

Anna Coote was another important hiring. More poised and half a decade older than Hewlett, like him she had an activist background: she had been involved in British feminism from its early 1970s flowering to the muddier struggles of Greenham. 'All I knew about TV was as a viewer,' she told me. 'But I had some ideas about TV and TV news, about the quality of representation of women etc. By going to Diverse, I was going to test out some of these.' She was recruited as editor of *The Friday Alternative*, as *Friday Perspective* was soon renamed. 'I had to learn *everything*. But I was just up for the risk. It was a bit like when the new universities were built in the 70s, and a lot of people became professors.'

Diverse ended up with fifty staff, most of them young, all of them initially working on its one and only programme. There were also consultants, including Greg Philo of the Glasgow Media Group, a fashionable left-wing research cell that conducted partisan but persuasive analyses of mainstream journalism's biases against the left and in favour of capitalism and the establishment. 'There was a preponderance of lefties,' said Hewlett, 'some rightists, and some floating around in the middle. It was a very open and argumentative culture. People's politics weren't secret – that's why they were there. Usually, TV is full of small "p" politics but big "P" politics is kept quiet.'

As for Graham himself, after his *Panorama* investigations of the welfare state and the radical right, and after becoming an entrepreneur himself, he was no longer sure what his politics were – except that they were shifting. 'Those experiences sort of reconfigured me,' he said – an apt metaphor for a technophile. But in the early 1980s he still liked the eagerness of left-wing journalists to challenge power. 'At that time, the critique of TV that had been best articulated was a left-wing critique. If you are statistically led, and you want evidence, at least the left had a whole bunch . . . They'd monitored hundreds of telecasts about unions. So you'd got a bit of a story there. The right-wing presence on the team was very hard to mobilize. The right had not yet properly squared up to TV. They wrote articles about its biases for the *Spectator* instead.'

To broaden minds, Graham organized seminars for the staff. The astringent left-wing cultural critic Stuart Hall took part, but so did the emollient Conservative intellectual Ferdinand Mount, who in 1982 succeeded John Hoskyns as head of the Downing Street policy unit. For a start-up, Diverse had a very good address book.

Originally, Graham and Donebauer had wanted to run Diverse as a cooperative, inspired by the famous Spanish workers' collective Mondragon. Graham and Donebauer's desire to steer Diverse closely made that unrealistic, but an egalitarianism and an irreverence towards authority figures lingered in the company's raw, barely decorated spaces. Including towards the co-founders: 'Peter was slightly hippyish,' said Hewlett. In 1982 Donebauer had feathery mid-1970s hair, elfin features and a faraway air. 'He looked after the technology, but his gadgets didn't always work. David was much more intense, and up for an argument. He wore the stress.' As for the outside world, 'We had a mission to be anti-consensus. If you see a consensus, take a pop at it. Do things with graphics that everyone says don't work – clashing colours, running crawlers [of text] across the bottom of the screen while interviewees are talking. In interviews, be a bit naive. Ask another question. Don't accept things. Try anything.'

By the time I spoke to Hewlett he had become a rather different broadcaster: the urbane, seen-it-all host of *The Media Show* on the establishment's favourite station, BBC Radio 4. But he still talked with intensity about his early Diverse years: 'The liberal consensus that had dominated British politics since the war was breaking up. British TV was breaking up. You could feel the place changing. Thatcher was anti-consensual. Although she was from a different part of the spectrum [from us], she was doing the same thing. I did feel that we were part of a moment in history. *The Friday Alternative* was meant to be a new way of looking at a new world.'

The first edition was broadcast on Guy Fawkes Night in 1982. It was Channel 4's fourth day on air. True to Isaacs' television philosophy of eclecticism and something for everyone, and to the need to keep costs down, during its opening week the channel had already shown a cheap and cheerful adaptation of a French gameshow, *Countdown*; a rather severe literary programme with interviews, *Book Four*, featuring a rather startled Len Deighton, the blokeish spy novelist, having to insist that 'my descriptions of women are not less valid because I'm a man'; a crass Australian sketch show starring the comedian Paul Hogan in tight shorts and younger women in less; a feminist cabaret, *In the Pink*, with a monologue about how men 'squeeze' women in relationships until 'your mind pops'; and *Walter*, a harrowing, empathetic film about a disabled man in an asylum.

But *The Friday Alternative* still stood out. For much of the programme most of the screen was black: no presenters, no studio shots, no people at all. In the centre of the blackness were just words – in giant, glowing letters, in jarring typefaces, flashing up and then quickly disappearing, or forming brief sentences and phrases that giddyingly mixed up programme content with self-promotion, polemic with appeals to viewers: 'Less Bias', 'Interviews With Famous People', 'Arthur Scargill: The Man They Love To Hate', 'Sanitary Protection. We Can Now Reveal The Great Rip-Off', 'Week after week the same people decide what's news and what isn't. What would you have put in this week's news?'

The pace was fast, verging on manic. An item about the House of Lords, during which members of the public were asked to rank it alongside eight other institutions, including the Queen, the Stock Exchange and the Trades Union Congress, lasted a minute. 'You placed it bottom,' announced a perky, faintly mocking voiceover, as tinny synthesizer music skipped along in the background. (Interestingly, and ominously for left-wingers, the Stock Exchange came second, and the TUC second last.) There was a cheap sound effect of an explosion: 'Maybe Mr Fawkes was a good guy after all?'

'I liked the idea of a really pacy show,' Graham told me. 'In America they like pace, and American media is much more impactful. And I'd been in advertising, when I was in Canada, as a copywriter. I wasn't afraid of short items.' It was a style that would soon spread to youth TV all over the world. Yet on *The Friday Alternative* it was often applied to subjects that TV, youth or otherwise, never touched. One opening-night item was about the annual conference of the moderately right-wing employers' body, the Confederation of British Industry. The report criticized the conference for failing to debate a resolution attacking monetarism. You didn't get things like that on MTV.

Only twice did the first *Friday Alternative* calm down. The Scargill item just let him speak for several minutes, without questions, in his small, implacable voice. He had been elected president of the National Union of Mineworkers seven months earlier. He had been agitating almost continuously since for a strike against the accelerated running down of his industry being overseen by the government, and was fast becoming as much of a media ogre as Tony Benn and Ken Livingstone. 'He seldom gets a chance to explain his own case in his own words,' *The Friday Alternative* argued, persuasively, introducing the piece. Some of what followed was a prescient Scargill critique of the BBC and ITV, which would be borne out by their slanted coverage of him and his union when he finally managed to get the miners out on strike sixteen months later, in 1984. But sceptical *Friday Alternative* viewers might have noted that Scargill's arguments dovetailed neatly with the concerns of Diverse's consultants, the Glasgow Media Group, and with the interests of Diverse's patron, Channel 4.

The show's treatment of Scargill was also part of a bigger break with the conventions of political broadcasting. 'We wanted to just let people say their piece,' remembered Coote. 'It was a reaction against the classic studio ding-dong. The idea was that the audience was mature enough to make up their own minds.' In some ways this was a left-wing approach, and a fresh one: giving unrestricted media access to previously excluded or misrepresented groups and individuals. But in other ways it was more politically ambiguous. It implied that Britain was a patchwork of separate interests who should be allowed to 'say their piece', rather than a simple layering of a few large collective entities such as social classes, as the left had traditionally believed. In this, as in many things, *The Friday Alternative* was prophetic. Five years after its first edition, in September 1987, Margaret Thatcher told the magazine *Woman's Own*: 'Who is society? There is no such thing! There are individual men and women.'

In another innovation, *The Friday Alternative* organized groups of viewers to discuss the programme and TV news in general, and then help shape the show's coverage. There were twenty-three of these 'contributor groups', about a dozen people in each, spread around the country and intended to be representative of national voting patterns and demographics. They met in each other's homes, and their conversations were filmed. It was an extension of the fly-on-the-wall and encounter-group work that Graham had done for *Panorama*. 'I was interested in what you were told if you stepped outside the Westminster consensus and went down to the grass roots.' Mixed in with this idealism was professional pragmatism: 'You could source a person speaking for a particular point of view, in a way that was difficult for other programmes to do. And we'd know that their perspective was genuine. The contributor groups were easy to recruit. They loved doing it.'

With the same uncharacteristic reverence that it presented Scargill, the first *Friday Alternative* featured a roomful of people, most of them white and elderly, sitting around a trestle table with cups of tea in what looked like a community hall. 'They did alert us to interesting stories,' remembered Hewlett. 'There was a private health insurance salesman in one group who'd had to be rushed from a private to an NHS hospital, because the private hospital wasn't able to treat him. And as a sounding board, the groups were really quite good. But it took us a while to learn how to use them. If you said, "What's important to you, as an issue?" they'd all say, "Too much dogshit on the street."' Or something even less palatable. Coote recalled: 'There was a group out in Barking, somewhere out there in east London – I never went out to these places where the groups were – that was very right-wing and anti-immigration: "too many blacks". We didn't know how to handle that. We didn't want to give it airtime.' More often, she said, the Diverse staff found the groups 'a bit formulaic. We didn't think they said anything particularly innovative. Not so interesting to follow their suggestions, we thought, as we have brighter ideas of our own.' Diverse had discovered focus groups and interactivity and anti-elitism and citizen journalism decades before most of the British media; but the company was also raising an elite of its own.

At first, all the contradictions and risk-taking appeared not to matter. 'Nothing prepared me for the sheer elan of *The Friday Alternative*,' Isaacs wrote of the first programme. 'It had spark . . . It had a visual wit. It caught the attention . . . It made my weekend.' Hewlett remembered, 'We got a reputation very quickly among other TV journalists. Whenever we turned up at a political event, a look of panic or concern would flash across their faces: what are *they* going to do this time? We would film press conferences sideways, film the journalists rather than the event. It was really juvenile, some of it. I'd been on *Panorama* and *Nationwide* for nine months before Diverse, and I was one of the most experienced people there.'

Items would be added to programmes at the last minute. Editing schedules would be dangerously compressed. Then there were the unreliable early personal computers that Graham insisted they use instead of typewriters; the idiosyncratic graphics apparatus that Donebauer was determined they incorporate – 'We were cutting it ridiculously fine,' said Coote. 'One week, we just didn't finish in time. David drove to Channel 4 with the tape along the Marylebone Road with all his hazards on, going through all the red lights. Channel 4 had to broadcast something else. We were carpeted by Jeremy.'

At first, *The Friday Alternative* also struggled with what seemed an incongruous and old-fashioned problem for an ultra-modern, left-wing programme. 'We recruited people who weren't in the unions,' said Donebauer. Graham recalled: 'When setting up Diverse, we refused to negotiate with the NUJ [National Union of Journalists] and ACTT [Association of Cinematograph Television and Allied Technicians]. Didn't want anything to do with them. We all knew that an ACTT crew consisted of up to 12 people when you only needed two. The NUJ . . . I had seen them operating at the BBC, and I didn't particularly like what they did. I didn't go on strike at the BBC, because BBC operatives had a good standard of living.' Donebauer went on: 'I suppose we couldn't pay the salaries that the unions expected . . . [But] we were giving everyone a break. And then, *everyone* on our team wanted to do this union stuff! In our little, funky, Mondragon-inspired attempt to do something different . . . And we said, "No, that was the 70s! We want to get away from that."'

In the early 1980s the epic, economically questionable, socially catastrophic, still-ongoing British counter-revolution against unions was in its initial stages. Union membership had only just peaked, in 1979 or 1980, depending on which set of the highly fluid, politically loaded membership statistics you favoured. For its first two and a bit years the Thatcher government, weighed down with other problems, did little to reduce the unions' potency. In 1980 a national strike by steelworkers for a 20 per cent pay rise – their management had offered 6 per cent – ended with the mainly state-employed workers getting 16 per cent. In January 1981, the mere threat of similar action by the miners against government-supported pit closures had ended in humiliation for Margaret Thatcher – a humiliation omitted by the Thatcher legend and by most historians in favour of the miners' strike she defeated, in much more favourable political circumstances, four years later. In 1981 her administration, which had failed to prepare for a strike, was forced to let the Coal Board withdraw its entire pit-closure plan. Simultaneously, the government increased its subsidy to the coal industry, and improved miners' employment terms, asserting in public through gritted teeth that, as Thatcher put it, 'Coal was a special case.' 'SURRENDER', fumed the front page of the *Sun* on 19 February.

Seven months later, in September 1981, she finally took the initiative against the unions. She replaced her accommodating first employment secretary Jim Prior with the much more sharp-clawed Norman Tebbit. Tebbit understood trade unionists much better than most Tory politicians: unlike them, he had been one. Before becoming an MP, he had worked briefly as a clerk for the *Financial Times* and then as an airline pilot, and in both jobs had joined a union. He had experienced their sometimes oppressive post-war clout: at the *FT* he had been 'bullied' into joining a union, he wrote afterwards. But as a pilot he had also taken part in 'a bruising work-to-rule . . . as well as a full-blown strike' against 'management stupidities'.

Yet by the early 1980s Tebbit had come to believe that unions should be economically subservient, essentially apolitical organizations. 'Their prime role,' he told the general secretary of the TUC Len Murray in 1983, 'should be to help improve the performance of their firms which provided their members with jobs.' With unemployment rampant, it would be easier to persuade trade unionists to settle for such a minimal role. But even Tebbit moved slowly against them at first. He told me, '[Thatcher] wanted me to do something. But she wasn't very clear about exactly what.' It took him over a year, until October 1982, after victory in the Falklands had made the Tories more politically secure, to produce his first Employment Act. It reduced the power of unions in some crucial ways, such as opening up their funds to claims for damages, and therefore discouraging the spur-of-the-moment, illegal walk-outs that had been a fact of British industrial life since the late 1960s. But the Act was portrayed by Tebbit as 'modest', and he held back from introducing measures demanded by the Tory right such as secret ballots before strikes.

'The media – I wanted them to be urging me all the time to go further,' Tebbit recalled with a sly, satisfied look, 'and for me to be saying, "Hold on, chaps." Because that would give me a better standing not only in parliament but with the public. I was half-pleased when the *Daily Express* denounced me one day as "Timid Tebbit."' Behind his public image as a blunt instrument, Tebbit had a subtle understanding of the ever-shifting balance of forces in British politics and society, and he sensed that in the early 1980s the time was not yet right for an overt confrontation with the unions. That would wait until the government had been entrenched by the 1983 election.

At Diverse, Graham and Donebauer's attempt to do without unions and union pay rates did not last long. 'For a few months,' said Graham, the company was 'blacked by the NUJ': the union instructed its members not to work for Diverse. Usually, blacking was a tactic used in Britain to try to isolate and shame stubborn right-wing employers and Fascist foreign governments. 'It was a bizarre situation, this little left-wing programme being blacked,' said Graham. But he insisted: 'It had little impact on us. We didn't use freelances very much, and our employees who were NUJ members didn't go on strike, because they were loyal to the project.' Yet after this show of resistance the company allowed an NUJ chapel to be set up, with Hewlett as father. 'We had to negotiate with the chapel,' said Donebauer. 'We had to start paying union rates. We felt let down, on a personal level . . . by people asking for more money, and for punitive rates. For the first six months David and I hadn't been getting overtime or' – his dreamy, slightly New Agey voice suddenly became contemptuous – '*days off in lieu*, I can tell you.' He looked out over the dirty Thames from his pristine apartment. 'I hate, hate being an employer.'

But it was external rather than internal frictions that sank *The Friday Alternative*. For Isaacs, for the Channel 4 board, for the government, for the channel's regulator the Independent Broadcasting Authority, and for the broadcasters that it constantly taunted and criticized, particularly Channel 4's collaborator ITN, the show quickly became grating. It 'appeared consistently if not exclusively to present only one alternative standpoint, that of the left,' wrote Isaacs. And not his clubbable, Tory-respecting brand of leftism; nor the consensual, SDP-leaning, semi-leftism of the Channel 4 board; but a much ruder variety.

On 7 January 1983, with the programme only two months old but already causing exasperated splutterings inside the political-broadcasting establishment – the IBA told Isaacs that *The Friday Alternative* needed 'rectification' – an edition appeared entirely devoted to one of the most provocative topics imaginable: the government-manipulated but highly popular British coverage of the Falklands War. Midway through the conflict, the programme reported, the *Sunday Times* had avoided printing a story about widespread doubts in Whitehall over Britain's claim to the islands. 'Thank you for your memo about the British claim to the Falklands sovereignty,' the editor of the paper, Frank Giles, had written to a British academic who had studied the relevant documents. 'You are obviously onto something quite interesting here. But ... publishing this information at the moment ... would be highly demoralizing to servicemen.' Using internal BBC documents leaked to Hewlett, the programme also reported that local radio stations had been prevented by the BBC hierarchy from broadcasting interviews with widows of servicemen killed in the war, except of those deemed heroic enough to have received posthumous medals. Finally, the show included detailed revelations about disquiet among BBC executives at the government's generally bullying attitude to Falklands reporting, and at the lack of airtime given to the large minority of Britons who opposed the war.

The programme presented all this heretical material in its usual, gleefully finger-pointing, student-rag style. The government was furious, especially when a follow-up edition included an amateur radio enthusiast's accidental recording of a browbeating Falklands conversation between Thatcher's domineering press secretary, Bernard Ingham, and the BBC's Assistant Director General, Alan Protheroe. The Channel 4 chairman Edmund Dell, a strait-laced Whitehall insider who had been uncomfortable with the channel's wilder impulses from the start – and had been appointed for exactly that reason – wrote to Isaacs after the first Falklands show: 'This programme was appalling once more ... Discipline must be exercised over these people very quickly.'

It never really was. By the summer of 1983 *The Friday Alternative* had taken to filming politicians' mouths only, and asking viewers to guess which party they belonged to. Hewlett interviewed MPs in a bear costume. Items attacked Channel 4 itself. That the programme was evolving, becoming anarchic rather than left-wing, and perhaps beginning to sense the intellectual hollowing-out and ideological convergence that was to come in British politics, went seemingly unnoticed by the show's overseers and viewers. Its audience deflated from a modest but promising 671,000 in November 1982 to a derisory 188,000 in July 1983. That month, after thirty-six editions, and four months before the end of its initial contract, the show was cancelled. 'The Chairman considered that certain public perceptions about the channel needed to be changed,' the minutes of the Channel 4 board meeting on 20 July recorded, 'and it would be wise to sacrifice the programme.'

'We failed,' said David Graham, in his undersized boardroom in Taunton. 'We tried to do too much. And we just weren't crafty enough to know that the challenges . . . had to be very deftly handled.' Hewlett, less self-doubting, felt something valuable had been achieved: 'It was the first time the nuts and bolts of TV production had been exposed.'

Either way, you might have expected Diverse to disappear, one casualty among many in the early 1980s TV free-for-all. But Channel 4 had invested in the company's hardware, so even Dell did not want to see it go bust. Instead he envisaged its premises becoming a facility for the production and editing of other companies' programmes. Graham had a less prosaic idea. He proposed a more professional, politically balanced version of *The Friday Alternative*. It would have a more seasoned staff, some hired specifically for their right-wing views, and a new name, Diverse Reports. Isaacs, who still had an exasperated fondness for the original programme, liked the notion, and the Channel 4 board were persuaded. The first edition of Diverse Reports was broadcast in January 1984. It was calmer, and more conventionally investigative: a typical show probed Israel's arms trade with apartheid South Africa. The show ran to respectable reviews for three and a half years. Hewlett, who was retained to help make it, considered Diverse Reports 'the best thing I ever did'. But he conceded there was 'not quite the same sense of collective passion' as with its predecessor. 'Diverse became less intense, more of a normal TV production company. In the end, we were there because David and Peter were making money out of it.'

Graham insisted, 'I didn't really care about money much. Mine and Peter's salaries were ridiculously low when we started the company. My ending salary at *Panorama* might have been £15,000, and we paid ourselves something like that.' The average national salary in 1981 was about £7,000. Graham went on: 'And then suddenly all that changed. Around '84, I was suddenly on quite a large salary. Suddenly people were saying, "You're on your way to your first million, in what your company's worth." Quite quickly, we were always travelling round London in taxis, and running up large bills, and living *rather well*.' He drew out and relished the words. 'I started going to restaurants for professional reasons. You didn't take *Panorama* producers out to restaurants!'

In 1984 Donebauer finally moved out of his semi-squat in Brixton. 'I was able to get a mortgage, get married. That was amazing. But then you get used to these things. You realize there's no way back.' We sat in silence for a moment on his balcony, no helicopters overhead for once, the relentlessly wealthy riverside of post-1980s west London stretching for miles around us. Then Donebauer continued: 'The intellectual basis for the left was crumbling. It had got very stale. I'd been at Manchester University in '68 – marches, sit-ins, I'd seen it all. Now I was on a different path. All my artist friends said, "What the fuck are you doing at Diverse? You're an artist." I said, "This is actually a lot more creative."'

Graham remembered, 'A lot of people said to me, "You've set up your left-wing company, and now you're a capitalist." I thought, "Yep, probably." All the independent producers quickly became capitalists. In 1983 or 1984, I got a call from someone at 10 Downing Street who said, "I'm being told independent producers are all left-wing. It's a kind of trade union." I said, "They're not. They're independent businesses."'

In 1986 Graham completed his ideological journey when Diverse broadcast its celebratory series about the international right, *The New Enlightenment*. Besides co-writing the accompanying book, he was executive producer. Margaret Thatcher was one of those who watched it. Isaacs writes in his memoirs, 'When the Prime Minister challenged [me] to name a single [Channel 4] series which had supported her point of view I named this one. "Ah yes," she said. "But that is the only one."'

Graham was invited to 10 Downing Street in 1987, to explain to Thatcher why independent production companies were, as he told the

Tories he increasingly mixed with, 'an important business sector'. The occasion was a lunch seminar for television executives. 'I was at the far end of the table from her,' he recalled. But when his turn came to speak, Thatcher listened, and he felt he did well. 'It was a good moment,' he said, almost dreamily, as the afternoon shoppers of Taunton fussed around in the car park outside the boardroom window. 'It was a good moment.' Then his self-critical side returned: 'I didn't get any great sense of warmth. I'd got a beard, and she didn't like men with beards.'

During the late 1980s his interest and involvement in Diverse gradually dwindled. 'It went off the boil for me. I didn't think the programmes were as good as I'd been making at the BBC.' According to Hewlett, who left the company in 1987 to go back to the BBC, 'David and Peter had a falling out.' With me, they both skirted around the subject, referring to each other respectfully, when they did at all. But Donebauer said obliquely, 'Having our own kit was a blessing and a curse. The company became driven by a need to keep all our facilities going. We always needed turnover' – here it was the accountant's son speaking – 'because business is all about cashflow. We did corporate programmes. We made programmes for unions. We did a lot of early interactive and Web stuff.' In 1991 Graham finally left. Donebauer stayed on. Diverse lasted another decade and a half – a very long existence, all told, for an independent production company. When I went to look at its old premises in 2012, its logo was still beside the intercom. But a sign on the wall above said, 'Sold'.

Channel 4 gradually turned into something else as well. In 1983 it showed the first property programme on British television, *A Cottage in the Country*. In 1988 Isaacs stepped down as chief executive. In 1993 the channel started selling its own advertising. In 1994 it moved from its skinny office conversion in raffish Charlotte Street to a purpose-built glass spread in Horseferry Road in Westminster, respectfully close to the ministers and civil servants whom *The Friday Alternative* used to ridicule. Around this time, the channel settled into a pattern that has continued ever since, broadcasting well-made, youth-oriented programmes, which were superficially controversial, ratings-savvy, good for revenues.

On 3 November 1982 the writer Peter Ackroyd, then slumming it as a TV reviewer for *The Times*, had described the channel's opening night as 'trying to get it both ways, to be "innovative" but not too innovative, distinctive but not too distinctive . . . offering approximately the same material as the other channels'. He was wrong then, but he would not be in the long run. Some of the early 1980s' liberations did not last.

15
'Loonies'

Of all the risky experiments in early 1980s Britain, cultural, economic or political, one attracted particularly wide derision. On 17 February 1982 the usually polite *Guardian* published a mocking three-paragraph item about 'a new wheeze' from the spectacularly unpopular, seemingly doomed political curiosity that was Ken Livingstone's Greater London Council. 'This is a Womens [*sic*] Committee,' explained the unnamed journalist, 'which will monitor all council activities to check that they are looking at things from a woman's as well as a man's point of view.' The report continued even more condescendingly: 'Sexism – albeit of a cheery and trivial sort – still lurks at County Hall . . . Valerie Wise, one of the councillors most enthusiastic for the scheme, wants "a committee that is going to be able to interfere with every decision of the council".'

By 1982, for journalists, even some *Guardian* ones, feminism was an old story. Women's Lib, in its modern British incarnation, had been going for a dozen years now. Some veterans of the struggle were slipping away to do other things, like Anna Coote with her new television career at Diverse Production. Meanwhile even feminists with fresh campaigning ideas, such as the peace camp at Greenham, struggled to get the attention of the media and Britain's overwhelmingly male politicians – sometimes, even, of the ideologically curious and unusually gender-conscious Livingstone himself. 'We had no proposal for the women's committee in the 1981 GLC manifesto,' he told me, despite the document's hundreds of pages and wide-ranging ambitions. 'We had a proposal to set up an ethnic minorities committee, and on the back of that, people like Valerie said we should do something for women. So it was an afterthought.'

In February 1982 Wise was twenty-seven. She had been a GLC councillor, her first elected office, for barely a year. Tall and slightly gawky, her narrow face dominated by her trademark circular, thick-rimmed glasses, she spoke in a youthful, upbeat, slightly grating voice, with non-London tinges to her vowels (she had also lived in the Midlands and the north). She was still in awe of her mother, Audrey, a political prodigy herself who had been a prominent feminist from the late 1960s onwards, and a stubbornly outspoken left-wing Labour MP in the late 1970s. 'I feel very privileged to have been the daughter of Audrey Wise,' Valerie said, with oddly stiff affection, when I interviewed her in 2013. Two walls of her living room were given over to volumes of Hansard covering her late mother's years in Parliament.

Socialism was the prime political faith passed from mother to daughter. 'I've called myself a feminist for some time, but coming to the GLC has meant my first contact with the women's movement,' Valerie admitted to the feminist magazine *Spare Rib* in July 1982, two months after the women's committee had officially started work. Her frankness was either naive, faux-naive, or immensely self-confident – or most likely a mixture of all three. 'It's been an amazing learning process for me, and I hope that's going to be mutual.'

In 1982 Livingstone's GLC badly needed a new purpose. 'What we'd really wanted to do was build housing and modernize the transport system, and those we were blocked on,' he told me. The council's attempt to revitalize the capital's economy and make it more socially just, through the Greater London Enterprise Board, was proceeding modestly at best. Livingstone was trying to wean himself off giving endless provocative quotes to hostile journalists, his original approach of leadership by outrage having proved increasingly counter-productive. The euphoria of the precocious London Labour left's seizure of the GLC in 1981 – 'London's Ours!' – seemed very distant a year on. As two of the many young, questing left-wing thinkers and activists who joined the Livingstone administration, Maureen Mackintosh and Hilary Wainwright, wrote in the slightly chastened 1987 book they co-edited about their experience, *A Taste of Power*: 'No one in the GLC thought we were creating socialism now.'

This GLC rethink was part of a wider retreat by the British left from 1982 onwards, as Tony Benn's Alternative Economic Strategy began to lose momentum after his failure to win the Labour deputy leadership, and Thatcherism finally started to create a new economy as well as destroy the old one. But if 'Red Ken' had given up on building socialism in one city, his GLC still had enough power, money and chutzpah for a different radical project. This was a new relationship between the state and the citizen, and between the increasingly disparate groups of citizens in London. It would have implications for the whole of Britain. And it would rival, and in some ways undermine, the psychological revolution being driven through by the Thatcherites.

The idea of the women's committee had crystallized during 1981. When Wise arrived at the GLC, she knew a lot more about politics and bureaucracies than her innocent manner suggested. She had worked for her mother Audrey in Parliament. She had also worked for a groundbreaking group of union shop stewards at the military-industrial conglomerate Lucas, who sidestepped the company management to develop worker-designed green technologies and other non-military products. Finally, during her curries in Tooting with Livingstone and Michael Ward, she had helped arrange the left's seizure of County Hall.

When she became a GLC councillor, Wise told me briskly, 'Because of my involvement with the Lucas shop stewards, I became vice-chair of Mike Ward's industry and employment committee – straightaway. Industry and employment were key parts of our manifesto. It was one of the most important GLC committees.' She nodded with satisfaction. 'I was in the right place at the right time.'

At industry and employment she became interested in how the GLC might alter the London economy to better suit women. She told *Spare Rib* that she 'tried meeting regularly with women['s groups] outside the GLC but . . . it just didn't work. The only way to get a proper strategy, to ensure things happen, is by a committee.' Otherwise, 'You get swallowed up by the system . . . becoming "the statutory woman" on things . . . just a front.' She wrote a proposal for a women's committee. She remembered, 'I went to Ken, and he was very receptive. I put it immediately to the Labour Group [of councillors].' She smiled: 'It was hard for them not to agree to it, given that there was already an ethnic minorities committee.'

The first annual budget of the women's committee was £332,000. The total GLC budget was then slightly under £850 million. The committee initially had eleven members, all councillors. Wise was chair – 'a curious GLC word', wrote the *Guardian* journalist Hugh Herbert, interviewing her a little uncomprehendingly on 22 July 1982. Of the other ten members, only seven were women and only six Labour. There were also three Conservative councillors and one from the SDP. But the political balance was immediately shifted leftwards when the Tories decided to boycott the weekly meetings, having had second thoughts about taking part in such a radical-sounding enterprise. To act as a minature civil service for the committee, in keeping with GLC practice, a women's support unit was set up with an initial staff of fourteen. The GLC had a staff of 37,000.

Even by the standards of the Livingstone administration, the official aims of the women's committee were optimistically broad:

> 1. The promotion of the welfare and interests of women in Greater London.
>
> 2. The implementation of policies to promote equal opportunity for women . . . within the [Greater London] Council . . . [and] the adoption by London borough councils and other employers in Greater London of equal opportunity policies.
>
> 3. Advocacy of the abolition of policies which discriminate against women.

But Wise and her comrades believed that fundamental change was the only approach worth trying. As Femi Otitoju, an even younger and brisker feminist than Wise who joined the support unit in 1984, put it to me: 'We were saying, "The way things have worked here [in London] have not worked for women. So everything is up for grabs!"'

The women's movement had already changed the capital – but not enough. Since the late 1960s the mostly male-designed city had been dotted with women's centres, women's cooperatives, women's bookshops, feminist consciousness-raising groups. But many women were still too scared to use the Underground at night, or even to go out after dark – for fear of being harassed, or worse. Whole areas of central London such as King's Cross and Soho were leering male-oriented quarters of sex shops and kerb-crawlers. Many public buildings were not open to people with prams. Many Londoners assumed that people with prams should be female. A majority of low-paid municipal employees in the capital were female. The previous Labour GLC, which only left office in 1977, had a single female councillor. Under Livingstone there were nine – still under a fifth of the Labour total. Wise remembered, 'Some of the older men on the Labour Group – Ken used to tell me, "Valerie go and be nice." I really couldn't do it. I felt I had nothing in common with them.'

Most London feminists had long avoided getting involved in local government. Although feminists were generally on the left, even the more open-minded Labour councils tended to be male-dominated, and clumsy and domineering in their dealings with non-Labour groups – if they dealt with them at all. Besides, such was the intensity and freshness of the women's movement, to many of those involved party politics seemed almost irrelevant: right up until the 1979 election, it featured little in feminist publications such as *Spare Rib*.

Around the turn of the decade, this all began to change. The coming to power of Margaret Thatcher was a big prompt. Some feminists voted for her; others – and some of the former – were horrified when her government began to unravel the post-war Britain that, however sexist, had supported women through its welfare state and increasingly female trade unions. By 1980, 38 per cent of trade unionists were women. In *Beyond the Fragments: Feminism and the Making of Socialism*, an influential 1979 collection of left-leaning feminist essays by Sheila Rowbotham, Lynne Segal and Hilary Wainwright, the latter warned prophetically: 'Our fragmented movements and campaigns are that much weaker without . . . political focus and back-up. This will become more and more painfully obvious as a strong, determined Tory government makes isolated victories more difficult.'

A more optimistic case for getting involved in initiatives such as the women's committee was put by Jan Parker in an expansive April 1983 piece for *Spare Rib* headlined 'A Feminist Takeover in Local Government?':

> There's ... some strong arguments for moving inside for a while and seeing how the system will budge ... There could be mass consciousness-raising ... a transport system that took women's needs into account; encouragement of women's sport; strong policies on positive discrimination and sexual harassment at work ... [And] precedents may be set ... for future feminist dealings with political parties and powerful institutions.

Yet she cautioned:

> It's far from straightforward aiming to import feminist ideas into male-dominated and hierarchical council structures ... [There is] the possibility of local councils picking only the parts that are consistent with their own policies and don't threaten [the status quo] ... National government policies mean money is getting even tighter and services are disappearing ... Women's committees can all too often just end up papering over the cracks.

As early as 1978, Labour-controlled Lewisham council in south London had set up a Women's Rights Working Party, a sort of prototype women's committee, with a membership evenly split between councillors and people from local women's groups. In 1982 a succession of Labour councils right across gentrifying, novelty-seeking, politically active inner London – Camden, Islington, Hackney, Greenwich, Southwark – set up women's committees. But it was the GLC one that mattered most. It was partly a question of resources: 'The second time I negotiated for a budget,' said Wise, 'I went for £8m. The Labour Group practically fell off their seats! But I got £6.9m.'

Wise's nous and cheery, insistent personality gave the committee impetus. So did her County Hall status as a valued Livingstone ally. At times he presented her almost as his deputy, the pair of them appearing in endless photocalls, shoulder to shoulder on formal occasions, arm in arm on goofier ones such as the GLC pantomime, both of them surprisingly photogenic and the same height, both of them younger and skinnier than the stout, well-lunched municipal fixers to which London and Britain were accustomed. It looked like a new generation had taken power. Although the sight of Wise showing some leg in spiked heels, next to Livingstone in tights, a panto Maid Marian to his Robin Hood, may not have been the municipal revolution some feminists had in mind.

But Livingstone's support for the women's committee was genuine. Despite all his GLC problems and responsibilities, he often came to its meetings. During the 1970s he had read and been influenced by feminist writers such as the exposer of male sexual violence, Andrea Dworkin. He had encountered feminist activists who made him aware that childcare and contraception and housework were political issues. And since his first days as a borough councillor, in Lambeth in the early 1970s, he had been interested in opening up and diversifying local government. Much quicker than most politicians, Livingstone spotted that 'London was now a collection of minorities', as he put it in 1987. 'We needed to listen to each of those groups . . . [That was] the only way it could work as a city.' As London's industry disappeared, and much of Labour's traditional union power base with it, Livingstone realized early that making alliances with other social groups was also the only way Labour would carry on getting elected.

The women's committee regarded listening to female London as its first task. Within days of its official establishment in May 1982, the committee set in motion a chain of public meetings, both at County Hall and across the capital; began drawing up and distributing waves of public questionnaires about how London should change for women; and began seeking people from outside the GLC as additional, 'co-opted members'. The latter were to be elected annually at the County Hall gatherings, and were intended to be ordinary citizens, not professional politicians. Unprecedentedly and contentiously for Britain, a fixed proportion were to be women from ethnic minorities, with smaller quotas for lesbians and the disabled.

Other Labour councils had occasionally allowed tiny numbers of co-opted members onto their committees. But the GLC women's committee would feature half a dozen or more of these citizen-politicians at a time – potentially a decisive voting bloc. Just as riskily and importantly, Wise and Livingstone prevented their Labour colleagues from requiring that these people be Labour Party members. Wise and Livingstone were still sometimes fierce left-wing tribalists. She told the socialist magazine the *Leveller* in 1982, 'I'd always vote for a left-wing man over a right-wing woman. Socialism has to come first.' But in other contexts their politics was evolving. 'At Lucas,' Wise told me, 'I had learned from Mike Cooley' – the shop stewards' leader and guru at the manufacturing conglomerate – 'who really believed that the real experts were the workers themselves. So I went to the GLC thinking, "The real experts for what should happen to women in London are the women – any women."' It was similar to the thinking that had led to the viewers' groups on *The Friday Alternative*: a prefiguring of the bottom-up, anti-elite mood of the Internet age to come.

The public meetings were well attended and often hard to manage. Women of all kinds came: severe or delighted, factional or open-minded, in wheelchairs, in business suits, with babies, in African dress, in pensioners' cardigans, representing the whole fragmenting spectrum of 1980s feminism, from class-driven socialist feminists to gender-separatist radicals. They squeezed into workaday meeting rooms and sometimes County Hall's much grander debating chamber, a presumptuously lavish, high-ceilinged horseshoe of wood and leather that rivalled the Tory-held House of Commons itself. 'The great thing was that we had the money to advertise these open meetings, on the radio, in magazines,' said Wise. 'We could pay bus fares, pay for carers so people could come.'

'The meetings were hard,' she said. 'There were some women who were really difficult – all the Wages for Housework lot. They would come to the meetings and try to take them over. You did come in for quite a lot of stick. I was accused of "chocolate box feminism" because the leaflets we sent out were all glossy. But we chose the suffragette colours for them, purple, green and white. And I thought, "Look, women are really busy. They haven't got time to pick up some boring-looking leaflet . . . Why do advertisers spend all this money, advertising Daz or Surf or whatever? You've got to produce your literature attractively, grab people's attention, before you can get them to participate . . ."'

Three decades on, in her living room, Wise was persuading herself and an audience once more. She suddenly beamed, bright as a saleswoman: 'Nothing at the GLC had the rank-and-file participation that we had!'

As in the wider women's movement, the gatherings were meant to be open and inclusive. 'Everyone is given a chance to speak,' reported Sue Goss in an essay for the 1984 collection *Local Socialism? Labour Councils and New Left Alternatives*. '[Yet] inevitably,' she went on, the evening meetings 'have tended to attract women already involved in women's rights or in the voluntary sector ... who are articulate, who are used to, and able to, travel around London at night, and who have no childcare difficulties. They run the risk of being "middle class".' Similarly, Goss found that at the GLC and elsewhere, 'The councillors heading women's committees and the majority of officers in the new women's [support] units are young professional women.'

During the second half of 1982 the GLC committee set up working groups of female Londoners to explore the main issues raised at the public meetings, and then make suggestions towards what it called, with typical purpose, the 'Programme of Action for Women in London'. One of the first working groups, reported the monthly *Bulletin on the GLC Women's Committee*, which quickly grew from a few stapled pages in crude type to an illustrated magazine, concerned itself with 'Media and Arts'. It proposed that GLC 'finance [be] given to a women's arts centre ... women's theatre ... film-making groups etc'.

Other working groups had more of a raw, unpredictable edge. 'Women Against the Law' invited *Bulletin* readers to its first meeting at King's Cross on 13 October 1982:

> We plan to explore all the ways in which women are being forced into illegal or semi-illegal activities in order to survive the worsening economic crisis ... [and] cuts in social services ... Whether we work as prostitutes or go shop-lifting in order to feed and clothe ourselves and our children; whether we're illegal immegrants [*sic*] or we are on SS [social security] and do a job on the side; whether we fiddle the bus and tube fares or carry a knife to defend ourselves, women are continually confronting the law, the police, the courst [courts] and the establishment ... We'll discuss what action the GLC can and should take to protect women who find themselves up against the law.

By the spring of 1983 Wise felt that the energies unlocked by the committee needed focusing. 'Working groups ... their success has varied,' she wrote in the April *Bulletin*. Like a headmistress or a school inspector, she continued: 'Some are good and attendance has been satisfactory, while others are poor and poorly attended. [The committee had] listened and taken into account much of what women have said. [But] we don't want to meet for the sake of meeting . . . It is really important that women . . . actually set up projects, to put ideas into practice.'

Some of these projects would be undertaken by the GLC itself. The women's committee pressured London Transport to 'ban sexist advertisements' on the Underground 'that show women as sexually available'. Aware as always where power lay, Wise knew the GLC funded London Transport. The women's committee won the argument. She gave me a satisfied look. 'Change does require people with power.'

But on other occasions the committee worked by giving power away. The Livingstone GLC's version of socialism was influenced by the do-it-yourself radicalism of the 1960s; by the Italian left's decentralizing city governments in the 1970s; by the ongoing modern decline of deference towards politicians – and also by the fact that the GLC had limited powers, which the Conservatives were making more limited by the day. This socialism held that truly modern left-wing politicians should not just consult individual voters, interest groups and community organizations; they should empower them. 'People have to do it for themselves,' Livingstone told the *Guardian*'s star interviewer, the professionally sceptical, politically cautious Terry Coleman, on 21 December 1981. 'You can't hinge it all on a small group of politicians doing it for you.' According to Coleman, who was fond of subtly taming his interviewees by paraphrasing them, in an ideal world Livingstone 'would want each factory run by its own workers, and each school by the parents and teachers'. But surely, asked Coleman, 'Few people could run anything?' Livingstone was not thrown off his stride: 'That potential's there in everybody.'

The GLC strategy that followed, to change London by giving out grants, was a dangerous challenge to the British right – one of increasingly few as the 1980s wore on and the Conservatives' parliamentary and wider supremacy became more and more entrenched. Firstly, Livingstone, like all of the period's demonized left-wing politicians, was supposed to be a control freak – the *Daily Mail*'s 'Commissar of

County Hall' – and not a delegator. Secondly, letting citizens run their own affairs was supposed to be the radical right's big idea. 'The GLC,' commented the usually pessimistic journal *Marxism Today* admiringly in April 1986, 'denied Thatcherism the high ground in the argument about initiative, enterprise and decentralization.'

However, as another Tory government, David Cameron's, would discover decades later, with its faintly Livingstonian 'free schools' and 'Big Society', decentralizing rhetoric is the easy part. In a questioning modern democracy, most voters are in favour of freedom and local initiatives and against centralized bureaucracy – in theory. But handing out taxpayers' money to non-government bodies while the British media look on with an unforgiving eye is much more difficult.

The women's committee distributed its grants from a ground-floor office in County Hall. Under Livingstone, being on one of the lower floors of the enormous complex was a sign of status: you were closer to the entrances and to the many lobbies and meeting spaces that his administration had pointedly opened up to the public. The women's long windowed room was open-plan but slender. The rapidly growing staff of the support unit, which reached almost a hundred at its peak, sat in teams at clusters of desks, separated by padded screens to provide some order and privacy, and to keep the noise down. 'The place had an *entirely* different atmosphere from the rest of the building,' remembered Femi Otitoju, 'which was much more muted, much more male.'

> There were no balloons, and very few posters in the rest of County Hall. In the women's unit, there was just this mass of women, who were different shapes, different colours, different sizes. Most of us had short hair. Obviously, there was less make-up in the room because we were feminists. We wore tailoring – the dungarees had gone by then – but we wore more colour than you saw in other places in County Hall. We just didn't collude with the skirts and tights and heels that women wore there. The trappings of female power were different for us.

Visitors to the women's unit

> would come to the door and hover nervously. We didn't have a reception, and our hierarchy didn't allow for minions to whisk you in and look after you. Visitors would . . . look into the room, and wait to be

rescued. You were fine if you came with an appointment, or saw someone you knew. Otherwise, you kind of hopped from foot to foot. I think people were aware that they had to be very very careful, because this was the beginning of identity politics: people weren't au fait with what language they should use. They weren't sure what would make some scary feminist kick off!

Otitoju was twenty-six when she joined the women's unit. She had been brought up by foster parents in sedate Worthing: 'My mother went back to Nigeria,' she told me, baldly. After Worthing, she was educated at a grammar school in more combustible Hackney. By the time she got to the GLC she was already a seasoned player in the new game of politics dominated by gender, race and sexuality. Self-confident, comfortable in different social contexts, with an unyielding stare and a steamroller of a smart southern English voice, she had come out as a lesbian in her late teens – 'practically unheard of, as a black woman' – and had been involved for years in radical organizations such as Women Against Violence Against Women and the London Lesbian and Gay Switchboard.

She had encountered Livingstone in this milieu before she joined the GLC: 'He was as eloquent as the rest of us on the issues, and apparently signed up.' But she had no time for his party-political side. 'I wasn't Labour ... I was a radical revolutionary feminist, which meant that the milkman left the milk at the *end* of the balcony of the block of flats where I lived, and the postman was *encouraged* not to touch my door knob.'

To earn a living, Otitoju sold advertising space for the *Observer* and the *Voice*, a paper for black Britons founded in 1982, and the first one to treat them primarily as British rather than immigrants. Then she was headhunted by the GLC. 'I was already kind of in and around the GLC by then: they'd funded a lesbian and gay centre where I worked, loads and loads of women's centres I'd been involved in. I had some anxieties that local government would bring you in, ostensibly to listen to you, but then nothing would happen. Or that I was being co-opted by the establishment. But at the end of the day' – she suddenly began to giggle with remembered glee – 'the GLC resources beat everything!'

Another women's unit recruit was Linda Bellos. Like Otitoju, she was hired in 1984, did not suffer fools gladly, and was black and a lesbian. But she was older, thirty-three, and came from a fairly standard left-wing background. She had read Marx 'at the age of 12' while her mother was out working as a junior manager for Sainsbury's. Bellos had studied politics at famously right-on Sussex University, and was a lapsed member of the Labour Party. She had come to feminism late. 'I went to Sussex in 1978 as a married heterosexual with two children,' she told me. 'Some of the tutors, usually male, encouraged us to think about feminism, and I'd say, "Yes, but my man's different." I certainly didn't see myself as a feminist. Then, Easter of my second year, I realized I was a lesbian – it really, seriously, had not occurred to me – and . . . the scales fell from my eyes. I was a Marxist, and the focus on power relationships and exploitation which I had learned from him – I began to apply it to gender and other forms of discrimination.' She joined the collective running *Spare Rib*. But she found the house journal of the women's movement too full of 'middle-class drivel' – too dominated by comfortably off white writers, as she saw it, wanting to do pieces about disadvantaged women when she felt those women should speak for themselves.

In 1983 someone from the GLC women's unit visited the magazine and asked whether the collective would like to apply for a grant. Similar encounters between the unit and London feminism's busy but cash-poor institutions were beginning to take place all over the capital. So keen was the unit to distribute money, it offered training sessions on how to apply for grants, and checklists of suggested items that women's groups could get GLC funding for. 'We had a discussion at *Spare Rib*,' said Bellos, 'and I remember strongly arguing that we shouldn't apply. It would compromise our independence. Instead of being accountable to our readers, we would become accountable to a public body.' The collective decided not to seek a grant. 'But what the meeting did do was introduce me to a local authority that was doing things in a different way.'

Later in 1983, Bellos, who was half-Jewish, left *Spare Rib* after an internal row over the 1982 Israeli invasion of Lebanon (she was against it). The re-election of the Thatcher government persuaded her to rejoin the Labour Party. She was unemployed for a few weeks, then she took a job advising women on how to set up voluntary bodies. In 1984 she saw a GLC ad in the *Guardian* for a 'team leader of equalities and grants monitoring'. The women's unit already had its own particular way with words.

Bellos agreed to be paid 'about £26,000'. She thought it was 'a bloody good salary'. Although Livingstone made the GLC's hierarchical pay structures more equal, and although he noisily insisted on a drastically reduced leader's salary that was 'not much more than [that of] County Hall cleaners', his administration was pragmatic, essentially market-driven in its approach, when it came to hiring talented outsiders.

The grants team was in semi-chaos when Bellos arrived. They were receiving hundreds of applications, and there were not enough people to process them. A backlog was building up, piles and piles of unread forms in an overcrowded department already notorious in County Hall for generating too much paper. On 10 August 1984 Jenni Fletcher of the women's committee admitted to *The Times* that the grants team had become 'extremely overworked . . . exhausted and emotional'. Otitoju worked in a related department, outreach, going out into London to make contact with women's organizations. She told me, 'The grants team – you didn't go there. They were absolutely swamped . . . It was awful for those of us who had encouraged women to apply, then sat up late at night with them, filling in the application forms.'

Bellos restored a degree of order. Lean, crop-haired, with large spectacles like Valerie Wise, but which sat disapprovingly halfway down her nose, Bellos was a fierce talker. In parallel with her political explorations she had worked at the Inland Revenue for five years. 'When I got to the GLC,' she told me, 'there was £17.3m that had been agreed for the women's unit, and most of it hadn't been spent. My target was to get the money out of the building – which meant that I had to get organizations ready to receive that money, in terms of their constitutions, employment practices.' She slipped into bureaucratese: 'Conditions of grant had to be met.' And then she extricated herself: 'Small groups of women on estates – they didn't know how to do that. I worked bloody hard. But I got the money out.'

Sometimes this involved dealing with the splits and tensions that ran through the women's movement and women in London generally. Bellos would encounter groups seeking grants who 'thought it was OK to be homophobic – not allow lesbians to be employed, that sort of thing'. But as the 1985 *GLC Women's Committee Information Pack* made clear, with a sternness about inclusivity that had yet to enter the wider British state bureaucracy, 'All projects funded are required to show what steps they have taken to make their activities accessible and suited to black and ethnic minority women, women with disabilities and lesbians.' Sometimes grants would be refused – or terminated.

But mostly the women's unit tried to see the best in female London. Along with three colleagues in the outreach team, Otitoju was given a GLC car – 'a zippy little Metro' – and an area of the capital to cover. 'I had south London. My job was to build alliances with the women of south London.' She laughed. 'What sort of remit is that? . . . A stupidly big remit. The women's unit said to me, "Go forth. And bring us women: get them to campaign and organize [locally] around the work of the unit." But it was also an *amazing* job. I was so lucky to have it – just the freedom. The unit saying to me, "However you get these women, bring them to us."'

County Hall had its own petrol pump for staff. To save time, Otitoju would get the attendant to fill her Metro right up, while she crammed the ingeniously spacious boot with boxes of leaflets about the women's committee, and surveys to be filled in, and application forms for grants, and posters and balloons for possible community events that the GLC might end up backing. Then, like Peter Turlik setting off to rescue Docklands in his Alfa Romeo, or even a little like a colonial district officer heading out to administer their territory – not a comparison the GLC would have welcomed – Otitoju would disappear into the green and grey immensity of largely working-class, often rather laddish south London. Being from north London, she found some of the geography baffling. 'I couldn't understand Kidbrooke' – a suburb near Greenwich dominated by an epic, multi-level council estate. 'If I got onto the estate, I couldn't get out! So I didn't do much work round Kidbrooke for ages.'

If possible, she would ring 'women who might be sympathetic' to GLC feminism beforehand: sometimes cold-calling them, sometimes using contacts: she had been hired by the women's unit partly for her connections. 'You'd say, "Can I come and see you? What are you doing for women locally? What else would you like to do?"' Once she had some leads, 'I was knocking on doors. I was sitting in women's centres. I was trying to explain what the GLC was – so it was a kind of evangelist's role as well. There was a little bit of suspicion sometimes. Women who knew of me, and of my type, were OK. But there were others who would go' – she dropped her voice to an apathetic drone – '"You're from the council."'

If the encounter went well, 'You'd introduce them to the grants team. Sign them up. Even if they didn't get substantive funding for an ongoing grant,' for a women's group or project, 'they might get money for an event, to celebrate children, some kind of ethnic minority day . . . It brought women together who were often isolated on big estates. And then sometimes they'd join in other things: we filled buses with women for women's committee campaigns. They'd get drawn into the wider GLC agenda.'

Otitoju worked on all this frenziedly. Even the loading of boxes of leaflets into her car: 'It was manic. You had to be fit to do that job!' Partly the urgency was down to the sheer size of her assigned territory. Partly it was her background: 'If you work around domestic violence, you have to get that woman out of the house *now*, and I think I went into the women's unit at the same sort of speed.'

But also she had a sense that things at the GLC were too good to last. 'You know that in local government there will be changes of political control.' With the London electorate evenly divided between Labour and the Conservatives, with the history of single-term GLC administrations, and with Livingstone's regime still intensely controversial and vulnerably constructed around a Labour faction, time felt as pressing for the women's unit as it did for the London Docklands Development Corporation and many other empire-builders in the early 1980s. Otitoju remembered: 'You felt, "Come on . . . this is our chance. Let's really go for it. How quickly can we build something that will stick for the long term?"'

In 1984, the *GLC Women's Committee Information Pack* proudly recorded, 'Nearly £11m was spent [by the committee] on over 500 grants . . . services and resources.' Of these, the committee 'funds

66 projects for, or run wholly or predominantly by, black and ethnic minority women, 4 for women or children with disabilities and three for lesbians'. In addition, 'The committee now funds more than 12 per cent of all full-time childcare places in London' – in 1984, as now, a precious commodity. The *Information Pack* emphasized, 'Over half [our] budget is spent on childcare projects.' All of this, the exhaustive publication went on, had been 'set in motion more quickly than could be done by a large organization'; had been conceived in a way that was 'more responsive to women's needs'; and had been overseen by a body that was 'based in the community, and run by women and for women'.

Yet there were legitimate questions to be asked about this revolution in social policy. Since the committee chose who and what to fund, and wrote the cheques, how fully was it empowering the women of London? Was it tactful of the County Hall professionals in the committee and women's unit to talk up the virtues of voluntary activity? As Maureen Mackintosh and Hilary Wainwright noted cuttingly in *A Taste of Power*, 'Many people found themselves giving up much unpaid time to work with well-paid GLC employees.'

And was there any meaningful difference between distributing money to groups whose working practices and mix of personnel the GLC approved of, and using that money to create supporters and activists for, as Otitoju put it to me, 'the wider GLC agenda'? The council's deputy leader John McDonnell told one of Livingstone's biographers, John Carvel, that 'within three months' of the grant system starting, 'Each constituency member [councillor] was realizing that the political returns were absolutely enormous.' Of course councils, like British governments, were allowed to implement politically advantageous policies; but they were not allowed to treat their income from taxpayers as party funds.

Finally, was the whole grant-giving experiment justifiable or sustainable in an age of state austerity? In 1983 one of the first grants officers on the women's committee, Kate Flannery, told *Spare Rib* that grants 'are a right to be demanded, not a privilege. Women as ratepayers and taxpayers have so far had a raw deal whenever local authorities have been handing out cash.' The second statement was hard to argue with – council-funded sports facilities, for example, tended to be male-oriented; but the first suggested some feminists had not yet realized that the fat years of the post-war state were over.

Fleet Street's many GLC-watchers were not much interested in these issues. They had cruder things to say about the women's committee. On 11 August 1984 a leader in the *Daily Telegraph* declared:

> Nobody can create equality for women, a fortiori [all the more] local government cannot create it. Noise can be made, pamphlets written . . . and the high screech of office politics of the most malignant kind may be indulged in. But what is the use of it? . . . Women's support units (not a happy title) . . . flourish on redistributed rate revenue like so many play groups . . . GLC undertakings of this sort are as much use as a GLC peace-keeping force for the Iran–Iraq war and just about as much within its province.

For sexist nudges (Women's support units!), sour misogyny ('high screech') and unthinkingly patronizing dismissals ('like so many play groups'), the *Telegraph* piece set quite a benchmark. But *Private Eye* frequently rivalled the paper for gentleman's-club sneers at the women's committee. A typical item on 7 October 1983 began:

> Nepotism and jobs for the comrades continue to be the watchwords at Our Ken's County Hall . . . the newly-formed Support Unit to the Women's Committee, it emerges, has recuited nothing but WIMMIN . . . [At] an open meeting called by Valerie 'Olive Oyl' Wise . . . several hundred screaming Wimmin conspired to wreck proceedings when the photographer requested by Ms Wise to record the proceedings for posterity turned out to be a MIN! The poor chap entered the hall to a torrent of abuse.

No matter that 'Ms Wise', or 'Miss Valerie Wise' as the *Telegraph* article called her, was actually married: to an optician, as was her mother – rather conventional, even bourgeois behaviour for a supposedly man-hating revolutionary. Facts were not the priority when it came to most press coverage of the women's committee. Nor was engagement with the social issues the committee was trying to address. On 21 February 1982, under the headline 'Red Ken Hands Out Cash With Gay Abandon', the *News of the World* approvingly quoted the crusty Tory right-winger, education minister and London MP Rhodes Boyson: 'The reality in London is madder than anything we could write for the stage.' The 'news' story continued, 'He said [GLC] grants included £750 to Lesbian Line and £8,000 for Women Against Rape.'

In the same saloon-bar spirit, *Private Eye* asked its readers to send in 'loony feminist nonsense'. Examples considered outrageous enough to print included a south London women's bicycling cooperative, set up in response to 'being patronized by men in bike repair shops'; and a logo for the works department of Sheffield city council, which was pursuing GLC-style policies on a more modest scale, featuring a woman in overalls holding a length of wood and a toolbox.

Given the leftie-bashing habits of most of the British press, and its preference for showing women with their clothes off rather than giving them senior jobs, the caricaturing of the women's committee did not come as a total shock at County Hall. 'Most of us had had some of it before the GLC: I'd been at Greenham,' said Otitoju. 'We were hurt by it, obviously . . . But we weren't really demoralized by it. After a while, we began to see that if the work that we were doing was making the front page, we were reaching women who might be interested. The papers mock the lesbian self-defence classes, but it means that lesbians get to hear about them.' Yet such rationalizations only drew the sting so far. When I first contacted Wise, over a quarter of a century after her involvement with the committee had ceased, and introduced myself as a writer who would give her a fair hearing, it took quite a few tiptoeing minutes on the phone to persuade her to meet. 'I can talk forever about the women's committee of the GLC,' she said with feeling. 'But I don't want to help people who just rubbish it.'

During the summer of 1984 the rubbishing reached a climax. In the same week that the government announced what the *Daily Telegraph* called a 'Clamp on Big-Spend Councils' – partisanly defined as the GLC and other Labour authorities – a two-day training retreat in Brighton for three dozen of the women's unit staff, costing a modest £2,250 in total, was given pages of forensic coverage in the Conservative papers. The women had travelled from London in a hired coach. They stayed, reported the *Telegraph* on 25 July, in the 'luxury'

Bedford Hotel – in reality a grey 1960s seafront tower. 'Use of a creche for two children who accompanied the group cost £15 a day.' The report went on: 'The group was easily identifiable among conference goers and holidaymakers milling in the hotel lobby. Spiky hair, boiler suits and sandles [*sic*] were de rigueur. They made an occasional sortie to the beach before breakfast or during the early afternoon, but most of the time remained in secret session in the second floor Arundel Room.'

The *Daily Mail* deployed a photographer with a long lens, and printed a sequence of pictures, in the style of police surveillance shots, of the women paddling, throwing stones into the sea, and chatting in the sunshine. Other reporters from the paper loitered in the corridors outside the women's 'twin' bedrooms, to see if there was any night-time 'naughtiness' from 'the girls', as a 24 July '*Daily Mail* Special' put it.

Amid all the innuendo and stereotyping and feigned outrage was the half-glimpsed outline of a much more important story. While the GLC blandly told the *Daily Mail* that the retreat was to help the women 'function effectively within their new teams and within the unit as a whole', on 23 July the paper quoted one of the staff of the unit itself. 'There have been arguments about the allocation of grants that have almost ended in blows,' the anonymous source said. 'A lot of people [in the unit] think they can achieve their ends by shouting . . . The Afro-Caribbeans dominate and the Asians have little to say in what goes on . . . The power struggle is still going on.'

In the crowded office of the women's unit, perhaps for the first time in Britain, a politics was being worked out and practised that sought to accommodate the full range of British identities. It was a process that was long overdue in a country that had been a hybrid place for centuries, but it was not proceeding smoothly. And it was producing consequences that were unsettling not just for conservatives but for left-wingers and liberals.

'It was very hierarchical in the women's unit,' Otitoju remembered. There was the official hierarchy: the team leaders, and the head of the unit, Louise Pankhurst, who was white and middle class – facts that would become increasingly significant. And then there was another hierarchy. 'Some of us brought our own power bases with us,' said Otitoju. She continued carefully: 'That is to say, we were unassailable in our communities. So you'd sit in a meeting, and ostensibly this person you were talking to was your superior. But actually you could mobilize forces that would . . . stop them doing something they wanted to do.' These 'forces' might be contacts or comrades beyond County Hall, in London feminism, or in other areas of activism. 'If something needed to be lobbied for, if a meeting needed to be . . . stormed – you could make that happen.'

This leverage depended not just on who you knew but on who you were. 'I was an out lesbian,' said Otitoju, 'and unlike Linda [Bellos] I was called a gold star lesbian, because I'd never married and never been in that kind of [heterosexual] relationship. Being black as well was just the icing on the cake. I had three of those equality points. In that room, it gave you currency . . . I was unassailable a lot of the time.' Even being called Femi seemed to underline her sisterhood credentials.

There was a bureaucratic logic to this elaborate identity politics. 'My little team consisted of me, the black, African woman; Shadnan, the Asian woman; Fay, who was the Irish woman; and Monica, the white, English woman. It was all very carefully engineered. The unit didn't have time to consult with every community, so it had better be representative.'

Meanwhile, entwined with all these status systems, was yet another: 'There were some women who'd joined the unit simply because they were already in the GLC . . . They were different from the women who'd come in as professional feminists. You didn't get currency from being a black woman if you were a black woman who came in after languishing over in . . . Parks or Licensing or something.'

Otitoju explained all this to me as if it was the most natural set of arrangements imaginable. It was 2013: May Day, the one day of the year when many left-wingers feel the world could still be remade to their specifications. We were in the office kitchen of Challenge Consultancy ('helping organizations embed equality and diversity'), a company Otitoju founded in 1988. The building that Challenge part-occupied was low and flaking, next to railway tracks in a prosaic north London suburb, but the company and its founder still had a confidence. The kitchen fridge was an expensive Smeg in shocking pink. The toilet handwash was pink. Otitoju was still active as an 'equality and human rights activist', on Twitter as @pinkfemi. 'I felt like an incredible creature by the time I came out of the GLC,' she told me, her women's-unit stare intact behind oval glasses. 'I was completely unstoppable.' Wearing a sharp black suit with white-trimmed, knife-like lapels, she still talked with dominating fluency.

What had she thought of Valerie Wise during their GLC days? She slipped into the first-person plural, as if speaking on behalf of a collective: 'Honestly, we didn't rate her. She didn't have a separate power base [outside County Hall]. You had to have someone in charge of the women's committee who was acceptable to the Labour party, and that wasn't going to be one of us. But you couldn't have somebody who was wholly one of them [the Labour mainstream]. So she suited everybody. She was malleable, if you got the right message to her.'

Other management figures in the women's unit or committee, who were more junior and less connected to Livingstone, often had their authority steadily undermined. Louise Pankhurst was one. Otitoju sighed. 'Everything was wrong with Louise. She didn't have a power base. She couldn't manage us, because she didn't really understand the politics.' Her voice softened with contempt: 'I'm sure that she would have *called* herself a feminist. But she wasn't the type of feminist that we were. She bought into the corporate, County Hall approach; whereas the rest of us were there to make County Hall different. So she didn't stand a chance. She might have had support when she went to meetings outside the unit, but at meetings in the unit the rest of us weren't there for her.'

In August 1984, halfway through a four-year contract, Pankhurst resigned as head of the unit. On the 10th, the London *Evening Standard* published fragments from a GLC report into the episode, which revealed frictions in the unit ranging from 'personal hostility' to internal allegations that Pankhurst had 'failed to tackle institutional racism'. Pankhurst told the *Standard* that she had been 'completely exonerated of all charges of racism'; but also that some of her experiences at the unit had been 'nightmarish'. The GLC report said that she had 'lacked help' from elsewhere in County Hall. It concluded: 'The policy, organization and operational difficulties with which she [Pankhurst] contended cannot be overstated.'

I asked Otitoju whether there had been a nasty atmosphere during

Pankhurst's final days. 'No,' she said, without emotion. 'It's not a nasty atmosphere when you have something undesirable cut off. You breathe a sigh of relief: it's done. Let's get on with the work at hand.'

After 1984 the women's unit and committee settled down in some ways. Valerie Wise herself turned thirty in 1985. She began to think more carefully about her public image. 'I was never a person that wore dungarees,' she told me. 'I dress appropriately to the role I'm carrying out. That's a working-class trait – my mum was always smart as an MP. But at first when I was on the women's committee I didn't have any suits.' She wore open-necked blouses and V-necked jumpers that made her look like a student politician. 'Then, when I was away at a Labour Party conference in Blackpool, I went to C&A and bought a couple of suits. I came back to London with a changed image.' Neat, always coordinated, with high-buttoned jackets and neck bows and frills, she looked a little like a younger Margaret Thatcher. 'You wouldn't have looked at me and thought, "Oh, she's a feminist."'

Fleet Street apart, the outside world began to regard the women's committee as less of an eccentric novelty. The Conservative GLC councillors ended their boycott of it, and a few became members. In 1985 Wise was invited to Scotland to speak about the committee's work, and ended up meeting seven different councils from Edinburgh to Kilmarnock. Edinburgh District Council had already set up a women's committee, and the *Glasgow Herald* photographed Wise with its chair, Val Woodward, in front of the City Chambers. Wise wore one of her most sensible suits, Woodward wore a practical tanktop, and against the stuffily magnificent Edinburgh buildings the two young women looked animated but quite at home, like municipal leaders of the future.

Back in London, Wise pushed through a scheme to give the women's committee a base – almost a kind of embassy – that was separate from County Hall. She found suitable premises on the broad boulevard between the barristers' quadrangles of Holborn and an increasingly buffed-up Covent Garden. 'I went and bought a building for a million pounds [£3 million now]. It felt very grand, buying a building on Kingsway.' The towering Victorian property, Wesley

House, a little gloomy and rundown, had previously been a Methodist mission, and had also housed 'the first full-time creche in Britain if not in Europe', the women's committee *Bulletin* excitedly noted. It had six floors and over fifty large rooms, including a lecture theatre. The committee envisaged the building housing GLC-backed women's organizations, hosting feminist public events and private activists' meetings, providing women with computer and printing facilities, concerts and other performances, perhaps a 'peace cafe', an 'alternative health centre', 'alternative feminist education' – a whole self-sustaining ecosystem of feminist activity. Readers of the *Bulletin* were asked for further suggestions, including a new name for the complex: 'We have long thought that Wesley House (after a male religious leader) or the Kingsway project (after a street named for a king)' – as the building had become informally known after the committee bought it – 'were not suitable.'

The committee eventually settled on the London Women's Centre – plain to the point of blandness, but cannily uncontroversial: a sign that the committee was becoming interested in feeding feminism more quietly into the bloodstream of British life. Builders were hired to refurbish the interior. Along with the originally envisaged amenities, a gym was installed, a video-editing suite and a Jacuzzi. It was announced that the centre would open 'by spring 1986'.

But before then the government intervened. Between 1983 and 1986 a Tory idea that had been around since the early 1970s – ever since Livingstone's Labour predecessor as GLC leader, Reg Goodwin, briefly threatened to upset the capital's established order – finally went from manifesto promise to law. As the Conservative 1983 general election manifesto put it: 'The Greater London Council [has] been shown to be a wasteful and unnecessary tier of government. We shall abolish [it].' Or as Norman Tebbit explained more frankly, and chillingly, in a speech to London Tories on 14 March 1984: 'The Labour Party ... in its present form ... represents a threat to the democratic values and institutions on which our parliamentary system is based. The Greater London Council is typical of this new, modern, divisive form of Socialism. It must be defeated. So, we shall abolish the GLC.'

Erasing London's elected government was hardly protecting British 'democratic values and institutions', and for the next three years the Livingstone administration fought an ingenious rearguard action against this transparently party-political policy. The GLC deployed all its PR flair. 'London's Not For Turning,' said one slogan on the County Hall roof, stealing Thatcher's catch-phrase, '74% Of Londoners Oppose GLC Abolition.' Red Ken recruited an army of unlikely allies, from peers and Tory backbenchers to right-wing tabloids. By September 1984 the usually Livingstone-phobic *Evening Standard* was describing the abolition plans as 'a hugely unpopular mess'.

Meanwhile the poll ratings for Livingstone and his administration went from awful to respectable to stronger than Thatcher's. A cartoon in the *Observer* on 1 July 1984 depicted him smashing a tennis ball insouciantly through her racquet – his moustache suddenly making him look like a tennis-club charmer rather than some beardless south London Che Guevara – as the prime minister was thrown backwards, off-balance, startled. After her twin victories in the Falklands and the 1983 election, she was not used to being outwitted or losing the initiative.

But in Britain governments with big majorities usually get what they want in the end. 'In the women's unit, there was this sense of foreboding,' remembered Otitoju. As abolition went from a possibility to a probability to a certainty, and a date for it was set – midnight on Easter Sunday, 31 March 1986 – so the already hectic work of the unit became frantic. In the outreach team, said Otitoju, 'We got bigger cars. I was given an estate, a great big white Ford – so I could put more GLC stuff in the boot to hand out.'

During the final days of the GLC, new office protocols raced along the long corridors of previously staid, by-the-book County Hall. 'It got a bit naughty,' said Otitoju. She produced a sly look: 'We *heard* a mandate: "Get whatever resources you can out of the building and into the community." Whether those words were actually said, that is how the message was received. Photocopiers disappeared – huge, almost room-sized photocopiers. Men in brown coats would come and take them away.' Where did she think they ended up? 'In some voluntary sector project.' In a sense, it was the grants revolution taken to its logical conclusion.

Two weeks before the GLC was abolished, Wise opened the London Women's Centre. With an enormous smile that hovered between delight and keeping up appearances, she stood holding a sheaf of papers, wearing one of her most Thatcher-like outfits, a ruffled blouse held in check by a strict jacket, in front of a huge dark plaque that read in lightly chiselled, non-macho white capitals: 'This building was developed as a resource for the women of London by the Greater London Council's Women's Committee. Opened by Valerie Wise 18 March 1986.'

She was thirty-one years old.

Epilogue: Whose Miracle?

In the bright, early spring of 1982, shortly before the Falklands War, I bought one of my first pop records. 'Promised You a Miracle' by Simple Minds was a shiny, repetitive strut of a single. Guitars jangled like jewellery. Disco drums popped and thumped. Keyboards splashed everything with frothy, liquid phrases. The singer chanted the title, which was also the chorus, right through the song from the first seconds – interrupted only by more drifting, ecstatic passages when the instruments blurred and he half-murmured a babble of tantalizingly cryptic, optimistic-sounding sentences. The one that stirred me most and stuck in my twelve-year-old head was 'Everything is possible.'

Simple Minds had started out in 1977 as a tinny Glasgow punk band called Johnny & The Self Abusers. They had come from the city's half-demolished, raucously left-wing dock hinterland, had changed their name, smartened up, and expanded and polished their sound – all the usual moves for the unusual glut of clever, upwardly mobile pop musicians as the 1970s turned into the 1980s. Yet for half a decade they had impressed music journalists much more than record buyers. Before 'Promised You a Miracle' they had released nine flop singles, and I had never heard of any of them.

But I saved up for the extended, more expensive twelve-inch version regardless. In February 1982 the song became Simple Minds' first hit, in Britain and six other countries from Sweden to New Zealand. Later that year it became part of their first top-ten album. The title of the euphoric, expansive LP seemed even more in tune with the country Britain was becoming: *New Gold Dream (81-82-83-84)*.

I never got round to buying it, or any of their two dozen

subsequent hits. But I held onto the single. In some ways, it looks and sounds pretty good still, in its creamy, marble-effect sleeve, overlaid with strips of blurred photo-collage and blocky 1980s computer digits. These days there are references to early Simple Minds in the songs and reviews of rated bands such as The Horrors and The War on Drugs. You can hear whole mornings of grandiose early 1980s British pop in the hipster cafés of Dalston in east London. I live just up the road, and if I took my unscratched twelve-inch to one of the knowingly analogue music shops that thrive there, I might get more than I paid for it.

Yet in other ways 'Promised You a Miracle' has aged less well. In the video, a blank silent blonde in heavy lipstick and an aristocratic tweed jacket saunters through airport security, then sunbathes alone on a beach. The band – all gawkily handsome young men – bob earnestly over their instruments, except for the singer, bare-chested except for a scarf, who crouches and writhes imploringly on another stretch of sand as he mimes the words, tormented, heroic. The gender roles feel old-fashioned, even by pop video standards. The frantically changing backdrops look like an early *Dr Who* set, stagey and cheap. The tune, for all its impetus, doesn't really go anywhere; it just repeats, and then protractedly fades.

After 'Promised You a Miracle', Simple Minds' hits became steadily more bombastic and broad-brush: sketches for stadiums of fans to fill in. By the late 1990s – a great run but not outstanding for a famous band – the hits had dwindled away.

Sometimes during the research for this book, I wondered whether the same had happened to the rest of Britain's early 1980s miracle – or whether the miracle had even happened at all. In the dark, late spring of 2012, I spent an afternoon looking for the Metro car factory. When I got off the train at Longbridge in thick noon rain, there was nothing but levelled red soil mixed with broken bricks and a few new office buildings. Where the car-making hub of Birmingham and Britain had once extended for miles, there was now a sign: 'New Longbridge Town Centre. Outstanding Retail and Restaurant Opportunities'.

Eventually, I came across a chipped and bent metal gate that was still painted in the corporate pale blue of the Austin Rover Group, the state-owned conglomerate formed in the early 1980s to produce the Metro and other models. A muddy lane disappeared downhill beyond it, through scrappy young woods sliced by old industrial culverts, towards what I estimated was the site of the New West Works, the purpose-built Metro factory that Prince Charles opened in 1980. As I walked down the gently curving lane, trying to keep out of the worst of the mud, huge rain-slicked dumper trucks loaded with red rubble kept roaring round the corner towards me. After dodging half a dozen, I reached another gate. Through it, uphill in the near distance, was a long high bank of the same rubble, like an ancient hill fort; and behind the bank, hidden from most vantage points, an immense wet apron of concrete. A small set of ruined steps and a single thick industrial tap poked up from one of its edges. A few painted factory-floor markings still ran across it in purposeful diagonals. A lone, moaning yellow digger swivelled back and forth on top of the bank, relentlessly filling more dumper trucks. Otherwise, there was nothing happening at the former New West Works except seagulls picking through the puddles.

'Longbridge now – it breaks your heart,' Tony Ball, who marketed the Metro for Austin, told me. 'But there is one consolation. Although we don't have a British motor industry any more, through the Metro we were instrumental in bringing the world's motor industry to Britain.' He began listing all the foreign companies with British plants, from BMW in Oxford to Nissan in Sunderland. Then he went back to his treasured Metro: 'What we were doing, as part of our patriotic thing – a British Car to Beat the World – was saying to the foreign manufacturers, "Hey, we don't want your finished cars coming to Britain. Set up here, and we'll do a good job of building them."' He gave an example. During the late 1970s and early 1980s, as well as promoting the Metro as the answer to all the problems of the British car industry, and commissioning the TV ad which suggested that the Metro would stop the country being 'invaded . . . by the Japanese', he was also, he said, 'out in Japan a lot . . . trying to secure an arrangement with Honda to bring some of their robotic technology to build a car entirely in this country: the Triumph Acclaim, which was based on the Honda Ballade.'

But didn't that make the Metro campaign basically dishonest? In the expensive glass office in London where we were talking, a long way from Longbridge, Ball dropped his voice. 'It was treading on eggs. You had to be very, very diplomatic. But it was a recognition on our part, that you had to involve the people who had the wherewithal to make manufacturing at a higher level of quality.' The 'British Car to Beat the World' was not so much the beginning of something as the beginning of the end.

Other voids left where the great arenas of the early 1980s had been were more uplifting. When I first went to Greenham Common in 2011, the cruise missiles and most of the military perimeter were long gone. The runways had been dug up. The United States Air Force had departed with their awful armoury in the early 1990s, as the Cold War thawed. The peace camp, praised for its part in the latter by the Soviet leader Mikhail Gorbachev, had been finally wound up in 2000.

On the site of the airbase, people were rolling prams and walking dogs across a sunlit upland of wild flowers and gorse, as if enacting one of the most madly optimistic fantasies from the 1981 peace march. The one part of the former base that remained closed off was the missile silos. They still had menace, crouching and enormous inside their webs of densely meshed fencing, their exteriors seemingly little altered. But the sign on the fence said 'Scheduled Ancient Monument'.

'I go to Greenham now to forage for funghi,' Ann Pettitt told me. We were strolling along a valley below the smallholding in Wales where she had first thought of the peace march. She and her partner Barry still lived in the farmhouse, its renovation long finished, a lovely, cosy vision of red and black floor tiles, bottling jars and home-made flapjacks, an Aga. In the shaggy garden, she had a painting studio in an outbuilding, and two hens were up a tree. There was the air of hippyish lefties in satisfied retirement.

'The last time I went to Greenham,' Pettitt continued, 'I stood there looking at this two-year-old – he was right by the silos on a red tricycle. I went to the peace camp in 1981 with one of my sons once, when he was a two-year-old with a red tricycle. When I saw the boy on the tricycle this time, I felt immensely glad. It's a wonderful public space now.' We had stopped in a strip of late afternoon sunlight, and she was silent for a second. Then she terminated the Hollywood moment. 'They should turn it into a Cold War theme park,' she said, her usual irreverent glint returning. 'Fibre-glass cruise missiles on transporters. And the Maggie Thatcher and Ronald Reagan *Spitting Image* puppets looming up in the woods.'

That evening, as she drove me to the station, her talk ranged freely for an hour in the racing country darkness. She and Barry, both in their sixties, were still working, making bespoke tiles and kitchens respectively – in their entrepreneurship Margaret Thatcher would have sensed a victory – but business was thin, as the Iron Lady's careless imitators in the coalition government made a mess of the economy. 'Barry is laying off workers. I've had no orders for weeks. That's why I've got time to see you.'

'Margaret Thatcher – you could admire some aspects of her thinking,' Pettitt continued. 'The trade unions *were* undemocratic. Barry and I were in the Labour party then. Awful meetings in Carmarthen. I could see they were making themselves pretty unelectable. And they weren't capable of putting the argument for nuclear disarmament forcefully enough to the public.'

What did she think about the situation with nuclear weapons now? 'It's less scary than in the 80s. But Cruise, Pershing, the SS20: those are the only weapons that have been destroyed completely. Yet nukes as an issue? Politically, it's dead.' And nuclear power? She had changed her mind since the 1980s, she said matter-of-factly. 'Less environmental damage than renewables.'

We moved onto weaponry and wars in general. 'I was at Greenham in '82 when the Falklands happened,' she said. 'You gradually realized that we were at the peace camp with our perspective, but the rest of the country . . . was right behind her.' A few months before I saw Pettitt, another Conservative prime minister, David Cameron, had ordered another risky military campaign in a location where vital British interests were not obvious: Libya. Like the Falklands, the 2011 Libyan war, after a slow start and widespread domestic doubt, had been won in a few months. Colonel Gaddafi, 2011's General Galtieri, a vain army despot who made a perfect villain for the keyboard warriors of the British press, had been killed the week before Pettitt and I met. She told me she had supported the war. 'As a humanitarian intervention,' she explained. And she would support further British wars if they had that justification. The founder of the Greenham Common peace campaign then left me at Swansea station.

The ease with which modern Britain goes to war is largely a legacy of the early 1980s. So much of what seemed extraordinary during the Falklands – Parliament recalled, bombing raids launched, British personnel actually fighting, rather than practising or peacekeeping, as most of them had been doing for most of the previous quarter century – is now such a regular and familiar ritual as to be almost invisible, at least to those not directly involved or not following current affairs. My father retired from the army decades ago, but he still complains to me, as he first did during the Falklands, about politicians who think soldiers can save them from their foreign-policy problems. Soon there won't be any serving soldiers left who can remember the less bellicose Britain of the 1960s and 1970s.

The early 1980s also changed the British landscape. 'When I first came to London it seemed a great deal like Lancashire, where I'd come from,' the pop musician John Foxx, the original singer of Ultravox, told the cultural critic Mark Fisher in 2014:

> Lancashire had fallen into ruin. The factories had closed . . . I grew up playing in empty factories, huge places which were overgrown . . . I went to Shoreditch [in east London], in 1982, and made a studio there.
>
> When we first went into the studio building it had trees growing out of the windows on the upper storeys . . . That whole area was derelict, had been abandoned.

Not many would say east London and Lancashire feel the same now. Industrial ruins still stick up like dinosaur bones in Pennine towns, and across other neglected, depopulating, Thatcher-damaged corners of northern England, from Liverpool to Middlesbrough. But since the early 1980s east London, and London in general, has diverged so far from this downward path that it is a commonplace to say it might be a different country.

In 1981, 6.6 million people lived in the capital, the lowest number for three-quarters of a century. At some point early in the 1980s the decline stopped, and then went into reverse. By the next census, in 1991, London's population had grown for the first time since the

Second World War. It has risen ever since, faster and faster. By 2050, according to a 2014 report by the cocky administration of mayor Boris Johnson, the population will be 11 million, cementing the capital's place as Europe's pre-eminent city. Until the early 1980s few post-war politicians and planners dreamt of London becoming that.

At Canary Wharf in the lunch hour, when the bankers pour out of their thick glass towers, and the wide gleaming floors of the ever-multiplying malls can barely cope with the river of striding, clacking, male and female, multi-ethnic, British and foreign, young, habitually suited London, as it looks for a sandwich that costs the same as three in Preston, and perhaps nips into the Porsche accessories shop afterwards – so you can feel the modern dominance of the capital at its most exhilarating and least subtle, a dominance that was partly established right here, by the bulldozing Isle of Dogs visionaries of the London Docklands Development Corporation.

For some people who know its story intimately, this new British landscape is a disaster. When I contacted Bob Colenutt, the LDDC's old 1980s foe, who was still campaigning against socially callous London planners and developers three decades later, he said he would meet me anywhere, 'as long as we don't go anywhere near the Isle of Dogs. To go there makes me physically sick. It is a place of defeat.' Canary Wharf makes it crushingly clear that the sleepier, kinder Britain which Thatcherism and its converts began to demolish in the early 1980s is mostly gone for good.

In the *Phaidon Architecture Guide: Docklands* (1993), Stephanie Williams writes, 'Nowhere has the changing economic structure of Britain in the late 20th century had such a dramatic impact on the built environment.' The result is:

> one of the worst collections of late 20th century buildings to be seen anywhere in the world . . . massed so closely, and incongruously . . . one plastic-looking facade against another . . . a boomtown of overheated development . . . a whole new city centre.

From his delicate Georgian home just to the west in Limehouse, David Owen has watched it go up. In a sense, during the 1980s every crass and shiny new arrival on his eastern horizon was a sign, like profits on a bar graph, that Thatcherism was strengthening and that his rival solution to Britain's troubles, the SDP, would soon be running out of political customers. At the 1983 election, with Roy Jenkins as party leader, the SDP and their Liberal allies won a combined 25.4 per cent of the vote and twenty-three seats – a disappointment after all his 'bweakthwoo' talk in 1981 and 1982. But the SDP was never so successful again.

'I never really believed that we would break through,' Owen insisted to me. 'I believed that politics is a long, hard grind.' His tastefully artisanal living-room coffee table was covered in neatly stacked policy journals, which he still read and contributed to as a lone 'independent social democrat' peer at the age of seventy-four. 'I always thought our epitaph would be that we changed the Labour Party' – into the centrist, pro-capitalist, SDP-ish party that was built during the 1980s and 1990s by Neil Kinnock and Tony Blair.

We went out onto one of Owen's riverside terraces for a breather. Seeing Canary Wharf looming overbearingly in the near distance, I asked him what he thought of it. He paused for quite a few seconds. 'Err . . . It is not my taste,' he finally said. 'But they maintain it terribly well. It's like Montreal.'

Even Peter Turlik, ex-LDDC, had regrets about the development. 'We had to be realistic, and get what we could for the Isle of Dogs,' he told me. 'But I find Canary Wharf alienating. It's quite foreign-looking. It's not consolidated enough with the rest of London. If you go to Paris, they've built that whole [office] complex at La Défense. But Paris itself hasn't been harmed.' He also worried that the owners of Canary Wharf were making a similar mistake to the nineteenth-century speculators who filled the Isle of Dogs with docks and little else. 'If I was the landlord of Canary Wharf,' he said, 'with predominantly financial services companies as tenants, I'd think, "We need to diversify."' When the 158-year-old American firm Lehman Brothers went bankrupt during the last financial crisis, its European headquarters was at Canary Wharf.

For the wider British economy, more banking is one early 1980s remedy that looks less shrewd now. Property ownership may be another. In 2014 the proportion of English homes lived in by owner-occupiers fell to 63 per cent, the lowest percentage since 1985. The figure has been dropping for 11 years, as property prices and wages for most people have moved in ever more incompatible directions. In 2015, the trade magazine *Inside Housing* reported that nearly 40 per cent of council flats sold in England since the early 1980s were now being let out again – but by private landlords, and at much less affordable rents than in their time as municipal properties. State spending on housing benefit has ballooned accordingly. Much of the Right to Buy revolution, revered though it still is by political strategists and historians, and however hard the current Conservative government may try to revive it by extending it to housing association tenants, has effectively unravelled.

Meanwhile even some who got on the bandwagon in time have discovered downsides to their appreciating assets. The Right to Buy turned tenants into leaseholders. Councils retained the freeholds to the properties, and with it what you might call the Right to Charge – for exterior maintenance and major repairs to blocks of flats, and for supplying common services used by both owners and tenants. In 2012 I met a tired-looking man at a party who worked in the housing department of the east London borough of Tower Hamlets. He told me that his borough, still one of the capital's poorest, and still patchily carpeted with miles of council estates, was full of pensioners who had exercised their Right to Buy in their more prosperous younger days, and now lived in fear of an unaffordable repair notice from the council. 'We're still really their landlord,' he said, with resignation. Britons' ties to the state were not so easily shed as many Thatcherites imagined.

But surely the early 1980s property revolution produced some unambiguous winners? In 2012 I went to the model Docklands estate that Michael Heseltine opened in 1982, Savage Gardens, expecting to find some. At first as I poked around the villagey squares and cul-de-sacs, the little houses looked as appealing as in the old newspaper cuttings. People had maintained their homely porches and gables. Their gardens had filled out.

It was a weekday mid-afternoon, grey and still, and there were only a few residents about. All the ones I spoke to were from Russia. The fact that they lived on an estate that had been built as a Thatcherite prototype when their country was still Soviet began to seem a good metaphor for capitalism's victory over communism. But none of them had lived at Savage Gardens for long or knew anything about its history.

I was about to leave when two reverberating East End voices strode round the corner. Pat and Jenny were in their fifties, in matching sportswear with anoraks tied round their waists, and had lived on the estate from the beginning. The development had turned out pretty well, I suggested to them. They looked astonished. 'There's no space at all,' said Pat. 'There's not enough room for all the cars. The rooms are too small. All I can get in my lounge is a two-seater.' Jenny interrupted: 'In the show home, they had mirrors and no doors, to make the rooms look bigger. Cupboard space is minimal. We both had to throw so much away. When we moved in, the removals lorry took more away than it left!' Pat added: 'The gardens are very, very small. There's no privacy – it's like living in a goldfish bowl.' I asked whether there was anything good about the houses. 'They're very warm,' said Pat. Jenny said, 'It was nice when we first moved in – peaceful. After we bought the houses, before they were finished, every week or so we'd come round to see what new things they'd installed. There was a list of extras you could have.'

Pat broke in: 'But it sinks! Because it's marsh! The garden walls, the road over there, where the puddle is' – she pointed – 'it's sunk!' I looked at the puddle. It was inches deep, not a pothole – the surface of the road was intact – but a sort of minature sinkhole. Then I noticed that the pavements too were startlingly uneven. Every few dozen yards, random sections of paving stones or brick suddenly rose or fell, sometimes at 45-degree angles. Exploring the estate earlier, I had stumbled puzzlingly often but had been peering too hard at the houses to work it out. Lots of the garden walls were also falling apart. Inch-wide cracks zigzagged through some; others were simply shearing off from the backs of the houses.

Pat and Jenny walked off, still grumbling. 'It's terrible, the way it's sinking,' said Pat to no one in particular. There was little sign on the estate of any repairs, but the two women, for all their dissatisfactions, had stayed for three decades anyway, in the landscape Thatcherism built, unable or unwilling to try something else. Like the rest of us, you could say.

Ten months later I went to Thatcher's funeral. On the bus from Hackney, which was the usual morning scrum of competitive modern London, only one person was reading any of the Thatcher coverage, which had plumped the papers for a week but had little to say about her other than that she saved or wrecked the country – rather than both, perhaps, or neither. The man was wearing a flat cap and had a copy of the *Sun*, her old press muscle, but his cap was a hipster appropriation and he was young, snappily dressed, Afro-Caribbean. He lingered over the paper's reprint of the funeral order of service for thirty seconds, then turned the page to 'We Celebrate Blue Blood's Boobs'. It was an adaptation of a feature from *Tatler*. The magazine had shed a certain subtlety since its early 1980s glory days.

Along the funeral procession route on the Strand an hour before it started, as many people were rushing to work as were securing spots behind the thinly lined police barriers. I bought a delicious coffee from a cart in a churchyard – Thatcherism made British consumer capitalism more pleasurable and ingenious, and more unthinkingly ubiquitous – and chose a vantage point opposite another church, St Clement Danes, where her coffin was to be unloaded from a hearse and transferred onto a gun carriage. In public at least, she was never a subtle politician: in many ways that was her great power. The amount her success as prime minister owed to the Falklands War and the military was trumpeted by the procession's choreography, which featured a parade of guns and uniforms absent from the funerals I had attended for her less warrior-like Downing Street predecessors, Edward Heath and James Callaghan. St Clement Danes is the official church of the Royal Air Force. As I waited for the hearse under a lid of barely moving clouds, I also realized it was the venue for another patriotic funeral, for Harold Abrahams in the first and last scenes of *Chariots of Fire*.

The crowd that collected around the church, half a dozen deep and pressing in close, was not big enough to block the pavement. People wore country and Home Counties clothes: tweed, Barbours, quilted jackets. A few wore old-style City pinstripes. There were more men than women, a lot of people over fifty, and a decent chatter of tourists. Everyone I saw was white. Quite a few had well-off winter tans. I heard nobody speak in a northern accent. Most of the Britons in the crowd did not speak at all. They looked like Thatcherism's long-term supporters and winners, lost in their own thoughts.

Thatcher had died at the Ritz. She had been living in a suite for three months, the nightly cost of which, according to the *Daily Mail*, was 'up to £3,660'. Hushed, claustrophobically gold-trimmed, with staff in epaulettes and the oligarchs and hedge funds of Mayfair directly across the road – the Thatcherite makeover of Britain taken to its logical conclusion – the hotel was 'one of her favourite places', the *Mail* reported. During her infirm final days, 'She was invited by its owners the Barclay brothers to stay there for the foreseeable future.' The *Mail* speculated, 'Lady Thatcher may have been paying for the [suite] at a reduced rate or getting it for free.'

The route of her funeral procession was also over-rich in symbolism. It passed some of the places where Thatcherism's fate was decided in the early 1980s: Covent Garden, where her vital, inadvertent allies the SDP officially launched, and where Ron Arad began to turn post-war discards into designs for millionaires; and Fleet Street, which helped sell her backfiring first government and Falklands gamble to doubting Britons. The procession followed some of the path of the 1982 Falklands victory parade. Both processions ended at St Paul's, in the City of London – her most contentious beneficiary.

The hearse appeared. The crowd tightened, and a sudden clammy breeze blew up the Strand. After the coffin had been carried into the church, a military band somewhere in the distance played 'Jerusalem', the same song that soared over the church in the final scene of *Chariots of Fire*. I felt a prickle of sadness, despite myself. Then I reflected that British patriotism has a pretty limited official repertoire.

I followed the coffin on its gun carriage towards St Paul's, taking the backstreets with part of the crowd, some of them clapping, some of them running. The previous year, the activists of Occupy London had surrounded the cathedral for four and a half months, with their carnival of demands that the version of capitalism Thatcher had helped make possible be abolished or at least reformed. The protest had got so much media interest, some surprisingly sympathetic, that it had just seemed possible that a change in the political weather was under way. But by the time her coffin entered St Paul's, not a shred of the Occupy stickers or a letter of their graffiti remained. All the money-lenders' buildings around the cathedral had been scrubbed clean.

When the funeral was over, I walked north through the City, back towards Hackney. As soon as I got two or three blocks away from the cathedral, there were bankers on the pavements as usual, fetching lunch-hour sushi and burritos. It was barely noon, but since the 1980s the City has started work early. The sun had come out, it was suddenly spring, and people seemed a little carefree. There was no sense of London paused in contemplation, as there had been when Thatcher's idol and role model, Winston Churchill, was given a state funeral half a century earlier. In a busier, more cosmopolitan, less political age, we are less inclined to notice how much big leaders have changed us.

Two days after the funeral, I did my interview with Valerie Wise. She was living in the Lancashire countryside outside Preston, in a large but dim cottage, not in a village but beside a busy road. Since the GLC, she had gradually but not completely withdrawn from public scrutiny. During her thirties and forties she had tried to make an orthodox political career in the Labour Party. She missed out on a succession of parliamentary candidacies. 'I was always beaten by left-wing men,' she told me, her brightness deserting her for once. In the mid-1990s she became leader of Preston council, and ran an attention-getting, GLC-style administration that campaigned for equal opportunities and against domestic violence. But her style did not fit the city's more traditional Labour politics, and she was ousted after eighteen months. Since then she has been chief executive of a respected small charity, Preston Domestic Violence Services.

'I sometimes feel I've under-achieved,' she said, with her usual jolting frankness, almost as soon as we met. 'I can run an organization. I could've been a minister.' Later she said of the GLC women's committee: 'They were the best four years of my life.' After we had talked for hours in her underlit living room, she took me upstairs to a study stacked to the ceiling with box files of committee publications and papers. Yet at the desk was a more unexpected relic: a silvery metal folding chair, more solid and expensive-looking than such chairs usually are, with a large logo embossed on the backrest. The logo was an adaptation of the female Venus symbol, with what looked like two cupped hands holding a small sphere inside the original circle. The effect was slightly 1960s hippy, slightly 1970s sci-fi – especially in the shiny metal, it might have been the emblem of some interstellar empire on *Blake's Seven*. In fact it was the official logo of the women's committee. It was devised by 'a woman in the GLC Design Team' and 'chosen by a panel of women', the committee *Bulletin* reported in February 1983. Wise assured me that the chair still functioned perfectly.

According to the catalogue of the Women's Library in London, the committee's other physical legacy, the London Women's Centre, was 'demolished in 1998 to make way for a hotel'. But one lunchtime when I wanted a change from the library I decided to go to the site anyway, and see if there was anything to be gleaned.

The building was still there. The GLC plaque had gone, and so had any trace that I could see of the address's brief feminist heyday – except, perhaps, for some walls in upbeat 1980s colours in its deserted basement café. The complex had become a business college, an outcome that would have pleased Margaret Thatcher more than the GLC. Only the café and a scuffed stairwell were public. When I asked at reception if I could have a quick look around the rest, I was given a phone number to call. The young-sounding man who answered had never heard of the GLC, let alone the London Women's Centre, and said that permission should be requested in writing. Before I left, wondering whether to bother, I had a last look at the café and stairwell. There was an ornate wooden door leading off the stairs that I had assumed was locked. This time I gave it a push.

A deep rectangular room opened out: a small lecture theatre, with a stage at one end. The room was empty and dim, with rows of dark wooden desks facing the stage. And behind the desks, glowing in the half-light, like an assembly of ghosts, or aliens, were the silvery, skull-shaped logos and backrests of a roomful of women's committee chairs.

Up close, the chairs were rusty in places, but they still felt firm and folded smoothly. And like the room they were clean and purposefully arranged: they were still being used. The business college was an outpost of a Welsh university, and after three years of Conservative and Liberal Democrat austerity, and three decades of intermittent skimping by governments of all the main parties, the British state was increasingly living off the more generous provision of the post-war years, of which the GLC women's committee was one of the last examples.

But the committee had also been the start of something. Outside the lecture theatre, on one of the college's grimy walls, were a couple of posters advertising its business courses. Beaming, improbably enthusiastic students crowded the photographs. Almost all of them were women, and of different races. It was a completely generic and uncontentious modern panorama. In the early 1980s it would have been an outrageous GLC leaflet.

In those years Britain had a burst of energy. Some of its effects are wearing off now – or wore off long ago. Some of them, not always noticed, are still rippling outward.

Acknowledgements

First, I would like to thank these people for talking to me, and for telling me things that weren't in the books: Ron Arad, Tony Ball, Eran Bauer, Linda Bellos, Bob Colenutt, David Cooksey, Anna Coote, Peter Donebauer, Danny Dorling, Norman Duckworth, John Fowler, Martin Fry, David Graham, Michael Heseltine, Steve Hewlett, Mark Hollingsworth, John Hoskyns, Geoffrey Howe, Hugh Hudson, Judith Hunt, Stuart Innes, Jeremy Isaacs, Jimi Jagne, Helen John, Nigel Lawson, Ken Livingstone, Nick Logan, Gerry Miller, Patrick Minford, Paul Morley, John Nott, David O'Keefe, Femi Otitoju, David Owen, Ann Pettitt, Nancy Poole, David Puttnam, Phil Redmond, David Rhodes, Danny Silverstone, Norman Tebbit, Peter Turlik, John Turner, Nigel Vinson, Michael Ward and Valerie Wise. I'm sorry that I didn't have room for all their wildly varying perspectives. Other interviewees preferred not to be named; but I am very grateful to them.

I would also like to thank these authors, whose books (detailed in the list of sources) were particularly valuable: Anthony Barnett, Alastair McLellan and Rob Steen, Martin Middlebrook, Ann Pettitt and Simon Reynolds. I would like to thank Kathleen Dixon at the British Film Institute; the staff of the British Library's Social Science and Science 2 reading rooms; and Louis and Shaun at Noble Espresso for helping me through the library's slower afternoons.

Alex Butterworth, Adam Curtis, Charlotte Higgins, Dan Hillman, Stuart Kerr, Paul Laity, Conrad Leach, Tim Marsh and Jenny Turner all helped refine my thoughts about the early 1980s, and sometimes usefully made me talk about something else. Larry Elliott helped me to (sort of) understand monetarism. Ian Katz, Mark Oliver, Dan

Roberts and Emily Wilson helped me get to the Falkland Islands. Phil Jones and Paddy Blagden briefed me pithily before I went. In Port Stanley, Arlette Betts and Robert Rowlands kindly steered me through the minefields of Falklands history and psychology; and my travelling companion Martin Argles helped me, occasionally, not to take it all too seriously.

In Gastard in Wiltshire, Octavian Vaults generously let me look around their underground empire. In the Isle of Dogs in London, E. Klein & Co. arranged an impromptu tour of their riverside one. At the *Guardian*, Melissa Denes, Becky Gardiner, Tim Lusher, Malik Meer and Katharine Viner helpfully gave me commissions with early 1980s elements.

My editors at Penguin, Helen Conford and Tom Penn, have been consistently encouraging, challenging, full of ideas about the early 1980s, and fun to meet up with. Their offices have also been handy for one of the period's key locations, Covent Garden. Richard Mason copyedited with great patience what I wrote about such places.

I would also like to thank my agent Sarah Chalfant, for her strategic thinking, intense interest in this book's subject, and for being so generous about the manuscript at a crucial moment. Her colleague at The Wylie Agency, Alba Ziegler-Bailey, also treated this project with great care and energy.

Jean Holloway, Richard Holloway, Elizabeth Beckett and Robert Milnes helped me to maintain a writing schedule during school holidays and at other times that Margaret Thatcher might have been proud of. Lorna and Gillen, by being so lovely and engrossing, made sure that my real working habits remained a bit more social democratic. Anne and Clive backed me in more ways than they know. And Sara gave me the support and advice you can only get from the best ex-editor in Britain. If it was not always taken, well, that's the early 1980s for you: a touch reckless.

Bibliography

SOURCES

These were the sources I found most useful. Those that contributed to more than one chapter are listed by their first relevance. Newspaper and magazine references not given here are in the main text. All the national government documents cited are in the National Archives.

PROLOGUE: RON'S CHAIR

Arad, Ron, author interview, 10 September 2013

British Design 1948–2012: Innovation in the Modern Age, London: Victoria and Albert Museum, 2012

Collings, Matthew, *Ron Arad Talks to Matthew Collings*, London: Phaidon, 2004

Halsey, A. H., and Josephine Webb, *Twentieth-Century British Social Trends*, Basingstoke: Macmillan, 1999

Postmodernism: Style and Subversion 1970–1990, London: Victoria and Albert Museum, 2011

Ron Arad: Restless, London: Barbican Art Gallery, 2010

Social Trends, London: HMSO, 1982, 1983, 1984, 1985, 1986, 1987, 1988

Sudjic, Deyan, *Ron Arad: Restless Furniture*, London: Fourth Estate, 1989

INTRODUCTION: 'A SMALL NUMBER OF DETERMINED PEOPLE'

Bellini, James, *Rule Britannia: A Progress Report for Domesday 1986*, London: Jonathan Cape, 1981

Clarke, Peter, and Clive Trebilcock (editors), *Understanding Decline: Perceptions and Realities of British Economic Performance*, Cambridge: Cambridge University Press, 1997

Collins, Bruce, and Keith Robbins (editors), *British Culture and Economic Decline*, London: Weidenfeld and Nicolson, 1990

English, Richard, and Michael Kenny (editors), *Rethinking British Decline*, Basingstoke: Macmillan Press, 2000

Gamble, Andrew, *Britain in Decline: Economic Policy, Political Strategy and the British State*, London: Macmillan 1981

Harris, Robin, *Not For Turning: The Life of Margaret Thatcher*, London: Corgi, 2014

Olson, Mancur, *The Rise and Decline of Nations: Economic Growth, Stagflation and Social Rigidities*, London: Yale University Press, 1982

Policy Unit Response To 'It Took a Riot', PREM 19/578

Raban, Jonathan, *Coasting*, London: Picador, 1986

Thatcher, Margaret, *The Revival of Britain: Speeches on Home and European Affairs 1975–1988*, London: Aurum, 1989

Theroux, Paul, *Kingdom by the Sea: A Journey Round the Coast of Great Britain*, London: Hamish Hamilton, 1983

Wiener, Martin J., *English Culture and the Decline of the Industrial Spirit, 1850–1980*, Cambridge: Cambridge University Press, 1981

CHAPTER 1: A BRITISH CAR TO BEAT THE WORLD

A British Car to Beat the World, London: Leo Burnett, 1980

Ball, Tony, author interview, 23 April 2012

British Leyland in Crisis: Defend the Unions Stop the Sabotage, London: Militant, November 1979

Broadbent, Simon (editor), *The Leo Burnett Book of Advertising*, London: Business, 1984

Dymock, Eric, *Rover: The First Ninety Years 1904–1994*, Torksey: Dove Publishing Ltd., 2013

East Anglian Daily Times, 5 August 1980

Edwardes, Michael, *Back from the Brink: An Apocalyptic Experience*, London: Collins, 1983

Ipswich Evening Star, 5 August 1980

Miller, Gerry, author interview, 23 April 2012

Robson, Graham, *Metro: The Book of the Car*, Cambridge: Patrick Stephens, 1982

Robson, Graham, *The Rover Story*, Cambridge: Patrick Stephens, 1981

CHAPTER 2: THE YEAR OF FLAGS

Botham, Ian, *Botham: My Autobiography*, London: CollinsWillow, 1994
Botham, Ian, *The Incredible Tests*, London: Sphere, 1981
Botham's Ashes: The Miracle of Headingley '81, BBC DVD, 2005
Bradford, Sarah, *Diana*, London: Viking, 2006
Brearley, Mike, *Phoenix from the Ashes: The Story of the England–Australia Series 1981*, London: Unwin, 1982
Campbell, Beatrix, *Diana, Princess of Wales: How Sexual Politics Shook the Monarchy*, London: Women's Press, 1998
Chariots of Fire, Enigma Productions, 1981
Dimbleby, Jonathan, *The Prince of Wales: A Biography*, London: Little, Brown, 1994
Hill, John, *British Cinema in the 1980s: Issues and Themes*, Oxford: Oxford University Press, 1999
Hudson, Hugh, author interview, 26 April 2012
Jarman, Derek, *The Last of England*, London: Constable, 1987
Kipps, Charles, *Out of Focus: Power, Pride and Prejudice – David Puttnam in Hollywood*, London: Century, 1989
Morton, Andrew, *Diana: Her True Story in Her Own Words*, London: Michael O'Mara Books, 1998
Puttnam, David, author interview, 1 May 2012
Ryan, Christian, *Golden Boy: Kim Hughes and the Bad Old Days of Australian Cricket*, London: Allen & Unwin, 2009
Steen, Rob, and Alastair McLellan, *500–1: The Miracle of Headingley*, London: John Wisden & Co., 2010
Willis, Bob, *Lasting the Pace*, London: Collins, 1985
Wisden Cricketers' Almanack 1982, London: MacDonald & Co., 1982
Yule, Andrew, *Enigma: David Puttnam – The Story So Far*, London: Sphere, 1988

CHAPTER 3: THE LIVERPOOL MODEL

Bayley, Stephen, *Liverpool: Shaping the City*, London: RIBA, 2010
Beckett, Andy, *Pinochet: Britain and Chile's Hidden History*, London: Faber and Faber, 2002
Beckett, Andy, *When the Lights Went Out: Britain in the Seventies*, London: Faber and Faber, 2009
Beynon, Hugh, *Working for Ford*, London: Allen Lane, 1973, 1984
Bleasdale, Alan, *Boys from the Blackstuff*, London: Hutchinson, 1985

Booth, Philip (editor), *Were 364 Economists All Wrong?* London: Institute of Economic Affairs, 2006

Brannon, Ike, 'Remembering the Man Behind Rational Expectations', *Regulation*, Spring 2006

Bruce-Gardyne, Jock, *Mrs Thatcher's First Administration: The Prophets Confounded*, London: Macmillan 1984

Economic Strategy/Records of the Prime Minister's Office: Correspondence, 2 January 1981 to 10 June 1981, PREM 19/423, PREM 19/424

Economist, The, 4 July 1981

Field, Frank, *Inequality in Britain: Freedom, Welfare and the State*, London: Fontana, 1981

Free to Choose, episode 9: *How to Cure Inflation*, PBS, 1980

Friedman, Milton, and Rose D. Friedman, *Two Lucky People: Memoirs*, London: University of Chicago Press, 1998

Graham, Paul, *Beyond Caring*, London: Whitechapel Gallery, 2011

Graham, Paul, *A1: The Great North Road*, London: Whitechapel Gallery, 2011

Hooson, Tom, and Geoffrey Howe, *Work for Wales*, London: Conservative Political Centre, 1959

Howe, Geoffrey, author interview, 20 June and 22 November 2011

Howe, Geoffrey, *Conflict of Loyalty*, London: Pan, 1995

Killip, Chris, *What Happened: Great Britain 1970–1990*, London: The Photographers' Gallery, 2013

Lawson, Nigel, *The View from No. 11: Memoirs of a Tory Radical*, London: Bantam, 1992

Letter to Brezhnev, Yeardream, 1985

McCloskey, Donald N., *The Rhetoric of Economics*, Madison: University of Wisconsin Press, 1985

Minford, Patrick, author interview, 3 June 2011

Minford, Patrick, 'Mrs Thatcher's Economic Reform Programme', in Patrick Minford, *The New Classical View of the Economy*, Birmingham: Society of Company & Commercial Accountants, 1983

Minford, Patrick, *The Problem of Unemployment*, London: Selsdon Group, 1981

Minford, Patrick, *The Supply Side Revolution in Britain*, Aldershot: Edward Elgar Publishing Ltd., 1991

Muth, John F., 'Rational Expectations and the Theory of Price Movements', *Econometrica*, July 1961

O Lucky Man! Memorial Enterprises/Sam, 1973

Pandora's Box: The League of Gentlemen, BBC2, 1992

Public Expenditure/Records of the Prime Minister's Office: Correspondence, PREM 19/418

Skidelsky, Robert (editor), *Thatcherism*, London: Chatto & Windus, 1988

Thatcher, Carol, *A Swim-On Part in the Goldfish Bowl: A Memoir*, London: Headline Review, 2008

The Reunion: Boys from the Blackstuff, BBC Radio 4, 28 August 2011

Tory! Tory! Tory! episode 3: *The Road to Power*, BBC4, 2006

Walters, Alan, *Britain's Economic Renaissance: Margaret Thatcher's Economic Reforms 1979–1984*, New York: Oxford University Press, 1986

CHAPTER 4: WAIT UNTIL DUSK

Belchem, John, and Bryan Biggs (editors), *Liverpool: City of Radicals*, Liverpool: Liverpool University Press, 2011

Brief for a Debate on Recent Outbreaks of Civil Disorder in Great Britain, in *HAC* (81) 8

Civil Disorder: Disturbances in Brixton, Bristol, Liverpool, Manchester and London Districts; Prime Minister's Meetings with Community Leaders, 2 April 1980 to 29 October 1981, PREM 19/484

Cornelius, John, *Liverpool 8*, London: John Murray, 1982

Dahrendorf, Ralf, *On Britain*, London: University of Chicago Press, 1982

Frost, Diane, and Richard Phillips, *Liverpool '81: Remembering the Riots*, Liverpool: Liverpool University Press, 2011

Gifford, Anthony, Wally Brown and Ruth Bundey, *Loosen the Shackles: First Report of the Liverpool 8 Inquiry into Race Relations in Liverpool*, London: Karia Press, 1989

Hansard, 7 July 1981, 16 July 1981

Hatton, Derek, *Inside Left: The Story So Far*, London: Bloomsbury 1988

Hoskyns, John, author interview, 22 June 2011

Hoskyns, John, *Just in Time: Inside the Thatcher Revolution*, London: Aurum, 2000

Jagne, Jimi, author interview, 23 September 2011

Kettle, Martin, and Lucy Hodges, *Uprising! The Police, the People and the Riots in Britain's Cities*, London: Pan, 1982

LeRoy, Michael G., *Riots in Liverpool 8*, Evangelical Coalition for Urban Mission, 1983

L8: A Timepiece, Urbeatz Films, 2010

On This Day, BBC, 5 July 1985

Scarman, Leslie, *The Scarman Report: The Brixton Disorders 10–12 April 1981: Report of an Inquiry by Lord Scarman*, London: Penguin, 1982

Time, 16 February 1981
Wells, John, *Anyone for Denis?* London: Faber and Faber, 1982

CHAPTER 5: DOOM CITY

Bauer, Eran, author interviews, 21 October 2011, 24 October 2011, 25 October 2011
Blake's 7, episode 1: *The Way Back*, BBC1, 2 January 1978
Briggs, Raymond, *When the Wind Blows*, London: Penguin, 1982
Campbell, Duncan, *The Unsinkable Aircraft Carrier: American Military Power in Britain*, London: Michael Joseph, 1984
Campbell, Duncan, *War Plan UK: The Truth about Civil Defence in Britain*, London: Burnett, 1982
Civil Defence: Why We Need It, London: Central Office of Information, 1981
Daily Mail, 23 January 1981
Defence of the Realm, Enigma Films, 1985
Duckworth, Norman, author interview, 31 October 2011
Goodwin, Peter, *Nuclear War: The Facts*, London: Macmillan, 1981
Hackett, Sir John, and others, *The Third World War: August 1982*, London: Sidgwick and Jackson, 1978
Hackett, Sir John, and others, *The Third World War: The Untold Story*, London: Sidgwick and Jackson, 1982
Hall, C. J., *Corsham: An Illustrated History*, Corsham: C. J. Hall, 1983
Hennessy, Peter, *The Secret State: Preparing for the Worst 1945–2010*, London: Penguin, 2010
London Under Attack: The Report of the Greater London Area War Risk Study Commission, GLC, 1986
McCamley, N. J., *Cold War Secret Nuclear Bunkers: The Passive Defence of the Western World During the Cold War*, London: Leo Cooper, 2002
McCamley, N. J., *Secret Underground Cities: An Account of Some of Britain's Subterranean Defence, Factory and Storage Sites in the Second World War*, Barnsley: Leo Cooper, 1998
Miller, Lt. Col. D. M. O., Col. William V. Kennedy, John Jordan and Douglas Richardson, *The Balance of Military Power: An Illustrated Assessment Comparing the Weapons and Capabilities of NATO and the Warsaw Pact*, London: Salamander Books, 1981
Muir, John Kenneth, *A History and Critical Analysis of Blake's 7, the 1978–1981 British Television Space Adventure*, Jefferson: McFarland & Co., 2000

Mullin, Chris, *A Very British Coup*, London: Hodder & Stoughton, 1982
Myrdal, Alva, *The Game of Disarmament: How the United States and Russia Run the Arms Race*, New York: Pantheon Books, 1976
Nazzaro, Joe, and Sheelagh Wells, *Blake's 7: The Inside Story*, London: Virgin, 1997
New Scientist, 11 September 1975
Protect and Survive, London: HMSO, 1980
Protect and Survive Monthly, January 1981, May 1981
QED: A Guide to Armageddon, BBC1, 26 July 1982
Sibley, C. Bruce, *Surviving Doomsday*, London: Shaw and Sons, 1977
Stafford, James, '"Stay at Home": The Politics of Nuclear Civil Defence, 1963–83', *20th Century British History*, September 2011
Thompson, E. P., 'Notes on Exterminism, the Last Stage of Civilization', *New Left Review*, May/June 1980
Thompson, E. P., *Protest and Survive*, London: CND, 1980
Towle, Philip, Iain Elliot and Gerald Frost, *Protest and Perish: A Critique of Unilateralism*, London: Alliance Publishers for the Institute for European Defence and Strategic Studies, 1982
Turner, John, author interview, 31 October 2011
WarGames, United Artists, Sherwood Productions, 1983
Whoops Apocalypse, London Weekend Television, 1982

CHAPTER 6: WINTER THAW

Crewe, Ivor, and Anthony King, *SDP: The Birth, Life and Death of the Social Democratic Party*, Oxford: Oxford University Press, 1995
Gow, Ian, letter about SDP Christmas card, 21 January 1982, THCR 1/3/7 f77
Jenkins, Peter, *Mrs Thatcher's Revolution: The Ending of the Socialist Era*, London: Jonathan Cape, 1987
Jenkins, Roy, *Home Thoughts from Abroad*, BBC, 1979
New Statesman, 24 January 2011
Owen, David, author interview, 14 November 2012
Owen, David, *Face the Future*, London: Jonathan Cape, 1981
Owen, David, *Time to Declare*, London: Penguin, 1992
Owen, David, *Time to Declare: Second Innings*, London: Politico's, 2009
Owen, David, David Marquand and John Mackintosh, 'Change Gear! Towards a Socialist Strategy', *Socialist Commentary*, 1967
Powell, David, *Tony Benn: A Political Life*, London: Continuum, 2003
Rodgers, William, *The Politics of Change*, London: Secker & Warburg, 1982

Stephenson, Hugh, *Claret and Chips: The Rise of the SDP*, London: Michael Joseph, 1982

Williams, Shirley, *Politics is for People*, London: Allen Lane, 1981

CHAPTER 7: 'LONDON'S OURS!'

Ali, Tariq, *Who's Afraid of Margaret Thatcher? Tariq Ali in Conversation with Ken Livingstone*, London: Verso, 1984

Bew, Paul, Peter Gibbon and Henry Patterson, *Northern Ireland 1921–2001: Political Forces and Social Classes*, London: Serif, 2002

Carvel, John, *Citizen Ken*, London: Chatto & Windus, 1987

Citizen Smith, pilot episode, BBC1, 1977

Citizen Smith, BBC1, 1977–80

Cockburn, Cynthia, *The Local State: Management of Cities and People*, London: Pluto, 1977

Hollingsworth, Mark, *The Press and Political Dissent: A Question of Censorship*, London: Pluto, 1986

Hosken, Andrew, *Ken: The Ups and Downs of Ken Livingstone*, London: Arcadia, 2008

Jaggi, Max, Roger Muller and Sil Schmid, *Red Bologna*, London: Writers and Readers Publishing Cooperative, 1977

Livingstone, Ken, author interview, 11 March 2013

Livingstone, Ken, *If Voting Changed Anything, They'd Abolish It*, London: Collins, 1987

Livingstone, Ken, *Monetarism in London*, London: GLC, 1982

Livingstone, Ken, *You Can't Say That: Memoirs*, London: Faber and Faber, 2011

Pimlott, Ben, and Nirmala Rao, *Governing London*, Oxford: Oxford University Press, 2002

Vote Labour in London, May 7th: A Summary of Labour's GLC Election Proposals, London: Greater London Labour Party, 1981

Ward, Michael, author interview, 15 March 2013

Ward, Michael, *Job-Creation by the Council: Local Government and the Struggle for Full Employment*, *Workers' Control: Bulletin of the Institute for Workers' Control*, 1981

Wise, Valerie, author interview, 19 April 2013

Whitehouse, Wes, *GLC – The Inside Story*, Sunbury-on-Thames: James Lester, 2000

Working for London, the Final Five Years: A Summary of the GLC's Major Achievements 1980–1985, London: GLC, 1986

CHAPTER 8: ARE YOU THE CLEANERS?

Aubrey, Crispin, and John Shearlaw, *Glastonbury: An Oral History of the Music, Mud and Magic*, London: Ebury, 2004

Campbell, Beatrix, *The Iron Ladies: Why Do Women Vote Tory?* London: Virago, 1987

Cocroft, Wayne D., and Roger J. C. Thomas, *Cold War: Building for Nuclear Confrontation 1946–1989*, Swindon: English Heritage, 2003

Cook, Alice, and Gwyn Kirk, *Greenham Women Everywhere: Dreams, Ideas and Actions from the Women's Peace Movement*, London: Pluto, 1983

Crick, Michael, *Michael Heseltine: A Biography*, London: Penguin, 1997

Daily Mail, 13 December 1982

Denselow, Robin, *When the Music's Over: The Story of Political Pop*, London: Faber and Faber, 1989

Fairhall, David, *Common Ground: The Story of Greenham*, London: I. B. Tauris, 2006

Greenham Common Trust, www.greenham-common-trust.co.uk

Guardian, 16 November 1981

Hipperson, Sarah, and Beth Junor (editors), *Greenham: Non-Violent Women v the Crown Prerogative*, London: Greenham Publications, 2005

Hollingsworth, Mark, author interview, 27 March 2013

John, Helen, author interview, 4 November 2011

Jones, Lynn (editor), *Keeping the Peace: Women's Peace Handbook*, London: Women's Press, 1983

Kerr, Andrew, *Intolerably Hip: The Memoirs of Andrew Kerr*, Norwich: Frontier, 2011

Liddington, Jill, *The Long Road to Greenham: Feminism and Anti-Militarism in Britain Since 1820*, London: Virago, 1989

London Evening Standard, 2 December 1981

McKay, George, *Glastonbury: A Very English Fair*, London: Gollancz, 2000

Pettitt, Ann, author interview, 27 October 2011

Pettitt, Ann, *Walking to Greenham: How the Peace-Camp Began and the Cold War Ended*, Dinas Powys: Honno, 2006

Ruddock, Joan, *CND Scrapbook*, London: Macdonald and Co., 1987

The War Game, BBC, 1965

Webber, Philip, Graeme Wilkinson and Barry Rubin, *Crisis over Cruise: A Plain Guide to the New Weapons*, London: Penguin, 1983

CHAPTER 9: SECRET THATCHERITES

Barr, Ann, and Peter York, *The Official Sloane Ranger Handbook: The First Guide to What Really Matters in Life*, London: Ebury, 1982
Brideshead Revisited, Granada Television, 1981
Fry, Martin, author interview, 17 August 2012
Kemp, Gary, *I Know This Much: From Soho to Spandau*, London: Fourth Estate, 2009
Kureishi, Hanif, and Jon Savage, *The Faber Book of Pop*, London: Faber and Faber, 1995
Logan, Nick, author interview, 23 August 2012
Mantrap, Midnight Films, 1983
Morley, Paul, author interview, 18 July 2012
Morley, Paul, *Ask: The Chatter of Pop*, London: Faber and Faber, 1986
New Musical Express, 20 December 1980
O'Hanlon, Redmond, *Into the Heart of Borneo*, Edinburgh: Salamander, 1984
Reynolds, Simon, *Rip It Up and Start Again: Post-Punk 1978–84*, London: Faber and Faber, 2005
Rimmer, Dave, *Like Punk Never Happened: Culture Club and the New Pop*, London: Faber and Faber, 1985
Sherman, Alfred, and Mark Garnett (editor), *Paradoxes of Power: Reflections on the Thatcher Interlude*, Exeter: Imprint Academic, 2005
testpressing.org, Nick Logan interview, 16 April 2012
Travis, John, *Spandau Ballet: The Authorised Story*, London: Sidgwick & Jackson, 1986
Vermorel, Fred, and Judy Vermorel, *Adam & The Ants*, London: Omnibus Press, 1981
York, Peter, *Modern Times: Everybody Wants Everything*, London: Heinemann, 1984
York, Peter, *Style Wars*, London: Sidgwick & Jackson, 1980

CHAPTER 10: SCAMS

Cockett, Richard, *Thinking the Unthinkable: Think-Tanks and the Economic Counter-Revolution 1931–1983*, London: HarperCollins, 1994
Cooksey, David, author interview, 29 September 2011
Gray, Colin, *Allowing for Enterprise: A Qualitative Assessment of the Enterprise Allowance Scheme*, London: Small Business Research Trust, 1986
Hansard, 23 July 1984

Jones, Colin, and Alan Murie, *The Right to Buy: Analysis & Evaluation of a Housing Policy*, Oxford: Blackwell, 2006

Kavanagh, Dennis, and Anthony Seldon (editors), *The Thatcher Effect: A Decade of Change*, Oxford: Clarendon, 1989

Kerr, Marion, *The Right to Buy: A National Survey of Tenants and Buyers of Council Homes*, London: HMSO, 1988

King, Peter, *Housing Policy Transformed: The Right to Buy and the Desire to Own*, Bristol: Policy, 2010

Meantime, Central Production, Mostpoint, Channel 4 Television Corporation, 1983

Sampson, Anthony, *The Changing Anatomy of Britain: The Handbook for the 80s*, Sevenoaks: Hodder and Stoughton, 1982, 1983

Sanders, David, Hugh Ward, David Marsh and Tony Fletcher, 'Government Popularity and the Falklands War: A Reassessment', *British Journal of Political Science*, July 1987

Tebbit, Norman, author interview, 26 April 2013

Tebbit, Norman, *Upwardly Mobile*, London: Weidenfeld and Nicolson, 1988

The Conservative Manifesto 1979, London: Conservative Central Office, 1979

The Explosive Eighties, episode 1, Channel 4, 2005

The Great Estate: The Rise and Fall of the Council House, BBC4, 11 April 2011

Vinson, Nigel, author interview, 14 September 2011

Young, Hugo, *The Hugo Young Papers: Thirty Years of British Politics – Off the Record*, London: Allen Lane, 2008

CHAPTER 11: OUR FRIENDS IN THE SOUTH

Argentina Falklands, 21 September 1979 to 15 December 1981, PREM 19/612

Argentina Falklands, 1 January 1982 to 30 March 1982, PREM 19/613

Barrow-in-Furness Dock Museum

Carrington, Peter, *Reflect on Things Past: The Memoirs of Lord Carrington*, London: Collins, 1988

Economic Survey of the Falkland Islands, HMSO, 1976

Falkland Islands Economic Study, HMSO, 1982

Fowler, John, author interview, 26 February 2012

Freedman, Lawrence, *The Official History of the Falklands Campaign. Volume 1: The Origins of the Falklands War*, London: Routledge, 2007

Geraghty, Tony, *Who Dares Wins: The Story of the Special Air Service, 1950–1982*, London: Fontana, 1983

Hansard, 2 December 1980, 9 February 1982, 3 March 1982

Hastings, Max, and Simon Jenkins, *The Battle for the Falklands*, London: Pan, 1983

Leach, Henry, *Endure No Makeshifts: Some Naval Recollections*, London: Leo Cooper, 1993

Moore, Charles, *Margaret Thatcher: The Authorized Biography*, London: Allen Lane, 2013

Nott, John, author interview, 14 December 2012

Nott, John, *Here Today, Gone Tomorrow: Recollections of an Errant Politician*, London: Politico's, 2002

Parkinson, Cecil, *Right at the Centre: An Autobiography*, London: Weidenfeld and Nicolson, 1992

Poole, Nancy, author interview, 26 February 2012

Ridley, Nicholas, *My Style of Government: The Thatcher Years*, London: Hutchinson, 1991

Saving the Great Britain, Nonesuch Expeditions, 1970

Vinen, Richard, *Thatcher's Britain: The Politics and Social Upheaval of the Thatcher Era*, London: Simon & Schuster, 2009

West, Nigel, *The Secret War for the Falklands: The SAS, MI6 and the War Whitehall Nearly Lost*, London: Warner Books, 1998

Who Dares Wins, Richmond: Light Horse Productions, 1982

Winchester, Simon, *Outposts*, Sevenoaks: Hodder and Stoughton, 1985

CHAPTER 12: WE WON

Barnett, Anthony, *Iron Britannia: Time to Take the Great out of Britain*, London: Faber and Faber, 2012

Beckett, Andy, *Pinochet in Piccadilly: Britain and Chile's Hidden History*, London: Faber and Faber, 2002

Chester Chronicle, 5 April 2012

Clark, Alan, *Diaries: Into Politics, 1972–1982*, London: Weidenfeld and Nicolson, 2000

Connaughton, R. M., *A Brief History of Modern Warfare*, London: Robinson, 2008

Falkland Islands Crisis: Argentine Invasion, 1 January 1982 to 31 December 1982, FCO 7/4490

Falkland Islands Crisis: The Visit of the Foreign and Commonwealth Secretary to New York, 3 May 1982 to 5 May 1982, PREM 19/624

Falkland Islands Review Committee (Franks Inquiry): Transcript of Oral Evidence by the Prime Minister, 25 October 1982, CAB 292/47

Freedman, Lawrence, *The Official History of the Falklands Campaign. Volume 2: War and Diplomacy*, London: Routledge, 2007

Gow, Ian, warning minute to Margaret Thatcher, 4 December 1981, THCR 1/4/17 f17

Greenhalf, Jim, *Electric Century: To Commemorate the Centenary of the School of Electronic and Electrical Engineering at the University of Leeds*, Leeds: Filtronic Plc/University of Leeds, 1999

Haig, Alexander M. Jr., *Caveat: Realism, Reagan, and Foreign Policy*, New York: Macmillan, 1984

Hall, Stuart, and Martin Jacques (editors), *The Politics of Thatcherism*, London: Lawrence and Wishart, 1983

Hansard, 23 March 1982, 30 March 1982, 2–3 April 1982

Hunter, Ian, *The Story of Filtronic*, London: James and James, 2003

Jolly, Rick, *Doctor for Friend or Foe: Britain's Frontline Medic in the Fight for the Falklands*, London: Anova Books Company Ltd., 2012

Major, John, *John Major: The Autobiography*, London: HarperCollins, 1999

Middlebrook, Martin, *The Argentine Fight for the Falklands*, Barnsley: Pen & Sword Military Classics, 2003

Pimlott, John (editor), *British Military Operations 1945–1984*, London: Hamlyn, 1984

Rhodes, David, author interview, 19 December 2012

Seymour, Richard, *Unhitched: The Trial of Christopher Hitchens*, London: Verso, 2012

Thatcher, Margaret, *Memoir of the Falklands War*, 1983

Thatcher, Margaret, *The Downing Street Years*, London: HarperCollins, 1993

The Downing Street Years, BBC2, 1993

The Falklands War: The Day by Day Record from Invasion to Victory, London: Marshall Cavendish, 1983

The Living Dead, episode 3: *The Attic*, BBC2, 1995

The Ploughman's Lunch, Greenpoint Films, 1983

Thompson, Julian, *No Picnic: 3 Commando Brigade in the South Atlantic: 1982*, London: Guild Publishing, 1985

War Cabinet Minutes, 6 April 1982 to 15 July 1982, CAB 148/211, CAB 148/212

Woodward, Sandy, and Patrick Robinson, *One Hundred Days: The Memoirs of the Falklands Battle Group Commander*, London: HarperCollins, 2003

CHAPTER 13: COCAINE AND GLASS

Ambrose, Peter, and Bob Colenutt, *The Property Machine*, London: Penguin, 1975

Aviation Market Studies: Report to the London Docklands Development Corporation, The Economic & Transport Planning Group, September 1982

Ballard, J. G., *High-Rise*, London: Jonathan Cape, 1975

Banks, Leslie, and Christopher Stanley, *The Thames: A History from the Air*, Oxford: Oxford University Press, 1990

Bentley, James, *East of the City: The London Docklands Story*, London: Pavilion, 1997

Bird, James, *The Geography of the Port of London*, London: Hutchinson University Library, 1957

Brownhill, Sue, *Developing London's Docklands: Another Great Planning Disaster?* London: Paul Chapman Publishing Ltd., 1993

Colenutt, Bob, author interview, 21 June 2012

Cox, Alan, *Docklands in the Making: The Redevelopment of the Isle of Dogs 1981–1995*, London: The Athlone Press, 1995

Docklands: Redevelopment Proposals for East London, London Dockland Study Team, 1973

Farson, Daniel, *Limehouse Days: A Personal Experience of the East End*, London: Michael Joseph, 1991

Foster, Janet, *Docklands: Cultures in Conflict, Worlds in Collision*, London: UCL Press, 1999

Four Year Review of the LDDC, The Docklands Consultative Committee, 1985

Hardy, Dennis, and Eleonore Kofman (editor), *Making Sense of the London Docklands: People and Places*, Enfield: Middlesex Polytechnic, 1983

Hardy, Dennis, and Eleonore Kofman (editor), *Making Sense of the London Docklands: Processes of Change*, Enfield: Middlesex Polytechnic, 1983

Heseltine, Michael, author interview, 28 September 2011

Hollamby, Ted, *Docklands: London's Backyard into Front Yard*, London: Docklands Forum, 1990

Howe, Geoffrey, *Enterprise Zones and the Enterprise Culture: Ten Years On*, London: The Bow Group, 1988

Howe, Geoffrey, *Liberating Free Enterprise: A New Experiment*, London: The Bow Group, 1978

Innes, Stuart, author interview, 8 June 2012

Isle of Dogs: A Guide to Design and Development Opportunities, LDDC, 1982

Keefe, Barrie, *The Long Good Friday*, London: Methuen, 1984, 1998

Law, Roger, interview, www.vice.com, 1 October 2010

Lloyd, John, interview, www.vice.com, 1 October 2010
London Docklands Development Corporation Annual Report and Accounts 1982/3, London: LDDC, 1983
Lyons, Charles Barker, *London – Isle of Dogs*, London: LDDC, 1981
Nairn, Ian, *Nairn's London*, London: Penguin, 1966
O'Keefe, David, author interview, 20 June 2012
Omnibus, BBC1, 9 May 1982
Rodrigues, David, and Peter Bruinvels, *Zoning in on Enterprise: A Businessman's Guide to the Enterprise Zones*, London: Kogan Page, 1982
Shawcross, William, *Rupert Murdoch: Ringmaster of the Information Circus*, London: Pan, 1993
Stewart, Graham, *The History of The Times. Volume 7, 1981–2002: The Murdoch Years*, London: HarperCollins, 2005
Sudjic, Deyan, *Norman Foster: A Life in Architecture*, London: Weidenfeld and Nicolson, 2010
Sudjic, Deyan, *The 100 Mile City*, London: Andre Deutsch Ltd., 1992
Sudjic, Deyan (editor), *From Matt Black to Memphis and Back Again: An Anthology from Blueprint Magazine*, London: Architecture Design and Technology Press, 1989
The Long Good Friday, Black Lion Films, 1979
Travers, Tony, Reg Ward obituary, *Guardian*, 22 February 2011
Turlik, Peter, author interview, 27 June 2012
Turlik, Peter, *Initiating Urban Change: London Docklands Before the LDDC*, London: LDDC, 1997
Widgery, David, *Some Lives! A GP's East End*, London: Sinclair-Stevenson, 1991
York, Peter, and Charles Jennings, *Peter York's Eighties*, London: BBC Books, 1996

CHAPTER 14: A JOURNEY

Bailey, Nick, *Fitzrovia*, New Barnet: Historical Publications/Camden History Society, 1981
Bonner, Paul, and Lesley Aston, *Independent Television in Britain. Volume 6: 1981–92*, Basingstoke: Palgrave Macmillan, 2003
Brown, Maggie, *A Licence to be Different: The Story of Channel 4*, London: BFI, 2007
Coote, Anna, author interview, 2 July 2012
Coote, Anna, and Beatrix Campbell, *Sweet Freedom: The Struggle for Women's Liberation*, Oxford: Basil Blackwell, 1987

Crick, Michael, *Scargill and the Miners*, London: Penguin, 1985
Donebauer, Peter, author interview, 29 May 2012
Ellis, John, *What Did Channel 4 Do for Us? Reassessing the Early Years*, in *Screen*, Autumn 2008
Farrell, Terry, *Terry Farrell*, London: Academy Editions, 1984
Farrell, Terry, *Terry Farrell: Selected and Current Works*, Mulgrave: Images Publishing, 1994
Graham, David, author interview, 11 May 2012
Graham, David, and Peter Clarke, *The New Enlightenment: The Rebirth of Liberalism*, London: Macmillan, 1986
Harvey, Sylvia, 'Channel Four Television: From Annan to Grade', in Edward Buscombe (editor), *British Television: A Reader*, Oxford: Clarendon Press, 2000
Hewlett, Steve, author interview, 17 May 2012
Isaacs, Jeremy, author interview, 25 June 2012
Isaacs, Jeremy, *Look Me in the Eye: A Life in Television*, London: Little, Brown, 2006
Isaacs, Jeremy, *Storm Over 4: A Personal Account*, London: Weidenfeld and Nicolson, 1989
Lambert, Stephen, *Channel Four: Television with a Difference?*, London: BFI, 1982
Redmond, Phil, author interview, 13 June 2012
Routledge, Paul, *Scargill: The Unauthorized Biography*, London: HarperCollins, 1993
Taylor, Robert, *The Trade Union Question in British Politics: Government and Unions Since 1945*, Oxford: Blackwell, 1993

CHAPTER 15: 'LOONIES'

Bashevkin, Sylvia B., *Tales of Two Cities: Women and Municipal Restructuring in London and Toronto*, Vancouver: UBC Press, 2006
Bellos, Linda, author interview, 19 March 2013
Bulletin on the GLC Women's Committee, London: GLC, 1982–6
Curren, James, Ivor Gaber and Julian Petley, *Culture Wars: The Media and the British Left*, Edinburgh: Edinburgh University Press, 2005
Flannery, Kate, and Sarah Roelofs, 'Local Government Women's Committees', in Joy Holland (editor), *Feminist Action 1*, 1984
Forrester, Andrew, Stewart Lansley and Robin Pauley, *Beyond Our Ken: A Guide to the Battle for London*, London: Fourth Estate, 1985
GLC Women's Committee Information Pack, London: GLC, 1985

Goss, Sue, 'Women's Initiatives in Local Government', in Martin Boddy and Colin Fudge (editors), *Local Socialism? Labour Councils and New Left Alternatives*, London: Macmillan, 1984

Hunt, Judith, author interview, 8 May 2013

Lefties, episode 2: *Angry Wimmin*, BBC4, 2007

Lovenduski, Joni, and Vicky Randall, *Contemporary Feminist Politics: Women and Power in Britain*, Oxford: Oxford University Press, 1993

Mackintosh, Maureen, and Hilary Wainwright (editors), *A Taste of Power: The Politics of Local Economics*, London: Verso 1987

Marxism Today, April 1986

Mona Lisa, Palace Pictures, 1986

Otitoju, Femi, author interview, 1 May 2013

Programme of Action for Women in London, London: GLC, 1982

Rowbotham, Sheila, Lynne Segal and Hilary Wainwright, *Beyond the Fragments: Feminism and the Making of Socialism*, London: Merlin, 1980

Wainwright, Hilary, *Labour: A Tale of Two Parties*, London: Hogarth Press, 1987

Wainwright, Hilary, and Dave Elliott, *The Lucas Plan: A New Trade Unionism in the Making?* London: Allison & Busby, 1982

EPILOGUE: WHOSE MIRACLE?

Fisher, Mark, *Ghosts of My Life: Writings on Depression, Hauntology and Lost Futures*, London: Zero Books, 2014

Sweeting, Adam, *Simple Minds*, London: Sidgwick & Jackson, 1988.

Williams, Stephanie, *Docklands*, London: Phaidon, 1993

Index

ALLEN LANE
an imprint of
PENGUIN BOOKS

Recently Published

Slavoj Žižek, *Against the Double Blackmail: Refugees, Terror, and Other Troubles with the Neighbours*

Lynsey Hanley, *Respectable: The Experience of Class*

Piers Brendon, *Edward VIII: The Uncrowned King*

Matthew Desmond, *Evicted: Poverty and Profit in the American City*

T.M. Devine, *Independence or Union: Scotland's Past and Scotland's Present*

Seamus Murphy, *The Republic*

Jerry Brotton, *This Orient Isle: Elizabethan England and the Islamic World*

Srinath Raghavan, *India's War: The Making of Modern South Asia, 1939-1945*

Clare Jackson, *Charles II: The Star King*

Nandan Nilekani and Viral Shah, *Rebooting India: Realizing a Billion Aspirations*

Sunil Khilnani, *Incarnations: India in 50 Lives*

Helen Pearson, *The Life Project: The Extraordinary Story of Our Ordinary Lives*

Ben Ratliff, *Every Song Ever: Twenty Ways to Listen to Music Now*

Richard Davenport-Hines, *Edward VII: The Cosmopolitan King*

Peter H. Wilson, *The Holy Roman Empire: A Thousand Years of Europe's History*

Todd Rose, *The End of Average: How to Succeed in a World that Values Sameness*

Frank Trentmann, *Empire of Things: How We Became a World of Consumers, from the Fifteenth Century to the Twenty-First*

Laura Ashe, *Richard II: A Brittle Glory*

John Donvan and Caren Zucker, *In a Different Key: The Story of Autism*

Jack Shenker, *The Egyptians: A Radical Story*

Tim Judah, *In Wartime: Stories from Ukraine*

Serhii Plokhy, *The Gates of Europe: A History of Ukraine*

Robin Lane Fox, *Augustine: Conversions and Confessions*

Peter Hennessy and James Jinks, *The Silent Deep: The Royal Navy Submarine Service Since 1945*

Sean McMeekin, *The Ottoman Endgame: War, Revolution and the Making of the Modern Middle East, 1908–1923*

Charles Moore, *Margaret Thatcher: The Authorized Biography, Volume Two: Everything She Wants*

Dominic Sandbrook, *The Great British Dream Factory: The Strange History of Our National Imagination*

Larissa MacFarquhar, *Strangers Drowning: Voyages to the Brink of Moral Extremity*

Niall Ferguson, *Kissinger: 1923-1968: The Idealist*

Carlo Rovelli, *Seven Brief Lessons on Physics*

Tim Blanning, *Frederick the Great: King of Prussia*

Ian Kershaw, *To Hell and Back: Europe, 1914–1949*

Pedro Domingos, *The Master Algorithm: How the Quest for the Ultimate Learning Machine Will Remake Our World*

David Wootton, *The Invention of Science: A New History of the Scientific Revolution*

Christopher Tyerman, *How to Plan a Crusade: Reason and Religious War in the Middle Ages*

Andy Beckett, *Promised You A Miracle: UK 80–82*

Carl Watkins, *Stephen: The Reign of Anarchy*

Anne Curry, *Henry V: From Playboy Prince to Warrior King*

John Gillingham, *William II: The Red King*

Roger Knight, *William IV: A King at Sea*

Douglas Hurd, *Elizabeth II: The Steadfast*

Richard Nisbett, *Mindware: Tools for Smart Thinking*

Jochen Bleicken, *Augustus: The Biography*

Paul Mason, *PostCapitalism: A Guide to Our Future*

Frank Wilczek, *A Beautiful Question: Finding Nature's Deep Design*

Roberto Saviano, *Zero Zero Zero*

Owen Hatherley, *Landscapes of Communism: A History Through Buildings*

César Hidalgo, *Why Information Grows: The Evolution of Order, from Atoms to Economies*

Aziz Ansari and Eric Klinenberg, *Modern Romance: An Investigation*

Sudhir Hazareesingh, *How the French Think: An Affectionate Portrait of an Intellectual People*

Steven D. Levitt and Stephen J. Dubner, *When to Rob a Bank: A Rogue Economist's Guide to the World*

Leonard Mlodinow, *The Upright Thinkers: The Human Journey from Living in Trees to Understanding the Cosmos*

Hans Ulrich Obrist, *Lives of the Artists, Lives of the Architects*

Richard H. Thaler, *Misbehaving: The Making of Behavioural Economics*

Sheldon Solomon, Jeff Greenberg and Tom Pyszczynski, *Worm at the Core: On the Role of Death in Life*

Nathaniel Popper, *Digital Gold: The Untold Story of Bitcoin*

Dominic Lieven, *Towards the Flame: Empire, War and the End of Tsarist Russia*

Noel Malcolm, *Agents of Empire: Knights, Corsairs, Jesuits and Spies in the Sixteenth-Century Mediterranean World*

James Rebanks, *The Shepherd's Life: A Tale of the Lake District*

David Brooks, *The Road to Character*

Joseph Stiglitz, *The Great Divide*

Ken Robinson and Lou Aronica, *Creative Schools: Revolutionizing Education from the Ground Up*

Clotaire Rapaille and Andrés Roemer, *Move UP: Why Some Cultures Advances While Others Don't*

Jonathan Keates, *William III and Mary II: Partners in Revolution*

David Womersley, *James II: The Last Catholic King*